£30 00   920.0092   QuicRef

KT-294-598

BLACK WHO'S WHO FOR THE MILLENNIUM

Published by

New Nation

& Caribbean Times

Edited by John Hughes

BLACK WHO'S WHO

First published in 1999, London, England

Published by:
Ethnic Media Group

Publisher:
Sarwar Ahmed

Compiled & Edited:
John Hughes

Production Manager:
Nadeem Khan

Researchers:
Kiran Lyall
Fatema Sheikh
Bimla Lyall

Photo Editor:
Sohail Anjum

Software Consultant:
Faiz Parkar

Printed and Bound in UK by:
Alden Press, Oxford.

British Library Cataloguing in Publication Data
A catalogue record for this book is available at the British Library and Book Data

ISBN: 0-9533744-1-6

Ethnic Media Group, 1st Floor, 148 Cambridge Heath Road, London E1 5QJ, England, Tel: 0171 702 8012, Fax: 0171 702 7937

CONTENTS

BLACK WHO'S WHO

BLACK WHO'S WHO

Marketing Manager *Mits Sahini* • Circulation Manager *Chris Piper* • Advertising Manager *Wayne Bower*
• Corporate Advertising *Asif Yusuf*

Black Who's Who is published by Ethnic Media Group
148 Cambridge Heath Road, London E1 5QJ Tel: 0171 702 8012 Fax: 0171 702 7937
1999 © All Rights reserved. No part of this publication may be reproduced or stored electronically without permission of the publisher.
Printed by Alden Press, Oxford

EDITOR'S NOTE

The Black Who's Who is the first directory of Black achievers in Britain that includes not only high-flyers and famous people, but more significantly, a great many unsung heroes as well as many hard-working individuals who are an inspiration and role models for us all.

In the hundreds of years that Black people have been in Britain no single document has been produced to record their contributions and achievements, outside the worlds of sport and entertainment, the Black Who's Who only scratches the surface of today's Black society in Britain to reveal a vast wealth of talent.

Most entries have been through a process of nominations. The public were invited through the pages of New Nation and Caribbean Times, community radio programmes and a telephone Hotline to nominate those who have been successful in their occupations and professions, or who have made positive contributions to the community, or who have been achievers in many other ways – the Black Who's Who profiles over 500 people

Nominees were sent an entry form to be filled in and returned with a photo. We have only used information submitted on the entry forms and while every attention was paid to accuracy we will have made unintentional errors. Some forms were handwritten and difficult to decipher, in these cases we attempted to contact the entrants with queries. A small number of entries did not get their form to us before publication deadline. I felt these achievers profiles should be included. (Courtesy Hearsay Communications).

The general reaction to a Black Who's Who from people has been overwhelming positive, though some expressed a definite desire to be excluded, many nominees felt that they had not achieved sufficiently at this time to be in the first edition. Many Black people in senior positions and in successful businesses have decided to wait and evaluate this edition before committing themselves.

I have included covers of the Caribbean Times which record some of the leading issues over the past few years. New Nation's Countdown to the Millennium features some of the issues that affected us in 1999.

I want to thank all those who returned their entry forms and all those who took the time to make nominations. Immediately after the racist London bombings I was inundated with requests not to publish addresses and telephone numbers. For those wishing to contact these entries I will forward correspondence providing it is in a stamped envelope.

My thanks go to the publisher, Sarwar Ahmed for his belief in my project and to the entire staff at Ethnic Media Group - sincere thanks. A special thanks goes to Faiz Parkar for his computer genius and especially to Nadeem Khan who worked tirelessly on design and the technology to create, single handedly, this book. I also thank those in the acknowledgements for their contributions. To the boss and his cheerful team at the Yellow Advertiser, South Woodford, who were a great help in our moment of need - thanks David. My assistant Kiran Lyall proved an invaluable asset to the project.

John Hughes
Compiler & Editor

I would like to thank the following for their help with this book:

ACKNOWLEDGEMENTS

Michael Eboda
Ron Shillingford
Anthea Lee
Hennriette Cole
Emmannuel Dunseath
Anita Toussaint
David Wheaton
Hasna Begum Ali
Ghazala Ahmed
Fiona Waye CVCP

Tony Atille (Photo credit: Angie Greaves)
Trevor Leighton (Photo credit: Lenny Henry)
Commission for Racial Equality
Bobby Syed Hearsay Communications
Ansell Wong
Dr Christopher Johnson
Paul Pearson
Roger Kopsis
Anne - Arista Records
Sharon Aitkins

Reaching the _heart_ of multi-cultural Britain

Ethnic Media Group represents Britain's diverse Black and Asian communities. The group's four nationally circulated newspapers, NEW NATION, EASTERN EYE, ASIAN TIMES and CARIBBEAN TIMES, reach over 500,000 readers every week and are the main source of news, views and information for this prosperous and growing sector of Britain. The papers' recruitment section, Jobs Direct, has already helped thousands find employment and is packed every week with hundreds of job opportunities. 'Public Sector', a weekly pull-out section in ASIAN TIMES and CARIBBEAN TIMES, is unique, being the only supplement covering news and features for Britain's ethnic minority workers in this important field. Together the papers cater for every taste, every kind of reader and reach the people who really matter. Ethnic Media Group titles provide a gateway to the British Black and Asian communities.

For more information call: 0171 702 8012

MAIN INDEX

Giscombe	Junior	47
Goddard	Patricia (Trisha)	48
Gorham	Clare	48
Graham	Llewellyn	48
Grant	Kim	48
Grant	Simon	48
Greaves	Angie	48
Greaves	Sonia May	48
Gregory	Phil	48
Griffin	Angela	49
Griffith	Eddie	49
Griffiths	Derek	49
Groves	Howard Deland	49
Guy	Enid	49
Guy	Kevin	49

H

Hall	Lynden David	51
Hamlett	Nathan	51
Hammond	Mona	51
Harper	Jacqui	51
Harper-Wills	Doris	51
Harriott	Ainsley	51
Harriott	Ernie	51
Harriott	Veronica	51
Harris	George William	52
Harris	Volney	52
Harris	Wayne	52
Hart	Merrick	52
Hayles	Barry	52
Hayles	Maxie Alphonso	52
Headley	Gary-Tyrone	52
Headley	Stella	52
Heath	Carlton Charles	53
Hector	Tony	53
Hendrickson	Claude 'Hopper'	53
Henry	Dollie	53
Henry	Lenny	53
Hibbert	Colette	53
Hibbert	Maureen	53
Higgins	Herbie	53
Holder	Hazel	54
Holland	June	54
Holloway	Lester	54
Holmes	Esther	54
Hooley	Joan	54
Hoyles	Asher	54
Hutchinson	Ruby - Marie	54
Hyatt	Gloria	54

I

I'Anson	Lisa	55
Ifill	Paul	55
Ikeazor	Chukwudum	55
Ikezue	Veronica	55
Iloghalu	Miriam Afoma	55
Ince	Paul	55
Inoniyegha	Josephine	55
Insular	Anthea	55

J

Jackson	Alan Anthony	57
Jackson	Blossom	57
Jackson	Carl	57
James	David	57
James	Lennie	57
Jarrett	Rene	57
Jasper	Lee	57
Jaye	Tee	58
Jee	Jocelyn	58
Jegede	Kunbi	58
Jerome	Mary-Theresa	58
Jesuorobo	Osagumwengie	58
John	Errol	58
John-Jules	Danny	59
Johnson	Christopher Adrian	59
Johnson	Linton Kwesi	59
Johnson	Morgan	59
Johnson	Neil Anthony	59

Johnson	Veronica	59
Johnson	Wil	59
Jones	Cecily	59
Jones	Quincy	60
Jones	Valentino A.	60
Jordan	Jennifer	60
Joseph	Bertha Joan	60
Joseph	Ellin Joyce	60
Joseph	Kamy	60
Joseph	Marc	60
Joseph	Michelle	60

K

Karlsson	Richard	61
Kennedy	Carol	61
Kid	Glamma	61
Kinch	Don	61
King	Rowena	61
Kisanga	Aida	61
Knight	Carmen	61
Kolah	Ardi	61
Kossoko	Aicha	62
Kwhali	Josephine	62
Kyd	Michael	62

L

Laing	Yvonne	63
Laniyan	Junior	63
Lawrence	Donovan K	63
Lawrence	Meranda M	63
Lawrence	Roydelle A.J	63
Leary	Denise	63
Lee	Samuel Richard	63
Lester	Adrian	63
Lewis	Linda	64
Lewis	Thelma	64
Liandu	Namasiku Donald	64
Linton	Eric Lloyd	64
Lloyd Garrison	Ruth	64
Loewenthal	Alexander	64
Longmore	Wyllie	64
Lowe	Alison	64
Luthers	Vibert Clarence	65
Lynch	Reuben Simeon	65

M

Macauley	Edith Joan Christabel	67
MacCormack	Cecil Bunting	67
Mack	Jerome	67
Mahoney	Louis	67
Mambu	Yomi	67
Mark	Constance	67
Masjid	Iman Abdul	67
McCarthy	Dean Monrose	67
McDermott	Shelly-Ann Desree	68
McDowell	Katrina	68
McFarlane	Harold Carl	68
Mckay	Lespaul Anthony	68
McKen	Eileen	68
McLean	Joseph	68
McLean	Suzann	68
McLean	Sylvia Doreen	68
McLeod	Maurice	69
McNaughton	Bernice	69
Meade	Leonard	69
Medford	Paul J	69
Mensa-Kuma	Kobby	69
Michaels	Angela	69
Miller	Patrick	69
Moffatt	Nigel	69
Moodie	Tanya	70
Moore	Nicole	70
Morris	Andrew	70
Morris	Tia	70
Morris	William	70
Morrison	Mark	70
Mullard	Christopher	70
Mwangi	Sophia	70

N

Nayles	Renville	71
Nelson	Trevor	71
Noble	Joseph	71
Nobrega	Cecile	71
Noel	Terry	71
Nri	Celeste Veronica	71
Nwanji	Tony Ike	71
Nwoko	Chinedu Munir	71

O

O'Brien	Leyland	73
Oba	Tunde Ona	73
Obano	Rex	73
Ofoegbu	Anthony	73
Ogilvie	John	73
Oguntimoju	Dele	73
Ohajah	Joyce	73
Okai	Omar F	73
Oke	Femi	73
Okeke	Uchenna O	74
Okoro	Innocent	74
Okorodudu	Roli Mejebi	74
Olayiwola	Abdur-Rahman	74
Oleforo	Laz Maduabuchi	74
Olomu	Ekundayo	74
Olowo	Femi	74
Olumegbon	Monsuru Adetunji	75
Oni	Lola	75
Oniya	Oladele	75
Onyenka	Justin	75
Opara	Marvel	75
Oppong-Wiafe	Jonathan	75
Osawe	Benson	75
Osborne	Hyacinth	75
Oshiyemi	Dapo	76
Oshungbure	Michael	76
Ouseley	Herman	76
Oyenigba	Olu	76

P

Packer	Susanne	77
Padmore	Stephen	77
Palmer	Carl	77
Palmer	Emmanuel	77
Palmer	Geoffrey Henry	77
Panton	Janice	77
Paris	Micia	77
Parish	Yvette Lorraine	77
Parkes	Shaun	78
Parris	Mabel Christobel	78
Pascal	Yvonne	78
Patten	Shirley Doreen	78
Patterson	Colin Roy	78
Patterson	Drew John Perigrine	78
Pearson	Paul	78
Peters	Sonia M	78
Philbert	Martin Ray	79
Philip	Darell	79
Phillips	Barbara	79
Phillips	Dave-Benson	79
Phillips	Marta R	79
Phillips	Richard	79
Phillpotts	Laurent	79
Phinn	Marcia	79
Phoenix	Sybil	80
Pickett	Justin	80
Pollendine	Yoyo	80
Pollitt	Jason Peter	80
Pope	Stephen	80
Pottinger-Noble	Valerie	80
Poyser	Daniel	80
Preece	Corrina	80
Prescod	Michael Sinclair	80
Price	Wordsworth	81
Purkiss	Bob	81
Praag	Barbara Van	81

R

Rabbatts	Heather	83
Ramdin	Ron	83
Rand	Jimi	83
Raymond	Neil	83
Reddie	Anthony George	83
Reece	Sherelle	83
Reid	Carl	83
Reid	Steven	83
Reids	Bernice	84
Rennis	Benjamin A H	84
Reynolds	Richard	84
Richards	Donald	84
Richards	Judy	84
Richards	Sandra	84
Ricketts	Shannen	84
Roberts	Adrienne Patricia	84
Roberts	John Anthony	85
Roberts	Norma	85
Robinson	Anthony	85
Robinson	Mae-Louise	85
Rochester	Vivienne	85
Rock	Lisa	85
Rockson	Amy	85
Rollins	Adrian Stewart	85
Rollins	Marva Yvonne	86
Romain	Ryan	86
Romano	Ken	86
Rose	Chrystal	86
Rose	Marcia	86
Ross	Catherine	86
Rowe	Clive	86
Rowe	Hyacinth	86

S

Salako	John	87
Salmon	Elijah Sylvester	87
Sam-Bailey	Bridgit Agatha	87
Samuel	Anslem	87
Sandy-Lee	Alex	87
Sandy-Lee	Inkla	87
Santiago	Michael	87
Sanusi	Bala Mohammed	87
Sapani	Danny Kwesi	88
Sapara	Ade	88
Sarpong	Kwasi	88
Sealy	Joseph	88
Sealy	June-Alison	88
Sealy	Philemon	88
Setchfield	Mark	88
Sharpe	Jimmy	88
Shodeke	Babafemi Olatunde	89
Shokoya-Eleshin	Christopher	89
Simon-Sarkodee	Melissa	89
Smalling	George	89
Smith	Alma	89
Smith	Jason Justin	89
Smith	Michael	89
Smith	Oswald	90
Snape	Tsagaza Hab	90
Spencer	Bill	90
Springer	Dorothy	90
Springer	Mark	90
Stennett	Enricho Alphanso	90
Stephenson	Steve	90
Strachan	Olive	90
Straker	Carol	91
Straker	Ralph Adolphus	91
Stubbs	Margaret	91
Suandi		91
Subryan	Carmeletta	91
Sunmonu	Lanre Adio	91
Superville	Dale	91
Sutherland	June	91

T

Tachie - Menson	Michael	93
Tapper	Natalie	93
Tate	Shirley	93
Taylor of Warwick	John	93
Terry	Todd	93
Theodore	Gloria Patricia	93
Thomas	Ebony	93
Thomas-Shell	Katryna	93
Thomason	Marsha	94
Thompson	Yvonne	94
Trusty	Len	94
Tui-tt	Akqiwa Catherine	94
Turay	Charlene	94
Turner	Ruby	94
Tywang	Monica-Joan	94

U

Uhlenbeek	Gus	95
Umana	N H R	95

V

Valley	Clinton	97
Vassel	Nevel Anthony	97
Vaughan	Winston Theodore	97
Vera	Joe	97
Victory	Danielle Merissa	97
Victory	Dennis	97
Victory	Grace Francesca	97
Vuli	Ludmilla	97

W

Waithe	Keith	99
Walker	Larrington	99
Walker	Rudolph	99
Walker	Sam	99
Walters	Roy Blake	99
Warner	Tony	99
Watson	Maxine Elizabeth	99
Watson-Druee	Neslyn	99
Webbe	Claudia	100
Webley	Emma	100
Weekes	Paul	100
Weir	Karen Marie	100
Wheeler	Robert Anthony	100
White	Densign	100
White	Jean Veta	100
White	Patsy	100
Whyte	Lorna	101
Wilkinson	Anthea	101
Williams	Alex	101
Williams	Denise	101
Williams	Marcia	101
Williams	Nadia	101
Williams	Sabra	101
Wilmot	Gary	101
Wilson	Carmen	102
Wilson	Eileen	102
Wilson	Granville A	102
Wilson	Precious	102
Woodley	Lorraine	102
Woodley	Stephanie	102
Woolford	Charlotte	102
Worthy	Johnny	102
Wright	Neal	102

Y

Yates	Salim-Geddes	103
Yeboah	Afua	103
Yinusa	Babatunde	103
Young	Jason	103
Young	Vince	103

Z

Zephaniah	Benjamin	103

ENTRY FORMAT IN BLACK WHO'S WHO

Each entry is in a standard format for easy reading. First we use the title followed by a first name, surname and honours where applicable. This is followed by a profession/occupation, the next entry is the current position/occupation, the name of an organisation/company and/or an address where given. All other information is standard. The personal profiles are either in the first or third person as submitted. Contact telephone numbers and addresses have been left out at the request of entrants. Nominations are not attached to every entry at the request of those making nominations.

INDEX OF
LATE ENTRIES

Abbreviations

This list of abbreviations is included merely as a guide to most of those contained in this directory and it does not necessarily imply any professional or other qualifications

ABAA	British Association of Accountants & Auditors
ABIM	Association of British Insecticide Manufacturers
ACA	Associate, Institute of Chartered Accountants
ACCA	Associate, Association of Chartered Certified Accountants
ACEA	Association of Cost and Executive Accountants
ACFI	Advisory Committee on Flight Information
ACGI	Associate of the City Guilds Institute London
ACIB	Associate, Chartered Institute of Bankers
ACLS	American Council of Learned Societies
ACMA	Associate, Chartered Institute of Management Accountants
ACP	Associate, College of Preceptors (Teachers/Trainors) Association of Clinical Pathologists.
ADV ST	Advance Stoppage (MUGU)
AFA	Associate, Institute of Financial Accountants
AFBPS	Associate Fellow, British Psychological Society
AFCS	Automatic Flight Control System
AGS M&D	Associate Guildhall School of Music and Drama
AGSM	Associate Guildhall School of Music and Drama
AHCIMA	Associate of Hotel, Catering and Institutional Management Association
AIDPM	Associate of the Institute of Data Processing Management
AIEC	Associate, Institution of Civil Engineers Associate of the Institute of Sales and Marketing Management
ALA	Associate Library Association
ALAM	Associate London Academy of Music and Dramatic Art
ALCM	Associate London College of Music
ALSTD	Associate of the Imperial Society of Teachers of Dance
AMIEE	Associate Member, Institution of Electrical Engineers
ARAM	Associate Royal Academy of Music
ARCM	Associate, Royal College of Music
ARCS	Associate Royal College of Science
ASA	Associate Member Society of Actuaries
ATCL	Associate Trinity College of Music, London
ATI	Associate Textile Institute
ATII	Associate Member of Chartered Institute of Taxation
B.Com	Bachelor of Commerce
B.Ed	Bachelor of Education
B.Eng	Bachelor of Engineering
B.Mus	Bachelor of Music
B.Pharm	Bachelor of Pharmacy
BA	Bachelor of Arts
BAJ	Bachelor of Arts in Journalism
BAMS	British American Minesweeper
BBA	Bachelor of Business Administration, British Bankers Association
BD	Bachelor of Divinity
BFA	Bachelor of Fine Arts
BL	Bachelor of Law, British Library
BLitt	Bachelor of Letters
BMA	British Medical Association
BOV	Burntout Velocity
BSc	Bachelor of Science
BT	Bachelor of Teaching / British Telecommunications
BTEC	Business and Technology Education Council
BVC	Bushveldt Carabineers

C Chem	Chartered Chemist
C.Eng	Chartered Engineer
C Math	Chartered Mathematician
C Phys	Chartered Physicist
C.Text	Chartered Textile Technologist
C&G	City & Guilds
CA	Chartered Accountant
CAA	Civil Aviation Authority
CAM	Communications, Advertising and Marketing
CBiol	Chartered Biologist
CCPR	Central Council of Physical Recreation
CD	Canadian Forces Decoration, Commander, Order of Distinction, Civil Defence, Compact Disc
Cert Ed	Certificate of Education
CIBSE	Chartered Institution of Building Services Engineers
CIDESCO	International Committee for Esthetics and Cosmetolgy
CIFP	Committee for Instrumental Flight Plans
CIMA	Chartered Institute of Management Accountants
CISA	Certified Information System Auditor
CMA)	Certified Management Accountant
CMS	Church Mission, Church Missionary Society, Certificate in Management Studies
CNAA	Council for National Academic Awards
CQSW	Certificate of Qualification in Social Work
CRCCYP	Certificate in the Residential Care of Children and Young People
CRSW	Certificate in Residential Social Work
CSM	Certificate Shopping Centre Manager
CTD	Certificate of Tax Deposit/ Corporate Technology Database
D.Med	Doctor of Medicine
D.Phil	Doctor of Philosophy
DA	Diploma of Arts, Diploma of Anaethesia, Doctor of Arts
DASE	Diploma in Advanced Studies in Education
DCH	Diploma in Child Health
DD	Doctor of Divinity
DDS	Doctor of Dental Surgery
DHMSA	Diploma in the History of Medicine
DHO	Director of Home Operations
DHY	Derelet Hara Yollon
DIC	Diploma of the Imperial College
Dip Ed	Diploma in Education
Dip HE	Diploma of Higher Education
DLitt	Dotor of Literature, Doctor of Letters
DMA	Diploma in Municipal Administration
DMC	Design Module Controller
DMH	Dept of Mental Health
DMRD	Diploma in Medical Radiological Diagnosis
DMS	Director of Medical Services
DOMS	Diploma in Ophthalmic Medicine and Surgery
DPEd	Doctor of Pedagogy
DPhil	Doctor of Philosophy
DPM	Diploma in Psychological Medicine
DRCOG	Diploma of Royal College of Obstetrictians and Gynaecologists
DSc	Doctor of Science
DSSc	Doctor of Social Science
DSW	Director of Special Weapons
DTCD	Diploma in Tuberculosis and Chest Diseases
DTM&H	Diploma in Tropical Medicine and Hygiene
DTP	Driver Training Platoon
EMRT	Ethnic Minority Recruiting Team
ENB	English National Board Careers Advisory Centre

ENG	Engineer Officer	HNC	Higher National Certificate
Eur-Ing	European Engineer	HND	Higher National Diploma
F InstCM	Fellow of the Institute of Commercial Management	IDTA	International Differential Treatment Association
F InstSMM	Fellow, Institute of Sales and Marketing Management	IEEE	Institute of Electrical and Electronics Engineers
		ITEC	Information Technology Electronics and Computers
FAAI	Fellow, Institute of Administrative Accounting Data	IWO	Institution of Water Officers
FBCO	Fellow British College of Optometrists		
FBHI	Fellow, British Horological Institute	LDSRCS	Licentiate in Dental Surgery of the Royal College of Surgeons
FCA	Fellow, Institute of Chartered Accountants, Fellow, Institute of Chartered Accountants in Australia, Fellow, New Zealand Society of Accountants, Federation of Canadian Artists	LJ	Lord Justice
		LL.B	Bachelor of Laws
		LLM	Master of Law
FCCA	Fellow Chartered Association of Certified Accountants	LMPA	Qualified Member of the Masters Photographers Association
FCCP	Friends Coordinating Committee on Peace	LMSSA	Licentiate in Medicine and Surgery
FCIB	Fellow, Corporation of Insurance Brokers, Fellow, Chartered Institute of Bankers	LRAM	Licentiate, Royal Academy of Music
		LRCP	Licentiate,Royal College of Physicians, London
FCIOB	Fellow, Chartered Institute of Building	LRSM	Licentiate, Royal Schools of Music
FCIS	Fellow, Institute of Chartered Secretaries and Administrators	LTCL	Licentiate of Trinity College of Music
FCIT	Fellow, Chartered Institute of Transport		
FFA	Fellow, Faculty of Actuaries, Fellow, Institute of Financial Accountants	M.Com	Master of Commerce
		M.Ed	Master of Education
FFAEM	Fellow, Faculty of Accident and Emergency	M.Imgt	Member, Institute of Management
FFARCS	Fellow, Faculty of Anaesthetists, Royal College of Surgeons of England	M. Mus	Master of Music
		M.Phil	Master of Philosophy
FFBA	Fellow. Corporation of Executives and Administrators	M Soc Sc	Master of Social Sciences
		MA	Master of Arts
FFPHM	Fellow, Faculty of Public Health Medicine	MAAT	Member, Association of Accounting Technicians
FFRRCSI	Fellow, Faculty of Radiologists, Royal College of Surgeons of Ireland	Maj	Major General
		MASC	Member, Australian Society of Calligraphers
FIAP	Fellow Institution of Analysts and Programmers	MASCE	Member, American Society of Civil Engineers
FIBiol	Fellow, Institute of Biology	MB	Medal of Bravery, Bachelor of Medicine
FICA	Fellow, Commonwealth Institute of Accountants, Fellow Institute of Chartered Accountants in England and Wales	MBA	Master of Business Administration
		MBBChin	Bachelor of Medicine
		MBBS	Bachelor of Medicine/ Bachelor of Science/Batchelor of Surgery
FIEE	Fellow of the Institution of Electrical Engineers	MBIM	Member, British Institute of Management
FIIA	Fellow, Institute of Industrial Administration, Fellow Institute of Internal Auditors	MCIH	Member of Chartered Institute of Housing
		MCIOB	Member, Chartered Institute of Building
FIM	Fellow Institute of Materials	MCIT	Member, Chartered Institute of Transport
FIMechE	Fellow Institution of Mechanical Engineers	MCIWEM	Member, Chartered Institution of Water and Environmental Management
FMAAT	Fellow Member, Association of Accounting Technicians		
FPC	Family Practitioner Committee	MD	Doctor of Medicine, Military District
FRAeS	Fellow, Royal Aeronautical Society	MED	Master of Education
FRAS	Fellow, Royal Astronomical Society	MFA	Master of Fine Arts
FRC.Path	Fellow of Royal College of Pathology	MFPHM	Member, Faculty of Public Health Medicine
FRCO	Fellow, Royal College of Organists	MIED	Member Institution of Engineering Designers
FRCP	Fellow, Royal College of Physicians	MIEE	Member Institution of Electrical Engineers
FRCPCH	Fellow, Royal College of Paediatrics and Child Health	MIFM	Member Institute of Fisheries Management
		MIIA	Member, Institute of Industrial Administration
FRCPE	Fellow, Royal College of Physicians	MIMI	Member, Institute of the Motor Industry
FRCPsych	Fellow, Royal College of Psychiatrists	MIMM	Member, Institution of Mining and Metallurgy
FRCR	Fellow, Royal College of Radiologists	MInst P	Member, Institute of Physics
FRCS	Fellow, Royal College of Surgeons of England	MIPD	Member, Institute of Personnel and Development
FRCSEd	Fellow, Royal College of Surgeons of Edinburgh	MIRSE	Member, Institute of Railway Signal Engineers
FRGS	Fellow, Royal Geographical Society	MIRTE	Member, Institute of Road Transport Engineers
FRHS	Fellow, Royal Horticultural Society	MLitt	Master of Letters
FRICS	Fellow, Royal Institution of Chartered Surveyors	MRCGP	Member, Royal College of General Practitioners
FRNS	Fellow Royal Numismatic Society	MRCP	Member of Royal College of Physicians, London
FRPharmS	Fellow, Royal Pharmaceutical Society		
FRSA	Fellow Royal Society of Arts	MRC	Member Royal College of Psychiatrists
FRSH	Fellow, Royal Society for the Promotion of Health	MRPharms	Member, Royal Pharmaceutical Society
		MRTPI	Member, Royal Town Planning Institute
FRSM	Fellow, Royal Society of Medicine	MS	Master of Surgery, Master of Science
		MSA	Master of Science, Agricure (US), Mineralogical Society of America
GPI	Greenpeace International/Grocery Price Index	MSc	Master of Science
HCS	Higher Civil Service		
HETC	Computer & Commercial Industries/Heavy Equipment Test Chamber	NCA	National Certificate of Agriculture
		NCDT	National Council of Drama Training

NCTJ	National Council for the Training of Journalists
NDN	National Diffusion Network
NEBSS	National Examinations Board for Supervisory Studies
ONC	Office of New Careers
OND	Ordinary National Diploma
PA	Pakistan Army, Personnal Assistant
PADI	Professional Association of Diving Instructors
PGCE	Post Graduate Certificate of Education
PhD	Doctor of Philosophy
PHEC	Human Ecology
PPA	Periodical Publishers Association
PQ	Physically Qualified/Province of Quebec
QTS	Qualification Test Specification
RADA	Royal Academy of Dramatic Arts
RAMC	Royal Army Medical Corps
RCA	Member, Royal Canadian Academy of Arts, Royal College of Art, Royal Cambrian Academy
RCOG	Royal College of Obstetricians and Gynaecologists
RCR	Royal College of Radiologists
RGN	Registered General Nurse
RIBA	Royal Institute of British Architects
RICS	Royal Institution of Chartered Surveyors
RJ	Royal Jordanian Airlines
RM	Royal Marines, Resident Magistrate, Registered Midwife
RMN	Registered Mental Nurse
RN	Royal Navy, Registered Nurse
RNT	Registered Nurse Tutor, Royal National Theatre
RSA	Royal Society of Arts
SCM	State Certified Midwife, Student Christian Movement
SFA	Securities and Future Authority
SMIEEE	Senior Member, Institute of Electrical and Electronics Engineers
SMO	Senior Medical Officer, Sovereign Military Order
SRN	State Registered Nurse
SWA	State Welfare Agency
TD	Territorial Army Efficiency Decoration
TESOL	Teaching English to Speakers of Other Languages
UPI	United Press International
USPTR	US Professional Tennis Registry
YMCA	Young Men's Christian Association

BLACK
WHO'S
WHO

First Edition

ETHNIC MEDIA GROUP

publishers of

 Caribbean Times  ASIAN TIMES

MS DIANE ABBOTT MP

DATE OF BIRTH: 27.9.53
PERSONAL PROFILE: Diane Abbott is the first Black woman ever elected to the British parliament. Miss Abbott has an Honours Degree in History from Cambridge University. She has served on the Treasury Select Committee of the House of Commons.

MR CHARLES ABOMELI (ACTOR)

215 Lansdowne Road, Tottenham, London, N17 0NU

PLACE OF BIRTH: London, 28.10.72
MARITAL STATUS: Single
COLLEGE: Kent University, Mountview and Central Drama Schools
ACADEMIC QUALIFICATIONS: BA in Politics
PROFESSIONAL QUALIFICATIONS: Postgraduate Diploma in Acting and Musical Theatre
MEMBERSHIPS: Equity
HOBBIES AND INTERESTS: Keeping fit, playing basketball, a regular funk fiend
PERSONAL PROFILE: Has a BA in Politics (Kent University) trained at Mountview Theatre School (Dame Judi Dench Scholarship) and is a private acting coach. Has worked consistently in Britain and Europe and received critical acclaim in roles such as Sophocles' Ajax and Othella at the Wycombe Swan. An actor to watch in 2000.

PROF BRIAN STANLEY ABRAHAMS (MUSICIAN-TEACHER)

9 Culross Buildings, Battlu Bridge Road, London, NW1 2TJ

PLACE OF BIRTH: South Africa, 26.6.47
MARITAL STATUS: Single
CHILDREN: One (Louis William)
PROFESSIONAL QUALIFICATIONS: Master Drummer. Prof of South African Jazz Studies
EMAIL: Brianabrahams@hotmail..com
PERSONAL PROFILE: Thirty years professional musician played with Archie Shepp, Abdullah Ebrahim, Dewey Redman, Don Cherry, Ronnie Scott and Grand Union Orchestra. Teacher of music at Guildhall School of Music and Drama, also at Southampton University and Royal Academy London - well travelled and well known in England, Europe and America. Bandleader of the celebrated group 'District Six'.

MR DERRICK WINSTON ACCRA (YOUTH LEADER)

Senior Youth Worker, Accra Centre for the advancement of young people, Accra-Crawford Youth Centre, Kenbury Street, London, SE5 9BS

PLACE OF BIRTH: Guyana, 6.8.49
MARITAL STATUS: Single
CHILDREN: Seven (Derrick, Alex, Nandi, Akua, Marlon, Kwame, Tane)
MEMBERSHIPS: Unison
HONOURS/AWARDS: ACYC Merit Award for contribution to youth work
HOBBIES AND INTERESTS: Football, fishing, young people, community
PERSONAL PROFILE: A visionary, influential community leader in central Brixton since 1979, Derrick recognised the lack of facilities and foresaw the effect of idle and disenchanted youth on a community. Thus he founded an organisation, which for 20 years has instilled a sense of pride and purpose in local youngsters by providing constructive activities in their leisure time. He was formerly a prison lay visitor and a member of the police consultative committee. He's currently chair of his Estates TA and the Area Housing Forum.
NOMINATED BY: Jackie Walsh

> 'I am associated with a lot of pastors and churches to help promote Christianity'
>
> **THOMAS ADDY**

DR OWOAHENE KWAKU ACHAMPONG JP
(UNIVERSITY LECTURER)

London Guildhall University MPD Department, Ghanaian Immigrants' Advisory Council, 69 Canterbury Road, Croydon, CR0 3PT

PLACE OF BIRTH: Ghana, 18.7.32
MARITAL STATUS: Married
CHILDREN: Four (Abena, Robin, Kofi, Kwabena)
COLLEGE: University of London
ACADEMIC QUALIFICATIONS: MA, LLB, PhD, Minor: Accs; HND
DIRECTORSHIPS: Director and Chairman of, New World Business Services Ltd (Ex)
MEMBERSHIPS: Commonwealth Judges and Magistrates Association
HONOURS/AWARDS: Justice of the Peace, ILEA Sponsorship for Doctoral Research
HOBBIES AND INTERESTS: Reading, writing, public speaking
PERSONAL PROFILE: Dr Kwaku Achampong taught in the School of Legal, Political and Social Sciences from 1991-1994. He is a competent lawyer of considerable experience both in the academic and administrative worlds. He has taught a number of the law core courses including company law, civil liberties and constitutional and administrative law. In addition, he has also taught business law on a number of business courses. Dr Achampong is a reliable colleague, who takes his classes very seriously and who is willing to help younger and junior members of staff.

NOMINATED BY: Mr Ameyan Kyereh

MR WILFRED ACHILLE (ARCHITECT)

MODE 1 Architects, Unit 220, Aberdeen House, 22-24 Highbury Grove, Islington, London, N5 2EA

PLACE OF BIRTH: London, 7.12.58
MARITAL STATUS: Married
CHILDREN: Two (Alexandra, Victoria)
COLLEGE: University of East London
ACADEMIC QUALIFICATIONS: BSc Dip Arch
PROFESSIONAL QUALIFICATIONS: RIBA
MEMBERSHIPS: Royal Institute of British Architects
HOBBIES AND INTERESTS: Black films, music
EMAIL: Mode1@compuserve.com
PERSONAL PROFILE: Wilfred Achille founded Mode 1 Architects who combine art, architecture, cultural backgrounds, well travelled experiences and debates as part of the ingredients required in the formulation of their specific design language. Projects include - Black Cultural Archives - Brixton, African Caribbean Centre in Leyton - Oxford Angoll Estates - Acton and Stonebridge Estate

MISS MARISSA ADAMS (SCHOOLGIRL-ACTRESS)

Jackie Palmer Stage School Agency, 30 Daws Hill Lane, High Wycombe, HP13 5DP

PLACE OF BIRTH: England, 7.2.92
HOBBIES AND INTERESTS: Tap, ballet, drama, tai kwondo, singing

PERSONAL PROFILE: Bright energetic girl, with lots of enthusiasm. She has been dancing since the age of four at the Jackie Palmer Stage School and has taken part in school shows and concerts. Recently she appeared in a BBC children's programme titled 'Within Living Memory'.

MR THOMAS ADDY (SHIPPING EXECUTIVE)

Manager, Poth Hille & Co. Ltd, 37 High Street, Stratford, London, E15 2QD

PLACE OF BIRTH: Ghana, 11.2.62
MARITAL STATUS: Married
CHILDREN: Four (Thomas Junior, Miles, Larisa, Tamsin)
COLLEGE: University of East London
ACADEMIC QUALIFICATIONS: O-Levels, A-Levels (East Ham College)
PROFESSIONAL QUALIFICATIONS: Dip in Shipping, Dip in Marketing, Degree in Sociology
DIRECTORSHIPS: Dashwood Shipping Agencies, Tomay Shipping Co.
MEMBERSHIPS: Institute of Freight Forwarders Association, C.I Transport Association, Institute of Marketing

HOBBIES AND INTERESTS: Debating, politics, singing, squash, swimming, reading, Christian activities
PERSONAL PROFILE: Radio presenter for Radio Afrique on Sundays for Christians. In the process of putting some Christian songs together. Also writing a book titled 'Container, Enemy or Friend' with the help of my father, Mr TT Addy - the former director of the port of Ghana. I also run my own company Tomay Shipping Co. I am associated with a lot of pastors and churches to help promote Christianity. Helping the youth gain self confidence to achieve their aims, especially the underclass.
NOMINATED BY: Gerrard Knight

MR DOTUN ADEBAYO (Publisher)

The X Press, 6 Hoxton Square, London, N1 6NU

PLACE OF BIRTH: Nigeria, 25.8.60
MARITAL STATUS: Married
CHILDREN: One (Temisan)
COLLEGE: University of Essex
ACADEMIC QUALIFICATIONS: BA Philosophy
PERSONAL PROFILE: Formerly a journalist with the Voice newspaper, he kicked off a publishing revolution with the release of the best seller 'Yardie' in 1992. He hosts the Dotun Adebayo show on BBC GLR 94.9 (London) every Tuesday night, and is a columnist with Pride magazine and New Nation.

MR VICTOR ADEBOWALE (Chief Executive)

Centrepoint, 2 Swallow Place, London, W1R 7AA

PLACE OF BIRTH: Wakefield, 21.7.62
MARITAL STATUS: Single
CHILDREN: One
DIRECTORSHIPS: Public Management Foundation, Rich Mix Centre, Tomorrow Project
MEMBERSHIPS: Member of the Government's New Deal Advisory Task Force, SITRA, Homeless Network, DEMOS Advisory Council, Fellow Royal Society of Arts
HOBBIES AND INTERESTS: Saxaphone, kite-flying
PERSONAL PROFILE: He is currently chief executive of Centerpoint which runs emergency shelters, hostels and flats in Greater London. Each year Centerpoint helps over 3,000 newly homeless young people with temporary accommodation, advice and assists them with finding a job and securing a permanent place to live. He is a member of SITRA (Special Needs Information Training and Resource Agency) which provides training and policy information to the special needs housing sector.
NOMINATED BY: Sarah Macaulay

MR ADE ADENIJI (Employment Law Officer)

Foreign and Commonwealth Office, Employment Law and Equal Opportunities Section, 1 Palace Street, Room 329, London, SW1E 5HE

PLACE OF BIRTH: London, 14.7.68
MARITAL STATUS: Single
COLLEGE: University of East London, South Bank University
ACADEMIC QUALIFICATIONS: LLB Hons - MSc
PROFESSIONAL QUALIFICATIONS: PG Diploma Legal Practise; IPD
MEMBERSHIPS: IPD
HOBBIES AND INTERESTS: Reading, travelling, cinema, theatre, personal development
PERSONAL PROFILE: Previously worked with the Cabinet Office dealing with development of policy on race and ethnicity issues. Also worked with the National Mentoring Consortium as co-ordinator of a scheme aimed at enhancing the skills of ethnic minority undergraduates. Former member of Tower Hamlets Citizens Advice Bureau Management Committee. Currently completing MSc in Human Resources, specialising in consultancy.
NOMINATED BY: Ms C.A Lufkin, Foreign & Commonwealth Office

MR KOLA ADESINA (News Editor)

West Africa Magazine, 43 - 45 Coldharbour Lane, Camberwell, London

PLACE OF BIRTH: Nigeria, 16.11.59
MARITAL STATUS: Married
CHILDREN: Three (Adesola, Dayo, Tope)
COLLEGE: South Bank University
ACADEMIC QUALIFICATIONS: MSc Development Studies
PROFESSIONAL QUALIFICATIONS: BSc Mass Communications Lagos Nigeria
MEMBERSHIPS: National Union Journalist (NUJ) UK, Consultant to United Nations Industrial Development Organisation UNIDO on media relations
HONOURS/AWARDS: Finalist - Best written feature Emma Awards 1998
HOBBIES AND INTERESTS: Football, reading
EMAIL: Kolaa@btinternet.com
PERSONAL PROFILE: As news editor of West Africa magazine, I cover media assignments in over 50 countries world-wide. I started my career as a trainee reporter with the Village News, a community newspaper published in Lagos, Nigeria. In 1986 I was appointed editor of Flight Africa, Africa's premier aviation and travel magazine. The next year I was transferred to London as head of international operations to open the Western Europe bureau of the magazine.

MR JOHN ADEWOLE (Actor)

Artistic Director, The Zuriya Theatre Company, 53 Lambeth Walk, London, SE11 6DX

PLACE OF BIRTH: Sierra Leone, 24.11.48
MARITAL STATUS: Married
CHILDREN: Several (Kahina, Afamefuna, Chioma, Iyaniwura, Adesimi)
COLLEGE: Darlington College of Arts
ACADEMIC QUALIFICATIONS: BA Hons Diploma in Journalism
MEMBERSHIPS: Equity
HONOURS/AWARDS: Society of Black Arts 1995 Outstanding Achievement in Promotion
HOBBIES AND INTERESTS: Cricket, architecture
PERSONAL PROFILE: Originally from Sierra Leone. Trained at Darlington College of Arts. Theatre appearances include: 'The Coventry Mystery Plays', 'Night and Day' (Sherman Theatre), 'Murmuring Judges' (Royal National Theatre). I am a regular contributor to the BBC World Service and a member of its African Theatre company.

MS ADENIKE ADEWUYI (Teacher)

PLACE OF BIRTH: London, 31.3.62
MARITAL STATUS: Separated
CHILDREN: One (Caroline, Oduja)
COLLEGE: Universities of Lagos and Huddersfield
ACADEMIC QUALIFICATIONS: BSc Hons Biology
PROFESSIONAL QUALIFICATIONS: PGCE, Education, RSA Computing
HOBBIES AND INTERESTS: Music, church
PERSONAL PROFILE: I am a professional with over six years experience in the retail industry. Well presented, friendly and computer literate, with excellent communication skills. I am now seeking to progress my career in education or in retail within a supervising or management role.

DR ANN ADEYEMI (Educator)

Co-ordinator History, Levenshulme High School,

PLACE OF BIRTH: Manchester, 9.3.51
MARITAL STATUS: Single
COLLEGE: University of Liverpool, Manchester University, Newscastle University
ACADEMIC QUALIFICATIONS: B Ed. History Eng. B Ed. Drama , MEP Drama in Education
PROFESSIONAL QUALIFICATIONS: PhD Race and Ethnic Studies
DIRECTORSHIPS: Bridgewater Hall, Manchester 2 Schools Curriculum
MEMBERSHIPS: Awards panel 3 ITC, Regional panellists
HOBBIES AND INTERESTS: Music, theatre, the arts, archaeology, education, travel, Black history
EMAIL: AA@DOL.UK.
PERSONAL PROFILE: An educator, artist and researcher who has been actively involved in developing projects and curriculum resources to profile Black and Asian arts and history. Ambitions - I would like to be elected to the new upper chamber of government with Black and Asian people taking a leading role.
NOMINATED BY: Chris Mullard

HRH PRINCE MALIK ADO-IBRAHIM (Businessman)

Arrows Grand Prix, Leafield Technical Centre, Leafield, Witney, 0X8 5PF

PLACE OF BIRTH: Nigeria, 22.12.60
MARITAL STATUS: Divorced
CHILDREN: Three (Azad, Alia, Asia)
COLLEGE: IUE
ACADEMIC QUALIFICATIONS: BSc, MBA (Soaltern cal)
HONOURS/AWARDS: Keys to the city of Dallas

HOBBIES AND INTERESTS: Polo, tennis, driving, reading
PERSONAL PROFILE: HRH Prince Malik Ado Ibrahim is a significant shareholder of Arrows Grand Prix, the Formula One racing team. He was responsible for leading the consortium that purchased 70% of Arrows Grand Prix over the past decade. Recently he brokered the sale of Lotus cars. Malik comes from a successful and established Nigerian family who once held a 40% share in Nestle Nigeria. His primary focus for 1999 is to develop the team's global marketing strategy by broadening its appeal to several unexploited international audiences.

MR RAZAAQ ADOTI (Actor)

Peters, Fraser & Dunlop, 503-4 The Chambers, Chelsea Harbour, Lots Road, London, SW10 0XF

PLACE OF BIRTH: London, 27.6.73
MARITAL STATUS: Single
COLLEGE: Central School of Speech and Drama
ACADEMIC QUALIFICATIONS: BA in Acting, BTEC National Diploma in the Performing Arts
HOBBIES AND INTERESTS: Gym, football, boxing, singing
PERSONAL PROFILE: Fortune favours the brave so I'm just trying to keep it real!

MISS PATRICIA ADUDU (Sports Journalist)

Channel 5, 200 Grays Inn Road, London, WC1X 8X2

PLACE OF BIRTH: Bristol, 30.5.69
MARITAL STATUS: Single
COLLEGE: Birmingham University, Warwick University
ACADEMIC QUALIFICATIONS: BA Sports Science, MA Sport, Media and Culture
PROFESSIONAL QUALIFICATIONS: (2.I)
DIRECTORSHIPS: Prerequisite Formats Company

MEMBERSHIPS: Pact
HOBBIES AND INTERESTS: Writing, cooking
PERSONAL PROFILE: I intend to create an 'active' base for young black media professionals to develop and initiate ideas for TV and radio so that they can gain true autonomy in media.

HE JAMES EMMANUEL KWEGYIR AGGREY-ORLEANS (Diplomat)

High Commissioner, Ghana High Commissioner, 13 Belgrave Square, London, SW1X 8PN

PLACE OF BIRTH: Ghana, 11.10.37
MARITAL STATUS: Married
CHILDREN: Two (James Junior, Bertrand Leslie)
COLLEGE: Universities of Ghana, Bordeaux University, Oxford University
ACADEMIC QUALIFICATIONS: BA Hons
PROFESSIONAL QUALIFICATIONS: Diploma in Public Administration
MEMBERSHIPS: Garrick Travellers
HONOURS/AWARDS: Officier Dans L'ordre Des Palmes Academiques
HOBBIES AND INTERESTS: Music, travel, heraldry, dancing
PERSONAL PROFILE: Joined Ghana Foreign Service in 1963 served at various posts in New York and Accra. Was chief of protocol then clerk to the Parliament of Ghana. Served also as assistant director for ten years at the International Tropical Timber Organisation (an organisation set up by the UN and based in Yokohama, Japan. Approved High Commissioner (Ambassador) for Ghana UK in October 1997.

DR BEULAH AINLEY (Journalist-Writer)

Freelance, 41 Vaughan Gardens, Ilford, IG1 3PA

PLACE OF BIRTH: Jamaica, 23.11.54
MARITAL STATUS: Married
CHILDREN: One (Adam)
COLLEGE: London School of Economics
ACADEMIC QUALIFICATIONS: BA Hons English, PhD
PROFESSIONAL QUALIFICATIONS: Social Science
MEMBERSHIPS: National Union Journalist
HONOURS/AWARDS: PhD LSE
HOBBIES AND INTERESTS: Politics, reading, walking, theatre, music, gardening
PERSONAL PROFILE: I am a journalist-writer, specialising in race and the media. Did research study at the London School of Economics for eight years on race and the media. I was awarded a PhD. I have recently written a book 'Black Journalists White Media'. Published by Trentham Books. I also lecture in journalism in Europe and the United States.
NOMINATED BY: Patrick Ainley

DEACON OLUMUYIWA OLU AIYEGBUSI (Engineer)

Chairman-CEO, Olu Olu Industries Ltd, Unit 5, Burwell Industrial Estate, Burwell Road, London, E10 7QJ

PLACE OF BIRTH: Nigeria, 23.10.53
MARITAL STATUS: Married
CHILDREN: Five (Funke, Yomi, Deji, Korede, Fola)
COLLEGE: Igbobi College, Nigeria
ACADEMIC QUALIFICATIONS: BA Hons, MSc Chemical Engineering
DIRECTORSHIPS: Upland Flour Mills (Nigeria) Ltd, Yem Yom Co., Monipat Ltd.
MEMBERSHIPS: National Society of Black Engineers and Chemists, IKOYI Club-Lagos, President Country Club, Efon Alaaye
HONOURS/AWARDS: Who's Who American Students,1976,1977, 1st Natwest/African Business Executives Merit Award,1997.
HOBBIES AND INTERESTS: Youth enlightenment programmes, church affairs, sports, music
PERSONAL PROFILE: Started engineering practice in 1980. Formed Olu Olu Winery (bottling Palm Wine) 1984. Profiled in publications as innovative engineer in the Guardian and Punch newspapers of Nigeria in 1985. Pioneered and popularised instant pounded yam flour in 1988. Wholesale importer and exporter, food processor, distributors Europe, US and Canada. Ordained deacon.
NOMINATED BY: Sam Jenyo

PRINCE RIBA AKABUSI (Actor-Poet)

Kimberley Weeks Management, 116 Earlham Grove, Forest Gate, London, E7 9AS

PLACE OF BIRTH: London, 27.12.60
MARITAL STATUS: Single
COLLEGE: City & Guilds
ACADEMIC QUALIFICATIONS: Security Procedures, RTITB International Forklift Driving Certificate
PROFESSIONAL QUALIFICATIONS: Black Belt 4th Dan Wado-Ryu-Karate (1978), Trained at Anna Scher Children's Theatre
MEMBERSHIPS: Full Equity Membership, Member of BECTO, Member of International Society of Poets (Distinguished)
HONOURS/AWARDS: Former Junior World Champion 1976, Former vice captain British Junior Team
HOBBIES AND INTERESTS: TV, cinema, reading, poetry, music, economics
PERSONAL PROFILE: Riba Akabusi has appeared hundreds of times on television, the big screen, radio, documentaries, theatre and video.

MR SEGUN AKINDAYINI (Managing Director)

African Video Centre,

PLACE OF BIRTH: Nigeria, 18.9.57
MARITAL STATUS: Divorced
ACADEMIC QUALIFICATIONS: BSc (Eng), MSc, MSc Molucular Science of Materials
PROFESSIONAL QUALIFICATIONS: Liceniate of City and Guilds (LCG) Incorporated Engineer (I.ENG)
HOBBIES AND INTERESTS: Music, films, travel
PERSONAL PROFILE: Segun developed the concept of the African Video Centre from a home based business (mail order only) to the formation of the UK's first and largest stockists of African, Caribbean and Black Hollywood films. AVC is used as a resource centre for colleges, universities and libraries
NOMINATED BY: Sam Jenyo

MR DELE AKINLADE (Managing Director-Publisher)

UK Black Links Ltd, Suite 102 - 1st Floor Cumberland House, 80 Scrubbs Lane, Willesden, London, NW10 6RF

PLACE OF BIRTH: London, 3.1.68
MARITAL STATUS: Single
COLLEGE: South Bank University
ACADEMIC QUALIFICATIONS: BSc Hons Industrial Biotechnology
PROFESSIONAL QUALIFICATIONS: SFA
DIRECTORSHIPS: UK Black Links Ltd
MEMBERSHIPS: Nigerian Chamber of Commerce
HONOURS/AWARDS: Numerous sales achievement and athletics awards
HOBBIES AND INTERESTS: Art, music, reading, motivational, personal development books, charitable work on sickle cell
EMAIL: dakinlade@uklinks.com
PERSONAL PROFILE: Ex-city stockbroker and managing director of UK Black Links, publishers of the Black business directory. His driving ambition is to put the UK Black business community firmly on the map as a strong economic force. He is on his way to achieving this by increasing public awareness through showcasing the true levels of Black businesses in the UK and their contribution to the overall economy.

MR ADEWALE AKINNUOYE-AGBAJE (ACTOR)

PLACE OF BIRTH: London, 22.8.67
MARITAL STATUS: Single
COLLEGE: King's College
ACADEMIC QUALIFICATIONS: BA, MA in Law
HOBBIES AND INTERESTS: Making music, capoeria writing arts, culture travel
PERSONAL PROFILE: A musician, holder of a Bachelors and Masters Degree in Law . One of Europe's prominent Black male models and now fast becoming Hollywood's 'new man on the block'. Debuting in Speilberg's 'Congo' and starring with Jim Carey in 'Ace Venturer'. Michael Caine in '20,000 Leagues Under The Sea'. He is currently starring in the much acclaimed 'HBO Trans OZ' He's only just getting warm.

MR ABIDEEN ABBEY AKINOSHUN
(PSYCHOLOGIST/ LAW STUDENT)

Employment Advisor, Voluntary Employment Advisory Services for Ethnic Minorities, 68 Gloucester House, Cambridge Road, London, SE28 8EA

PLACE OF BIRTH: Nigeria, 5.12.64
MARITAL STATUS: Married
COLLEGE: University of Sofia, Bulgaria. King's College London
ACADEMIC QUALIFICATIONS: Master of Arts in Social Psychology
PROFESSIONAL QUALIFICATIONS: Diploma of Higher Education in Mental Health Nursing
DIRECTORSHIPS: Voluntary Employment Advisory Services for Ethnic Minorities
MEMBERSHIPS: Labour Party, Discrimination Law Association, TGWU
HONOURS/AWARDS: Award Nominee for the 1998 The Voice Black Community Awards
HOBBIES AND INTERESTS: Politics, sport, travelling, music
PERSONAL PROFILE: Akinoshun is currently studying for a post graduate diploma in law at Southbank University, London. He is also a co-founder of Voluntary Employment Advisory Services of Ethnic Minorities in London. He has worked tirelessly on behalf of others within the Black community.
NOMINATED BY: Olusagun Ajisafe

MR JUDE AKUWUDIKE (ACTOR)

Hamilton Asper Management, Ground Floor, 24 Hanway Street, London, W1P 9DD

COLLEGE: RADA
ACADEMIC QUALIFICATIONS: Dip RADA
PROFESSIONAL QUALIFICATIONS: Dip RADA
HONOURS/AWARDS: Martini Rossi Regional Theatre Awards 1994, Best Supporting Actor
HOBBIES AND INTERESTS: Visual arts, soccer, other sports, music
EMAIL: Hamiltonasper@compuserve.com
PERSONAL PROFILE: Has worked in many theatres in England and abroad. Productions include: At Royal Court, 'Our Countries Good', 'Marching For Fausa', 'Recruiting Officer 'for RNT', 'Richard II', 'Not About Nightingales'. Television credits include: 'Roger Roger' 'Theebbtide', ' Under The Sun'. Films: 'A World Apart', 'Home & Away' . Radio: Worked extensively in radio drama for BBC World Service and Radio 4. Has co-written 'It's Good To Talk' at Theatre Royal Stratford. Have also directed.

MISS DONNA ALEXANDER (ACTRESS)

c/o Sally Hope Association, 108 Leonard Street, London, EC2A 4RH

PLACE OF BIRTH: Manchester, 16.4.65
MARITAL STATUS: Single
COLLEGE: Arden School Theatre
PROFESSIONAL QUALIFICATIONS: Acting Diploma Certificate
HOBBIES AND INTERESTS: Fitness, cooking, music, reading
PERSONAL PROFILE: Mixed race from a single parent family only child, mother West Indian, father Norwegian and Welsh. Joined drama school at 25, acting professionally for five years, played Penny Hutchens 'Para Medic' for 18 months. Love riding my Kawasaki Ninji.

MR GODFREY ALLEN (CHIEF EXECUTIVE)

Apex Trust, St Alphage House, Wingate Annexe, 2 Fore Street, Moorgate, London, EC2Y 5DA

PLACE OF BIRTH: London, 14.4.60
MARITAL STATUS: Single
COLLEGE: South Bank University
ACADEMIC QUALIFICATIONS: MSc, Public Services Management
PROFESSIONAL QUALIFICATIONS: Certificate in Training and Development
DIRECTORSHIPS: OPP International Limited, South Thames College Corporation
MEMBERSHIPS: Fellow, Royal Society of Arts; Fellow, Institute of Directors; Fellow, Institute of Management, MENSA, Inner London JP's
HONOURS/AWARDS: 1985 Recipient of the Certificate of Welcome - Los Angeles City Council
EMAIL: apexho@globalnet.co.UK
PERSONAL PROFILE: Former Task Force leader, DOE W.Midlands 1993-95, MD, OPP International Ltd 1990-93. CEO (formerly regional manager) Fullemploy Training Ltd 1987-90, Race equality officer (formerly neighbourhood worker) Ealing REC 1980-87. Major sporting honours: International Union of Martial Arts Championships.Team Gold Medalist -1985 and 1989.

MISS SONITA ALLEYNE (COMPANY DIRECTOR)

Somethin' Else, Unit 1-3, 1a Old Nichol Street, London, E2 7HR

PLACE OF BIRTH: Barbados, 16.3.67
MARITAL STATUS: Single
COLLEGE: Cambridge University, Fitzwilliam College
ACADEMIC QUALIFICATIONS: MA Hons CANTAB-Philosophy
DIRECTORSHIPS: Somethin'Else, Sound Directions Ltd
HONOURS/AWARDS: Nominated for 2 Bafta Awards
HOBBIES AND INTERESTS: Writing, film, cordon bleu cookery, wine
EMAIL: Sonita@somethin-else.com
PERSONAL PROFILE: Founded Somethin' Else, independent radio and television production company in 1991. The company makes programmes for BBC networks, international syndication, multimedia CD Roms, websites, inflight entertainment and corporate videos. In her spare time she is a presenter and journalist having worked for Radio's 4, 5 and GLR.
NOMINATED BY: Sharon Aitkin

MISS SHOLA AMA (ARTIST)

WEA Records, The Warner Building, 28 Kensington Church Street, London, W8 4EP

HONOURS/AWARDS: Brit Award for Best Female Solo Artist, 2 MOBO Awards for Best R&B Act and Best Newcomer
PERSONAL PROFILE: Shola Ama is a prodigious performer with a remarkable voice and a host of exquisite self-penned songs. She began 1997 with her astonishing debut single, 'You Might Need Somebody', which has already sold nearly 500,000 copies. A television documentary devoted exclusively to her was aired on ITV as part of LWT's 'Fresh' series. Shola joined 3T on a ten date tour, she also played at Jamiroquai's Jam In The Park and appeared on the Kiss Stage at the Notting Hill Carnival. Her meteoric rise has been incredible and the story behind her discovery is equally astonishing.

MR MICKEY AMBROSE (ACTOR-CHARITY FUNDRAISER)

PC Mick Tate, The Bill, 1 Deer Park Road, Merton, London, SW1G 3TL

PLACE OF BIRTH: Lambeth, 2.8.61
MARITAL STATUS: Married
CHILDREN: Three (Christina, Aaron, Kobie)
COLLEGE: East Ham College
ACADEMIC QUALIFICATIONS: 5 O-Levels
PROFESSIONAL QUALIFICATIONS: Football Coaching Certificate
HOBBIES AND INTERESTS: Football, basketball, jogging
PERSONAL PROFILE: Ex professional footballer Charlton Athletic and Chelsea. Freelance commentator for Sky Sports, actor in TV programme 'The Bill' as PC Mick Tate 541. Only registered football choreographer in England credits include 'Eastenders', 'The Bill', 'Casualty' and films 'Fever Pitch'. Organises charity celebrity football matches. Manager and founder TV All Stars X1, which has raised £400,000 for variety of charities.

MR JOHNNY AMOBI (ACTOR-SINGER-DANCER)

Writer, International Artists Ltd, Mezzanine Floor, 235 Regents Street, London, W1R 8AX

PLACE OF BIRTH: London, 18.7.65
MARITAL STATUS: Common Law Wife
CHILDREN: Two Stepchildren (Ocean, Daimali)
COLLEGE: London Studio Centre
ACADEMIC QUALIFICATIONS: 5 O-Levels (PCSC) Diploma in Social Work
PROFESSIONAL QUALIFICATIONS: Starlight Express, Miss Saigon, Joseph and Five Guys Named MOE.
MEMBERSHIPS: Music Union & Equity
HONOURS/AWARDS: Dame Anna Neagle Scholarship Awarded by Cameron Mackintosh, Sheila O'Neil Cup for Best All Round Performer
EMAIL: info@ h webber.co.UK
PERSONAL PROFILE: Raised in London of Nigerian and Scottish parents. Labelled maladjusted by the education system, I went on to achieve relative academic success, realising my lifes dream by winning a scholarship at one of Londons top performing arts colleges. In two years I became a principal artiste in the West End theatre. After travelling to Africa and Asia I became a writer, recording artiste and facilitator in African dance, voice and meditation workshops.

MS MOJIRAYO BOLA AMOLE (BUSINESSWOMAN)

Director, Bims African Food Store Ltd, 102 Rye Lane, Peckham, London, SE15 4RZ

PLACE OF BIRTH: Nigeria, 16.12.60
MARITAL STATUS: Ms
CHILDREN: One (Adejumo Mary Abimbole)
COLLEGE: Oyo State College of Education, Ilesa (Affliated to University Ibadan Agricultural Science
ACADEMIC QUALIFICATIONS: National Certificate of Education, Agricultural Scientist
DIRECTORSHIPS: Bims African Foods
HONOURS/AWARDS: Nigeria Businesswoman of the Year 1994, African Businesswoman of the Year 1997, African Personality Award 1998
HOBBIES AND INTERESTS: Reading, meeting people of like mind
PERSONAL PROFILE: Started business seven years ago. Worked four nights a week to support the business (auxiliary nurse). Trained as an agricultural science teacher, worked 14 hours all week in the shop. Import from seven different countries and export to more than 16 countries worldwide Canada, Brazil, Italy etc. Business started with a £1000. Strong ambition in politics.
NOMINATED BY: Dapo Oshiyemi

MR VIV ANDERSON (ASSISTANT MANAGER)

Middlesbrough Football Club, Cellnet Riverside Stadium, Middlesbrough, TS3 6RS

PLACE OF BIRTH: Nottingham, 29.7.56
PROFESSIONAL QUALIFICATIONS: 30 Caps For England
HONOURS/AWARDS: Won 2 League Championships & 2 European Cup Medals (Nottingham Forest)
PERSONAL PROFILE: Viv joined Boro as assistant manager with Bryan Robson in the summer of 1994 and has experienced all the ups and downs of promotion, relegation and three major cup finals ever since. He began his career under Brian Clough at Nottingham Forest where he won two League Championships and two European Cup medals before going on to have successful spells at Arsenal, Manchester United and Sheffield Wednesday before a year as player-manager at Barnsley.

MS BEVERLY ANDREWS (ACTRESS-WRITER)

PLACE OF BIRTH: US, 24.10.64
MARITAL STATUS: Single
COLLEGE: York University
ACADEMIC QUALIFICATIONS: Bachelor of Fine Arts
HONOURS/AWARDS: Talawa Theatre's Black Female Writers Award
HOBBIES AND INTERESTS: Diving
PERSONAL PROFILE: As an actress I have worked for BBC radio, Newcastle Playhouse, Perth Rep, Directors Ken Russell, Peter Greenaway. As a writer I've currently been commissioned to write a play for Soho Theatre Company 99.

MR AFOLABI ADEWALS ANDU
(MANAGING DIRECTOR)

Integral Consultants Group, 69 Harrowdens Road, North Wembley, HA0 2JQ

PLACE OF BIRTH: Ibadan, 16.4.62
MARITAL STATUS: Married
CHILDREN: Two (Adeture, Tolulade)
COLLEGE: Andrew Jackson University, US
ACADEMIC QUALIFICATIONS: BA Hons MBA
MEMBERSHIPS: Fast Track. Producing Nigerian News, AIMET magazine
PERSONAL PROFILE: Afolabi Andu was born to the Royal family of the Andus from Odosenly Town in the province of Ijeby in Nigeria. His father is Nigeria's first water engineer. Afolabi a committed Christian is married to Bridgst Oluyomisi Adenisi a medical practitioner.

DR ADRIEN ANTOINE (RESEARCHER-PUBLISHER)

Research Director, First Page, 62B Millais Road, Leytonstone, London, E11 4HD

PLACE OF BIRTH: West Indies, 5.3.50
COLLEGE: London
ACADEMIC QUALIFICATIONS: BSc, MSc, PhD
DIRECTORSHIPS: First Page
HOBBIES AND INTERESTS: Tennis, golf, sailing, theatre, music
PERSONAL PROFILE: Experienced researcher, writer and trainer. Research director of First Page, a research and publishing business specialising in socio-economic development issues in Africa and Caribbean. Considerable experience of work in higher education, including research and teaching and several more years experience in policy research in local government and private enterprise.

MS JANICE AQUAH (ACTOR-PRODUCER)

Michael Ladkin Management, Suite 1, 1 Duchess Street, London, W1N 3DE

PLACE OF BIRTH: Ghana, 23.2.67
MARITAL STATUS: Not Single
COLLEGE: University of York
ACADEMIC QUALIFICATIONS: BSc Hons, Environmental Biology
MEMBERSHIPS: Equity
EMAIL: janice@ourhq.freeserve.co.UK
PERSONAL PROFILE: Grew up in Ghana. After university, established Sparks Theatre Company. Currently presenter on the 'Really Wild Show' and the BBC Wildbunch. Have worked as an actor in theatre, film, television and radio. Have produced two videos. Community work in spare time for Friends of the Earth and Homelessness.

MISS EMMA ARCHIBALD (STUDENT-ACTRESS)

112 Charlton Road, Edmonton, London, 8EN

PLACE OF BIRTH: London, 20.11.79
MARITAL STATUS: Single
COLLEGE: The London Institute
ACADEMIC QUALIFICATIONS: GCSE's, Advanced GNVQ, 1st Year BA International Travel & Tourism Management
MEMBERSHIPS: Heart Line Association
HOBBIES AND INTERESTS: Writing poetry, karate, skating, dancing, modelling, athletics
EMAIL: emmaarchibald@hotmail.com
PERSONAL PROFILE: My inspiration is my mother - seeing how hard she works and all the things she has achieved. I see myself as an enthusiastic and outgoing person. I like trying out new things and achieving. I am 19 years old but look very young which leads to me having a crazy and great personality. My dreams and goals are to finish my degree and then make it into a film or be an MTV presenter. 'I have faith' Emma.

Afolabi Andu was born to the Royal family of the Andus from Odosenly Town in the province of Ijeby in Nigeria

MS JASMIN ARCHIBALD (MIDWIFE-MAGISTRATE)

Ward Sister-Magistrate, Haringey Magistrate Court, 112 Charlton Road, Lower Edmonton, London, N9 8EW

PLACE OF BIRTH: Jamaica, 27.4.51
MARITAL STATUS: Divorced
CHILDREN: Three (Nathaniel, Lawrence, Emma)
COLLEGE: Middlesex University
PROFESSIONAL QUALIFICATIONS: Registered Nurse, Registered Midwife ENB 402; 997; 907 and 807
MEMBERSHIPS: Chairperson of St Ann's C of E school governors
HOBBIES AND INTERESTS: Reading, charity work, travel
PERSONAL PROFILE: Arrived in England with brother and sister to join mum and dad in December 1966 aged 15 years. Finished school at Maryboon Secondary Technical in South Kensington. Went straight into nursing, worked hard to became a magistrate 1989. Now vice chairman of family court, also chair of governors of St Ann's Primary School. Two of my three children are at university. Busy with charity work.

NOMINATED BY: Emma Archibald

DR UDUAK ARCHIBONG (LECTURER)

Research Adviser, University of Bradford,

PLACE OF BIRTH: Nigeria, 2.2.63
MARITAL STATUS: Married
CHILDREN: Four (Emem, Medara, Ndifreke, Ifiok)
COLLEGE: University of Nigeria, University of Hull
ACADEMIC QUALIFICATIONS: PhD, BSc Hons, HETC
PROFESSIONAL QUALIFICATIONS: RN, RM, RPHN, RNT
MEMBERSHIPS: Racial Equality Council, Nigeria Friendship Society, Trans-cultural Nursing Health Association
HONOURS/AWARDS: The Outstanding Young Person of Nigeria in Health Care Development (1990) and other academic awards
HOBBIES AND INTERESTS: Sewing, dancing, badminton, table tennis, reading
EMAIL: U.E.ARCHIBONG@BRADFORD.AC.UK
PERSONAL PROFILE: TOYP 1990; Key roles in development of nursing practise, research and education in UK and Nigeria; high publication profile through peer review articles and conference papers, presentation of papers at national and international conferences, publications in academic journals and author; chair of research advisory board on trans-cultural care; steering committee member of Northern Ethnic Women's Network; advisor to black groups on health and women's issues; research interests; research utilisation; African extended family system and health and consumerism.

MR TONY ARMATRADING (ACTOR)

Scott Marshall, 44 Perryn Road, London, W3 7NA

PLACE OF BIRTH: Birmingham, 24.8.61
MARITAL STATUS: Married
DIRECTORSHIPS: Director Way Out West Ltd Multimedia
HOBBIES AND INTERESTS: Computers, cinema
PERSONAL PROFILE: Tony has worked extensively throughout British arts with leading roles at both the Royal National Theatre and RSC. He has also appeared as a regular in some of Britan's most popular soap operas. He and his wife Suzie Catso, an actress, live in London.

MR STEWART AVON ARNOLD (CHOREOGRAPHER)

Teacher-Dancer,

PLACE OF BIRTH: London, 7.4.55
MARITAL STATUS: Single
COLLEGE: London School of Contemporary Dance
PERSONAL PROFILE: Original cast of Andrew Lloyd Webber's 'Song & Dance'. Dancer/choreographer for Kate Bush. International teacher (Europe & Japan). Principle dancer choreographer for Channel 4 'Streets Ahead'. Director of 'Souls In Motion' dance company. Choreographer 'The Wiz' (London). Director choreographer - 'Singer and Dancing the Blues' European Tour

MS LOLA AROUN (DIRECTOR)

Innovative Black Women, 62D Stanmford Hill, London, N16 6XS

PLACE OF BIRTH: London, 10.6.66
MARITAL STATUS: Single
CHILDREN: One (Abdul)
COLLEGE: South East London
ACADEMIC QUALIFICATIONS: Maths, English, Human Biology, Art, Design, Literature
PROFESSIONAL QUALIFICATIONS: RIPHH Cert, 706/1-706/2-77/1
HONOURS/AWARDS: Too many to mention
HOBBIES AND INTERESTS: Writing, reading, sport, current affairs, Black film, positive art
EMAIL: 16W@blacknet.co.uk
PERSONAL PROFILE: Lola Aroun is the director of the arts organisation Innovative Black Women she is a performing artiste and the writer and producer of the hit comedy 'Sidebusters'. Lola has worked alongside a range of celebrities. 'My work is to promote the artistic and industrial skills of black women and to open avenues for a group that has almost no proper and supportive representation'.
NOMINATED BY: Anthea Lee

MR PETER KINGSLEY ASANTE (WRITER-PUBLISHER)

Proprietor, Astek Publishing, 10 The Beeches, Gladstone Avenue, Manor Park, London, E12 6NT

PLACE OF BIRTH: Ghana, 21.10.44
MARITAL STATUS: Married
CHILDREN: Four (Five) (Rhoda, Ellen, Teddy (deceased), Twins Judy, Peter)
COLLEGE: University College Ghana, Sussex College of Technology
ACADEMIC QUALIFICATIONS: Diploma Ed (1969), M.Ed (1978)
HOBBIES AND INTERESTS: Soccer, table tennis, music, dancing
EMAIL: pasante@globalnet.co.uk
PERSONAL PROFILE: Formerly a science teacher now UK writer/publisher. Originator of the book 'Sex Education'; now a subject in UK schools curriculum published (Astek), 1992 brought awareness and solutions to sexual problems. Forthcoming titles: 'Soccer Perfect' and 'Rape, Child Abuse and Social Ills'; Homework books for schools.

MISS ABENA ASARE (STUDENT)

University of Lancashire, Department of Built Environment, Preston, PR1 2HE

PLACE OF BIRTH: Ghana, 5.8.75
MARITAL STATUS: Single
COLLEGE: University of Central Lancashire
ACADEMIC QUALIFICATIONS: B Eng Hons Building Services Engineering (2 year), 9 GCSE O-Levels, GCE A-Levels in Maths, Physics, Chemistry
MEMBERSHIPS: Student member, Chartered Insitute of Building Services Engineers - CIBSE American Society of Heating, Refridgeration & Air Conditioning Engineers - Ashrae
HONOURS/AWARDS: 'Most Promising Student'1998 Award, Presented By CIBSE
HOBBIES AND INTERESTS: Reading, travelling, martial arts (Tae Kwondo)
EMAIL: apeaa@hotmail.com
PERSONAL PROFILE: I am 23 years old B Eng Hons, Building Services Engineering student, currently on a year out with consulting engineers IBSEC Ltd. I love travelling and discovering diverse cultures and would like to see more women join the engineering profession where they can be assured of a rewarding career.

> 'My work is to promote the artistic and industrial skills of black women and to open avenues for a group that has almost no proper and supportive representation'
>
> **LOLA AROUN**

MS RASHEDA ASHANTI (Publisher)

Director, 4 Hall Drive

PLACE OF BIRTH: Jamaica
CHILDREN: Four (Nyah, Kumanie, Jahzeal, Yohanes)
COLLEGE: City University
ACADEMIC QUALIFICATIONS: BAJ
MEMBERSHIPS: Vice chair of the West London African-Caribbean Women's Development Association
HONOURS/AWARDS: Working Mother of the Year Award, The 'Black Business Woman 1990', Claudia Jones Award from CBS for Juggling Family and Business 1993, 2nd Place - Acer Penmanship Award for Young Black Writers (1983) and A Written Critique For Entry For BBC 2's Debut 2 for Young Playwrights (1984)
HOBBIES AND INTERESTS: Reading, travelling, meditating, listening to music, spending time with family.
PERSONAL PROFILE: Rasheda Ashanti was the architect of 'Candice' magazine, the bi-monthly black women's publication launched in 1992. For her achievements Rasheda has received the Publishing Award from the National Black Women Achievement Awards in 1994, she was runner-up in She magazine working mothers competition, and voted Black Business Women in 1990. Rasheda is the vice-chair of the West London based African-Caribbean Women's Development Association, a director of the Black Media Institute and a patron of Innovative Black Women.
NOMINATED BY: Lola Aroun, Innovative Black Women

MR OGHENEOVO JOSHUA ATIKPAKPA
(Solicitor-Advocate)

Managing Partner, Joshua & Usman Solicitors, Lord Denning Court, Grummant Road, London, SE15 5PZ

PLACE OF BIRTH: Nigeria, 5.12.57
MARITAL STATUS: Married
CHILDREN: Four (Jeff-Jones, James, Joyce, Iasha)
COLLEGE: Lancaster University
ACADEMIC QUALIFICATIONS: LLM, LLB Hons
PROFESSIONAL QUALIFICATIONS: Barrister-at-Law (Lincoln's Inn) formerly, Currently Solicitor of the Supreme Court
DIRECTORSHIPS: Director/Publisher of Urhobo Voice
EMAIL: ojatikpakpa@joshua.usman.com
PERSONAL PROFILE: Managing partner in a medium sized firm of solicitors employing over 28 staff. President of Nigerian Council of Lawyers. Also president of Delta State Union UK. Keen interest in politics, dream of democracy in Nigeria.

MR CHARLES L AUGINS (Choreographer)

Director, 31 Wheatash Road, Chertsey, Addlestone, KT15 2ER

PLACE OF BIRTH: Washington DC, 17.9.43
MARITAL STATUS: Single
PROFESSIONAL QUALIFICATIONS: Studied with Arlington Recreation Department and the Jones Heywood School of Ballet in Washington DC, dancer with the Baltimore City Ballet Company, The Talley Beatty Company, The DC Repertory Dance Company for which he was a ballet master
HONOURS/AWARDS: Olivier Award Winner for Best Choreographer,The EMMA Award for Children Zone & 'Let My People Come', the Broadway production
PERSONAL PROFILE: Charles directed and choreographed 'Five Guys Named Moe', his last film 'The Tall Guy' - Mel Smith. He has taught jazz at Boston University and jazz and ballet at Boston Conservatory. Charles enjoys an exceptionally varied career as an actor, dancer, choreographer and teacher.

MICHELLE AUSTIN (Actress)

Burdett-Couts Associates, Riverside Studios, Crisp Road, London, W6 9LR

PLACE OF BIRTH: London, 1.3.70
MARITAL STATUS: Living with partner
COLLEGE: Rose Bruford College
ACADEMIC QUALIFICATIONS: BA Hons in Theatre Arts
HOBBIES AND INTERESTS: Learning to make clothes, cooking, most importantly drinking with my friends
PERSONAL PROFILE: Most important work to date with Mike Leigh, playing Dionne Daniels in 'Secrets and Lies'. Television work includes: 'The Perfect Blue'; 'Comedy Nation'; 'Home and Away'; 'Eastenders'. Theatre work includes: 'Our Century's Good' directed by Max Stafford - Clark, 'Been So Long' at the Royal Court. 'It's a great big shame!', written and directed by Mike Leigh.

REV FRANK DAYO AWONUSI (Managing Director)

Atlas Security (UK) Limited, 20 Winslow House, Kinglake Street, London, SE17 2RT

PLACE OF BIRTH: Nigeria
MARITAL STATUS: Married
CHILDREN: Five (Tusin, Kemi, Bukky, Biola, Joseph)
ACADEMIC QUALIFICATIONS: BA Hons, Management Accounting, MSc Business Finance
PROFESSIONAL QUALIFICATIONS: Associate Institute of Cost & Executive Accountants
MEMBERSHIPS: Fellow Institute of Professional Finance Managers (FIPFM)
HONOURS/AWARDS: Doctor of Divinity - Trinity International University - US.
HOBBIES AND INTERESTS: Preaching the gospel
PERSONAL PROFILE: Came to Britain mid-eighties. Struggled up the ladder educating himself up to the master's level. Heard the call of God to preach the gospel. Proprietor and managing director of Atlas Security (UK) Ltd and founder/pastor of New Creation Gospel Church London.

MR TAYO AYENIYEGBE (Barber)

Proprietor, Mr Tee Barber Shops, 499 High Road, Leytonstone, London, E11 4PG

PLACE OF BIRTH: Nigeria, 25.12.64
MARITAL STATUS: Married
CHILDREN: One (Oyinkansola)
DIRECTORSHIPS: Felicitas Co Ltd, Ultimate Promotions Ltd
HONOURS/AWARDS: Natwest and Western Union, 2nd African Business Executives Award 1998
HOBBIES AND INTERESTS: Lawn tennis, tavelling, music
PERSONAL PROFILE: Tayo Ayeniyegbe - aka Mr Tee comes from a dynasty of hair stylists. His father was a barber and he taught his children. Mr Tee opened his first salon in 1992 and the second one in 1997. Along with his professional staff they serve a wide spectrum of various nationalities and age groups.
NOMINATED BY: Sam Jenyo

MS RAKIE AYOLA (Actress)

Singer, Marina Martin Associates, 12-13 Poland Street, London, W1V 3DE

PLACE OF BIRTH: London, 11.5.68
MARITAL STATUS: Single
COLLEGE: Welsh College of Music and Drama
ACADEMIC QUALIFICATIONS: Three year Acting Diploma
PROFESSIONAL QUALIFICATIONS: Ten years doing theatre, film, television
MEMBERSHIPS: Women In Film and Television, SWS (Social, Welsh and Sexy)
HONOURS/AWARDS: Sunday Times and Royal National Theatre - Ian Charleson Award 1995
HOBBIES AND INTERESTS: Travel, reading, gardening, exercise, cycling
PERSONAL PROFILE: Cardiff actress has appeared in several stage productions and TV series, including 'Maise Raine', 'Soldier Soldier' and 'Tiger Bay'. Films include 'Great Moments in Aviation' opposite Johnathan Pryce and John Hurt and 'The Secret Laughter of Women' with Colin Firth. Recently played Ophelia in Birmingham Rep's acclaimed production of 'Hamlet'.

> Managing partner in a medium sized firm of solicitors employing over 28 staff. President of Nigerian Council of Lawyers. Also president of Delta State Union UK. Keen interest in politics, dream of democracy in Nigeria

OGHENEOVO JOSHUA ATIKPAKPA

Carribbean Times

COUNTDOWN TO THE MILLENNIUM

MR CHRISTOPHER B-LYNCH (Surgeon Specialist)

Consultant, NHS & Private Practise, 152 Harley Street, London, W1N 1HH

PLACE OF BIRTH: Sierra Leone, 1.10.47
MARITAL STATUS: Married
CHILDREN: Four (Joshua, Sarah, Emily, Isabelle)
COLLEGE: Oxford/Barts
ACADEMIC QUALIFICATIONS: MA Oxon MBBS
PROFESSIONAL QUALIFICATIONS: LRCP, FRCS, FRCOG, FLLA, MAE, ACI Arb. QDR, MEWI
MEMBERSHIPS: Academy of Experts (Council) Livery Company, The Athenaeum School
HONOURS/AWARDS: Hon Docorate of the Open University
HOBBIES AND INTERESTS: Rugby, cricket, golf, writing, publishing, teaching
EMAIL: cbLynch@ukconsultants.co.uk
PERSONAL PROFILE: Inventor of the B-Lynch surgical techniques, formerly chief assistant to the Queen's gynaecologist 1981-1983. Examiner for London University and professional bodies in obstetrics and gynaecology. Inventor of surgical procedures, lifesaving for obstetric haemorrhage, medico legal expert, witness and registered mediator. Founder chairman of the Milton Keynes District Ethical Committee. Tutor of the RWG. Chairman of the Oxford Committee for Milton Keynes Surgery Training Gynaecology.

MISS INDAY BA (Actress)

c/o **Envision Management,** 409 Santa Monica Blvd, Santa Monica, CA 90401

PLACE OF BIRTH: Sweden, 10.8.72
MARITAL STATUS: Single
COLLEGE: Webber Douglas Academy of Dramatic Art
ACADEMIC QUALIFICATIONS: Went to school in Sweden
HOBBIES AND INTERESTS: Life with music, madness, compassion
PERSONAL PROFILE: I am spreading good madness in Los Angeles as well as in London. Have been the only Black Swede in my home town I wanted to contribute to a 'healthier' world with more mixes. My need for acting combined with London's amazing mix of all, drew me here. London proved to be just that place and because of the multi ethnic mix here we can also offer inspiration to others all over the world. London's Rocking!!!

MR PHILIP (PHIL) BABB (Footballer)

Liverpool Football Club, Anfield Road, Liverpool, L4 0TH

PLACE OF BIRTH: London, 30.11.70
PROFESSIONAL QUALIFICATIONS: 26 Caps for Republic of Ireland and 150 Appearances for Liverpool
HONOURS/AWARDS: Coca-Cola Cup Winners Medal V Bolton1994/95
PERSONAL PROFILE: Signed from Coventry City in September 1994 after outstanding displays for the Republic of Ireland in that summer's World Cup in the US. Liverpool had previously tracked the player after noting his ability to mark dangerous opponents. Phil began his career at Millwall and has made over 150 appearances for Liverpool.

MISS NINA BADEN-SEMPER (Actress)

Collis Management, 182 Trevelyan Road, London, SW17 9LW

PLACE OF BIRTH: Trindad
MARITAL STATUS: Married
CHILDREN: Two (Caroline, Joseph)
PROFESSIONAL QUALIFICATIONS: State Registered Nurse, State Certificate Midwife
HONOURS/AWARDS: ITV Television Personality Award, PYE Television Award, The Scarlet Ibis.
HOBBIES AND INTERESTS: Party and banquet organiser, floral designer. Restoring old houses in Italy, London, West Indies. Writer, cookery editor for the Caribbean World magazine
PERSONAL PROFILE: Actress of stage, film and television. Born in Trinidad West Indies. First Black actress to star in the long running popular comedy series 'Love Thy Neighbour' in 1973 and recently starred in the all Black series 'Brothers and Sisters'. Has won several awards for her outstanding acting roles.

MR NICHOLAS BAILEY (Actor-Writer-Producer)

Divided Child Theatre Company, 101 Hamstead Hill, Handsworth Wood, Birmingham, B20 1BX

DATE OF BIRTH: 5.7.71
MARITAL STATUS: Single
COLLEGE: LAMDA
ACADEMIC QUALIFICATIONS: 11 O-Levels, 4 A-Levels
PROFESSIONAL QUALIFICATIONS: Drama School Training
DIRECTORSHIPS: Artistic Director - 'Divided Child Theatre Company'
MEMBERSHIPS: Old Foleyan's Association - Old Boys of Old Swinford School
HONOURS/AWARDS: Philip Sayer/Ian Charleston Award for Drama
HOBBIES AND INTERESTS: Writing poetry, screen plays, painting, drama teaching, singing, fitness, cinema, dance, socialising
PERSONAL PROFILE: Having been a professional actor for six years I want to contribute to art in the community by producing theatre and film and by continuing to teach drama to children. Hopefully Walter Tell's story will contribute to public knowledge of Black British history.

MS PAMELA BAILEY (Training Officer)

Birmingham Social Services Department, 2 Yew Tree Road, Moseley, Birmingham, B20 8QG

PLACE OF BIRTH: Neth Antilles, 27.8.49
MARITAL STATUS: Divorced
CHILDREN: Two (Nicholas, Christian)
COLLEGE: Birmingham Polytechnic
ACADEMIC QUALIFICATIONS: CGSW, CTD Diploma in Management
MEMBERSHIPS: National Organisation of Practice Teaching, UK Standing Conference of Diploma in Social Work Partnership
HONOURS/AWARDS: Advanced Social Work, Practice Teaching Award
HOBBIES AND INTERESTS: Reading, travel, community work, dancing
PERSONAL PROFILE: School governor specialist in social work education, member of Central Council for Social Work (England Committee), member of West Midlands Black Practice Teacher's Group, founder member of Birmingham Social Services Black Women's Training & Development Group.
NOMINATED BY: Nicholas Bailey

MS NATASHA BAIN (Actress)

Flat 8, Roma Read Close, Bess Borough Road, London, SW15 4AZ

PLACE OF BIRTH: London, 17.11.67
MARITAL STATUS: Single
COLLEGE: GuildHall School of Music and Drama, City University
ACADEMIC QUALIFICATIONS: 7 O-Levels, O/A Level, A-Level, AGSM Dip. BA Hons Degree in Acting
MEMBERSHIPS: Equity
HOBBIES AND INTERESTS: Music, reading, long walks, horse riding, animals, athletics.
PERSONAL PROFILE: In my sixth year out of drama school, I'm pleased to have been part of a BAFTA winning short, 'Zinky Boys Go Underground'. To have performed in an Olivier nominated musical 'The Threepenny Opera', at the Donmar Warehouse. Hopefully I have more potential to be fulfilled.

MR ADE BAKARE (Fashion Designer)

Ade Bakare (Couture) London, 26 Grosvenor Street, Mayfair, London, W1X 0BD

PLACE OF BIRTH: Bromsgrove, 22.6.66
COLLEGE: University of Lagos, Nigeria, Salford University, Manchester
ACADEMIC QUALIFICATIONS: BA Education History
PROFESSIONAL QUALIFICATIONS: BTEC HND Fashion Design
HONOURS/AWARDS: African Businessman of the Year Award 1998
HOBBIES AND INTERESTS: Travelling, art, jazz
PERSONAL PROFILE: Born in England, educated in Nigeria. Studied fashion design in Manchester. Worked for couture design house in London. Set up business in 1992 with loan from Prince's Youth Business Trust (PYBT) opened Mayfair salon in 1997. Lectures part-time in Manchester. Celebrity and royal clients.
NOMINATED BY: Sam Jenyo

MR DAVID BAKER (Actor-Writer)

PLACE OF BIRTH: Birmingham
MARITAL STATUS: Single
COLLEGE: Arts Education Schools
ACADEMIC QUALIFICATIONS: Diploma in Drama
HOBBIES AND INTERESTS: Sports, reading, writing, photography
PERSONAL PROFILE: Started acting in his early twenties in Birmingham and has appeared on TV, film and on stages all over the country. In my time as an actor, I have become increasingly aware of the need for good Black role models as we move towards a new century it is my hope to see more and more.

MR THOMAS BAPTISTE (Actor)

PLACE OF BIRTH: Guyana
PERSONAL PROFILE: Thomas began his theatrical career touring with Joan Littlewood's Theatre Workshop company in the early 1950's. In 1955 he made his first West End appearance in 'Summer Song'. Thomas has worked in most of the popular TV series, including 'Eastenders', 'Brookside'... and most recently as 'Lord Godfrey' in 'Love Hurts'. He has sung in the BBC's production of the opera 'Amahl and the Night Visitors'. Thomas performed as soloist at the Manchester Jazz Festival's celebration of George Gershwin.

MR PATRICK PAUL BARBER (Actor-Entertainer)

c/o London Management, 2-4 Noel Street, London, W1V 3RB

PLACE OF BIRTH: Liverpool, 18.3.51
MARITAL STATUS: Single
COLLEGE: Life
ACADEMIC QUALIFICATIONS: Lamda Gold Medal
PROFESSIONAL QUALIFICATIONS: Acting
MEMBERSHIPS: Equity, BEC
HONOURS/AWARDS: Screen Actors Guild Outstanding Performance US, BAFTA, UK
HOBBIES AND INTERESTS: Philosophy, watching King of the Hill and Fraser, listening to music, jazz
PERSONAL PROFILE: Started off in the musical 'Hair' followed that with 'Jesus Christ Superstar'. Moved into TV and film with TV credits in 'Lucky' (Granada), 'Gangsters' (BBC), 'Brothers McGregor' (Granada), 'Cracker' (BBC), 'Casualty' (BBC), 'Fools and Horses' (BBC), 'Boys From The Blackstuff' (BBC), 'Needle' (BBC), and in films, 'Curse of the Fire Beetle' (BBC/Arena), 'Long Good Friday' (Handmade), 'Priest' (BBC), 'Full Monty' (20th Century Fox).

MS PAULA KAY BARDOWELL (Actress)

'Forever On The Look Out', Clive Corner Associates, 73 Gloucester Road, Hampton, TW13 24Q

PLACE OF BIRTH: London
MARITAL STATUS: Single
COLLEGE: Welsh College Music and Drama
ACADEMIC QUALIFICATIONS: 3 O-Levels, 3 A-Levels, 7 CSEs
PROFESSIONAL QUALIFICATIONS: Advanced Diploma in Acting
MEMBERSHIPS: British Actors Equity on the boards of Whispering Eyes Theatre and Time Travellers in Newscastle
HOBBIES AND INTERESTS: Running, loud music, cinema, girlie nights out (and in), reading detective stories ala Lynda Le Plante
PERSONAL PROFILE: At 16 heard advert on the radio and went to audition for a musical 'Just Good Friends' at the Cockpit Theatre and has been acting ever since. Work includes: Premiere Tour of 'The House of Spirits'; 'The Footballers Wife'; 'The African Co Present Richard III' for Five Points Black American Theatre Company at Riverside Studios.

MR FITZROY JOHN BATCHELOR
(Community Relations Manager)

London Ambulance Service, Deptford Ambulance Station, 1 New Cross Road, London, SE14 5DS

PLACE OF BIRTH: Jamaica, 4.5.56
MARITAL STATUS: Married
CHILDREN: Three (Kevin, Sarita, Theodore)
COLLEGE: Sedgehill Comprehensive, South Bank University, Greenwich University
ACADEMIC QUALIFICATIONS: 2 A-Levels, 4 O-Levels
PROFESSIONAL QUALIFICATIONS: Cert MHS, PG Dip Ms
MEMBERSHIPS: Hospital Liaison Committee
HOBBIES AND INTERESTS: Football, religion-helping others to learn about the bible
PERSONAL PROFILE: John Batchelor has been given the task of encouraging more Black people and ethnic minorities to enter the London Ambulance Service. (LAS). Within the LAS John has the responsibility for race and cultural awareness training, equal opportunities and the development of a positive action programme for the recruitment, retention and development of ethnic minorities and other under representation groups.

MR BRENDON BATSON (Deputy Chief Executive)

Professional Footballers Association (PFA), 20 Oxford Court, Bishopsgate, Manchester, M2 3WQ

PLACE OF BIRTH: West Indies, 6.2.53
MARITAL STATUS: Married
CHILDREN: Two (Zoe, Jason)
DIRECTORSHIPS: PFA Enterprises, PFA Financial Management Ltd.
HOBBIES AND INTERESTS: Golf, scuba diving, theatre, music, reading
EMAIL: bbatson@thepfa.co.UK
PERSONAL PROFILE: Arrived in England aged nine spotted by Arsenal FC aged 13 and signed as a professional on 17th birthday. Played for Arsenal, Cambridge Utd. and West Bromwich Albion playing over 350 games. Won 3 England 'B' caps. Retired in 1984 due to knee injury. Took up present position with the PFA upon retirement.
NOMINATED BY: Gordon Taylor - PFA

MR GARY BEADLE (Actor-Writer)

c/o Lou Coulson Management, 37 Berwick Street, London, W1V 3RF

PLACE OF BIRTH: London, 8.7.65
MARITAL STATUS: Single
CHILDREN: One (Louis-Rae)
COLLEGE: Anna Scher Theatre
MEMBERSHIPS: Equity, MO
HONOURS/AWARDS: Many award winning productions
HOBBIES AND INTERESTS: Football
PERSONAL PROFILE: As one of Britain's first Black child TV actors, Gary is now a veteran in his profession. With over 25 years of experience under his belt, his unique style of acting, has earned him high acclaim and a choice of ground breaking roles.

MISS SANDRA BEE (Actress)

1 Kingsway House, Albion Road, London, N16 OTA

PLACE OF BIRTH: London, 22.6.72
MARITAL STATUS: Single
COLLEGE: Melody Urgurrt
ACADEMIC QUALIFICATIONS: Mastor School Laban Centre
PROFESSIONAL QUALIFICATIONS: Miss Melody's Cert in cabaret dance
MEMBERSHIPS: Equity
HONOURS/AWARDS: Jersey CI, Best Dance Professional.
HOBBIES AND INTERESTS: Videos, athletics
PERSONAL PROFILE: Sandra Bee actress from the first Black soap for twenty years 'Brothers & Sisters'. Her portrayal of the feisty Jamaican single mum Petronella brought street life to main stream TV. Multi talented Brent actress has also success on the Black comedy circuit.

Patrick Paul Barber has appeared in, 'Curse of the Fire Beetle' (BBC/Arena), 'Long Good Friday' (Handmade), 'Priest' (BBC) and the 'Full Monty' (20th Century Fox).

MISS BEEJAYE (Actress & Singer)

McIntosh Rae Management, Thornton House, Thornton Road, London, SW19 4NG

PLACE OF BIRTH: London
MEMBERSHIPS: Equity

MR NEWTON BELL (Financial Adviser)

Franchisee, Allied Dunbar, 584 High Road, Leyton, London, E10 6RL

PLACE OF BIRTH: Jamaica, 17.8.57
MARITAL STATUS: Married
CHILDREN: Four (Jermaine, Theresa, Nathaniel, Eythan)
COLLEGE: Central London Polytechnic
ACADEMIC QUALIFICATIONS: AC I.I (Part 1)
PROFESSIONAL QUALIFICATIONS: Financial Planning Certificate (Full)
MEMBERSHIPS: Life Insurance Association
HONOURS/AWARDS: Martial Arts Awards Senior Instructor (Tang Soo Do Moo Duk Kwan)
HOBBIES AND INTERESTS: Martial arts, cricket, thinking
PERSONAL PROFILE: Born Manchester Jamaica, arrived UK 1971. Former civil servant but left to develop own financial services franchise with Allied Dunbar since 1980. Set up private 'Saturday' school (Project for African Caribbean Educators) in 1996. Ambition to further assist development of African community.

MR BRIAN BENJAMIN

BB's Crabback Restaurant, 3 Chignell Place, West Ealing, London, W13 0TD

PLACE OF BIRTH: Grenada, 29.6.58
MARITAL STATUS: Married
CHILDREN: Four (Ashley, Seretse, Twins on the way)
PROFESSIONAL QUALIFICATIONS: Salon Culinaire Gold, Silver, Bronze Awards
MEMBERSHIPS: City & Guilds
HONOURS/AWARDS: 1999 Afro-Caribbean Master Chef
HOBBIES AND INTERESTS: Cricket, exotic holidays
PERSONAL PROFILE: Brian Benjamin, owner/chef, of BB's Restaurant, rapidly becoming one of the capital's best known Caribbean restaurants. Arriving from Grenada aged 11, Brian's love of cooking was already well established by his grandmother. His success he attributes to classical cuisine training combined with his knowledge of Caribbean food. Brian's awards include numerous Salon Culinaire along with the much-coveted 1999 Afro Caribbean Master Chef.

MS FLOELLA BENJAMIN (Chief Executive)

Floella Benjamin Productions,

PLACE OF BIRTH: Guyana
MARITAL STATUS: Married
CHILDREN: Two (Aston, Aluina)
ACADEMIC QUALIFICATIONS: GSE A-Levels
DIRECTORSHIPS: BAFTA - Women of the Year & Assembly - KTE Floella Benjamin Production
MEMBERSHIPS: Commonwealth Club BAFTA
HOBBIES AND INTERESTS: Golf, sports, travel, environment, children, reading, set up her own film and television production company
PERSONAL PROFILE: Floella found her way into theatre after a short career in the world of banking. West End shows including 'Jesus Christ Superstar', 'The Black Mikado', with Michael Denison and 'The Husband in Law' with Kenneth Williams. Television drama: 'Within These Walls'. Presenter of BBC's legendary children's programmes 'Play School' and 'Playaway'. In 1977, Floella appeared in her first feature film, 'Black Joy'. Since 1982, Floella has written over 20 children's books plus a guide to Caribbean food and cookery. Her latest book 'Coming To England' charts her journey from Trinidad to England as a young girl.

MR TREVOR (JUNIOR) BENJAMIN (Footballer)

Cambridge United, Abbey Stadium, Newmarket Road, Cambridge, CB5 8LN

PLACE OF BIRTH: Kettering, 8.2.79
PROFESSIONAL QUALIFICATIONS: 15 League Goals & 78 League Appearances
PERSONAL PROFILE: Trevor Benjamin is one of the latest youngsters to graduate into the first team from United's youth scheme, where he was prolific scorer. Trevor started out as a left-winger before becoming a centre-forward and he made his first team debut as a 16 year old trainee. A new four year contract with United. Trevor was recently filmed for a feature on Sky TV.

MISS LORREN BENT (Actress)

Jane Lehrer Associates, 5A The Crest, Hendon, London, NW4 2HN

PLACE OF BIRTH: Coventry, 20.3.70
MARITAL STATUS: Single
COLLEGE: Drama Centre London
ACADEMIC QUALIFICATIONS: Diploma in Acting
MEMBERSHIPS: Equity
HOBBIES AND INTERESTS: Play hockey for West Hampstead, sings jazz, rhythm and blues in regional venues
EMAIL: Lorraire.bent@rossJay.co.UK
PERSONAL PROFILE: 2000 will see my 12th year in London and despite hard work and a lot of tears I have realised many of my long time ambitions. I've still got a long way to go. Thank you EMG for this honour, may we inspire our future....Keep on moving!

MS DONNA BERLIN (Actress-Singer)

Dancer, Choreographer and Singer, 11E John Fisher Street, Whitechapel, London, E1 8JY

PLACE OF BIRTH: London, 27.6.69
MEMBERSHIPS: Equity, founding member of the London based club SWK
HONOURS/AWARDS: 'Best Production in Dance 1997' for the co-devised 2 Handed Show 'Tapping The Blue Away'
HOBBIES AND INTERESTS: Sports, poetry, photography, films
PERSONAL PROFILE: At a young age I attended two dance groups. I travelled to New York to work with the masters of rhythm tap and teach and lecture in the UK and Germany. I am now successfully furthering my acting and writing career.

MS CAROL BERNARD (Divisional Manager)

Middlesex Probation Service, Probation Office, Rosslyn Crescent, Harrow, HA1 2SR

PLACE OF BIRTH: Sheffield, 4.7.61
MARITAL STATUS: Divorced-Single
CHILDREN: Four (Makeda, Aaron, Elias, Tobias)
COLLEGE: Sheffield Hallam University
ACADEMIC QUALIFICATIONS: BA Hons Applied Social Studies, Masters Degree Policy and Professional Studies-Social Policy
PROFESSIONAL QUALIFICATIONS: Certificate of Qualification in Social Work (CQSW), Practice Teachers Award
MEMBERSHIPS: Association of Black Probation Officers
HOBBIES AND INTERESTS: Black history, health and fitness, martial arts, music
PERSONAL PROFILE: I joined South Yorkshire Probation Service in 1991 after training as a probation officer. Whilst there I developed a group work programme for Black offenders. In 1994 appointed semi-specialist practise teacher in Middlesex Probation Service. In 1995 promoted, senior probation officer. In 1998 promoted to divisional manager and one of few Black senior managers in the probation service. I am currently studying part-time for an MBA. My philosophy is that I continually strive for knowledge wisdom and understanding.
NOMINATED BY: John Walters, Chief Probation Officer

In 1998 promoted to divisional manager and one of few Black senior managers in the probation service

MS CAROL BERNARD

CLLR GEE BERNARD (Social Worker)

Councillor, London Borough of Croydon & Co-ordinator, CACFO,

PLACE OF BIRTH: Jamaica, 29.12.39
CHILDREN: Six
COLLEGE: North London University
ACADEMIC QUALIFICATIONS: CQSW, DSW, CD
PROFESSIONAL QUALIFICATIONS: DSW, CD, CQSW
HOBBIES AND INTERESTS: Dancing, gardening
PERSONAL PROFILE: I work to combat social inequality and deprivation within the Black community mainly in the area of education, housing and social services. This has been my work for 29 years, member of the Labour Party, NHS.

MR RONALD O'NEAL BEST (Teacher-Artist)

Teaching Part-time,

PLACE OF BIRTH: Barbados, 25.5.57
MARITAL STATUS: Single
COLLEGE: Royal College of Art
ACADEMIC QUALIFICATIONS: MA , RCA, Dip AD, Post Dip FA
PROFESSIONAL QUALIFICATIONS: Artist
DIRECTORSHIPS: (Helper) Visual Arts, Portobello Festival
MEMBERSHIPS: Portobello Group, Portobello Printmakers
HOBBIES AND INTERESTS: Football, walking
PERSONAL PROFILE: Intuition rather than concept has been the basis for work (psychological, philosophical references). I believe that there is an inextricable link between art and culture, contemporary art should reflect the Black and multicultural communities.

MR STERLING BETANCOURT (Bandleader-Musician)

Association Nostalgia Steel Band, 35 Mortimer Road, London, NW10 5QR

PLACE OF BIRTH: Trinidad, 30.3.30
MARITAL STATUS: Married
CHILDREN: Two (Benjamin, Simon)
ACADEMIC QUALIFICATIONS: Honorary Fellow UEL 1995
HONOURS/AWARDS: Scarlet IBIS, Sunshine Award 1996 Hall of Fame US, Trinidad Folk Art Institute 1993 US, Honorary Fellowship UEL London 1995
HOBBIES AND INTERESTS: Music, singing, teaching
PERSONAL PROFILE: 1951: Member of first steelband to come to Europe from Trinidad called Trinidad All Steel Percussion Orchestra. 1954: Played for the Royal Family. 1965 - Pioneer for Notting Hill carnival playing in the streets with only three members then every year after that. 1976: Pioneer for bringing steel drums to Zurich, making the drums, playing and teaching others the art of playing steel pan.

KEVIN BETSY (Footballer)

Fulham Football Club, Craven Cottage, Stevenage Road, London, SW6 6HH

PLACE OF BIRTH: Seychelles
HONOURS/AWARDS: Woking's Player of the Year 1997-98
PERSONAL PROFILE: Kevin was part-time at Woking but football was his life. Farnborough Town had signed him up as assistant community officer to coach schoolkids all over north-east Hampshire. Kevin is the first player of his surname to play postwar football at league level, he made his debut for Fulham against Liverpool in the Worthington Cup his first full game followed in the Auto Windscreens clash with Torquay, he played another cameo role at Old Trafford, and his aim now is to get a start in the League.

MS PAULINE BLACK (Singer-Actress)

18 Abercorn Road, Chapelfields, Coventry

PLACE OF BIRTH: Essex, 23.10.53
MARITAL STATUS: Married
COLLEGE: Coventry University
ACADEMIC QUALIFICATIONS: BSc Biochemistry Combined Science
PROFESSIONAL QUALIFICATIONS: Diploma of Royal Society Radiographers
DIRECTORSHIPS: Board Member of Tricycle Theatre, Kilburn High Road, London
MEMBERSHIPS: Equity, Performing Rights Society
HONOURS/AWARDS: Time Out (Best Actress) 1990, Manchester Evening News (Best Actress) 1993
HOBBIES AND INTERESTS: Tennis, computing, songwriting, piano, writing
EMAIL: pblack1@compuserve.com
PERSONAL PROFILE: Pauline Black is of Nigerian/Jewish descent. She has had an extensive career as singer/songwriter, actress, TV and radio presenter for 20 years. As founder member of The Selecter, she enjoyed many hits and a Gold selling album 'Too Much Pressure'. The band still record and tour successfully.

MR SONNY BLACKS (Impressario)

PERSONAL PROFILE: Sonny Blacks, Trinidad born impresario, came to UK in 1961, together with the 'Dixieland - Steel Orchestra'. Previous to this, had promoted concerts in Trinidad and other Caribbean Islands. He was the first person to promote steelband concerts and calypso shows at the Queens Hall in Port-of-Spain, Trinidad. The first impressario to present steelband and calypso music in European countries.

MISS SYAN BLAKE (Actress)

Tim Scott, 5 Cloister Business Centre, 8 Battersea Park Road, London, SW8 4BG

PLACE OF BIRTH: London, 14.9.72
MARITAL STATUS: Single
COLLEGE: Guildford School of Acting
ACADEMIC QUALIFICATIONS: 3 A-Levels, 7 O-Levels
PROFESSIONAL QUALIFICATIONS: Diploma in Acting
HOBBIES AND INTERESTS: Enriching my mind, soul
PERSONAL PROFILE: Being a woman of colour I am blessed: I wear all the hues of our world and have the gift of creating life, therefore I strive to harness these blessings by giving a voice to all. As the Jamaican motto tells us: 'Out of many one people'.

MS CORRINE BOUGAARD (Artistic Director)

Union Dance Co, Marylebone Dance Studio, 121 Lisson Grove, London, NW1 6TS

PLACE OF BIRTH: South Africa, 11.1.54
MARITAL STATUS: Married
CHILDREN: Two (Danielle, Lauren)
COLLEGE: London School of Contemporary Dance, Central St Martins
ACADEMIC QUALIFICATIONS: Diploma, MA in Design Studies
PROFESSIONAL QUALIFICATIONS: Dancer, Choreographer, Art Director
DIRECTORSHIPS: Board of Directors, Youth and Music, ADAD and Pan Project
MEMBERSHIPS: Equity
HONOURS/AWARDS: Lise Ullmann Travelling Scholorship, Winston Churchill Fellow
EMAIL: Bougaard@Gol.com.
PERSONAL PROFILE: Objective through dance 'infinite process of identity construction'. (Union Dance founded by C.B. as artistic director). Aim to make cultural nationalism and postmodernism less divisive and enrich the art form of dance and movement exploring programmes of dance with acknowledgement that race, history and mere physics do not enforce an identity - aim cultural improvement for youth.
NOMINATED BY: Sharon Aitkin

1965 - Pioneer for Notting Hill carnival playing in the streets with only three members - then every year after that

MR STERLING BETANCOURT

MR BEN BOUSQUET (Playwrites' & Poets' Agent)

Bousquet International (Playwrites' & Poets' Agents), Bouquet International, 165 Woodville Road, Ipswich, IP4 1PE

PLACE OF BIRTH: St Lucia
PERSONAL PROFILE: Active trade unionist. Elected councillor for Borough of Kensington & Chelsea, 1978/90. Obtained highest vote for each election in Kensington. Created Black Section movement in Labour Party. Parliamentary candidate in general election. Managed to get funds just in time to stop the anti-apartheid movement going bankrupt. Co-author of several pamphlets and have written for various Black newspapers. Co-author 'West Indian Women at War' with Colin Douglas. Presently involved in youth cricket and lectures on Black history.
NOMINATED BY: Cephas and Dave Williams & Staff

MR ROBERT (BOBBY) BOWRY (Footballer)

Millwall Football Club, The Den, Zampa Road, London, SE16 3LN

PLACE OF BIRTH: Croydon, 19.5.71
PROFESSIONAL QUALIFICATIONS: 109 League appearances, 5 goals & 12 Cup Appearances
HONOURS/AWARDS: First Division Champions 1994
PERSONAL PROFILE: Signed from Crystal Palace in July 1995, Bobby made his 100th League appearance for the Lions towards the end of the 1997/98 season. A neat skilful midfielder with the ability to make telling passes, it took him a while to win over the fans at the Den. However, he kept battling away and was one of Millwall's most consistent performers.

MR BRAINARD BRAIMAH MBE (Director)

Chapeltown HareHills Assisted Learning Computer School, Unit 5 Technorth, 9 Harrogate Road, Leeds, LS7 3NB

PLACE OF BIRTH: Ghana, 21.6.44
MARITAL STATUS: Married
CHILDREN: Two (Adam, Amina)
COLLEGE: Cape Coast & Leeds
ACADEMIC QUALIFICATIONS: BSc Hons Maths, MSc
PROFESSIONAL QUALIFICATIONS: BSc Ed
DIRECTORSHIPS: FE Business Support, CHEL, Ed 2000 (Ex.)
HONOURS/AWARDS: MBE
HOBBIES AND INTERESTS: Very little time for hobbies
EMAIL: Braimah@chalcs.org.uk
PERSONAL PROFILE: School governor, committee member for Children in Need, panel member for NCH Action Wades Charity. Instrumental in setting up CHALCS to address decades of under achievement of ethnic minority children. Firmly believe that every child is capable of learning and no child should be allowed to under-achieve.

JEAN BINTA BREEZE (Writer-Performer)

PLACE OF BIRTH: Jamaica, 11.3.56
MARITAL STATUS: Married
CHILDREN: Three (Gareth, Imega, Caribe)
COLLEGE: Jamaica School of Drama
HONOURS/AWARDS: Excelle UK Awards Poetry
HOBBIES AND INTERESTS: Dancing, reading
PERSONAL PROFILE: International writer and performer, four books published and two albums recorded.

MR RUFUS BREVETT (Footballer)

Fulham Football Club, Craven Cottage, Stevenage Road, London, SW6 6HH

PLACE OF BIRTH: Derby
PERSONAL PROFILE: Rufus joined up with Fulham for a fee of £350,000 and was quickly taken to by the fans. Rufus was a trainee before signing for Doncaster Rovers where he played under the likes of Dave MacKay, Joe Kinnear and Billy Bremner. He also played in the FA Youth Cup Final whilst at Belle Vue and was signed for QPR in 1991. Whilst at Rangers he was competing with Clive Watson and Robbie Herrera for the left-back position.

MRS BARBARA BREWSTER JP (Development Officer)

Sickle Cell Society, 20 South Croxted Road, West Dulwich, London, SE21 8BB

PLACE OF BIRTH: Barbados, 23.12.46
MARITAL STATUS: Married
CHILDREN: Two (Gayle Jeremy, Monica Denise)
ACADEMIC QUALIFICATIONS: Bsc With Honours Health Studies
PROFESSIONAL QUALIFICATIONS: Msc Health Promotion
MEMBERSHIPS: British Juvenille and Family Courts Society Magistrates Association
HONOURS/AWARDS: Justice of the Peace
HOBBIES AND INTERESTS: Travelling, reading
PERSONAL PROFILE: I was born in Barbados and emigrated to England on 29.12.64. Completed my SRN and midwife studies in 1970. I have been a foster parent since 1984. I gained a BSc in Health Studies in 1996 and a Masters Degree in Health Promotions in 1998. I was a appointed a JP in 1995 and now serve as a Youth Justice in West London. President of the Barbados Overseas Nurses Association.
NOMINATED BY: Brewster Family

MRS YVONNE BREWSTER OBE (Theatre Director)

Artistic Director, Talawa Theatre Company, 3rd Floor, 23-25 Great Sutton Street, London, EC1V 0DN

PLACE OF BIRTH: Jamaica, 7.10.38
MARITAL STATUS: Married
CHILDREN: One (Julian)
COLLEGE: Rose Bruford/Royal Academy
ACADEMIC QUALIFICATIONS: RBTC Diploma Teaching LRAM
PROFESSIONAL QUALIFICATIONS: FRSA
DIRECTORSHIPS: London Arts Board Theatres Trust, Riverside Mental Health Trust
HONOURS/AWARDS: Woman Achivements Award ACE, OBE Voice Community Award for the Arts 1998, Living Legend (US) etc
HOBBIES AND INTERESTS: London reading, Black history
EMAIL: yvonne@talawa.com
PERSONAL PROFILE: Yvonne Brewster OBE, artistic director of Talawa, works in radio, television, film, theatre, dance, schools and universities as director, lecturer, performer and analyst. She edits Black Plays (Methuen) and has sat on many boards including the British Council, London Arts Board, The Theatre's Trust and Riverside Mental Health Trust.

MR LESLIE BRISSETT JNR JP (Management Consultant)

Director, 20 Elmhurst Road, Bruce Grove, Tottenham, London, N17 6RQ

PLACE OF BIRTH: London, 31.10.67
MARITAL STATUS: Single
COLLEGE: Sunderland/King's College London
ACADEMIC QUALIFICATIONS: BSc Hons Health Studies, MSc Health Education
DIRECTORSHIPS: BCHP, Wessex Foundation
MEMBERSHIPS: Society of Health Education and Promotion Specialists
HONOURS/AWARDS: London Review of Books, Sedona, International Relations, Justice of the Peace 1996
HOBBIES AND INTERESTS: Psychology, regeneration, women's issue
PERSONAL PROFILE: Board member, College of North East London; chair of human resources. Chair of Tottenham Conservation Advisory Committee. Only Black independent sampling officer for UK Sport. Campaigning to regenerate Tottenham. Public health and voluntary sector consultant.

MR MARLON BROOMES (Footballer)

Blackburn Rovers Football & Athletic Plc, Ewood Park, Blackburn, BB2 4JF

PLACE OF BIRTH: Meriden, 22.11.77
PROFESSIONAL QUALIFICATIONS: England Under 21
PERSONAL PROFILE: Signed from YTS level. A product of the FA School of Excellence, he has already been capped by England at various levels and during the summer of 1998 was a member of the squad who took part in the World Youth Championship finals in Malaysia. He is so highly regarded that he was called up for training with the full England squad last season.

MR AARON BROWN (ACTOR)

84 Norman Road, Ilford, Essex, IG1 2NG

PLACE OF BIRTH: Britain
COLLEGE: College
MEMBERSHIPS: Equity Union
HOBBIES AND INTERESTS: Golf, rugby, boxing
PERSONAL PROFILE: I started acting from the age of five at drama school. At the age of eight I went to Sylvia Young Theatre School as a young helper, then got the opportunity to play parts in theatre and one small part on a TV programme. When I was 16 years old, I continued studying drama at the College of Redbridge, also taking two other subjects English and history.

MR HERBERT BROWN (TELECOMMUNICATIONS)

Security (BMA), 150 The Avenue, Tottenham, London, N17 6JL

PLACE OF BIRTH: Jamaica, 19.4.38
MARITAL STATUS: Single
COLLEGE: North London
ACADEMIC QUALIFICATIONS: Engineer
PROFESSIONAL QUALIFICATIONS: Telecom
DIRECTORSHIPS: None
MEMBERSHIPS: Guild of Freemen
HONOURS/AWARDS: TEM
HOBBIES AND INTERESTS: Football, music, cinema
PERSONAL PROFILE: Arrived in England in the early fifties from Jamaica. Attended school and college, North London. Served in British Army (RAMC) 1958-60. Reserves 1960-74: District commissioner (Scouts), 15 years. Chairperson, Hackney Area Youth 1985-90. Former chair, now patron Hackney Quest, Freeman of the City of London, councillor.

BISHOP HERMAN DARCUS BROWN (MINISTER)

Mount Shiloh Apostalic Church of Jesus Christ, 246 Stafford Road, Oxley, Wolverhampton, WV10 6DF

PLACE OF BIRTH: Jamaica, 16.2.24
MARITAL STATUS: Married
CHILDREN: Seven (Buman, Gilroy, Owen, Julie, Marcia, Ruth, Toel)
COLLEGE: Lee College Clevelands Ten, US.
ACADEMIC QUALIFICATIONS: Religious Studies
PROFESSIONAL QUALIFICATIONS: Ministerial
DIRECTORSHIPS: Bishop (12 Churches in Diocese)
MEMBERSHIPS: Member of Bishop Board Council of Churches
HONOURS/AWARDS: Black Achievers Award (Religion & Community)
HOBBIES AND INTERESTS: Reading, writing
PERSONAL PROFILE: Emigrated to England 48 years ago, served as an advisor for the Black community and race relations in Wolverhampton. Serve on many boards for local community organisations including the Black Council of Churches and interfaith, taught religious studies in local schools. Support many community mixtures in the church, ie. Mr Shiloh Health Advisory Centre and director of the Bible training school.
NOMINATED BY: Hyacinth Rowe

KARL 'TUFF ENUFF' BROWN (DJ-PRODUCER)

Tuff Jam, Fifty First Recordings, Alaska Building, 61 Grange Road, London, SE1 3BA

MEMBERSHIPS: Musicians Institute
HONOURS/AWARDS: BPI, Silver discs for Rosie Gaines and Tina Moore to recognise sales of 100,000
PERSONAL PROFILE: Karl Brown part of duo 'Tuff Jam'. A DJ, production duo who have hit the Top 20 with their remixes of Rosie Gaines 'Closer Than Close' and Tina Moore's 'Never Gonna Let You Go'. Travel the world DJing and own their own recording studio.

MS LORNA BROWN (ACTRESS)

PLACE OF BIRTH: London, 9.2.66
MARITAL STATUS: Single
COLLEGE: Central School of Speech & Drama
ACADEMIC QUALIFICATIONS: Degree
HOBBIES AND INTERESTS: Rambling, travelling
PERSONAL PROFILE: Trained at Central School of Speech & Drama. Theatre Credits: 'Once on this island' (West End); 'Zumbi' (Black Theatre Co-op); 'King', 'Mass Carib'. TV credits include: 'Dangerfield'; 'The Bill'; 'Anna Lee'; 'Murder Most Horrid' and 'Jill Bras'. Lorna has sung with Martha Reeves and supported Gladys Knight on tour.

MR RAY EMMET BROWN (ACTOR)

Marina Martin Associates, 12-13 Poland Street, London, W1V 3DE

PLACE OF BIRTH: Manchester
MARITAL STATUS: Single
COLLEGE: Guildhall School of Music and Drama
ACADEMIC QUALIFICATIONS: LLB, AGSMD
MEMBERSHIPS: Equity
HONOURS/AWARDS: 1995 The Manchester Evening News Theatre Award for Best Actor in a supporting role
HOBBIES AND INTERESTS: Birds of prey, handgliding, cycling
EMAIL: Mondo@globalnet.Co.UK
PERSONAL PROFILE: Jamaican descent, first role on television was in Alan Bleasdales acclaimed 'GBH'. 1995 won the Manchester Evening News theatre award for best actor in a supporting role. 1996 starred alongside Helen Mirren in the Emmy Award Winning 'Prime Suspects'. Just completed Law degree and new series with Pete Postlethwaite.

MRS MODUPE BROWNLOW (LECTURER BLACK STUDIES)

c/o Education Department, H.M.P Holloway, Parkhurst Road, London, N7

PLACE OF BIRTH: Nigeria, 18.12.24
CHILDREN: Two (Cynthia Adetokunbo, Philip Ayodeji)
COLLEGE: Residential Teacher
ACADEMIC QUALIFICATIONS: Training College (UMC) Nigeria
PROFESSIONAL QUALIFICATIONS: Higher Teaching Certificate State Registered. Nurse London 1955, Nursing Tutor 1965
MEMBERSHIPS: British Association for Counselling
HONOURS/AWARDS: Honorary Chieftaincy for Achievement Nigeria 1994
HOBBIES AND INTERESTS: Travelling, voluntary group therapy for cancer Black care
PERSONAL PROFILE: Qualified teacher (colonial Nigeria) 1943. Arrived in Britain 1949. Nursing career SRN returned to Nigeria 1956. Further studies London 1965 -1974, returned to Britain 1985 qualified counsellor, teaches Yoruba language and culture to mainly Caribbean people. Represented Nigeria in Australia 1961 at International Congress of Nurses.

MS ANGELA BRUCE (ACTRESS)

London Management, 2-4 Noel Street, London, W1V 3RB

PLACE OF BIRTH: Leeds, 6.5.51
MARITAL STATUS: Single
HONOURS/AWARDS: Best Actress 'Educating Rita', Derby
HOBBIES AND INTERESTS: Riding horses, tennis, sun-bathing
PERSONAL PROFILE: I have still no idea what I want to be when I grow up. Life begins at 48.

> ## Arrived in England in the early fifties from Jamaica. Attended school and college, North London. Served in British Army (RAMC) 1958-60
>
> **HERBERT BROWN**

MISS KAREN BRYSON (ACTRESS)

21 East Castle Street, London, W1N 7PA

PLACE OF BIRTH: London, 2.3.71
MARITAL STATUS: Single
COLLEGE: London Academy of Music and Dramatic Art
HOBBIES AND INTERESTS: Writing, dance, yoga, a keen interest in filmmaking
PERSONAL PROFILE: I have been writing professionally for five years after graduating from the London Academy of Music and Dramatic Art. I have worked in theatre, TV and film including 'The Longest Memory' adapted from the award winning book 'Fred D'agmar', I am currently working for the Royal Shakespeare Company.

MR JAK BUBEUIA-DODD (SOCIAL SCIENTIST)

Chief Executive, Nubian Jak, Unit 11, The Mulberry Centre, Ashmore Road, Maida Hill, London, W9 3DP

PLACE OF BIRTH: London, 4.7.63
MARITAL STATUS: Engaged
CHILDREN: Two (Qaina Minors-Dodd, Kaiyin Minors-Dodd)
COLLEGE: North London Polytechnic
ACADEMIC QUALIFICATIONS: 5 O-Levels
PROFESSIONAL QUALIFICATIONS: Youth and Community Work & Social Work Qualified
DIRECTORSHIPS: Two

MEMBERSHIPS: Various
HONOURS/AWARDS: Various
HOBBIES AND INTERESTS: Sport, leisure, speaking French, travel, women
EMAIL: Jak@nubianjak.com
PERSONAL PROFILE: Former model and the most successful Black British male model for single ad campaign - Interflora 1991-1995, Rapper and singer songwriter, social worker. Launched Nubian Jak in 1995 which became a world first in board games. Currently available all over UK and selected US states and as a computer game and book.

MASTER JAEDEN BURKE (SCHOOLBOY-ACTOR)

The Jackie Palmer Stage School, The Rise, Western Dene, Hazlemere, High Wycombe, HP15 7ET

PLACE OF BIRTH: High Wycombe, 14.1.92
COLLEGE: Hazlemere C of E School
HONOURS/AWARDS: Vuninal Gym Award
HOBBIES AND INTERESTS: Football, table tennis, computer games
EMAIL: JardenB@BurkeFamily.Freescrve
PERSONAL PROFILE: Jaeden is just beginning his debut in the West End musical 'Whistle Down The Wind' playing Winston. Jaedon is a gifted footballer whose main ambition is to play with Ian Wright.

MASTER NETHAN BURKE (SCHOOLBOY-ACTOR)

The Jackie Palmer Stage School Agency, The Rise, Western Drive, Hazlemere, High Wycombe, HP15 7ET

PLACE OF BIRTH: High Wycombe, 4.9.89
COLLEGE: Hazlemere C of E School
HOBBIES AND INTERESTS: Computer games
EMAIL: Nethannb@BurkeFamily.FreeServe
PERSONAL PROFILE: Nethan is just coming to the end of his five months performing at the Aldwych Theatre in 'Whistle Down The Wind'. Nethan is very academically gifted, an easy learner who is full of energy. His goal in life is to become a doctor.

'I came to England in 1956 started writing Westerns in 1965. Had my first two novels published that year. I have had nine novels published since I started writing'

MICHAEL BURROWES

YOLANDA BURKE (CHOREOGRAPHER-DANCE TUTOR)

Dancer, Yolanda Burkes School of Multi Cultural Dance, 48 Newington Green Mansions, Green Lanes, London, N16 9BT

PLACE OF BIRTH: US, 11.4.45
MARITAL STATUS: Married
CHILDREN: Two (Ama Gaffney, Antonio Rodrigues (deceased))
PROFESSIONAL QUALIFICATIONS: Graduated from Katherine Dunham, School of Cultural Arts
MEMBERSHIPS: Jean Leon Destine Talley Beauty Companies, Katherine Dunham Company
HOBBIES AND INTERESTS: Painting, cooking, teaching dance to all ages, music
PERSONAL PROFILE: I taught dance and advised for art in multi-cultural education for the Arts Council nationwide. I am currently doing the same independently. My home base is the Oval House Theatre, Kennington Oval.
NOMINATED BY: Sharon Aitkin

MR BERNARD BURRELL (JOURNALIST-SOCIAL WORKER)

Radio Jamaica Communications Group (RJR), 379 Witton Avenue East, Middlesex, UB6 0JT

PLACE OF BIRTH: Jamaica
MARITAL STATUS: Single
COLLEGE: London, Columbia-Chicago
ACADEMIC QUALIFICATIONS: BA Hons Humanities, BA Journalism, Postgrad-Social Work
PROFESSIONAL QUALIFICATIONS: Journalism BA Social Work - PGrad Diploma
MEMBERSHIPS: National Union of Journalist, British Social Workers Association
HONOURS/AWARDS: John Fischetti Scholar 1991, Columbia Journalism Award 1991
HOBBIES AND INTERESTS: Photography, travels, media, wild life, conservation and architecture
EMAIL: burrell.media@elara.net
WEB SITE: www.radiojamaica.com
PERSONAL PROFILE: Born in Clarendon, Jamaica. Graduate of Pindar's Valley School, London University and Columbia, Chicago. Worked as a journalist for various publications. Former press officer at the British Overseas Aid office. Senior reporter at the defunct JBC radio, Kingston. Producer, Fox 32, Chicago. Currently London correspondent Radio Jamaica and social work, Kensington.
NOMINATED BY: Mark Anthony Lobban

MR MICHAEL BURROWES (WRITER)

Own Business, M & J Cleaners, 15 Bellingham Cresent, Hove, East Sussex, BN3 7FA

PLACE OF BIRTH: Guyana, 7.5.37
MARITAL STATUS: Separated
CHILDREN: Four (David, Linda, Marianne, Robert)
COLLEGE: Queens College
ACADEMIC QUALIFICATIONS: 3 O-Levels, English Language, English Literature and Art
MEMBERSHIPS: LAPSED - FIBA
HOBBIES AND INTERESTS: Writing, reading, art, puzzles (crosswords, jigsaws)
PERSONAL PROFILE: I was born in Guyana, studied at St Starislaus and Queens Colleges. I came to England in 1956 started writing Westerns in 1965. Had my first two novels published that year. I have had nine novels published since I started writing.

MS JOSETTE BUSHELL-MINGO (ACTRESS-DIRECTOR)

Freelance Artiste, 60 Marmont Road, Peckham, London, SE15 5TE

PLACE OF BIRTH: London, 16.2.64
MARITAL STATUS: Ms
HONOURS/AWARDS: TMA Charrington and Manchester Evening News awards
HOBBIES AND INTERESTS: Singing
EMAIL: steffos@div.co.
PERSONAL PROFILE: As an actress Josette has worked with the following companies: The Royal National Theatre; Royal Shakespeare Co and Manchester Royal Exchange. Patron of the Arden Theatre School Manchester. Director of Aspect Theatre Productions. Also a teacher and workshop leader.

MS DAWN BUTLER (Trade Union Officer)

Regional Organiser, GMB London Region, Thorne House, 152 Brent Street, Hendon, London, NW4 2DP

PLACE OF BIRTH: East London, 3.11.69
MARITAL STATUS: Single
COLLEGE: Waltham Forest
ACADEMIC QUALIFICATIONS: 7 O-Levels, BTEC Diploma in Computer Studies
MEMBERSHIPS: Associate Member IPD
HOBBIES AND INTERESTS: Poetry, family
EMAIL: Dawn.Butler@GMB.ORG.UK
PERSONAL PROFILE: I am an independent strong Black woman who firmly believes in equality and family values. I feel that we need to develop a strong Black race who are proud of their colour and the achievements of others. We need role models and we need to support Black businesses.
NOMINATED BY: Allan Black, GMB - Britain's General Union

MR JAZZIE B (Musician-Producer-Entrepreneur)

Soul II Soul Limited, 36-38 Rochester Place, Camden, London, NW1 9JX

PLACE OF BIRTH: London
HONOURS/AWARDS: MOBO, 3 Grammies
PERSONAL PROFILE: Jazzie B co-founded the Soul II Soul Sound System in 1982. The recording group Soul II Soul has achieved world-wide acclaim. He is a true entrepreneur being involved in diverse projects ranging from radio and club DJ to TV presenter and role model.

Entrants in the Black Who's Who 1999 have

been nominated for their achievements and

contributions. You can nominate

someone who deserves

to be in the

Black Who's Who 2000,

nominate them today.

Entries are free

Send in your nominations, including name,

contact address and telephone number to:

Books Division, Ethnic Media Group,

148 Cambridge Heath Road, London E1 5QJ

MR EARL CAMERON (Actor)

Basement Flat, 41 Alfred Road, Acton, London, W3 6LH

PLACE OF BIRTH: Bermuda, 8.8.17
MARITAL STATUS: Married
HOBBIES AND INTERESTS: Tennis, reading
PERSONAL PROFILE: Earl Cameron is one of Britain's best known actors. Since his impressive film debut in 'Pool of London', 1951, he has acted in many films including: 'Sapphire'; 'Flame in the Streets'; 'Guns at Batasi' and 'Thunderball'. Having started his career in the theatre where he appeared in many plays in the West End of London and throughout the UK, Earl has also appeared in numerous TV and radio productions.

MISS CARINE CAMPBELL (Company Director)

Carmona, Carmona House, PO Box 16632, London, SE6 1ZR

PLACE OF BIRTH: London
MARITAL STATUS: Single
COLLEGE: Central London Poly
ACADEMIC QUALIFICATIONS: BA Hons, Business Studies
EMAIL: carmona@
WEB SITE: postmaster.co.uk
PERSONAL PROFILE: Silk products have been available for centuries, but have never been marketed as hair maintenance products. Carmona was born out of Carine's desire to stop her hair breaking. Before Carmona, silk pillow cases were regarded as a luxury. Carine was inspired to make silk night hats and pillow cases more accessible and market them in a revolutionary way, to prove their necessity for well maintained hair.

MR IRVIN ROY CAMPBELL (Carpenter-Youth Worker)

I.R Campbell. Carpentry & General Building Contractor, 10 Valentine Close, Whitchurch, Bristol, BS14 9NB

PLACE OF BIRTH: Jamaica, 10.7.57
MARITAL STATUS: Married
CHILDREN: Three (Lewis Irwin, Gillena Pearl, Alisha May Louise)
ACADEMIC QUALIFICATIONS: O-Level English Lit, History
PROFESSIONAL QUALIFICATIONS: Time Served Carpenter, Qualified Olympic Wrestling Coach, Qualified Football Referee
MEMBERSHIPS: BAWA Southern Representative, Sari committee member
HONOURS/AWARDS: 1995 & 1996 Top Coach Award (Soccer) 97 National Team Manager
HOBBIES AND INTERESTS: Sport, reading, collecting water colours, wine making, politics, Black history
PERSONAL PROFILE: Played soccer at amateur level, started wrestling at 16 years of age. After many years qualified as coach. Teaching in schools. Married and live with wife Angela and children (teenagers). Keen on Black history and politics, travel abroad often, go to Jamaica each year. I hate wasting time.
NOMINATED BY: Angela Campbell

MISS JOANNE CAMPBELL (Actress-Drama Therapist)

Churchill Priory, 80 Lambeth Road, London, SE1 7PW

PLACE OF BIRTH: Northampton, 8.2.64
MARITAL STATUS: Single
COLLEGE: Hertfordshire University, Arts Educational College
ACADEMIC QUALIFICATIONS: Post Graduate Diploma Drama Therapy
PROFESSIONAL QUALIFICATIONS: Diploma Performing Arts
DIRECTORSHIPS: Theatre Royal Stratford East
PERSONAL PROFILE: Joanne has worked as an actress in theatre, television and radio for the last two decades, this has included forming the female production company - The Bibi Crew. Following a return to acting she studied a post graduate. Joanne now combines working as a qualified drama therapist along with her acting career.

MISS NEENAGH CAMPBELL (Schoolgirl-Gymnast)

Manchester South Gym Club, 24 Albert Grove, Longsight, Manchester, M12 4WF

PLACE OF BIRTH: Manchester, 22.1.90
COLLEGE: St Richards R.C Primary
HOBBIES AND INTERESTS: Gymnastics, swimming, modelling
PERSONAL PROFILE: Neenagh trains at Manchester South Gymnastics Club Sharston, at nine she is the current primary level 4 Greater Manchester champion, and a full member of the Greater Manchester gymnastics squad. This year she has been tipped for the top in the compulsory level 4 competition and also the individual voluntary level 4.

TEVIN CAMPBELL (Artiste)

WEA Records, The Warner Building, 28 Kensington Church Street, London, W8 4EP

PERSONAL PROFILE: At the age of 12, Tevin Campbell had his first US No. 1 hit with 'Tomorrow' (A Better You, Better Me) featured on the legendary Quincy Jones' 'Back On The Block' album. Telvin also performed on the soundtrack to Prince's 'Graffiti Bridge'. This success was followed by the US multi-million selling albums 'TELVIN' (1992), 'I'm Ready' and 1996's 'Back to the World'.

LA CHELLE CARL (Actress)

McKenna Hazeldine, 5 Blenheim Street, London, W1Y 9LB

PLACE OF BIRTH: Pittsburgh
CHILDREN: One (Matteo)
COLLEGE: Point Park College
ACADEMIC QUALIFICATIONS: BFA Theatre Arts
DIRECTORSHIPS: British Actors Equity Member
HOBBIES AND INTERESTS: Fluent in Spanish, basic flying trapeze training
PERSONAL PROFILE: La Chelle has two BFA's in Theatre Arts from Point Park College Pittsburgh. Studied Sandford Meisner Technique in New York. Moved to London and earned a British actors Equity card and has worked with BBC in television and radio also performed in several feature films such as the original 'Batman'. Has performed in London's West End.

MS JANET CARON (Artist-Writer)

67 Mayfield Road, London, N8 9LN

PLACE OF BIRTH: Guyana, 26.11.51
MARITAL STATUS: Married
CHILDREN: Two (Rebecca, Sarah)
COLLEGE: City & Guilds: TV & Video Production - City & Islington College
ACADEMIC QUALIFICATIONS: Foundation Course Art & Design, GCSEs: English Language & Literature
PROFESSIONAL QUALIFICATIONS: Ceramics, Jewellery and Paint Works
MEMBERSHIPS: Wood Craft Folk -Youth Org. Word For Word - Writer's Group
HOBBIES AND INTERESTS: Film, reading, painting, drawing, ceramics, jewellery making
PERSONAL PROFILE: An artist and writer. Creating ceramics, oil paintings and illustrations, exhibited in galleries in London. Poetry and short stories published. On steering committee - 'Art in the Green' - Crouch-End's arts markets 1995-96. In 1991 a leader with Hornsey District Woodcraft Folk. Equipment Officer 1992-95, fund-raising 1995-97, publicity and PR 1998, Chair - Jamaica Delegation Committee from 1997, London Management Committee, 1998.
NOMINATED BY: Anthea Lee

'Silk products have been available for centuries,
but have never been marketed as hair maintenance products'

MISS CARINE CAMPBELL

MR DAVID OLIVER CARR (Actor)

Evans & Reiss, 100 Fawe Park Road, London, SW15 2EA

PLACE OF BIRTH: Nottingham, 16.7.63
MARITAL STATUS: Single
CHILDREN: Two (Daniel Oliver, Naydine Amanda)
COLLEGE: Central School of Speech and Drama
PROFESSIONAL QUALIFICATIONS: Actor
MEMBERSHIPS: Equity
HOBBIES AND INTERESTS: All sports, learning languages, theatre going, music
PERSONAL PROFILE: I was born in Nottingham and moved to Birmingham with my family aged two. I began my acting career at Midlands Art Centre, then left for London in 1987 to join the Central Drama School. Since then I have had several TV roles and many theatre roles.

MR TONY CEALY (Actor-Filmmaker)

Producer Writer, Noh Budget Films,

PLACE OF BIRTH: London, 28.1.66
MARITAL STATUS: Single
CHILDREN: One (Sergei)
COLLEGE: Brixton, Goldsmiths
ACADEMIC QUALIFICATIONS: MA Drama, BA, Communication Studies, HND Business and Finance
MEMBERSHIPS: BECTU, Equity, PACT
HONOURS/AWARDS: Lottery Funding, London Arts Board Funding, Arts Council of England Funding
HOBBIES AND INTERESTS: Training young people and senior citizens in drama and film production
PERSONAL PROFILE: As an actor/filmmaker/teacher who works in the film and TV industry, my specialist improvisation company tours nationwide. I teach film production and improvisation techniques to actors and non actors. Funded by Arts Council of England and Lottery Boards to produce local community video project looking at health, education and the environment.
NOMINATED BY: Ms Roli Okorodudu

MS MARIE ERETE CHAMBERLIN (Sole Principal-Solicitor)

Chamberlin Solicitors, 358/360 Goswell Road, Angel, London, EC1V 7LQ

PLACE OF BIRTH: Nigeria, 27.12.58
MARITAL STATUS: Married
CHILDREN: Two (Mary-Eileen McDowell, Maximilian)
COLLEGE: London Guildhall University
ACADEMIC QUALIFICATIONS: BA Hons Law
PROFESSIONAL QUALIFICATIONS: LSF
MEMBERSHIPS: Calabar Union of the United Kingdom
HOBBIES AND INTERESTS: Various
PERSONAL PROFILE: Marie is the sole principal at Chamberlin Solicitors. Born in Calabow, Nigeria she has extensive knowledge in criminal law and has established a reputation amongst her clients for the skill and tenacity with which she handles her cases. The mother of two also deals with human rights issues amongst other things. She covers other areas such as public law, immigration company/commercial and civil litigation.

DR EDDIE CHAMBERS (Curator)

62 Islington Road, Southville, Bristol, BS3 1PZ

PLACE OF BIRTH: Wolverhampton, 9.9.60
MARITAL STATUS: Single
COLLEGE: Sutherland Polytechnic, Goldsmiths College
PROFESSIONAL QUALIFICATIONS: BA Hons Fine Art 2:1, PhD History of Art
HOBBIES AND INTERESTS: Travel, Black history
EMAIL: Eddiechambers@pan@africa.demon.co.uk
PERSONAL PROFILE: Organising and curating a considerable number of artistes' exhibitions in the UK which began with 'Black Art an' done'. He has also written a large number of articles published in magazines such as Race Today, Circa... His work was also included in a major Hayward Gallery exhibition. Established the African and Asian Visual Artists' Archive which was the only research and reference facility in the country concerned with documenting the history, presence and work of British based Black artists.
NOMINATED BY: Clare Hardman Wilson, The London Institute

> 'My mother who taught me if I want anything in life I had to work hard for it'
>
> **IAN CHRISTOPHER**

MR JOSEPH CHARLES (Managing Director)

SOCA News Magazine Ltd, Suite 104, The Hiltongrove Business Centre, Hatherley Mews, Walthamstow, London, E17 4QP

PLACE OF BIRTH: London, 19.6.70
MARITAL STATUS: Single
COLLEGE: St Benedics Voc.
ACADEMIC QUALIFICATIONS: BTEC, O-Levels
DIRECTORSHIPS: 1 SOCA News
HOBBIES AND INTERESTS: Computers
EMAIL: Socanews@socanews.com
WEB SITE: WWW.SOCANEWS.COM
PERSONAL PROFILE: A strong, honest, hard-working, dedicated and friendly person. Someone who sees the best in everyone. I believe that we should pave the way to help the future generations achieve there goals in life, whatever they maybe.
NOMINATED BY: Stephen Spark

MRS RUTH CHIGWADA-BAILEY (Criminology Consultant)

Lecturer in Criminology, Birbeck College, University Of London, Dept. of Criminology, Mare Street, London, WC1

PLACE OF BIRTH: Zimbabwe, 29.12.54
MARITAL STATUS: Married
COLLEGE: Brunel University, Uxbridge
ACADEMIC QUALIFICATIONS: Bsc, University Msc
PROFESSIONAL QUALIFICATIONS: Criminologist
HONOURS/AWARDS: Black Women of the Year in Law 1994, Academic Excellence1997
HOBBIES AND INTERESTS: Reading, exercise, listening to music, going to dinner parties
PERSONAL PROFILE: I lecture in criminology and I am a consultant criminologist in areas of race and gender. I also run conferences addressing issues around race, gender and the criminal justice system.
NOMINATED BY: Sarah Brant

DR MARK CHRISTIAN (University-College Lecturer)

Co-ordinator, Charles Wooton College Centre for African & African Diaspora Studies, 14 Victoria Court, Parkfield Road, Liverpool, L17 8UL

PLACE OF BIRTH: Liverpool, 16.4.61
MARITAL STATUS: Single
COLLEGE: Liverpool Hope University College, Ohio State University, US, University of Sheffield
ACADEMIC QUALIFICATIONS: 1992 BA Honours Degree in Combined Subjects, Sociology and American Studies, 1993 MA Degree In Black Studies, 1997 PhD in Sociology
HONOURS/AWARDS: Senior Fulbright Recepient Fellow National Council for Black Studies
HOBBIES AND INTERESTS: Football, guitar, DIY, running
EMAIL: mchristain@cwcfe.ac.UK
PERSONAL PROFILE: He is the author of various articles and book reviews. He has recently been described as 'One of the best young scholars in the African Diaspora'. Among his numerous academic achievements, he is a Senior Fulbright Scholar recipient. In 1996 he was made a Fellow of the National Council for Black Studies at California State University graduating with Malcolm X's daughter: Malika Shabazz.
NOMINATED BY: Shirley Tate

MR IAN CHRISTOPHER (Lecturer-Writer)

7 Oxenford Street, Grove Vale, East Dulwich, London, SE15 4DF

PLACE OF BIRTH: London, 7.5.62
MARITAL STATUS: Single
ACADEMIC QUALIFICATIONS: BA Government and Economics, MA Int. Relations and Economics
PROFESSIONAL QUALIFICATIONS: PGCE PhD Education
MEMBERSHIPS: Treasurer: Martin Shaw King Trust
HONOURS/AWARDS: Slump Art Prize 1995 Gold Standard - New Impact-Short Story1997
HOBBIES AND INTERESTS: Reading, squash, football, writing brilliant short stories
PERSONAL PROFILE: I come from a hard-working Jamaican family and it was my mother who taught me if I want anything in life I had to work hard for it. I also had to be three times as good as anybody else in order to succeed.
NOMINATED BY: Mrs M Nixon

MRS CHINWE CHUKWUOGO-ROY (Artist)

Glevering Mill, Wickham Market, Woodbridge, 1P13 0EY

PLACE OF BIRTH: Nigeria, 2.5.53
MARITAL STATUS: Married
CHILDREN: Two (Rogan Chineda, Alasdair Nnonyeli)
COLLEGE: Middlesex Polytechnic
ACADEMIC QUALIFICATIONS: BA Hons
MEMBERSHIPS: Royal African Society
HOBBIES AND INTERESTS: African history, reading
PERSONAL PROFILE: Nigerian born, survived Biafran war before attaining BA Arts Degree in London. Major Black female portrait painter in UK. Commissions overseas and UK including Chief Anyaoku, Commonwealth Secretary General. Historical series featured on BBC and in the UK national newspapers. Presently organising free golf coaching for underprivileged children in Ipswich.
NOMINATED BY: Mrs Buchi Otung

MR NEVILLE ROY CLARE (Sickle Cell Advisor)

Director, Sickle Watch Registered Charity, The West Indian Centre, 9 Claredon Road, London, N8 0DJ

PLACE OF BIRTH: Jamaica, 8.5.46
MARITAL STATUS: Married
CHILDREN: Stepdaughter (Donas Douglas)
COLLEGE: University of Westminister
ACADEMIC QUALIFICATIONS: BA, MA Degrees
PROFESSIONAL QUALIFICATIONS: PG Diploma Counselling
DIRECTORSHIPS: None
MEMBERSHIPS: MSF Trade Union, Patient Representative FORUM
HONOURS/AWARDS: Caribbean Times Award 1992, Ethnic Minority Media Award 1998
HOBBIES AND INTERESTS: Reading, writing
PERSONAL PROFILE: In 1975 I founded OSCAR (Organisation for Sickle Cell Anaemia Research), the first charity of its kind not only to pioneer sickle cell awareness in the UK but to promote and support research and improved services. I am pleased that my contribution has assisted so many fellow sickle cell sufferers.
NOMINATED BY: Dolores Gray

MS ROXANNE CLINCH (Actress)

Visionary Mystique, 26D Quex Road, West Hampstead, London, NW6 4PG

PLACE OF BIRTH: London, 14.1.64
MARITAL STATUS: Divorced
CHILDREN: One (Elliot)
COLLEGE: Drama Studio London
PROFESSIONAL QUALIFICATIONS: Post Graduate Affirmation Granted by Church of England as Visionary Missionary
MEMBERSHIPS: Equity (British Actors)
HOBBIES AND INTERESTS: Jazz singer
PERSONAL PROFILE: Worked as an actress for many years, reviews for every show, in publications such as Time Out, the Guardian, What's On. Been a visionary all my life, giving lectures, talks to various bodies, conferences and scientists. Group work as missionary laying on hands for priests and churches.

MISS AMIRAH COLE (Black Arts Coordinator)

Kuumba Project, 20-22 Hepburn Road, St Pauls, Bristol, BS2 9DE

PLACE OF BIRTH: Bristol, 14.2.66
MARITAL STATUS: Single
CHILDREN: One (Amari)
HOBBIES AND INTERESTS: Sports, drama
PERSONAL PROFILE: I am an imaginative and innovative artist of 13 years experience in performing arts. For ten years I have been actively involved in community arts. In 1995 I formed an organisation called 'First Fruits' which has been successful in performing in the west region.
NOMINATED BY: Anthea Lee

'In 1975 I founded OSCAR (Organisation for Sickle Cell Anaemia Research), the first charity of its kind'

NEVILLE ROY CLARE

MR MARTIN COLE (Actor-Singer)

c/o Felix De Wolfe, Manfield House, 1 Southampton Street, London, WC2R 0LR

PLACE OF BIRTH: Cardiff, 1.5.76
MARITAL STATUS: Single
COLLEGE: Coleg Guan Hafren
MEMBERSHIPS: Equity
HOBBIES AND INTERESTS: Martial arts, basketball, collector of music, films
PERSONAL PROFILE: As a professional actor from an early age Martin has worked extensively in theatre and television. His stage work includes lead roles in three award winning productions. Martin has also excelled in music, from school choir to country choir, to signed singer/rapper on East West records.

MR SELTZER COLE (Writer-Communication Specialist)

Director, 17 TM Limited, 90 Hawtrey Road, London, NW3 3SS

PLACE OF BIRTH: London, 9.2.65
MARITAL STATUS: Single
COLLEGE: Westminster University
ACADEMIC QUALIFICATIONS: MA Journalism
PROFESSIONAL QUALIFICATIONS: Video Journalism Course VNI (New York) Inc.
DIRECTORSHIPS: Infrared Limited & 17TM Limited
MEMBERSHIPS: Royal Television Society and New Playwright's Trust
HOBBIES AND INTERESTS: Travel, cinema, languages
EMAIL: Seltzer@dircon.co.uk
PERSONAL PROFILE: Following a journalism career that has embraced radio, LBC, television, Channel One and print, I am now embarking on a career as editor of web magazine Urban Traveller.
NOMINATED BY: Ron Shillingford

MR FRASER COLLINS (Actor-Writer-Dancer)

G3 Group & Associates,

PLACE OF BIRTH: Luton, 19.5.71
MARITAL STATUS: Single
COLLEGE: Middlesex University
ACADEMIC QUALIFICATIONS: BA Hons in Performing Arts
HOBBIES AND INTERESTS: Music, theatre, books, composing,
EMAIL: fraser@ccom.co.uk
PERSONAL PROFILE: Fraser has played the trumpet since he was eleven years old, playing in the county orchestras. After majoring in dance at university he has appeared in musicals such as 'Five Guys Named Moe' and 'Smokey Joe's Cafe' and as a bass singer in 'The Flying Pickets'. Nowadays he enjoys songwriting, composing and recording.

MR WAYNE COLLINS (Footballer)

Fulham Football Club, Craven Cottage, Stevenage Road, London, SW6 6HH

PLACE OF BIRTH: Manchester, 4.3.69
PROFESSIONAL QUALIFICATIONS: 117 League Games, Scoring 14 Goals
PERSONAL PROFILE: Wayne is hard running midfielder who likes to get forward and support the attack. Manchester born Wayne was playing for non-league Winsford United when Dario Gradi spotted him and took him to Crewe Alexandra. In three seasons at Gresty Road, Wayne played 117 league games, scoring 14 goals. David Pleat signed Wayne for Sheffield Wednesday. Wayne scored some important goals for the Owls and then joined Fulham.

MR CARDIGAN CONNOR (Cricketer-Coach)

Director, Cricket Anguilla BWI,

PLACE OF BIRTH: Anguilla, 24.3.61
MARITAL STATUS: Married
HOBBIES AND INTERESTS: Keep fit, working with children
PERSONAL PROFILE: Became the first Anguillian to play first class cricket in England when making debut for Hampshire in 1984. Played for Hampshire for 15 years, taking over a thousand wickets in first class and one day matches. Currently coaching young cricketers on his native Auguilla.

MR EDDIE CONNOR (ACTOR)

c/o Character Artistes, 153 Battersea Rise, London, SW11 1HP

PLACE OF BIRTH: Rotterdam, 10.12.63
MARITAL STATUS: Single
ACADEMIC QUALIFICATIONS: Maths, English, History, German, French
PROFESSIONAL QUALIFICATIONS: BA I, BAZ, PSARA, Drama Degree
MEMBERSHIPS: Equity
HONOURS/AWARDS: Young Writers Award 1980
HOBBIES AND INTERESTS: Travel, languages, writing, swimming, wine, good food, stage/screen
PERSONAL PROFILE: Have written and performed several plays for Royal Court Theatre, Half Moon Theatre and several other well established venues. Have done film voice-overs, featured in commercials, photographic features and television. Featured in 'Maisie Raine', 'Crimewatch', 'A Certain Justice' and my all time favourite 'The Bill'. Ambition is to be in a soap opera.

GERALDINE CONNOR (UNIVERSITY LECTURER)

Programme Co-ordinator, College of the University of Leeds, The Gate House, 149 Commercial Road, Skelmanthorpe, Huddersfield, HD8 9DX

PLACE OF BIRTH: London, 22.3.52
MARITAL STATUS: Single
COLLEGE: SOAS London University
ACADEMIC QUALIFICATIONS: M Mus
PROFESSIONAL QUALIFICATIONS: LRSM and Dip. Ed
DIRECTORSHIPS: Youth Music Trust Carnival Musical NCPM, Ebony Steelband, 2000 Cultural Corporation, Firebird Arts Council of England-Music Panel
MEMBERSHIPS: Yorkshire and Humberside Arts Awards: Care Award 1995
HOBBIES AND INTERESTS: Music, theatre
PERSONAL PROFILE: Composer, musician and journalist.
NOMINATED BY: Mary Kershaw

MR CAVIN CORNWALL (ACTOR-SINGER)

52 Limes Grove, London, SE13 6DE

PLACE OF BIRTH: Bristol, 6.11.64
MARITAL STATUS: Single
COLLEGE: Doreen Birds Arts College/ Performing Wandsworth College
ACADEMIC QUALIFICATIONS: Six O-Levels
PROFESSIONAL QUALIFICATIONS: BTEC, HNC TV Productions
MEMBERSHIPS: Equity
HONOURS/AWARDS: English Junior Karate Champion
HOBBIES AND INTERESTS: Film production, karate
PERSONAL PROFILE: Cavin was English junior karate champion at 17 and at 21. He graduated from theatre school and has worked in all mediums of film, TV, theatre, voice-over artist and radio in front and behind the camera. Cavin has understudied many leading roles in West End theatres and will play his first in the musical 'Dreamgirls' (Autumn 1999).

MR LUKE CORNWALL (FOOTBALLER)

Fulham Football Club, Craven Cottage, Stevenage Road, London, SW6 6HH

PLACE OF BIRTH: London
PERSONAL PROFILE: Luke has progressed through the youth set-up at Fulham and has shown an eye for goal at every level he has played. A Londoner, Luke made his Fulham debut in September, playing his first full match against Southampton in the Worthington Cup. Marked his league debut four days later with his first goal for the club.

MR ANTHONY CORRIETTE (GENERAL MANAGER)

Talawa Theatre Co, Third Floor, 23-25 Great Sutton Street, London, EC1V 0DN

PLACE OF BIRTH: London, 26.8.66
MARITAL STATUS: Single
DIRECTORSHIPS: Black Theatre Forum
HOBBIES AND INTERESTS: Arts, technology
EMAIL: hq@talawa.com
PERSONAL PROFILE: Anthony Corriette has worked in the entertainment industry for 17-years achieving a variety of engagements in theatre, including management; marketing; producing and now general manager of Talawa, Britain's foremost Black theatre company. Formerly, an accomplished actor and singer, with work ranging from West End musicals to television dramas.

MR SEBERT COX (DEVELOPMENT ADVISOR)

Home Office, 50 Queen Anne's Gate, London, SW1H 9AT

PLACE OF BIRTH: Jamaica, 27.12.50
MARITAL STATUS: Married
CHILDREN: Two (Lauren, Rachel)
COLLEGE: Lancaster
ACADEMIC QUALIFICATIONS: MSc
PROFESSIONAL QUALIFICATIONS: Certificate of Residential Care
DIRECTORSHIPS: (Non-exec) Chairman North British Housing Group
MEMBERSHIPS: Member of the Institute of Directors
HONOURS/AWARDS: OBE
HOBBIES AND INTERESTS: Walking, music, cooking (followed by eating)
PERSONAL PROFILE: For more than 25 years, Sebert Cox has pursued a career in social work combined with housing. This career has been motivated by a strong sense of concern for people who are in some way disadvantaged. He now holds prominent positions in the Home Office and the North British Housing Group.
NOMINATED BY: David Omand

For more than 25 years, Sebert Cox has pursued a career in social work combined with housing. This career has been motivated by a strong sense of concern for people who are in some way disadvantaged. He now holds prominent positions in the Home Office and the North British Housing Group

SEBERT COX

MARTIN DAHLIN (Footballer)

Blackburn Rovers Football & Athetic Plc, Ewood Park, Blackburn, BB2 4JF

PLACE OF BIRTH: Sweden, 16.4.68
PROFESSIONAL QUALIFICATIONS: Caps for Sweden (60)
PERSONAL PROFILE: Signed for a £2 million fee from Italian giants AS Roma in July 1997. Scored four goals in the World Cup finals in America. He left Borussia for AS Roma, returning for a loan spell to Borussia. Left Blackburn in November 1998 to go on a loan spell to Hamburger, has now returned for the 1999/2000 season.

MR DEVON DALEY (Media and Arts Consultant)

Broadcaster-Journalist, BBC Radio Derby, Groove Genie - Media, Music/Marketing, PO Box 73, Derby, DE1 9PQ

PLACE OF BIRTH: Derby, 24.10.62
MARITAL STATUS: Single
COLLEGE: Nottingham Trent University
ACADEMIC QUALIFICATIONS: Business Studies HND
PROFESSIONAL QUALIFICATIONS: Institute of Sales and Marketing Management
DIRECTORSHIPS: Metro Cinema, Derby and Rotary Club Cultural Ambassador to Brazil 1995.
HONOURS/AWARDS: Windrush Achievement Award 99 - Finalist, Minority Broadcaster of the Year & Special Honours
HOBBIES AND INTERESTS: African diaspora travel, Black history, soul / jazz collector, ancient Egypt, world faiths, football
EMAIL: Devon.daley@bbc.co.uk
PERSONAL PROFILE: Media and arts entrepreneur specialising in broadcast/print journalism and edutainment events consultancy. Experienced radio/TV presenter, compere, PR/marketing co-ordinator within and beyond Black community. Business tenures in recruitment and sales management with British, European and American organisations. Established DJ/promoter.
NOMINATED BY: Karen Weir

EARL DALEY (Songwriter-Vocalist)

Entertainer, Down Beat Records, 132 Royal College Street, Camden Town, London, NW1 0TA

PLACE OF BIRTH: Jubilee, 9.9.58
MARITAL STATUS: Divorced
CHILDREN: Four (Gabriel, Jordon, Kymani, Ryan)
COLLEGE: Wandsworth
ACADEMIC QUALIFICATIONS: Electrical Engineering
PROFESSIONAL QUALIFICATIONS: Producer, Recording Artist, Entertainer
DIRECTORSHIPS: Sixteen Music Publishing
MEMBERSHIPS: BMG, PRS, MCPS
HONOURS/AWARDS: Platinum Disc For 'Release The Pressure'
HOBBIES AND INTERESTS: Cooking, driving, reading, lawn tennis
PERSONAL PROFILE: Born in Jamaica, took up professional singing at age 15 having several hits such as 'Don't Mash Up The Dance' and 'Love is a feeling'. Also recorded with Augustus Pablo, Lee Perry and Derrick Harriot. Moved to the UK in 1985, had several reggae hits and ultimately proved his crossover appeal with Leftfield and Dreadzone. Currently recording second solo album for Warners, in Germany.

DR PATRICIA DALEY (University Lecturer)

College Fellow, Oxford University, Jesus College, Oxford, OX1 3DW

PLACE OF BIRTH: Jamaica, 18.10.57
MARITAL STATUS: Single
CHILDREN: One (Sule Mandinso)
COLLEGE: Middlesex/SOAS/Oxford
ACADEMIC QUALIFICATIONS: BSc, MA, DPhil
PROFESSIONAL QUALIFICATIONS: PGCE
HOBBIES AND INTERESTS: Reading, walking, travelling, Black music
EMAIL: Patricia.Daley.Geog.ox.ac.UK
PERSONAL PROFILE: Dr Daley was born in Kingston, Jamaica and grew up in Claredon. She was educated in Jamaica and the UK. Since 1991 she has been working as a university lecturer in human geography and is a Fellow of Jesus College, Oxford. Her principal academic interests are in African development, forced migration and political ecology.
NOMINATED BY: Maria Anubi

MR MARK DALGETY (Herbal Tea Manufacturer)

Director, Dalgety Teas & Herbs, Regent House, Business Centre, 291 Kirkdale, Sydenham, London, SE26 4QD

PLACE OF BIRTH: London, 27.1.66
MARITAL STATUS: Divorced
CHILDREN: One (Farai)
COLLEGE: South Bank University
ACADEMIC QUALIFICATIONS: Hons Degree Chemical Engineer
PROFESSIONAL QUALIFICATIONS: Chemical Engineer
MEMBERSHIPS: Institute Chemical Engineers
HOBBIES AND INTERESTS: Cinema, reading
PERSONAL PROFILE: Dynamic chemical engineer with a passion for manufacturing systems. Vision-the application of the most appropriate technology in the processing of local raw materials found in the soils of the Caribbean, transforming them into useful products processed and packaged to the highest standard to be sold in any part of the world.

MR JON DANIEL (Art Director-Designer)

DMB & B Advertising, 123 Buckingham Palace Road, London, SW1W 9DZ

PLACE OF BIRTH: London, 31.5.66
MARITAL STATUS: Married
CHILDREN: One (Noah)
HOBBIES AND INTERESTS: Boxing, art - design, music
EMAIL: bigblackguy@angelfire.com
PERSONAL PROFILE: My first campaign sought to put historical Black Britons on the Royal Mail stamps. As co-author of the operation Black Vote advertising campaign for the 1997 General Election, I know Black issues are advanced by powerful campaigns. My aim: To create ideas that highlight the Black British dynamic.
NOMINATED BY: Sonita Alleyne

MR PAUL DASH (Lecturer-Artist)

Goldsmith University of London, Lewisham, London, SE14

PLACE OF BIRTH: Barbados, 25.6.46
MARITAL STATUS: Married
CHILDREN: Three (Luke, Nicholas, Rebecca)
ACADEMIC QUALIFICATIONS: Diploma in Art and Design, MA Education
DIRECTORSHIPS: 198 Gallery (Secretary Board of Management)
MEMBERSHIPS: National Society for Education in Art and Design
HOBBIES AND INTERESTS: Travelling, music, reading
EMAIL: edsOlpd!gold.ac.UK
PERSONAL PROFILE: PGCE (Secondary) Lecturer, Goldsmiths University of London. Research area art and design, education and Caribbean children. A practising painter, I have exhibited at Whitechapel Copend Royal Academy, Highgate Gallery, Commonwealth Institute Gallery. I have written 'Traditions' from the Caribbean, a childrens book published by Wayland 1998.
NOMINATED BY: Professor Clyde Chitty, Goldsmiths College

MR ROGER DAVIES (Actor)

The Jackie Palmer Agency, 30 Daws Hill Lane, High Wycombe, HP11 1PN

PLACE OF BIRTH: London, 30.7.81
MARITAL STATUS: Single
MEMBERSHIPS: Equity: Professional Name - Roger Roberts
HOBBIES AND INTERESTS: Theatre, sport
PERSONAL PROFILE: Actor/singer and dancer, former member of National Youth Music Theatre. Appeared in several TV programmes including lead roles in 'Dream Team' and 'Renford Rejects', later shown on Channel 4 and Nickelodeon. Was runner-up in childrens BAFTA drama section.

> 'I know Black issues are advanced by powerful campaigns. My aim: To create ideas that highlight the Black British dynamic'
>
> **JON DANIEL**

MR VINCENT PAUL DAVIES (ACTOR)

Amber Personal Management Ltd, 28 St Margaret's Chambers, 5 Newton Street, Manchester, M1 1HN

PLACE OF BIRTH: Manchester, 14.7.68
MARITAL STATUS: Single (Has Partner)
CHILDREN: Three (Nathan, Jordan, Cameron)
ACADEMIC QUALIFICATIONS: 3 A-Levels, BA Hons Degree
HOBBIES AND INTERESTS: Education, arts
EMAIL: info@amberltd.co.uk
PERSONAL PROFILE: Successful actor, lead role in forthcoming film 'Everybody Loves Sunshine'. Extensive TV and radio credits.

MS BEVERLEY DAVIS (ART CO-ORDINATOR)

Director, Black Women in the Arts, 18 Cleveland Park Avenue, Walthamstow, London, E17 7BS

PLACE OF BIRTH: Jamaica, 14.12.52
CHILDREN: Two (Nicolette Tanya, Jastine Claudette)
COLLEGE: Brunel
PROFESSIONAL QUALIFICATIONS: B.A Hons Youth and Community Work
HOBBIES AND INTERESTS: Badminton, kick boxing, reading
PERSONAL PROFILE: My background is Black Women in the Arts. I developed a love of the arts during adolescence. I am an ardent campaigner for the development and promotion of all art forms performed by African and African Caribbean artists. One of my happiest moments was realising the vision of the Young Artist Achievers Award.

MR JUNIOR DELGADO (ARTIST)

Smash Press, 99c Talbot Road, London, W11 2AT

PERSONAL PROFILE: One of Jamaica's most enduring reggae legends, Junior 'Jux' Delgado has a history in reggae music that spans three decades during which he has recorded with a virtual who's who of reggae superstars. In West Kingston, Jamaica, Jux recorded with Dennis Brown and Lee Perry. His debut album ('Taste Of The Young Heart') was released through Dennis Brown's DEB label in 1978. In 1998 Junior had re-recorded and re-mixed a number of his classic songs for his next project, 'Fearless'. 1999 sees Jux returning to his roots with his new album, 'Reasons'. Junior played at the Glastonbury Festival summer 1999 on the world and jazz stage.

MR ALAN DENNIS (MANAGEMENT CONSULTANT)

Mark II Management, Flat 9, 5 Station Road, Wood Green, London, N22 6UY

PLACE OF BIRTH: N. Ireland, 5.10.61
MARITAL STATUS: Single
COLLEGE: Kingston Polytechnic Business School, Newcastle-upon-Tyne Polytechnic
ACADEMIC QUALIFICATIONS: Postgraduate Diploma in Marketing, BA Degree in Sports Studies
PROFESSIONAL QUALIFICATIONS:

MEMBERSHIPS: Institute of Public Relations, Associate Member (AMIPR) Music Link
HOBBIES AND INTERESTS: Basketball, sport, music, communication, commerce, philosophy, politics, astrology, theology, reading, creative writing, cinema, theatre, socialising, fitness-training
PERSONAL PROFILE: Enterprising, resilient, marketing professional who has achieved a reputation for consistently delivering unique marketing solutions in the field of sports, music and art management. Current business activity focuses on media production and future projects include screen-writing and publishing.

One of Jamaica's most enduring reggae legends

JUNIOR DELGADO

MS ANNMARIE DIXON-BARROW (DIRECTOR)

Project Fullemploy, Wakeside, 15 Deans Farm, The Causeway, Reading, RG4 57Z

PLACE OF BIRTH: Wiltshire, 25.4.62
MARITAL STATUS: Married
CHILDREN: Two (Oscar Barrow-Townsend, Lucas Barrow-Townsend)
DIRECTORSHIPS: Camden ITEC Providence Housing Association
MEMBERSHIPS: New Deal Adviser Group, Prince's Trust Ethnic Minority Group and Fellow of RSA
HOBBIES AND INTERESTS: People, reading, social welfare, politics
PERSONAL PROFILE: A decade of experience at all levels across public, private and voluntary sectors. Developing programmes to generate employment opportunity for minority communities. Providing policy briefings to a range of sectors including government. An approach intergrating policy, process and promotion to achieve strategic impact.

CHIEF DR RAYMOND ALEOGHO DOKPESI
(MARINE ENGINEER)

Executive Chairman, Daar Communications (UK) Ltd. AIT, Suite 22, Pall Mall Deposit, 124-128 Barlby Road, London, W10 6BL

PLACE OF BIRTH: Ibadan, 25.10.51
MARITAL STATUS: Married
COLLEGE: Wyzssa Gdynia-Poland, University of Gdynia
ACADEMIC QUALIFICATIONS: MSc Marine Transportation Engineering, Doctor Of Economics Science (PhD)
PROFESSIONAL QUALIFICATIONS: Nigerian Institute of Shipping, Chartered Inst. of Transport (FCIT), Nigerian Inst. of Management., Inst. of Directors
DIRECTORSHIPS: President Chartered Institute of Transport (Nigeria) President Independent Broadcasters Association of Nigeria
MEMBERSHIPS: Committee on the Commercialisation of Nigerian Ports Authority
HONOURS/AWARDS: 'Men of Achievement' Corporate Press Services Inc. 1993
HOBBIES AND INTERESTS: Football, reading, travelling, music
EMAIL: ait@dokpesi.freeserve.com
PERSONAL PROFILE: Born 1951, travelled to Poland, obtained 1st class with distinction first of its kind in 50 years, for both masters and doctorate degrees. In Nigeria, I have held various public and political appointments. Managing director of the first private shipping company and proprietor of first private radio, television and satellite stations, post broadcasting deregulation in Nigeria.
NOMINATED BY: Johnson Onime

ANNI DOMINGO (ACTRESS-SINGER)

Aurora House, 5 Wimpole Street, Chatteris, Cambridgeshire, PE16 6ND

PLACE OF BIRTH: London
MARITAL STATUS: Married
CHILDREN: Three (Jeremiah, Joel, Zelda)
COLLEGE: Rose Bruford College
ACADEMIC QUALIFICATIONS: Trained Teacher
MEMBERSHIPS: Actors Equity
HOBBIES AND INTERESTS: Sewing, knitting, dancing
EMAIL: annidom@aol.com
PERSONAL PROFILE: Anni lives out in the country with her husband and three kids. She also runs a knitwear design company. She started acting and dancing at the age of three. She has worked in radio, TV, theatre and films. Work has taken her around the United Kingdom and as far as America and Australia.

MS TAMZIE DUARTE-AGYEMAN (SINGER-PERFORMER)

319 Neasden Lane North, London, NW10 0AG

PLACE OF BIRTH: London, 14.5.76
MARITAL STATUS: Single
COLLEGE: Richmond-upon-Thames College
ACADEMIC QUALIFICATIONS: French, Dance, Spanish A-Levels
PROFESSIONAL QUALIFICATIONS: (Bronze Medal) LAMDA , RAD (Honours)
MEMBERSHIPS: Full Equity
HOBBIES AND INTERESTS: Travel, history, sports, karate, cooking
PERSONAL PROFILE: I come from a Portuguese and Ghanaian background. I grew up in northwest London. From a young age I travelled to many countries with my parents. I grew up very cultured, I took an interest in languages and now speak five. I also took an interest in sports and dance, I became a Brown Belt in karate, I still enjoy travelling. At the moment I'm living in Germany and working as a singer. I'm enjoying it very much.

MISS SHARON DUNCAN-BREWSTER (ACTRESS)

c/o CAM, 19 Denmark Street, London, WC2H 8NA

PLACE OF BIRTH: London, 28.1.75
MARITAL STATUS: Single
COLLEGE: Raines Foundation and Tower Hamlets
ACADEMIC QUALIFICATIONS: 13 GCSE's, 3 A-Levels
MEMBERSHIPS: Equity
HOBBIES AND INTERESTS: Photography, singing, songwriting
PERSONAL PROFILE: I went to Anna Scher's Childrens Theatre where I acquired various acting skills. I got my first acting job when I was eight years old. I have appeared in numerous productions for radio, TV and theatre. I am currently working on 'Jailbirds' for Granada TV.

MR DAVID DURHAM (ACTOR-MUSICIAN)

The Really Useful Theatre Company, 23 Alexandra Mansions, 333 Kings Road, London, SW3 5ET

PLACE OF BIRTH: Liverpool, 27.4.65
MARITAL STATUS: Single
COLLEGE: Guildhall South Music and Drama
ACADEMIC QUALIFICATIONS: AGSM
PROFESSIONAL QUALIFICATIONS: Professional Actor and Musician
MEMBERSHIPS: Equity
HONOURS/AWARDS: Bursary from Prince of Wales Trust
HOBBIES AND INTERESTS: Astronomy, philosophy
PERSONAL PROFILE: Trained as a violinist and viola player at GSMD. Later becoming an actor appearing in productions for stage and TV. Currently playing 'Caiaphas' in the National Theatre of 'Jesus Christ Superstar'. Ambitions for classical straight theatre, particularly to do more 'Shakespeare' and opera?.... The sky's the limit!

MR GERRY DWIGHT (ACTOR)

30 Swancombe PT, Clarkson Road, Canning Town, London, E16 1EY

PLACE OF BIRTH: London, 31.12.68
MARITAL STATUS: Single
CHILDREN: One (Jay)
COLLEGE: Brunel
ACADEMIC QUALIFICATIONS: Undergraduate Music Industry MGT.
PROFESSIONAL QUALIFICATIONS: Diploma In Performing Arts
HOBBIES AND INTERESTS: Football, tennis, training, singing, drama
PERSONAL PROFILE: I am an actor, I have been involved with the theatre for fifteen years. I have been in various productions including 'West Side Story', 'Show Boat', 'Babes In Arms' in the West End and 'Billy Budd' at the Royal Opera House. Appeared in the 'Vanishing Man' for Carlton TV.

'I grew up very cultured, I took an interest in languages and now speak five. I also took an interest in sports and dance, I became a Brown Belt in karate'

TAMZIE DUARTE-AGYEMAN

Carribbean Times

Caribbean Times *Incorporating African Times*

◆Friday·11·June·1999◆ BRITAIN'S·ONLY·QUALITY·BLACK·NEWSPAPER◆ Issue·938◆ 50p

TRINIDAD HANGS NINE MURDERERS IN HISTORIC CASE

Privy·Council·rejects·appeals,·allowing·gang·to·be·executed

Emmanuel Dunoomh

TRINIDAD·and·Tobago·hanged three·killers·on·Monday,·the last·executions·in·an unprecedented·series·of·nine over·four·days·that·marked the·Caribbean·nation's resumption·of·capital punishment.

Joel·Ramsingh,·Stephen·Eversley and·Bhagwandeen·Singh·were·put to·death·within·three·hours·starting at·6am·EDT·(1000·GMT)·at·the Royal·Jail·in·Port·of·Spain,·Prison Commissioner·Ciprian·Baptiste said.

Denying·local·media·reports·that some·of·the·nine·killers·had·been eaten·to·the·gallows·kicking·and screaming,·Baptiste·said·all·of·the men·went·to·their·deaths peacefully.

Defying·years·of·pressure·from former·colonial·master·Britain·to end·capital·punishment,·Trinidad began·the·executions·last·Friday, sending·gang·leader·Dole·Chadee to·the·gallows.

It·was·the·first·execution·in·the southern·Caribbean·nation·in·five years.

Notorious

One·of·Trinidad·and·Tobago's most·notorious·criminals,·Chadee was·a·reputed·drug·lord·who·was never·convicted·of·a·drug·crime. But·he·and·eight·members·of·his gang·were·convicted·of·the·brutal 1994·shooting·deaths·of·a·family of·four·at·their·home·in Williamsville,·in·central·Trinidad.

A·large·crowd·gathered·outside the·jail·on·Monday·for·news·of·the hangings.·Trinidadians·are·overwhelmingly·in·favour·of·capital·punishment·as a·deterrent·to·rising·crime.

There·were·few·protesters·during the·three·days·of·executions.·But on·Monday,·abolitionist·Ishmael Samad,·who·has·waged·a·long campaign·against·execution,·was joined·outside·the·jail·by·several Catholic·nuns.

"No·human·life,·no·matter·how wretched,·is·without·worth,"·Sister Theresa·Deelha·said.·"[The·men]·are still·human·beings,·children·of·God."

Along·with·Chadee,·gang

Dead·and·buried:·prisoners·at·the·Golden·Grove·prison·bring·in·the·body·of·executed·murderer·Clive·Thomas·in·a·crude, wooden·casket·for·burial·at·the·Happy·Valley·cemetery

The·nine·men,·sentenced·to death·in·1996·for·the·killings were·hanged·after·failing·in·a lengthy·battle·to·get·their·local courts·and·the·British·Privy Council,·the·final·court·of·appeal for·many·former·and·current British·territories,·to·commute their·sentences·to·life·in·prison.

During·trial,·state·prosecutors said·Chadee·gave·orders·to·the gang·to·kill·Hamilton·Baboolal suggesting·Baboolal·was·a member·of·the·drug·gang·but wanted·out.·Baboolal's·father Deo,·his·mother·Rookmin·and sister·Monica,·also·were·shot·to death.

members·Joey·Ramiah·and Ramlchelawan·Singh·also·were executed·Friday.·Clive·Thomas, Robin·Gopaul·and·Russel Sankerath·were·hanged·Saturday.

The·executed·men·were·buried at·Happy·Valley·cemetery·in·the compound·of·the·Golden·Grove prison,·15·miles·east·of·Port·of Spain.

Their·executions·took·place despite·a·last-minute·plea·by Amnesty·International,·which·sent a·petition·to·the·government·with over·150·signatures·including those·of·Nobel·Peace·Prize winners·Rose·Ramos-Horta,·Sir Joseph·Rotblat·and·South·African Archbishop·Desmond·Tutu.

Robin·Gopaul:·hanged·on·Saturday

Dole·Chadee:·leader·was·first·to·go

COUNTDOWN TO THE MILLENNIUM

MR ROY EBANKS (MANAGER HR)

HR Strategy, BT Plc, BT Group HQ, 81 Newgate Street, London, EC1A 7AJ

PLACE OF BIRTH: London, 1.7.61
MARITAL STATUS: Married
CHILDREN: Three (Jordan, Adam, Leah Elaine)
ACADEMIC QUALIFICATIONS: 5 O-Levels, 2 A-Levels
PROFESSIONAL QUALIFICATIONS: Certificate - Advertising and Marketing, M.Inst. Admin Mgrs
MEMBERSHIPS: M.Inst Admin Mgrs MBIM
HOBBIES AND INTERESTS: DIY, reading, networking
EMAIL: Royebanks@bt.com
PERSONAL PROFILE: Committee and strategy team member of BT Ethnic Minority Network. Helped to set it's strategic direction, increased management support and exposure, Membership support EMN Britain's leading company sponsored staff network. In addition Roy has had a varied and interesting BT career encompassing sales marketing, operations regulatory and Human Resource strategy/policy.

CLLR ANDREW EDWARDS (MANAGEMENT CONSULTANT)

Kennet District Council, The Members' Rooms, Browfort HQ, Devizes, Wiltshire, SN10 2AT

PLACE OF BIRTH: Manchester, 20.2.62
MARITAL STATUS: Single
COLLEGE: Bolton Institute of Higher Education
ACADEMIC QUALIFICATIONS: HND in Finance
DIRECTORSHIPS: Sarsen Housing Association Devizes
MEMBERSHIPS: CBI Member Employment Tribunals
HONOURS/AWARDS: Bronze, Silver & Gold DOE Awards
HOBBIES AND INTERESTS: Railways
PERSONAL PROFILE: Andrew is the Labour Party councillor for the Army Town at Tidworth and Perham Down on Kennet District Council in Wiltshire, one of only three Black councillors in southwest England. He is also the party's spokesman on housing and homelessness. Single and self-employed and living in London, Andrew is busy trying to attract more industry and employment to the area.
NOMINATED BY: Niall Murphy - Sarsen Housing Association

MR DANNY EDWARDS (ACTOR)

c/o C.S.M Artistes, St Dunstans Hall, East Acton Lane, London, W3

PLACE OF BIRTH: London, 10.12.68
MARITAL STATUS: Single
COLLEGE: Lowlands 6th Form
ACADEMIC QUALIFICATIONS: 7 O-Levels
MEMBERSHIPS: Full Actors Equity
HOBBIES AND INTERESTS: Photography, dance, singing
PERSONAL PROFILE: Born in London to mixed race parentage in 1968. Began his professional career aged 12. Became the youngest actor to join the Belgrade Theatre in Education Company aged 17 in 1986. Has had a very diverse career since, ranging from cabaret artiste at Madam JoJo's to a leading role in 'Bands of Gold'.

MS FAITH EDWARDS (ACTRESS)

Shane Collins Associates, 39/41 New Oxford Street, London, WC1A 1BH

PLACE OF BIRTH: England, 4.8.66
MARITAL STATUS: Single
COLLEGE: Croydon College, Birkbeck University
ACADEMIC QUALIFICATIONS: Currently working towards a media studies degree: Screenwriting
PROFESSIONAL QUALIFICATIONS: Trained: Adam Darius Mime Centre, Eastis Acting School
MEMBERSHIPS: Equity, Actors Centre
HONOURS/AWARDS: 'Othello' BAC Nominated for 'The Independent ' Fringe Award 1993
HOBBIES AND INTERESTS: Writing, reading, current affairs, art, drawing, painting
PERSONAL PROFILE: Miriam Sisulu, Warner Brothers 'The Power of One'; Female Othello in BAC's 'Othello'; Amy in C4's 'Wavelengths', Annette in ITV's 'The Tomorrow People', Heidi in BBC1's 'So Haunt Me', in addition to numerous screen and theatre credits. A growing interest in cultivating my own scripts, in conjunction with the acting.

MS JEILLO EDWARDS-CLOTTEY (ACTRESS)

Freelance, Oriental Casting, 60 Downton Avenue, Streatham Hill, London, SW2 37R

PLACE OF BIRTH: Sierra Leone, 23.9.42
MARITAL STATUS: Married
CHILDREN: Three (Victoria, Edmund Junior, Andrew)
COLLEGE: Norwood Technical College
ACADEMIC QUALIFICATIONS: Licentiate of the Guild Hall School of Music and Drama (Performers)
PROFESSIONAL QUALIFICATIONS: Associate of the London Academy of Music (Public Speaking), City and Guilds Cooks Certificate
MEMBERSHIPS: Equity
HONOURS/AWARDS: Jackson Award 1964/5, Third Year Speech and Drama Prize
HOBBIES AND INTERESTS: Hosting functions, events
PERSONAL PROFILE: Born to the late Crispin and Victoria Edwards. Married in 1970 to Emund Clottey. Worked with several Black theatre groups and with the BBC African Theatre since 1964. I've had numerous roles on Radio 4, in theatre, television and film. I've also been a successful restaurateur, caterer and lecturer in wine-making.

CLLR JOSEPH EJIOFOR (SENIOR PARLIAMENTARY OFFICER)

Bandung Parliamentary Institute, Bendish Road, East Ham, London, E6 1JH

PLACE OF BIRTH: London, 16.7.64
COLLEGE: London Guildhall University
ACADEMIC QUALIFICATIONS: BA Hons Politics and Government
HOBBIES AND INTERESTS: Playing football, badminton, snooker, reading, walking, Black film, theatre
EMAIL: ejiofor@hotmail.com
PERSONAL PROFILE: Second term councillor on London Borough of Newham Council. One of only five African-Caribbean's on the Labour Party's approved GLA assembly panel. Work for Bandung Parliamentary Institute involves linking Black communities with parliamentarians, ministers and senior civil servants. Former assistant to Labour MP Marsha Singh.

REV EDEMEKONG SUNDAY EKONG (MINISTER)

President, Mboho Akwa Ibom State (UK & Eire), 4 Oxford Close, Lower Edmonton, London, N9 0NB

PLACE OF BIRTH: Nung Obong, 28.8.54
MARITAL STATUS: Married
CHILDREN: Three (Florence, Ruth, David)
COLLEGE: Southampton University
ACADEMIC QUALIFICATIONS: MSc (Advanced Structural Engineering)
PROFESSIONAL QUALIFICATIONS: MInst P
HONOURS/AWARDS: Okunnu Award - Best Student in Structural Technology 1981
HOBBIES AND INTERESTS: Badminton, DIY building, fixing, Bible teaching, training
EMAIL: Edemekong@aol.com
PERSONAL PROFILE: Trained as a structural engineer. Civil-structural engineering lecturer for several years at the Federal Polytechnic, Bauchi, Nigeria. Senior structural engineer with companies throughout England before leaving to serve as a pastor of a growing church in London. An outstanding community leader and visionary, president of an African community.

MR EFFIE EKPO (ACTOR)

Henry's Agency, 53 Westbury, Rochford, SS4 1UL

PLACE OF BIRTH: London, 16.4.69
MARITAL STATUS: Single
CHILDREN: One (Emma Louis)
COLLEGE: University of Calabar, London Academy of Performing Arts
ACADEMIC QUALIFICATIONS: Bachelor of Arts Degree, Theatre Arts
PROFESSIONAL QUALIFICATIONS: Post Graduate Diploma Acting
DIRECTORSHIPS: Director: Ekpo (Securities Limited)
HOBBIES AND INTERESTS: Music, reading, fitness
PERSONAL PROFILE: Effie Ekpo is a professional actor. Since graduating from drama school in 1985 he has appeared in various films i.e. 'On the eight' and 'All' and 'Mean City'. Plays: Impact Theatre. Adverts (TV): Midland Bank and numerous variety shows. He lives in Brighton with his partner and daughter.

MS REBECCA ELLA (ACTRESS-DIRECTOR)

56 Regents Park Road, London, NW1 7SX

PLACE OF BIRTH: Hatfield, 29.9.70
MARITAL STATUS: Engaged
COLLEGE: Drama Studio London, University of Kent at Canterbury
ACADEMIC QUALIFICATIONS: BA Single Hons Drama 2:1
PROFESSIONAL QUALIFICATIONS: NCDT Accredited, Postgraduate Acting Diploma
MEMBERSHIPS: Equity Co-operative Agency Member (Rosebury Man't)
HOBBIES AND INTERESTS: Surfing, travelling, dance, swimming, writing, politics
EMAIL: Rebecca@orangenet.co.uk
PERSONAL PROFILE: My passion is people. My profession is all about them I am an actress. My greatest desire is to work in films. I am mixed race. I am concerned with creating an appropriate racial distinction for myself and others like me; the race of the future.

MR PATRICK ELLAH (ARCHITECT)

EGM Associates, 216 Westbourne Park Road, Notting Hill, London, W11 1EP

PLACE OF BIRTH: Nigeria, 11.2.59
MARITAL STATUS: Married
CHILDREN: Two (Maxine, Xavier)
COLLEGE: Southbank University
ACADEMIC QUALIFICATIONS: BA Hons Arch P.G. Dip (Arch)
PROFESSIONAL QUALIFICATIONS: Member of the RIBA
MEMBERSHIPS: RIBA, ARCUK
HOBBIES AND INTERESTS: DIY projects, tennis, wind surfing and discovering snow boarding, computer art
EMAIL: Pellah@aol.com
PERSONAL PROFILE: Founded EGM Associates, an architectural practise based in London. The practise is renowned their creative approach to projects both here and abroad. Their work is informed by a cultural appreciation of the locality. Without losing sight of the advantages offered by technology in terms of environmental sustainability.

MS JULIET ELLIS (ACTRESS)

137 India House, 75 Whitworth Street, Manchester, M1 6HB

PLACE OF BIRTH: England, 18.8.69
MARITAL STATUS: Single
COLLEGE: Arden School of Theatre
ACADEMIC QUALIFICATIONS: BA Honours Acting Degree
MEMBERSHIPS: Equity, PRS, Musicians Union
HOBBIES AND INTERESTS: Yoga, Japanese cuisine, British films
PERSONAL PROFILE: Started career as a dancer appearing in many pop promos, later became a singer with pop band 'Funky Worm' with commercial and chart success reaching No.11. After finishing acting degree went on to work for Crucible Theatre with an invitation to Japan. In addition, teaches drama to teenagers in Manchester. TV work, new drama about Yorkshire Ripper.

SIR BENNET CHUKWUOGO ETIABA
(CHARTERED ACCOUNTANT)

Company Director, Thames Valley Services, 43-47 Rushey Green, Catford, London, SE6 4AS

PLACE OF BIRTH: Nigeria, 20.9.63
MARITAL STATUS: Married
CHILDREN: Three (Chinemelum, Chukwudifu, Tobenna)
COLLEGE: South Bank University, London
ACADEMIC QUALIFICATIONS: PGD Business Administration
PROFESSIONAL QUALIFICATIONS: ACCA, ACA
DIRECTORSHIPS: Thames Valley Services, Ben Etiaba and Co (Management Consultants)
MEMBERSHIPS: NNEW1 Community association, ACCA, ICAN
HONOURS/AWARDS: African Businessmen of the Year Commendation 1998, Knighthood (Church Of Nigeria 1998)
HOBBIES AND INTERESTS: Golf, tennis, reading
PERSONAL PROFILE: Did primary and secondary schooling in Nigeria. Arrived UK in November 1982. Resident in UK since then. Read business administration and accountancy. Happily married to Dr Enyinnaya Ifeoma Etiaba. A Knight of the Anglian Church of Nigeria.
NOMINATED BY: Sam Jenyo

MR TREVA ETIENNE (ACTOR-DIRECTOR)

Producer, Writer. Kerry Gardener Agent Management, 7 St George's Square, London, SW1V 2HX

PLACE OF BIRTH: London, 21.7.65
MARITAL STATUS: Single
CHILDREN: One (Haylie)
COLLEGE: City and Guilds Electronic Servicing
PROFESSIONAL QUALIFICATIONS: BBC TV Director Course, BBC Radio Drama Producer Course
MEMBERSHIPS: Government's Film Policy Review Group Action Committee
HONOURS/AWARDS: Stood in on behalf of HRH The Duke Of Edinburgh and HRH The Prince Edward at Buckingham Palace, to present the Duke of Edinburgh Awards to 200 young people along with other celebrities
HOBBIES AND INTERESTS: Football, movies, parties, travelling
EMAIL: KGM1@compusenve.com
PERSONAL PROFILE: Treva is best known for his portrayal of fireman Tony Sanderson in 'London's Burning', but has played leading roles in many other television dramas. Treva has been writing and directing stage plays and producing variety nights for the theatre since 1983 with his theatre company Afro-Sax. Treva is now in post production with his two short films 'Driving Miss Crazy' and 'A Woman Scorned'. Treva was joint artiste director/writer of AfroSax Theatre Company between 1983-89. Treva set up Crown Ten Productions and secured a £5000 loan from Prince's Youth Business trust.

MR SCOTT EUSTACE (FOOTBALLER)

Cambridge United FC, Abbey Stadium, New Market Road, Cambridge, CB5 8LN

PLACE OF BIRTH: Leicester, 13.6.75
PROFESSIONAL QUALIFICATIONS: 6 League Goals &15 League Appearances
PERSONAL PROFILE: Scott Eustace joined United on a monthly contract in February 1999 after an extended trial period. A powerfully-built central defender, he had impressed for the reserves and seems to have an eye for goal. The big defender joined Cambridge on trial in December last year and after doing very well for the reserves he was signed in February as cover for the young pairing of Andy Duncan and Marc Joseph. Scott made his debut for United at Leyton Orient in February, after Andy Duncan was sent off, and looked a solid and deceptively quick defender.

MS TANIA EVANS (SINGER)

Prospects Associations (Management), 28 Magpie Close, Forest Gate, London, E7 9DE

ACADEMIC QUALIFICATIONS: O-Levels and Childcare Qualifications
HONOURS/AWARDS: Echo Prize, Bravo, RSM, Writer Music Conference, Sweden Dance
HOBBIES AND INTERESTS: Many interests
PERSONAL PROFILE: One of the top Black female vocalists nominated for entry at Grammy Awards Feb 99 . Scored several with Culture based in UK, No.1 'Mr Vain', No.4 'Got To Get It', No.5 'Anything', No.20 'World In Your Hands' (23). Top awards including Germany's Echo Prize (6) Supported Micheal Jackson, Dangerous Tour.

MR MAYNARD EZIASHI (ACTOR)

c/o Conway Van Gelder Ltd, 18-21 Jermyn Street, London, SW1Y 6HP

PLACE OF BIRTH: London, 13.5.65
MARITAL STATUS: Single
CHILDREN: One (Saffron)
COLLEGE: Rose Bruford College of Speech and Drama
ACADEMIC QUALIFICATIONS: BA Hons in Theatre Arts, HNC Electrical Engineering
DIRECTORSHIPS: Granite Films Ltd
HONOURS/AWARDS: Silver Bear Berlin Festival 1991 For Best Actor For "Mr Johnson".
HOBBIES AND INTERESTS: Writing
EMAIL: Maynard@lounge10
PERSONAL PROFILE: I started my career with a film called 'Mr Johnson', this is probably my best experience, especially as I won an award for it. My favourite film was 'BOPHA' I had the opportunity of delivering the destructive message of apartheid and meeting Mr Mandela and working with Morgan Freeman among others.

PRINCE YOMI FABIKUN (CHARTERED ACCOUNTANT)

Sole Practitioner, Yomi Fabikun & Co, Suite 250 Camberwell Business Centre, 99-103 Lomond Grove, Camberwell, London, SE5 7HN

PLACE OF BIRTH: Nigeria, 30.11.39
MARITAL STATUS: Separated
CHILDREN: Eight
PROFESSIONAL QUALIFICATIONS: FCA, ATII
EMAIL: Abolade@oal.uk
PERSONAL PROFILE: Have been in professional practise since June 1970. I have one office in Kano, Nigeria and 3 offices in the UK- in Bradford, in Leeds and in London. Once served as director of a Nigerian bank, Owena Bank Plc for about 18 months.

MS TOYIN FANI-KAYODE (PRESENTER-ACTRESS)

Arlington Enterprises, 1-3 Charlotte Street, London, W1

PLACE OF BIRTH: Nigeria
MARITAL STATUS: Married
CHILDREN: One (Ruth)
COLLEGE: University College of London, The Actors Institute, Academy of Live and Recording Arts
ACADEMIC QUALIFICATIONS: BSc Psychology Hons
PROFESSIONAL QUALIFICATIONS: Post Graduate Actors Course, The Mastery Course, BBC World Service Training Journalism 1 & 2
MEMBERSHIPS: Equity
HONOURS/AWARDS: Nominated for Action Aid Award for an African Express Report, Presenter of United Nations Gold Cup Winner, Women Making a Difference
PERSONAL PROFILE: Television: 'Global Raiders'; 'Africa Express Series 1,2 & 3'; 'The Radical Option'; 'Reparations For Slavery'; 'People and the Planet 1,2 & 3'. Radio: 'Speakout'; 'Women Making a Difference'; 'The Deal With Drugs'; 'Sayyida Salma' (portrait of a 19th Century Zanizibari princess.); 'Aman': The Story of a Somali Girl. Theatre: 'Death and the Kings' 'Horseman'; 'Anowa' and 'For Coloured Girls who have considered suicide'.

MR OLU FASAN (CHIEF EXECUTIVE)

LEXCOM Consultants, Suite 4, 272 Queen's Road, London, SE14 5JN

PLACE OF BIRTH: Nigeria, 2.7.60
MARITAL STATUS: Married
CHILDREN: Two (Tomi, Toyo)
COLLEGE: King's College, London
ACADEMIC QUALIFICATIONS: LLB Hons, LLM, Dip Journalism, FRSA
HONOURS/AWARDS: Fellowship of the Royal Society of Arts (FRSA)
HOBBIES AND INTERESTS: Reading, networking, meeting people for intellectual stimulation, problem solving
PERSONAL PROFILE: Olu Fasan founded the business magazine, 'Market Finder International' in 1993 to advance trade and business between Africa and Britain. Mr Fasan also runs a legal and commercial consultancy, Lexcom, which specialises in all aspects of international commercial law transactions.
NOMINATED BY: Sam Jenyo

JOHN FASHANU (MANAGING DIRECTOR)

Blue Orchid Management Company Ltd, Warm Sea House, 23 Wellington Road, St John's Wood, London, NW8 9SL

PLACE OF BIRTH: London, 18.9.62
MARITAL STATUS: Married
CHILDREN: Three (Amal, Amir, Akim)
HOBBIES AND INTERESTS: Martial arts
PERSONAL PROFILE: The world famous footballer, John Fashanu, has played for England's top football teams including Wimbledon and Aston Villa. He is now a successful businessman and the host of a popular game show called 'The Gladiators'. John is equally well known for humanitarian work and his commitment to children and has received numerous international awards in recognition of these activities. He was officially appointed a UNICEF international spokesperson in June 1998.

JUMOKE FASHOLA (BROADCASTER)

c/o BBC GLR, 35c Marlyebone High Street, London, W1A 4LG

PLACE OF BIRTH: London, 14.1.63
MARITAL STATUS: Single
COLLEGE: Inchbald School of Design
ACADEMIC QUALIFICATIONS: Diploma in Interior Design, Diploma of Christian Ministries
DIRECTORSHIPS: Creative Director, (Chutney Media)
HOBBIES AND INTERESTS: Christianity, music, reading
EMAIL: jumoke.fashola@cms-uk.org
PERSONAL PROFILE: 'Jumoke' is the creative director of Chutney Media and the national youth work co-ordinator for CMS. Her television credits include: 'The Holiday Programme', 'Summer Praise' and 'Holidays Out' (BBC TV). On radio she hosts BBC GLR's Gospel Show and freelances for Radio's 2 and 4. She is currently writing her first book.

MR TAYO FATUNLA (CARTOONIST-ILLUSTRATOR)

Thamesmead Times, 13 Austin Close, Thamesmead, Greenwich, London, SE28 8AY

PLACE OF BIRTH: Wimbledon, 19.1.61
MARITAL STATUS: Married
CHILDREN: Two (Toyo, Jola)
COLLEGE: Joe Kubert School of Art, New Jersey US, Diploma Cartoon/Graphics
MEMBERSHIPS: Cartoonist & Writers Synidcate, New York/NUJ (UK)
HOBBIES AND INTERESTS: Watching wrestling, table tennis, football
EMAIL: Tayo.Fatunla@Btinternet.com
PERSONAL PROFILE: Tayo Fatunla is one of Britain's Black cartoonists and illustrators whose work is published nationally and internationally on a regular basis. He has designed numerous magazine and book covers, posters and calendars. His cartoons have been exhibited in the UK, US, Finland and Nigeria. His cartoons are on permanent display at a cartoon museum in Florida.

MR EARL FERGUSON (MAGISTRATE-RTD)

PLACE OF BIRTH: Jamaica, 12.3.31
MARITAL STATUS: Married
CHILDREN: Three
COLLEGE: Folkestone Technical College
ACADEMIC QUALIFICATIONS: GCEs
HONOURS/AWARDS: Service (HMF: Army) Medals, Justice of the Peace
HOBBIES AND INTERESTS: Weight-lifting, photography
PERSONAL PROFILE: After 30 years in the HMF Army, I am a magistrate on the Hereford and Worchester Bench, was involved as: board visitor/local review committee of Long Lartin Prison; racial advisor; Hereford and Worchester Probation Service; chair/executive member, Worchester CRE; regional panel member, National Lottery; executive member, Age Concern (local branch).
NOMINATED BY: Worchester Racial Equality Council

MRS MARJORIE FERGUSON (NURSE-COUNSELLOR)

Specialist Haemaglobinapthy Counsellor, George Marsh Centre, Haringey Health Care Trust,

PLACE OF BIRTH: Jamaica, 8.8.41
MARITAL STATUS: Widow
CHILDREN: Three (John, Dwayne, Sonya)
COLLEGE: City & Guilds Teaching Certificate
ACADEMIC QUALIFICATIONS: Certificate In Counselling, BE Certificate in Management, Open University
PROFESSIONAL QUALIFICATIONS: EN, RN, Health Visitor, Family Planning Certificate
HOBBIES AND INTERESTS: Voluntary work, public speaking, travel
PERSONAL PROFILE: I have had various roles in the NHS I am also involved in charitable and religious activities. I initiated a community service for sickle cell clients in Haringey. Was instrumental in getting funding for the a haemaglobinapthy centre in the Britain. I worked as a haemaglobinapthy counsellor. My children are all high achievers.

> I initiated a community service for sickle cell clients in Haringey.
>
> **MARJORIE FERGUSON**

MS SHEILA FERGUSON (Singer-Actress-Author)

PO Box 1400, Maidenhead, SL6 1HR

PLACE OF BIRTH: US, 8.10.47
MARITAL STATUS: Married
CHILDREN: Twins (Alicia, Alexandria)
ACADEMIC QUALIFICATIONS: High School Graduate
DIRECTORSHIPS: Pamra Director
MEMBERSHIPS: Equity, Counsellor, SAG, AFTRA, MU
PERSONAL PROFILE: Lead singer with the Three Degrees; 28 Gold records. Star of sitcom, 'Land of Hope and Glory', 'Desmond's' cameo role, 'Brookside' cameo role. Author of 'Soul Food-Classical Cuisine of the American South'. Solo performer around the world.

MS LAURA FISH (Television Researcher-Writer)

Writer, Gerald Duckworth & Company Ltd, The Old Piano Factory, 48 Hoxton Square, London, N1 6PB

PLACE OF BIRTH: London, 6.1.64
MARITAL STATUS: Single
CHILDREN: One (Joshua Betton)
COLLEGE: Bristol Old Vic Theatre School (BOVTS)
ACADEMIC QUALIFICATIONS: 5 O-Levels GCSE's, BOVTs - Stage Management & Technical Course
PROFESSIONAL QUALIFICATIONS: BBC Ealing Film Studios Assist. Film Editor Training Course
MEMBERSHIPS: Black Members Committee, BECTU (Broadcasting Union)
HONOURS/AWARDS: CRE Race in the Media Awards, Commendation for Documentary Producer, Society of Authors Grant/Hawthornden Castle Fellowship
HOBBIES AND INTERESTS: Reading, travel, horse-riding, hiking, cinema, arts, crafts
PERSONAL PROFILE: Freelance writer of Caribbean parentage. Over ten years experience in broadcast television as assistant film editor, researcher and producer/director. Two years reporting for BBC World Service. Has lived and worked in Africa and Australia. Most recent position: Visiting writer, St Andrews University. Publications: 'Flight of Black Swans'- A novel-Duckworth.

MISS AMANDA FOSTER (Stunt Double)

Equity Stunt Register, Guild House, Upper Street, Martin Lane, London, WC2H 9EG

PLACE OF BIRTH: Birmingham, 18.3.67
MARITAL STATUS: Single
CHILDREN: Three (Aaron, Azizi, Femi)
ACADEMIC QUALIFICATIONS: CCPR (PE Teacher)
PROFESSIONAL QUALIFICATIONS: Hand Gliding, CPC Kung Fu Loga, Black-Belt, Fencing Foil, Sabre, EPEE
MEMBERSHIPS: Equity Registered
HOBBIES AND INTERESTS: Music, fine foods
PERSONAL PROFILE: I'm an active and determined person - doing nothing is not my style. Although I came to my chosen career by accident, I am now Britain's first Black stuntwoman. It has also been my privilege to start my professional career by doubling for Whoopi Goldberg, and this is just the beginning.

MR ELRIDGE FOSTER (Team Leader-Civil Servant)

Team Leader, Department For Education & Employment, Sanctuary Buildings, Great Smith Street, London, SW1P 3BT

PLACE OF BIRTH: Barbados, 16.9.53
MARITAL STATUS: Married
CHILDREN: Three (Gordon, Louise, David)
ACADEMIC QUALIFICATIONS: A-Level Biology, Botany
MEMBERSHIPS: Chair, DFEE Ethnic Minority Advisory Group, Vice Chair, Governing Body Lemuel Findlay Supplementary School
HOBBIES AND INTERESTS: Current affairs, sports, DIY
EMAIL: elridge.foster@dfee.gov.uk
PERSONAL PROFILE: I have held a wide range of policy posts in education since the mid-1970s. Currently have national policy responsibilities relating to GNVQ qualifications, including the development of Part One GNVQ for 14-16 year olds, which will be available nationally from September 1999.
NOMINATED BY: Bernadette Hillon DFEE

MRS YVONNE FOSTER (Managing Director)

Company Director, Lotus Training Ltd, Etna House, 350 Kennington Road, London, SE11 4LD

PLACE OF BIRTH: Jamaica, 6.8.58
MARITAL STATUS: Divorced
CHILDREN: One (Lorraine)
COLLEGE: London University
ACADEMIC QUALIFICATIONS: BSc, MSc, MA
PROFESSIONAL QUALIFICATIONS: MA in Human Resource Management
HOBBIES AND INTERESTS: Practising Buddhist
EMAIL: Lotus.Training@dial.pipex.com
PERSONAL PROFILE: Lotus Training was established in 1994 and provides training consultancy to organisations such as the Cabinet Office and IPC magazines. The company employs eight staff and has established an excellent reputation for delivering well designed training programmes. Yvonne is a dynamic business leader whose vision is to grow Lotus Training to become a premier training provider.
NOMINATED BY: Christopher Johnson MBA

MISS LYNSEY FRANCE (Actress)

Member of Group Awaiting To Be Signed, 1st Avenue Records, 9 Greenheys Road, Flat 2, Liverpool, L8 0SX

PLACE OF BIRTH: Liverpool, 20.9.25
MARITAL STATUS: Single
COLLEGE: School of Performing Arts
ACADEMIC QUALIFICATIONS: HND Dance and Drama
MEMBERSHIPS: Equity Member
HOBBIES AND INTERESTS: Acting, singing, dancing, reading

MR ANDREW FRANCIS (Actor)

Chuck Julian Associates,

PLACE OF BIRTH: Bristol, 11.4.55
MARITAL STATUS: Single
HOBBIES AND INTERESTS: Salsa, motor cycling, theatre, food
PERSONAL PROFILE: During my 20 years in the business I've been fortunate enough to be able to cover a variety of subjects from Shakespeare, drama and comedy both on stage and television.

MR CURTIS ALLISTER FRANCIS MBE
(Project Development Officer)

Project Development Officer, Social Services Department Croydon Council, 156 Tenison Road, South Norwood, London, SE25 5NE

PLACE OF BIRTH: Grenada, 26.4.44
MARITAL STATUS: Married
CHILDREN: Three (Alicia, Gerald, Marlene)
COLLEGE: Bulmershe College of Higher Education
PROFESSIONAL QUALIFICATIONS: Certificate in Youth and Community Work
MEMBERSHIPS: Trustee, Grenada Arts Promotion Trust, St John's Library Project UK
HONOURS/AWARDS: MBE
HOBBIES AND INTERESTS: Writing, football
PERSONAL PROFILE: Born in Gouyave, Grenada. Attended the Grenada Boy's Secondary School (GBSS) before leaving for England in 1964. Has been working in the field of community development both in the voluntary and statutory sectors for over twenty-five years. Writes poetry and enjoys listening to music.
NOMINATED BY: Anthony John La Moth

MR SEAN FRANCIS (Actor)

JM Associates, 77 Beak Street, London, W1R 3LF

PLACE OF BIRTH: Coulsdon, 4.9.69
MARITAL STATUS: Single
COLLEGE: RADA Degree
PROFESSIONAL QUALIFICATIONS: BA
DIRECTORSHIPS: Sable Productions
MEMBERSHIPS: RADA Life, National Theatre, Hayward Gallery
HOBBIES AND INTERESTS: Sculpture, film, photography
EMAIL: Sean.francis@virgin.net
PERSONAL PROFILE: Sean graduated from RADA in 1994 and has worked in theatre, film and television. Theatre credits include 'As You Like It...', TV credits 'The Knock'... and film credits 'The Tribe'... He is currently entering negotiations to set-up his own production company which he says will help him achieve long-term goals within the industry.

MRS IFILIA FRANCOIS (Counsellor)

PLACE OF BIRTH: Dominica, 12.12.53
MARITAL STATUS: Separted
CHILDREN: Two (Andre, Rita)
ACADEMIC QUALIFICATIONS: O-Level: Maths, Science, Geography, English
PROFESSIONAL QUALIFICATIONS: City & Guilds Distinction: Arts, Counselling
HOBBIES AND INTERESTS: Philosophy, reading, walks, travel, theatre
PERSONAL PROFILE: Has worked for many years writing /compiling words of wisdom and counselling for character building and positive inner strength. Runs a positive awareness club. Started up and coming language exchange, where people learn any language for free in exchange for teaching their own language.

MISS JUANNE FULLER (Actress)

Evans & Reiss, 100 Fawe Park Road, London, SW15 2EA

PLACE OF BIRTH: London, 29.5.73
MARITAL STATUS: Single
MEMBERSHIPS: Equity
HOBBIES AND INTERESTS: Theatre, cinema, travel
EMAIL: JuJu@Twight1.Demon.co.uk
PERSONAL PROFILE: I have been working professionally as an actress for five years. I trained at Weekend Arts College in London for four years and undertook my first professional engagement in March 1991 on 'The Bill'. I've since gone on to do various TV roles including parts in 'Touch of Frost', 'Kavanagh HQ' and most recently 'Brookside'.

MS VERNELLA E FULLER (Lecturer-Businesswoman)

Fulani Residential Care,

PLACE OF BIRTH: Jamaica, 16.11.56
MARITAL STATUS: Divorced
CHILDREN: One (Alisha)
COLLEGE: University of Sussex in London University
ACADEMIC QUALIFICATIONS: BA, MA, Currently doing PhD (Education)
PROFESSIONAL QUALIFICATIONS: PGCE Achievement
DIRECTORSHIPS: Fulani Residential Care (Residential Care Home For Children)
HOBBIES AND INTERESTS: Running, gym, travel, cricket
EMAIL: vefanf@compuserve.com
PERSONAL PROFILE: Teacher for 20 years in schools, further education and higher education, currently doing doctoral research (PhD) in Education Achievement. Published work 'Going Back Home' (1992), 'Unlike Normal Women' (1995)... Foster carer for seven years, currently foster two teenage girls. Director of residential home for teenage boys with challenging behaviour - opening August 1999.
NOMINATED BY: Alisha N Fuller - Arman

'I have held a wide range of policy posts in education since the mid-1970s. Currently have national policy responsibilities relating to GNVQ qualifications, including the development of Part One GNVQ for 14-16 year olds, which will be available nationally from September 1999'

ELRIDGE FOSTER

Carribbean Times

Caribbean Times

incorporating African Times

Friday 14 May 1999 · BRITAIN'S ONLY QUALITY BLACK NEWSPAPER · Issue 934 · 50p

'I WANT THEM TO PAY'

Haitian immigrant accuses police of sexually torturing him in 1997

Justin Volpe (c), accused of putting his baton up Abner's rectum, and his lawyer arrive at court

Louima Abner: another NYPD victim

Emmanuel Dunseath

A HAITIAN immigrant told a New York court last week that he was beaten and sexually tortured by police officers in 1997, an incident that at the time lead to riots in the black community and drew national attention to alleged abuses and racism in the New York Police Department.

Former security guard Abner Louima accused two officers of beating him in a patrol car on the way to the 70th precinct station house in Brooklyn, where he alleged that a second officer held him down in the restroom and inserted a stick into his rectum and mouth.

Two years later and the four white officers are on trial in a Brooklyn federal court on the charges of violating Louima's civil rights. A police sergeant is also being charged for allegedly attempting to cover up the alleged assault on August 9, 1997, after Louima was arrested outside a nightclub.

All five officers have pleaded not guilty and are suspended from the job without pay.

Facing the officers for the first time since he made the shooting charges, Louima accused Officer Justin Volpe of taking an object believed to be a stick, and while Louima was still handcuffed, the police inserted it in my rectum and put it in my mouth. He said, "that's my shit"

Misconduct

It took three weeks for the jury to be selected for the trial, which is being held at a time when tensions over alleged police misconduct resurfaced again in New York City. Four officers were charged with the murder March 31 after unarmed West African immigrant Amadou Diallo was killed in a hail of 41 bullets in February.

Louima, 32, testified to the witness stand for further cross-examination throughout this week.

Louima is represented in the civil lawsuit by the well known legal team of Johnnie Cochran, Barry Scheck and Peter Neufeld, who helped defend former National Football League star OJ Simpson in his double-murder criminal trial.

The Haitian immigrant, who is a US citizen and has no criminal record, said he filed the civil lawsuit because "I want them to pay for all the pain and suffering they have caused me."

He described in court how he required three separate surgeries to repair the severe intestinal injuries he suffered in the alleged assault at the hands of the police officers.

Torturing

Police officers Justin Volpe, 26 and Charles Schwarz, 33, are accused of sexually assaulting Louima. They could be sentenced to life in prison if convicted. Officers Thomas Bruder, 32, and Thomas Wiese, 35, are charged with beating Louima in the police car. Bruder, Wiese and Sgt. Michael Bellomo, 37, could face up to 10 years in prison if convicted.

NEED A NEW JOB? SEE **Jobs Direct** ON PAGES 15-26

COUNTDOWN TO THE MILLENNIUM

MS GINA GANGAR (ACTRESS)

Pelham Associates, Brighton Media Centre, 9-12 Middle Street, Brighton, BN1 1AL

PLACE OF BIRTH: Kent, 16.11.69
MARITAL STATUS: Single
COLLEGE: Nottingham Trent University
ACADEMIC QUALIFICATIONS: First Class Honours Degree in Performing Arts
HONOURS/AWARDS: Prince's Trust Award
HOBBIES AND INTERESTS: Yoga, computers, travel, painting, drawing, the arts, aromatherapy
EMAIL: gina@gangar.freeserve.co.uk
PERSONAL PROFILE: Gina won a Prince's Youth Business Trust Award to train with a Russian director at the Ice. After gaining a first, Gina's degree show won entry to the 1994 National Review of Live Art at the ICA, which was also chosen to represent her university at the IPA Prague. Gina has played a wide variety of roles in the theatre and has worked extensively in theatre in education and training, particularly in equal opportunity 'awareness'.

MR ROBBIE GEE (MANAGING DIRECTOR)

Geestor Productions, 146 Glenarm Road, Geestor House, London, E5 0NB

PLACE OF BIRTH: Greenwich, 24.3.70
MARITAL STATUS: Single
CHILDREN: Three (Decosta, Luke-Karl, Harley-Jay)
ACADEMIC QUALIFICATIONS: 8 O-Levels: TD, PE, Ecms, Eng, Maths, Drama, Physics, Woodwork
HOBBIES AND INTERESTS: Football, tennis, fishing, badminton
EMAIL: Geestor@emart.com

MR GILBERT GEORGE (FINANCIAL ACCOUNTANT)

Health Education Authority, 35 Croydon Road, Plaistow, London, E13 8ES

PLACE OF BIRTH: London, 19.3.63
MARITAL STATUS: Married
CHILDREN: Two (Jean-Paul Anton, Clair-Marie Melody)
COLLEGE: Kesington School of Business
PROFESSIONAL QUALIFICATIONS: Chartered Secretary, Accounting Technicians
MEMBERSHIPS: Institute of Chartered Secretaries, Association of Accounting Technicians
HOBBIES AND INTERESTS: Bible, golf, history
EMAIL: Gilbert.George.Hea.org.uk
PERSONAL PROFILE: I currently work as the financial accountant for the Health Education Authority having responsibility for producing the authorities published financial statements. My previous positions include working for the committee of vice-chancellors and principals (1989-96), where I oversaw the financial affairs of five higher education companies.
NOMINATED BY: Seymour Fortescue - CE of Health Authority

MR MOHAMMED GEORGE (ACTOR)

Rosemore Personal Management, 31 Vallance Road, London, E1 5HS

PLACE OF BIRTH: Hackney, 30.6.82
COLLEGE: Currently doing 'Lift-Off' at Royal Court
ACADEMIC QUALIFICATIONS: 5 GCSEs in English, Art, Drama, Maths, Geography
PROFESSIONAL QUALIFICATIONS: Kids TV Series 'The Biz' for Three Summers (BBC), Theatre Includes 'Oliver' (Palladium), 'Jolson' (Victoria Palace), Seven Adverts, 'Bottom', 'Barrymoore' Twice, 'Blue Peter' Twice, Lenny Henry, 'French & Saunders', 'Lift Off' At Royal Court doing it now
HONOURS/AWARDS: LAMDA Junior Medalion Honours 1986, Honours 1988 Dunition Twice
HOBBIES AND INTERESTS: Acting, dancing, football, pool, films, music hip hop, swing, house & garage, reggae & ragga
PERSONAL PROFILE: I'm 16, 5 ft 7 inches, I'm quite small but have a big heart. I live with my dad, two brothers and a sister. I love having fun with friends or family and I encourage them to do things positively in their life. I'm happy my father sent me to stage school where I learned a lot about showbiz, as entertaining people has always been something I love doing.

MRS NORMA GIBBES (COUNCILLOR)

Former Headteacher,

PLACE OF BIRTH: Jamaica, 22.8.43
MARITAL STATUS: Married
CHILDREN: Two (Asquith Junior, Carla)
COLLEGE: Sussex
ACADEMIC QUALIFICATIONS: B Ed Hons MA
HOBBIES AND INTERESTS: Painting, reading, travel
PERSONAL PROFILE: A founder member of the Caribbean Teacher's Association and author of 'West Indian Teachers Speak Out', Norma has channelled much energy into voluntary work whilst pursuing her educational career. After nine years as the head of a secondary school she is now a councillor. Norma is married with two grown up children.

MISS LLEWELLA GIDEON (ACTRESS-WRITER)

Dual Impact Theatre & Film Productions, c/o Billy Marsh, 174-178 Gower Street, London, NW1 2NB

PLACE OF BIRTH: London, 27.9.67
MARITAL STATUS: Single
COLLEGE: Hammersmths & West London
ACADEMIC QUALIFICATIONS: 8 O-Levels, 3 A-Levels
DIRECTORSHIPS: Dual Impact Productions
HONOURS/AWARDS: CRE-Race In Media, Best Black Television
HOBBIES AND INTERESTS: Reading
PERSONAL PROFILE: A professional since 1989 also a pioneer in Black television. A core writer/performer of the 'Real McCoy' (BBC). Llewella has worked with Britain's top comedians including Lenny Henry and French & Saunders. Currently runs her own production company Dual Impact and has produced several hit one women shows.
NOMINATED BY: Ron Shillingford

MS CLARISCIA GILL (COUTURIER-DESIGNER)

Proprietor, C G Couture,

PLACE OF BIRTH: Derby, 9.3.59
MARITAL STATUS: Single
COLLEGE: London College of Fashion
ACADEMIC QUALIFICATIONS: City & Guilds, Tailoring Certificates, Diploma in Fashion Design & Pattern Construction
HONOURS/AWARDS: Cosmopolitan Award for Achievement, Black Women's Achievement Awards, London Business Women's Award
HOBBIES AND INTERESTS: Portrait painting, poetry writing, Latin American dance, charity fundraising fashion shows
PERSONAL PROFILE: I am of St Lucian, French Guyanese parentage, mother was a seamstress, father was a builder and decorator, five brothers and sisters. I have built up a portrait of private customers which includes business women, royalty, musicians and performers from classical to rock, jazz R&B. The business will be expanded end of 1999 into 2000 to include also overseas connections.
NOMINATED BY: Percy Savage

MR JUNIOR GISCOMBE (ARTIST)

Junior Music Ltd, 6 Sream's Buildings, London, EC4A 1HP

PLACE OF BIRTH: London, 6.6.57
MARITAL STATUS: Married
CHILDREN: Three (Dita, Jewique, Xyle)
COLLEGE: Hammersmith
ACADEMIC QUALIFICATIONS: 2 O-Levels, City & Guilds Computer Programming
MEMBERSHIPS: BRMB
HONOURS/AWARDS: Best New Comer Billbored 1981
HOBBIES AND INTERESTS: Football, reading, publishing, spending time with family
PERSONAL PROFILE: I began my career in 1980, my first hit being 'Mama used to say' it sold over 2 million copies worldwide in total. Writing and producing for myself and others, have sold over 15 million records and CDs in a career spanning over 19 years.

> A founder member of the Caribbean Teacher's Association and author of 'West Indian Teachers Speak Out'
>
> **NORMA GIBBES**

MS PATRICIA (TRISHA) GODDARD (TV Presenter)

Journalist, Anglia Television Limited, c/o Anglia House, Norwich, NR1 3JG

PLACE OF BIRTH: London, 23.12.57
MARITAL STATUS: Married
CHILDREN: Two (Billie Dee, Madison Mae)
ACADEMIC QUALIFICATIONS: 9 GCSEs
PROFESSIONAL QUALIFICATIONS: Conflict Resolution Counsellor, Mental Health Adviser
DIRECTORSHIPS: Own company (Australia C'est La Vie Productions)
MEMBERSHIPS: Australian Journalist Association (AJA) Australian Equity, Patron SANE (Australia)
HONOURS/AWARDS: Australia's Clear Speaking Award
HOBBIES AND INTERESTS: Rollerblading, reading, skiing, classical piano, mental health policy, planning
PERSONAL PROFILE: Was Australia's first Black TV news presenter. I have had parallel careers in a mental health advisory capacity. Formulating policy and planning for the Australian Government from 1991-1998. Journalist (print, radio and TV) since 1986. Ambition: balancing career, kids and love of my life, husband Peter Gianfrancesco.

MS CLARE GORHAM (Journalist-Broadcaster)

Presenter, Raw TV Action Time, 21 Midhope House, Midhope Street, London, WC1H

PLACE OF BIRTH: London, 31.1.66
MARITAL STATUS: Unmarried
COLLEGE: Sussex University
ACADEMIC QUALIFICATIONS: BA Hons in Combined Arts
MEMBERSHIPS: Groucho Club
HOBBIES AND INTERESTS: Painting, piano, guitar
PERSONAL PROFILE: As someone who comes from a family of nine, I have the ability to mix, integrate and compromise, this has helped me in the media industry. I paint successfully and I sing in a band - I'm a multi-achiever yet remain modest.

MR LLEWELLYN GRAHAM (Director Housing-Management)

Director, Nehemiah Housing Association Ltd, 6 Beacon Court, Birmingham Road, Great Barr, Birmingham, B43 6NN

PLACE OF BIRTH: Jamaica, 25.7.61
MARITAL STATUS: Married
CHILDREN: Three (Karise, Monique, Nicole)
COLLEGE: Middlesex University Wolverhampton University
ACADEMIC QUALIFICATIONS: BA Hons Ceramics, Post Graduate Diploma in Management
PROFESSIONAL QUALIFICATIONS: Final Year of Masters in Business Administration
MEMBERSHIPS: Member of the Institute of Directors
HOBBIES AND INTERESTS: Health fitness, gospel singing, travelling
EMAIL: Llewgm@aol.com
PERSONAL PROFILE: Director of Nehemiah since 1989. Former director of Wolverhampton African Caribbean Development Agency with responsibility for community and economic development work. His leadership at Nehemiah has seen the association grow from strength to strength. Nehemiah is the recipient of several awards including the Investor in People and the Gleaner, Jamaican National Overseas, 1997 Honour award for excellence in service delivery to the community.

MR KIM GRANT (Footballer)

Millwall Football Club, The Den, Zampa Road, London, SE16 3LN

PLACE OF BIRTH: Ghana, 25.7.72
PROFESSIONAL QUALIFICATIONS: 39 League Appearances, 8 League Goals. 6 Cup Appearances, 2 Cup Goals. 4 Caps for Ghana
PERSONAL PROFILE: Ghanaian international who signed for Millwall from Luton Town in August 1997 after a brief loan spell and scored ten goals in all competitions for the Lions last season, making him the second top scorer. Kim made his name with Charlton, where he played alongside Alan McLeary and under Steve Gritt, before ultimately moving on to Kenilworth Road. His spell at Luton was an unhappy one, and his Millwall career started brightly with a goal on his debut.

DR SIMON GRANT (Senior Development Chemist)

Victrex Plc,

PLACE OF BIRTH: Preston, 7.5.64
MARITAL STATUS: Married
CHILDREN: Two (Alexander, Naomi)
COLLEGE: Brunel, Lancaster, Warwick
ACADEMIC QUALIFICATIONS: BSc, MSc, PhD
PROFESSIONAL QUALIFICATIONS: C Chem
MEMBERSHIPS: Member of Royal Society of Chemistry
HOBBIES AND INTERESTS: Sports, basketball, football, cricket, reading, theatre
EMAIL: sgrant@victrex.com
PERSONAL PROFILE: Simon was born in 1964 and attended Archbishop Temple School and Preston College. He gained his BSc Hons in Applied Chemistry from Brunel University, MSc in Polymer Synthesis from Lancaster University and PhD in Chemistry from Warwick University. A research and development chemist, he joined BP Chemicals working in Specialities and Technical Services before moving to his current position with Victrex. Simon is married with two children and lives in Lancaster.
NOMINATED BY: I A Grant

MISS ANGIE GREAVES (TV-Radio Presenter)

BBC Greater London Radio, 35c Marylebone High Street, London, W1 4LG

PLACE OF BIRTH: London, 26.4.64
MARITAL STATUS: Single
COLLEGE: Kilburn Polytechnic
ACADEMIC QUALIFICATIONS: Maths, English, French, Commercial Studies
HONOURS/AWARDS: Ethnic Minority Media Award for Best Radio Presenter
PERSONAL PROFILE: Angie has been heavily involved in theatre, pantomime and cable television. Her terrestrial television debut came in October 1996 when she hosted BBC2's dating game show 'Get it on' which completed its third series in December of 1997. Angie's presence on GLR has been rapidly noticed and she now covers a lot of the daytime programming, she has also been approached by numerous television production companies with a view to developing her work on terrestrial television.
NOMINATED BY: Gloria Abramoof

MRS SONIA MAY GREAVES (Fundraising Co-ordinator)

Disabled Living, Redbank House, 4 St Chad's Street, Cheetham, Manchester, M8 8QA

PLACE OF BIRTH: Manchester, 28.7.64
MARITAL STATUS: Married
CHILDREN: One (Karl Andrew Evans Wood)
COLLEGE: South Trafford College of Further Education
HOBBIES AND INTERESTS: Music (Simply Red, Kenny G.), Man United, anything Italian
PERSONAL PROFILE: A lot of my education was at the University of Experience, for example eight years 'selling art-work in Italian. Now much of my effort goes in profile and fundraising for the disabled. It's challenging and satisfying, and helped me do a TV series in the north west.
NOMINATED BY: Vinni Davis

MR PHIL GREGORY (Student)

The Black Presence in Britain,

PLACE OF BIRTH: Manchester, 5.1.74
MARITAL STATUS: Single
COLLEGE: Staffordshire
ACADEMIC QUALIFICATIONS: 7 GCSE, 2 A-Levels
MEMBERSHIPS: Black Briton Webring Afoam.WR
HOBBIES AND INTERESTS: Black British history, computers, politics
EMAIL: Philgreg@easynet.co.uk
WEB SITE: http://www.geocities.com/athens/crete/9145
PERSONAL PROFILE: It is my wish to provide a comprehensive database of Black British history on the Internet. My site has already received good reviews, with more exposure I hope to expand the service further. It is my wish to see Black British history taught on the schools curriculum.
NOMINATED BY: Mark Dawson

MISS ANGELA GRIFFIN (ACTRESS)

Barbara Pemberton Associates, London House, 53-54 Haymarket, London, SW1Y 4RP

PLACE OF BIRTH: Leeds, 19.7.76
MARITAL STATUS: Single
ACADEMIC QUALIFICATIONS: 9 GCSEs
HONOURS/AWARDS: NTA for Best Newcomer 1995 National Television award
PERSONAL PROFILE: Began in 'Coronation Street' in 1992 and became a familiar face to many at the age of sixteen. After leaving in 1998, moved to the BBC's 'Holby City' and also presenting BBC's National Lottery. Not bad for a 22-year old mixed race girl.

MR EDDIE GRIFFITH (EDUCATIONALIST)

20 Crawley Road, London, N22 6AN

PLACE OF BIRTH: Barbados
MARITAL STATUS: Married
CHILDREN: One (Elwyn)
COLLEGE: Salford London
ACADEMIC QUALIFICATIONS: MA, BSc Hons, PGCE
PROFESSIONAL QUALIFICATIONS: FRSA
MEMBERSHIPS: NUT, BCA
HOBBIES AND INTERESTS: Sport, travel, politics, the theatre, dominoes, debating
PERSONAL PROFILE: Local political activist and educationalist. Chaired numerous committees on Haringey Borough Council. Social and political scientist and lecturer on educational issues. Believed to be the first and longest serving Black chair of governors of a secondary school and first Black chair of a standing advisory council for religious education.

MR DEREK GRIFFITHS (ACTOR-COMPOSER)

Marina Martin Associates, 12-13 Poland Street, London, W1V 3DE

PLACE OF BIRTH: England
MARITAL STATUS: Single
COLLEGE: LCM
PERSONAL PROFILE: Studied music at London College of Music. Greenwich Theatre for two years, many West End productions including: 'Ko-Ko'; 'Black Mikado'; 'The Engineer'; 'Miss Saigon'; 'Lumiere'; 'Beauty and The Beast'; 'Royal Shakespeare Company Feste'; In '12th Night'; Pompey in 'Measure for Measure'. Many TV and film appearances.

MR HOWARD DELAND GROVES (DETECTIVE INSPECTOR)

Metropolitan Police, Uxbridge Police Station, 1 Warwick Place, Uxbridge, Hillingdon, UB8 1PE

PLACE OF BIRTH: London, 25.9.57
MARITAL STATUS: Single
COLLEGE: Kingston College
ACADEMIC QUALIFICATIONS: Jamaica, 4 O-Levels
HOBBIES AND INTERESTS: Horse ownership, running the marathon
PERSONAL PROFILE: Joined police service 1980, promoted to sergeant 1989, served at Inner London Division - Complaints Branch. CID duties predominantly. Promoted 1998 to detective inspector. Serving at Uxbridge Police Station. Engaged in community work during and prior to joining the police in Brent, Harlesden.

MRS ENID GUY (OPERA-PIONEER)

c/o 3 Elmira Street, Lewisham, London, SE13 7BN

PLACE OF BIRTH: Guyana, 17.9.21
MARITAL STATUS: Married-Divorced
CHILDREN: Six (Bridget, Carl, Montroze, Dennis, Henry, Phillip)
MEMBERSHIPS: Chair Rose Apple, Calabash, Womans Own Management Committee
HOBBIES AND INTERESTS: Community development projects, handicrafts, singing
EMAIL: M.gousse@virgin,net
PERSONAL PROFILE: First Black women to sing in the Blackheath Opera - when Douglas Childs was the director. She has also sang in the Blackheath Woman's Choir and still sings presently. One of the pioneering persons on the St Mauritius and Deptford African Caribbean Group - now renamed the Rose Apple Day Centre. Went to Belarus to promote the Older Women's Project in 1991/2. 1998 went to Brussels as a representative for Lewisham.

MR KEVIN GUY (BRITISH CHAMPION-BUSINESSMAN)

Importer-Exporter, Guise International,

PLACE OF BIRTH: England
MARITAL STATUS: Single
COLLEGE: Allesbury
ACADEMIC QUALIFICATIONS: Qualified Electrician
PROFESSIONAL QUALIFICATIONS: Pro Tae-Kwondo Instructor, Electrician
PERSONAL PROFILE: British United Tae-Kwondo Federation. 1989-92 held the title of British Champion Heavyweight. 1990-93 held the title of English Champion Heavyweight. 1990-93 held the title of Welsh Champion Heavyweight. 1990 Scottish Champion Heavyweight.
NOMINATED BY: David John

Joined police service 1980, promoted to sergeant 1989,
served at Inner London Division - Complaints Branch. CID duties predominantly.

HOWARD DELAND GROVES

Carribbean Times

Caribbean Times
incorporating African Times

Friday 23 April 1999 · BRITAIN'S ONLY QUALITY BLACK NEWSPAPER · Issue 931 · 50p

RACE TERRORISM?

Cops follow far right lead for the evil Brixton nail bomber

Race Hater

UNLESS the Brixton bomb was left outside the Iceland store by some bizarre or random accident, the perpetrator must have intended the maximum possible number of black casualties.

That spot at 5.30pm on a Saturday afternoon is heaving. The bus stop is rammed with people waiting to go home and the market is full of shoppers, some looking for last-minute deals on fruit and veg, others making sure their hair problems are sorted for the night ahead.

That no-one was killed is nothing short of a miracle, although as we went to press 14 of the 40 victims remained in hospital and two were expected to lose their sight.

In the most amazing escape, a 23-month-old black boy had a four inch nail removed from two inches beneath his skull but everyone expects him to make a full recovery.

But Brixton's notable black enclave by any means and the fact's that many, perhaps most, of Saturday's victims were white, reflecting how diverse the area has become.

It is doubtful that the lunatic who packed six-inch nails into his box of death and then pinned it to explode would be aware of those subtle demographic shifts.

To most people in Britain, Brixton equals black people, or as some in the community put it, 'its black Britain's capital'.

Reluctant

The logic is hideous and frightening and many people watching the police's follow-up operation on Saturday evening were naturally reluctant to make the connection which may yet prove to be wrong.

Some spoke of the war in the Balkans and said the two events must be connected and others assumed it must have something to do with Northern Ireland.

Everyone spoke of their total shock and disbelief.

People were amazed by the size of the blast which could be felt almost a mile down the road on the Angel Estate and many thought there had been two explosions because a loud clap of thunder had followed minutes later.

The four of this brave student Don Magoose of this fantastic stood at a bus stop about 30 yards away. He was only there because his friend was late to meet him.

He recalled picking himself up and seeing people around him covered in blood, a child having facial cuts tended to in Boots, glass everywhere and one man, with a nail embedded in his leg, moaning over and over 'Who could have done this?'

Lee Jasper, the community activist, knew straight away who he considered the prime suspects and there hours later with the national press assembled, he outlined the circumstantial evidence: Far right groups have instructions for bomb making posted on the Internet and they have documented links to loyalist

+ continued on page 10 &11

COUNTDOWN TO THE MILLENNIUM

MR LYNDEN DAVID HALL (ARTIST)

Cooltempo, EMI House, 43 Brook Green, London, W6 7EF

PLACE OF BIRTH: London, 7.5.74
HONOURS/AWARDS: Best British Artist and Best Newcomer MOBO Awards
PERSONAL PROFILE: Lynden David Hall sings like an angel, writes songs of immense depth and funkiness, plays and produces most of it in his own studio. He is, without doubt, the most complete soul talent England's capital has produced in years.

MR NATHAN HAMLETT (ACTOR)

c/o Brain Taylor & Nina Quick Associates, 50 Pembroke Road, Kensington, London, W8 6NX

PLACE OF BIRTH: London, 17.12.68
MARITAL STATUS: Single
COLLEGE: Polytechnic Southwest
ACADEMIC QUALIFICATIONS: English BA Hons Degree
MEMBERSHIPS: Equity
HOBBIES AND INTERESTS: Play guitar, bass, piano, reading, going to theatre, films
PERSONAL PROFILE: Trained at the Academy Drama School and has been acting professionally since 1995. Theatre work has included a production at West Yorkshire playhouse and a tour of Germany as well as work with own theatre company, Awol. Television work includes: 'London's Burning' and 'Body Story' (Channel 4). Films: 'Underground', 'Day Release'.

MS MONA HAMMOND (ACTRESS)

8 Mallard Court, Petersham Road, Richmond, TW10 6UW

PLACE OF BIRTH: Jamaica, 23.3.35
MARITAL STATUS: Divorced
CHILDREN: One (Mulad)
PROFESSIONAL QUALIFICATIONS: Graduated Royal Academy Dramatic Art
MEMBERSHIPS: Equity
HONOURS/AWARDS: Achievement Award Jamaican in UK
HOBBIES AND INTERESTS: Dancing anytime anywhere
PERSONAL PROFILE: Jamaican Scholarship awarded to study in 1959, won scholarship to RADA 1962, graduated 1964 - Since then have worked extensively in theatre: RSC; National, Talawa; TV: 'Desmond's'; 'Eastenders'. Recently first film BBC 'Storm Damage'.

MS JACQUI HARPER (COMPANY DIRECTOR)

Crystal Media Training Ltd, 31 Southampton Place, London, WC1 A 2EA

PLACE OF BIRTH: Yorkshire
MARITAL STATUS: Married
COLLEGE: Sussex University
ACADEMIC QUALIFICATIONS: BA Hons, MA Hons
DIRECTORSHIPS: Crystal Media
MEMBERSHIPS: BAFTA
HONOURS/AWARDS: Honorary Fellowship
HOBBIES AND INTERESTS: Gym, theatre, movies, jazz
PERSONAL PROFILE: Jacqui grew up in London's East End. She has a BA from Sussex University and an MA from University of Westminster. She has anchored many programmes for GMTV, Sky News and BBC Television. She is very proud of her management training company, Crystal Media.

'As a child I always wanted to do something different and being a northern Black kid you would think the odds were stacked against me...'

VERONICA HARRIOTT

MS DORIS HARPER-WILLS (ARTISTIC DIRECTOR)

Carifesta UK, 59 Southlands Close, Coulsdon, Surrey, CR5 2HX

PLACE OF BIRTH: Guyana, 10.6.37
MARITAL STATUS: Divorced
CHILDREN: Three (Leslee, Peta, Leah)
COLLEGE: Avery Hill College, University of Guyana, University of London
ACADEMIC QUALIFICATIONS: BA Hons Associate, Institute of Education
DIRECTORSHIPS: London Entertains Carifesta UK
MEMBERSHIPS: CCL, RCS, Soroptomist Associate (Institute Of Education, London)
HONOURS/AWARDS: Carifesta Award (Guyana), International Women's Year Award (New York)
HOBBIES AND INTERESTS: Teaching, preaching to children / adults about our glorious African past / present contributions.
PERSONAL PROFILE: Described as 'a ball of fire' African Woman Magazine, 'Sheer Magic' (Commonwealth Institute Queen's Heritage Programme). Choreographed for Queen's Jubilee Celebrations (UK), Billie Holiday Theatre (New York), Africa Theatre Exchange (Zimbabwe), United Nations Celebrations (Zambia), Non-Aligned Nations (Guyana). Filmed as Queen Judgement (Channel 4 International Cinemas).

NOMINATED BY: Barbara Von Praag

MR AINSLEY HARRIOTT (TV CHEF-PRESENTER)

Chef de Cuisine, BBC Television, Jeremy Hicks Associates, 12 Ogle Street, London, W1P 7LG

PLACE OF BIRTH: England, 28.2.57
MARITAL STATUS: Married
CHILDREN: Two (Madeline, Jimmy)
ACADEMIC QUALIFICATIONS: 706-1-2 Catering City & Guilds
MEMBERSHIPS: Tennis Clubs, Harbour, Teatro, Soho House
HONOURS/AWARDS: TV Quick 97-98 Good Food, TV Personality 1997-98, Satellite TV 1 1998, Best Day Time B.B.Q Bible 1997
HOBBIES AND INTERESTS: Cycling, tennis, reading, Arsenal FC
PERSONAL PROFILE: Ainsley Harriott - a South London boy - has, over the last 40 years, been cooking up quite a career for himself in top restaurants, as a celebrities' caterer, on stage and television as a singer, comic and latterly as TV's most exciting personality chef. His first book - 'In the kitchen with Ainsley Harriott' - was published in Spring 1996 and his second - 'Can't Cook Won't Cook', was published in March 1997.
NOMINATED BY: Sharon Aitkin

MR ERNIE HARRIOTT (RADIO PRESENTER)

Businessman, Choice FM, Klassique Records, Unit 13, Wembley Market, Lancelot Road, Wembley, HA0 2BU

PLACE OF BIRTH: London, 18.1.56
MARITAL STATUS: Married
CHILDREN: Two (Andrez, Ryan)
HONOURS/AWARDS: 1987, 1990, 1994 British Industry Awards, 1991 Voice Readers Award - Best DJ, 1993 Sam Tu Dang Martial Arts, 1996 Soul and Reggae Trade Magazine
HOBBIES AND INTERESTS: Squash, football, swimming
PERSONAL PROFILE: Daddy Ernie host of Reggae Superjam on Choice FM London Monday to Friday between 7pm and 9pm. One of the most listened to shows on the station with a weekly average reach of 106,000 listeners. Daddy Ernie has been with Choice FM since its launch in March 1990 after serving his radio apprenticeship on private stations Time FM and LWR.

MISS VERONICA HARRIOTT (PERFORMER)

Lead In 'Whistle Down The Wind', Adrian King Associates, 33 Marlborough Mansions, Cannon Hill, London, NW6 1JS

PLACE OF BIRTH: Huddersfield, 28.7.74
MARITAL STATUS: Single
COLLEGE: Huddersfield Technical College
ACADEMIC QUALIFICATIONS: BTEC General/National Diplomas
PROFESSIONAL QUALIFICATIONS: Seven years In 'West End' musicals
HOBBIES AND INTERESTS: Tai yoga massage
PERSONAL PROFILE: As a child I always wanted to do something different and being a northern Black kid you would think the odds were stacked against me. I never ever saw colour as a disadvantage and always used every opportunity I could in a positive way. Ambition has no colour code!

MR GEORGE WILLIAM HARRIS (Actor)

ICM International Creative Management, Oxford House, 76 Oxford Street, London, W1N 0AY

PLACE OF BIRTH: Grenada, 20.11.46
MARITAL STATUS: Married
CHILDREN: Two (Aorja, Elior)
EMAIL: Harrisglo@aol.com
PERSONAL PROFILE: Royal National Theatre actor. Arrived in the UK aged 15 with £3.00 in his pocket. He has gone on to star in numerous international films, successful theatre and television productions with directors such as Steven Spielberg and Richard Eyre. His work includes: 'Wolcott'; 'Prime Suspect' and 'The Changeling' plus musicals.

MR VOLNEY HARRIS (Executive Manager)

Director, Agency for Economic Development Limited (AED), 44B Moss Lane West, Moss Side, Manchester, M15 5PD

PLACE OF BIRTH: Barbados, 18.3.52
MARITAL STATUS: Divorced
CHILDREN: Three
COLLEGE: Manchester Metropolitan
ACADEMIC QUALIFICATIONS: Diploma Training Management
PROFESSIONAL QUALIFICATIONS: BA Degree Business Studies Hons
DIRECTORSHIPS: AED Ltd, North West Network Ltd, MSHCDT Ltd, F.F Ltd
MEMBERSHIPS: IOD, MITD
HONOURS/AWARDS: Moss Side and Hulme Enterprise Award
HOBBIES AND INTERESTS: Computers, sport
PERSONAL PROFILE: I am committed to business training and economic development in our inner cities. My life is dedicated to the development of Black people.
NOMINATED BY: Mr W Patrick

MR WAYNE HARRIS (Furniture Specialist)

Director, W. Harris & Son (Specialist In Reproduction Furniture), 1206 Warwick Road, Acocks Cureen, Birmingham, B27 6BY

PLACE OF BIRTH: Jamaica, 1.7.61
MARITAL STATUS: Married
CHILDREN: One (Rashid)
COLLEGE: GT Rackstraw
PROFESSIONAL QUALIFICATIONS: Specialist in hand finished reproduction furniture. French polishing and spray polishing
DIRECTORSHIPS: Proprietor/Director
PERSONAL PROFILE: 20 years in furniture business. Trained at GT Rackstraw, Norfolk Manor, Brooke Yachts International, Windsor Reproductions, Beresford and Hicks and Elliot Crown.
NOMINATED BY: Joseph McLean

MR MERRICK HART (Administrator - Museums & Collections)

PCS, NEC Chair English Heritage, c/o Public & Commerical Services Union, 160 Falcon Road, London, SW11 2LN

PLACE OF BIRTH: London, 18.10.64
MARITAL STATUS: Single
COLLEGE: SouthgateTC-BTEC Engineering Science
ACADEMIC QUALIFICATIONS: Waltham Forest College BTEC Business & Finance
DIRECTORSHIPS: Director/Vice Treasurer-Hackney Caribbean Elderly Organisation
MEMBERSHIPS: PCS Union, Associate Member, ACA Lawyers, Pure Hart Services
HOBBIES AND INTERESTS: Raising funds to create, develop & promote British ethnic & diverse images, British cultural history and collections.
EMAIL: Purehart@easynet.co.uk
PERSONAL PROFILE: Elected PCS Union, NEC formerly CPSA 1995 and PCS chair/secretary at English Heritage since1994. Since April 1992, management committee, director and vice treasurer - Hackney Caribbean Elderly Organisation (HCEO). October 1993, founder Pure Hart Services-raising funds to develop, create and promote British ethnic and diverse images. Associate member: ACA Lawyers/ESM, Afro-Caribbean Golf Society.
NOMINATED BY: Joanne Mayers-Gaskin

MR BARRY HAYLES (Footballer)

Fulham Football Club, Craven Cottage, Stevenage Road, London, SW6 6HH

HONOURS/AWARDS: Player of the Season Award, 36 Goals, and a Conference League Winners Medal
PERSONAL PROFILE: At £2 million, Barry Hayles is one of Fulham's most expensive signings. A latecomer to the professional game, Barry is a Londoner who began his career at Stevenage. Initially playing as a full-back, Barry switched to attack after a successful upfront outing as a substitute saw him poach two goals in a friendly against Luton. His 26 goals last season helped Rovers secure a play-off place and established Barry as one of the best strikers in the division.

MR MAXIE ALPHONSO HAYLES
(Housing Project Worker)

Senior Worker, Sandwell Racial Harassment Unit, 13 Bull Street, West Bromwich, B70 6EU

PLACE OF BIRTH: Jamaica, 31.12.43
MARITAL STATUS: Married
CHILDREN: Two (Angeline Hayles, Maxie Hayles Junior)
COLLEGE: University of Central England
ACADEMIC QUALIFICATIONS: Housing Management Social Worker (Trained)
PROFESSIONAL QUALIFICATIONS: Diploma in ILEX CCAW in Advice Work
MEMBERSHIPS: Chair for four community organisations & affliliated to various local and national organisations.
HOBBIES AND INTERESTS: Reading, politics, music, cricket, football
PERSONAL PROFILE: Mr Maxie Hayles is a very prominent figure within the Black community. Maxie successfully led the Alton Manning Campaign for justice and was the only person who stood up and brought the Stephen Lawrence Inquiry to Birmingham Racial Attacks Monitoring Unit and Sandwell Racial Harassment Unit plus various other groups and committees.
NOMINATED BY: Mr Rajinder Singh Bhogal

MR GARY-TYRONE HEADLEY (Cricketer Ex Pro)

Human Resources-PR Manager, EMP Plc, 45 Stone Haven Road, Aylesbury, Bucks, HP19 3JG

PLACE OF BIRTH: Reading, 5.9.66
MARITAL STATUS: Single
CHILDREN: One (Daneka)
COLLEGE: CardiffT EC, Wales
ACADEMIC QUALIFICATIONS: 3 O-Levels, Credit in BTEC / Studying Contract Law Present
PROFESSIONAL QUALIFICATIONS: Senior Cricket Coaching Certificate
DIRECTORSHIPS: Headley Associates
MEMBERSHIPS: President of Barbados Overseas Youth & Friends Association, MMC at Lords Cricket Ground
HONOURS/AWARDS: Barbados 30th Year of Independence Awards for Bridging Gaps Between Generations
HOBBIES AND INTERESTS: Cricket, fundraising, history
EMAIL: GaryHeadley@Hotmail.com
PERSONAL PROFILE: Played for Derbyshire CCC and Middlesex CCC, 2nd 11. Spent three winters playing and coaching in Australia after five operations on knees. Stopped playing full time in 1993 and now studying contract law. I am a human resources /PR manager. Founded Barbados Overseas Youth and Friends Association in 1992 and was very active in first five years with 150 members, most of whom were between 15-35 years old. Our aim is to bond a closer relationship with Barbados. I also do radio and media KYTV, New Nation and GLR.
NOMINATED BY: Kevin Morris, BOYFA

MISS STELLA HEADLEY (Director-Radio Broadcasting)

First Love Radio Ltd, PO Box 1073, London, SE8 4WU

DATE OF BIRTH: 12.8.65
MARITAL STATUS: Single
CHILDREN: Two (Morni, Chi)
COLLEGE: HNC Radio Production and Broadcast Journalism, CSM Management
ACADEMIC QUALIFICATIONS: NVQ Senior Human Resource Development
DIRECTORSHIPS: First Love Radio Ltd, First Love Media Training
HONOURS/AWARDS: SOLOTEC achievers awards 1998 and skills for small business
HOBBIES AND INTERESTS: Interior design, cooking, writing, music
PERSONAL PROFILE: Stella Headley founder of First Love Radio (FLR.1073) and First Love Media Training in Lewisham. FLR.1073 is SE London's only radio station offering a unique service which caters for the tastes of it's local audience of some 420,000. Stella Headley has developed and maintained excellent working relations with businesses, organisations and individuals. With young children, Stella also studies as well as manages two successful businesses.
NOMINATED BY: Lloyd Mitchell - First Love Radio Ltd

MR CARLTON CHARLES HEATH (CHIEF ENGINEER)

Churchill Inter Continental, 30 Portman Square, London, W1A 4ZX

PLACE OF BIRTH: Jamaica, 26.1.54
MARITAL STATUS: Married
CHILDREN: Four (Collin, Carl, Curtis, Stuart)
COLLEGE: Hackney, East Ham
ACADEMIC QUALIFICATIONS: Electrical Engineering
PROFESSIONAL QUALIFICATIONS: CIBSE Member
MEMBERSHIPS: Chartered Institute of Building Services Engineer
HOBBIES AND INTERESTS: Cricket, golf
EMAIL: charles.heat@interconti.com
PERSONAL PROFILE: Born in Jamaica 1954. Secondary education - Acland Burghley Comprehensive; Electrical apprenticeship completed 1972; Electrical Engineering Higher National Certificate 1976. Joined Intercontinental Hotels 1980 as an electrician. Promoted to assistant engineer 1985. Chief engineer 1989 at Forum Hotel Glasgow. Joined Churchill Hotel 1993. Managed millions of pounds for refurbishment of property.

MR TONY HECTOR (ART DIRECTOR)

c/o Lowe Howard Spink, Bowater House, 68-114 Kinightsbridge, London, SW1X 7LT

PLACE OF BIRTH: London, 30.6.67
MARITAL STATUS: Single
COLLEGE: Newscastle College
ACADEMIC QUALIFICATIONS: HND Advertising
HONOURS/AWARDS: Cannes D&A Euro Best
HOBBIES AND INTERESTS: Sports, music
EMAIL: Thector@lhs.co.uk
PERSONAL PROFILE: Work hard, play hard and love my family not necessarily in that order.
NOMINATED BY: Jon Daniel

MR CLAUDE 'HOPPER' HENDRICKSON
(DEVELOPMENT MANAGER)

Chapletown Young People's 10-12 Club, 231 Chapletown Road, Leeds, LS7 4DX

PLACE OF BIRTH: Leeds, 5.2.60
MARITAL STATUS: Single
CHILDREN: Five (Chevone, Clifford, Tiah, Curtis, O'Shae)
COLLEGE: Thomas Danby College
ACADEMIC QUALIFICATIONS: Supervisory Management
HONOURS/AWARDS: Black Achiever 'Youth and Community' The Voice Newspaper (1997)
HOBBIES AND INTERESTS: Music, sport, travel
PERSONAL PROFILE: He is one of the most influential activists of his generation in the community. Claude is most noted for his six-year Frontline Community Selfbuild Housing Association project in 1994-5, which took 12 long-term unemployed African-Caribbean's from the Chapletown area of Leeds seven and in record time, built 12 two-bedroom houses on derelict land at Ravanscar Mount.

MS DOLLIE HENRY (DIRECTOR-CHOREOGRAPHER)

Artistic Director, BOP Productions Ltd, 10 Stayton Road, Sutton, SM1 1RB

PLACE OF BIRTH: Bridgewater, 30.6.62
MARITAL STATUS: Married
CHILDREN: One (Daniel)
COLLEGE: Laine Theatre Arts
ACADEMIC QUALIFICATIONS: 10 (CSE & GCSE)
PROFESSIONAL QUALIFICATIONS: Full Teaching Diploma with Imperial Society of Dance and Lamda Drama and Lecturer of Jazz Dance
MEMBERSHIPS: William Louther Foundation
HOBBIES AND INTERESTS: Writing, travel, cooking, working hard, living life
EMAIL: info@abop.demon.co.uk
PERSONAL PROFILE: Is one of the country's leading choreographers and teachers of British jazz dance. Her professional experience spans 20 years and includes a vast and extremely varied career as a lecturer, performer, choreographer and director of West End musicals, theatre and concert dance productions, films, TV and video nationally and internationally.
NOMINATED BY: Sharon Aitkin

MR LENNY HENRY (STAND-UP COMEDIAN-ACTOR-WRITER)

PBJ Management Ltd, 5 Soho Square, London, W1V 3DE

DATE OF BIRTH: 29.8.58
MARITAL STATUS: Married
CHILDREN: One Adopted
HONOURS/AWARDS: Won New Faces Talent Show 1975
PERSONAL PROFILE: TV appearances include: 'Fosters'; 'Tiswas'; '3 of a Kind'; 'Lenny Henry Show'; 'Chef'; Films: 'Coast To Coast'; 'Work Experience'; 'Alive & Kicking'; 'True Identity'; 'Lenny 's Big Amazon Adventure'. Publications: 'Quest for the Big Woof'; 'Charlie & The Big Chill', 1995; 'Charlie Queen of the Desert', 1996. Lenny has been a trustee of and the face of Comic Relief since it began in 1987.

MISS COLETTE HIBBERT (EDITOR)

The Weekly Gleaner Newspaper, Unit 220-223, Elephant & Castlle Shopping Centre, London, SE1 6TE

PLACE OF BIRTH: England, 25.3.73
MARITAL STATUS: Single
COLLEGE: Southampton Institute of HE
ACADEMIC QUALIFICATIONS: 8 GCSEs, 3 A-Levels, BA Hons Media with Cultural Studies
PROFESSIONAL QUALIFICATIONS: Postgraduate Certificate In Magazine Journalism
HOBBIES AND INTERESTS: Reading, socialising, karate, badminton, current affairs
EMAIL: Collette@gleaner1.demon.co.uk
PERSONAL PROFILE: Joined the Weekly Gleaner as a reporter, became editor at 23-years old when the current editor left the company. Main role is to provide our readers - the majority of whom are Jamaican nationals - with a weekly newspaper consisting of news from Jamaica and the UK. Ambition: To write a book.
NOMINATED BY: Ron Shillingford

MS MAUREEN HIBBERT (ACTRESS)

Student, Peters, Fraser & Dunlop, 503 The Chambers, Lots Road, Chelsea Wharf, London, SW10 0XF

PLACE OF BIRTH: London, 9.5.59
MARITAL STATUS: Single
CHILDREN: One (Chloe)
COLLEGE: Irie Dance Theatre/University of London
ACADEMIC QUALIFICATIONS: Dip HE BA Hons
PROFESSIONAL QUALIFICATIONS: SRN, RMN
MEMBERSHIPS: Board Member Oily Cart Childrens Theatre Co. Committee, Mary Seacole Memorial Association
HOBBIES AND INTERESTS: Writing, photography, travel, meditation - yoga, chanting
EMAIL: ethiopl@yahoo.com.
PERSONAL PROFILE: Daughter, sister, auntie, mother. Diversity of roles: nurse, actress, drama tutor, mas player, singer and poet: spanning two decades of communication. Through an emerging creative language, currently unified by African, Caribbean and contemporary dance, development in literacy and academic cultural studies, is a legacy for spiritual healing for future generations.

MR HERBIE HIGGINS MBE (VOLUNTEER WORKER)

Merseyside Caribbean Carnival, 60 Duke Street, Liverpool, L1 5AA

PLACE OF BIRTH: Jamaica, 13.5.29
MARITAL STATUS: Married
CHILDREN: Five (Herbert, Keith, Yvonne, Clifford, Kenneth)
DIRECTORSHIPS: Comtechsa
MEMBERSHIPS: MREC, Comtechsa Caribbean Council
HONOURS/AWARDS: CSV Volunteer Voice Award, FBHO Award, MBE
HOBBIES AND INTERESTS: Sports, cricket, dominos, football
PERSONAL PROFILE: Herbie Higgins has distinguished himself in community work for over 50 years. He runs the very successful carnival in Liverpool and is president of the Caribbean Centre. He has been honoured for his work in volunteering and community development receiving an MBE in 1997.
NOMINATED BY: Mrs A Wong - Jamaica Merseyside Association

MISS HAZEL HOLDER (ACTRESS-SINGER)

CAM London, 19 Denmark Street, London, WC2H 8NA

PLACE OF BIRTH: Luton, 18.2.69
MARITAL STATUS: Married
COLLEGE: Mountview Theatre School
ACADEMIC QUALIFICATIONS: Diploma in Musical Theatre
MEMBERSHIPS: Equity
HONOURS/AWARDS: First Recipient of The Kobler Trust at Mountview
HOBBIES AND INTERESTS: Walking, travel, yoga
PERSONAL PROFILE: Theatre credits include 'Carmen Jones' at the Old Vic 'Maskarade' with the Talawa Theatre Company, 'Ain't Misbehaving' at the Lyric. National tours of 'Morning Song' with Black Mime, 'Voyage in the Dark' with Sphinx and 'The Little Shop of Horrors'. Guest lead appearances include 'The Bill' and Radio 4 dramas.

MS JUNE HOLLAND (SENIOR HOUSING OFFICER)

Warden Housing Association, Unit 5, 14 Hogarth Cresent, Croydon, CR0 2JH

PLACE OF BIRTH: Grenada, 22.11.56
MARITAL STATUS: Married
CHILDREN: Two (Darren, Nia)
COLLEGE: Birbeck College, Middlesex Polytechnic
ACADEMIC QUALIFICATIONS: BA Hons, Diploma in Psychology
MEMBERSHIPS: Affiliate Member Chartered Institute of Housing
HOBBIES AND INTERESTS: Reading, current events, cultural activities, photography
PERSONAL PROFILE: I currently work as senior housing officer for a large housing association. I have been involved in the Black community from Caribbean Focus 1996 to setting up the first Black housing association in Croydon. Due to family commitments I am no longer actively involved in community work but keep abreast of what is happening.
NOMINATED BY: B O C A

MR LESTER HOLLOWAY (CONSULTANT-FREELANCE)

Journalist, National Assoc Of Black, Asian & Ethnic Minority Councillors, 49 Cathnor Road, Shepherds Bush, London, W12 9JB

PLACE OF BIRTH: London, 22.7.70
MARITAL STATUS: Single
ACADEMIC QUALIFICATIONS: 3 A-Levels, 6 O-Levels
DIRECTORSHIPS: Two voluntary organisations
MEMBERSHIPS: Labour Party and eleven other organisations
HONOURS/AWARDS: 1987 Winner Radio 4/ YMCA 'Best British Youth Award'
HOBBIES AND INTERESTS: Bird watching
PERSONAL PROFILE: Founder member and first secretary of National Association of Black, Asian and Ethnic Minority Councillors. Elected councillor to L.B. of Hammersmith & Fulham 1994-3. Chairman: Hammersmith Community Trust 1998. Environmental and 'Third World' development campaigner. Winner 1987 YMCA/Radio 4 'Best Of British Youth Award'. Executive member H & F Community Health Council; H & F Race Equality Council, school governor.

MRS ESTHER HOLMES (SENIOR TAX AUDITOR)

Rtd, Formerly HM Customs & Excise, 36 Broadlands Road, Bromley, BR1 5DE

PLACE OF BIRTH: Barbados, 17.8.38
MARITAL STATUS: Married
CHILDREN: Two (Winslow, Deborah)
HONOURS/AWARDS: Barbados High Commission 1996 Award to mark 30 Years of Barbados Independence, Custom & Excise Long Service Award
HOBBIES AND INTERESTS: Promoting and supporting young Black people with particular education needs
PERSONAL PROFILE: First African-Caribbean, female to have received an officer's commission from British Customs and Excise. Reached the grade of senior executive officer in Customs and Excise (1989). Completed 40 years public service in Customs and Excise, also first secretary and founder member of the first Barbados Overseas Community Association (founded 1966). First African Caribbean schools governor in Bromley.
NOMINATED BY: Barbados High Commission

MISS JOAN HOOLEY (ACTRESS)

Writer, 38A Highlever Road, North Kensington, London, W10 6PT

PLACE OF BIRTH: Jamaica, 13.11.36
CHILDREN: One (Julian Clark)
COLLEGE: University of London
PROFESSIONAL QUALIFICATIONS: S.R.N
HOBBIES AND INTERESTS: Art, riding
PERSONAL PROFILE: Trained as a nurse prior to being lured into the acting profession. Have also written professionally for several years. Published many short stories and wrote the Channel 4 series 'Desmonds'. At present in 'Eastenders'.

MRS ASHER HOYLES (LEARNING SUPPORT WORKER)

Additional Support Tutor, New Vic Sixth Form College, Prince Regent Lane, Plaistow, London, E13 8SG

PLACE OF BIRTH: Leeds, 12.12.66
MARITAL STATUS: Married
CHILDREN: One (Rosa)
COLLEGE: University of East London
ACADEMIC QUALIFICATIONS: BA Hons Degree in Education and Communication Studies
PROFESSIONAL QUALIFICATIONS: Teachers Certificate (NVQ) Certificate in Technical Training in the Entertainment Industry
MEMBERSHIPS: Poetry Society
HOBBIES AND INTERESTS: Poetry/Black studies, disability (especially dyslexia, as I am dyslexic.
PERSONAL PROFILE: Asher left home at sixteen with no qualifications and came to London. She now has a degree and teachers certificate and is a celebrated poet, performing her poems in major venues. Some of her poems (selected by Roger McGough) have appeared on London buses and she has taught her students about performance poetry.
NOMINATED BY: Martin Hoyles

MS RUBY - MARIE HUTCHINSON (ACTRESS-SINGER)

PLACE OF BIRTH: Gloucester
MARITAL STATUS: Single
COLLEGE: London Studio Centre
ACADEMIC QUALIFICATIONS: 6 O-Levels in Eng. Lang, French, Biology, Drama, Citizenship, Home Economics
PROFESSIONAL QUALIFICATIONS: Professional actress for 15 years
HOBBIES AND INTERESTS: Visiting yummy restaurants
PERSONAL PROFILE: I came to London from Gloucester at age 16 to continue my dancing training. Perseverance and determination has given me a great career, travelling to many countries all over the world. I've also retrained as a sports/holistic massage therapist which has taken off beyond what I ever expected. I now have a wonderful life working successfully as an actress and sports/holistic massage therapist.

MISS GLORIA HYATT (HEADTEACHER)

Elimu Study School, Dove Street, Toxteth, Liverpool, L8 0TU

PLACE OF BIRTH: Liverpool, 17.10.66
MARITAL STATUS: Single
CHILDREN: One (Marvin)
COLLEGE: John Moores University
ACADEMIC QUALIFICATIONS: Bachelor of Education with Honours Degree
PROFESSIONAL QUALIFICATIONS: Qualified Teacher Status
MEMBERSHIPS: Black Teacher Association; Parents of Black Children
HONOURS/AWARDS: Community Achievement Award
HOBBIES AND INTERESTS: Reading, writing, poetry, sports
PERSONAL PROFILE: Over a six year period after graduating from college with a six month contract of employment, created a full time educational service for Black pupils excluded from school and after school service, nine full time and six part time job's and an annual budget that increased from £40,000 per annum to £350,000.

Some of her poems (selected by Roger McGough) have appeared on London buses

ASHER HOYLES

MS LISA I'ANSON (Broadcaster)

c/o John Noel Management, 10 A Belmont Street, London, NW1 8HH

PLACE OF BIRTH: London, 31.5.65
MARITAL STATUS: Separated
CHILDREN: One (Dylan Kwamg)
COLLEGE: University of Westminster
ACADEMIC QUALIFICATIONS: O & A-Levels
PERSONAL PROFILE: Lisa I'Anson, one of Britain's most exciting radio and television presenters. Has worked for many major television networks since 1989, including Kiss FM, BBC 1, MTV, Channel 4, ILR and Sky Television. In 1995 Lisa was offered the prestigious job of presenting on BBC Radio 1. She has recently left the station to concentrate on her television career.

MR PAUL IFILL (Footballer)

Millwall Football Club, The Den, Zampa Road, London, SE16 3LN

PLACE OF BIRTH: Brighton, 20.10.79
PERSONAL PROFILE: Top scorer for the Millwall Youth side during 1997/98 with 17 goals, Paul will be looking to continue this form at reserve level. Signed a new professional contract at the end of last season.

MR CHUKWUDUM IKEAZOR (Writer)

143 Adare Walk, Streatham, London, SW16 2PP

PLACE OF BIRTH: London, 11.9.56
MARITAL STATUS: Single
COLLEGE: University of Nigeria
ACADEMIC QUALIFICATIONS: LLB Hons
PROFESSIONAL QUALIFICATIONS: BL
MEMBERSHIPS: Africa Centre, International Police Association, International Bar Association, Greenpeace, Royal Africa Society
HONOURS/AWARDS: Class Top Student Award, Metropolitan Police TRG Sch.Hendon 1990
HOBBIES AND INTERESTS: Writing, travelling, chess, current affairs ('Third World' bias)
PERSONAL PROFILE: Born to Nigerian parents. Attended St Gregorys College, Lagos, University of Nigeria, Police Staff College Nigeria, Merton College Morden and Police School Hendon. Has published four books - 'The Ethnic Factor', 'Nigeria 1966', 'The Report To The People' and 'The Ministry Syndrome' (co-authored), writes for West Africa and Trumpet Magazines.

MS VERONICA IKEZUE (Project Co-ordinator)

Caring for Carers Association,

PLACE OF BIRTH: Nigeria, 18.10.41
MARITAL STATUS: Married
CHILDREN: Five (Yemi, Robert, Late Georgina, David, Tony)
COLLEGE: Western College of Commerce
ACADEMIC QUALIFICATIONS: History, Geography, Arithmetic and English
MEMBERSHIPS: CHC Forword Project Mind Carers National
HOBBIES AND INTERESTS: Swimming, dancing, working
PERSONAL PROFILE: I was educated in Nigeria. Got my first job at Federal Census Office Lagos the first count of population in Nigeria 1961 as an IBM operator. After three years in Census, I left for England on June 1964. I worked and studied in the UK as secretary typist. I lost my second daughter in 1993 after a long illness. I set a project in 1991 to look after Black and other ethnic minorities in the borough of Hammersmith & Fulham. The project is still running to this date, it is called Caring and Carers Association it looks after people looking after their loved ones.
NOMINATED BY: Christopher Johnson MBA

MS MIRIAM AFOMA ILOGHALU (Management Consultant)

London Borough of Lewisham, Members Services Branch, Civic Suite, Catford, London, SE6 4RU

PLACE OF BIRTH: Nigeria, 24.10.54
MARITAL STATUS: Single
CHILDREN: Four
COLLEGE: London University
ACADEMIC QUALIFICATIONS: LLB Hons, Diploma in Business Studies
HOBBIES AND INTERESTS: Theatre-opera, classical, jazz music, horse-racing, political documentories, dining out, golfing
PERSONAL PROFILE: Black British, born to Obi Okotu I and Adazi Enu in Anambra State, Nigeria. Was married with four children. A self employed management consultant, lawyer and active politician serving my third term as an elected councillor. Held various positions including housing. Labour Party constituency womens officer, chair, General Election campaign organiser, London Borough Ambassador, as the Mayoress for two years, London University Mentor.

MR PAUL INCE (Footballer)

Middlesborough Football Club, Middlesborough

PLACE OF BIRTH: Ilford, 21.10.67
PROFESSIONAL QUALIFICATIONS: Caps for England (43). B team and Under 21. Occasional England Team Captain
PERSONAL PROFILE: One of the stars of England's World Cup in France, Paul was back to his forceful best scoring against Inter Milan in the pre-season clash at Anfield in early August. Signed in the summer of 1997 from the very highest levels to the Anfield midfielder. A former West Ham trainee moved to Manchester United in 1989, and he went on to win every domestic honour with the Old Trafford outfit.

MISS JOSEPHINE INONIYEGHA (Student)

3 Woodside Close, Alperton, Wembley, London, HA0 1UL

PLACE OF BIRTH: Nigeria, 4.9.77
MARITAL STATUS: Single
CHILDREN: One (Caius Owusu Antiwi)
COLLEGE: University of East London
ACADEMIC QUALIFICATIONS: GCSEs, A-Levels, Diploma in Acting
HONOURS/AWARDS: LAMDA Examination Bronze and Silver
HOBBIES AND INTERESTS: Reading, sporting activities i.e kempo karate
EMAIL: ino3278p@UEL.COM
PERSONAL PROFILE: I am currently studying for a BSc in Psychology. I have been interested in pursuing a career in the theatre or film industry and hope to do so after my degree. I have appeared in a number of amateur productions as well as professional productions such as Reata Fahodzls 'Booked'. My biggest achievement (and proudest) of 1999 so far is my new baby boy Caius.

ANTHEA INSULAR (Photographer)

Walsall Hospitals NHS Trust, 11a Frederick Road, Wednesfield, Walsall, WV11 1PQ

DATE OF BIRTH: 4.11.72
MARITAL STATUS: Single
COLLEGE: University of Central England
ACADEMIC QUALIFICATIONS: 5 GCSEs, 3 A-Levels, 2 City and Guilds, BA Hons Media and Communications
HOBBIES AND INTERESTS: Reading Black history, power-walking, running, photography
PERSONAL PROFILE: I am a motivated individual who is currently working towards a personal goal of starting my own photographic business. It will be achieved through perseverance and my strong will to get my foot in the doors that were previously closed to me, and leave to them ajar for those to follow.

'I worked and studied in the UK as secretary typist. I lost my second daughter in 1993 after a long illness. I set a project in 1991 to look after Black and other ethnic minorities'

VERONICA IKEZUE

Carribbean Times

Caribbean Times
Incorporating African Times

Friday 12 March 1999 • BRITAIN'S ONLY QUALITY BLACK NEWSPAPER • Issue 925 • 50p

BANANA SPLIT

CARICOM to review Clinton agreement as US take on EU in trade war

St Lucian women prepare for market. 80 per cent of the population of this small island are involved in the banana business.

NEED A NEW JOB? SEE **Jobs Direct** ON PAGES 15-26

COUNTDOWN TO THE MILLENNIUM

PROF ALAN ANTHONY JACKSON
(PAEDIATRICIAN, HONORARY CONSULTANT IN HUMAN NUTRITION)

Professor, School Of Medicine, University Of Southampton, Clinical Nutrition and Metabolism Unit, Level C (113), West Wing, Southampton General Hospital, Tremona Road, Southampton, SO16 6YD

PLACE OF BIRTH: Manchester, 22.11.45
MARITAL STATUS: Married
CHILDREN: Two (Josina, Akil)
COLLEGE: University of Cambridge, University College Hospital, University of London
ACADEMIC QUALIFICATIONS: BA, MA, MB, B Chir, MD
PROFESSIONAL QUALIFICATIONS: FRCP, FRCPCH, FRCPath
DIRECTORSHIPS: Scientific Director, British Nutrition Foundation. Chairman, Association of Professors of Human Nutrition
MEMBERSHIPS: Committee on Medical Aspects of Food and Nutrition Policy, Department of Health Council of the Carribean Health Research Council
HONOURS/AWARDS: Sir Lionel Whitby Prize 1983, Cuthbertson Visiting Lecturer 1996, Sri Prakash Visiting Lecturer 1998, British Nutrition Foundation Prize 1998
PERSONAL PROFILE: Formerly Director, Tropical Metabolism Research Unit, University of the West Indies. Interests: Research as driving force for personal and social development; nutrition as fundamental aspect of growth and development; rational approaches to nutrition care of seriously ill; training of doctors in nutrition care and prevention of nutritionally related health conditions.
NOMINATED BY: A J Strike

MRS BLOSSOM JACKSON (HEALTH VISITOR-LECTURER)

Managing Director, Paublo Books Ltd, Dentax House, South Hill Avenue, Northolt Road, South Harrow, HA2 0DU

PLACE OF BIRTH: Jamaica, 18.5.36
MARITAL STATUS: Divorced
CHILDREN: One (Dr John Pennington)
COLLEGE: OU, Surrey; East London Universities
ACADEMIC QUALIFICATIONS: MA, BA
PROFESSIONAL QUALIFICATIONS: RN, OND, HV, CHNT, RNT, HVT
DIRECTORSHIPS: Paublo Books Charities Evaluation Services UK (CES)
MEMBERSHIPS: RCN
HONOURS/AWARDS: Rubicon Community Award 1997
HOBBIES AND INTERESTS: Classical music, walking, cooking, gardening, writing, home decorating, travel
EMAIL: Blossom@paublo.demon.co.uk
PERSONAL PROFILE: Trained at Addenbrookes Hospital, Cambridge. Was senior nursing officer and health education officer LB of Camden. Senior lecturer and school course leader. Nursing course - East London University. Principle lecturers HV course. Director at Oxford Brookes University. Became health visiting officer and professional advisor at the UKCC. A post Blossom left to become a freelance consultant. Love gardening, cooking, travel and working.
NOMINATED BY: Dr Joan Pennington

MR CARL JACKSON (ORGANIST-TEACHER)

Director of Music, Chapel Royal, Hampton Court Palace, East Molesey, KT8 9AU

PLACE OF BIRTH: London, 13.9.58
MARITAL STATUS: Single
COLLEGE: RAM Downing College. Goldsmiths College London
ACADEMIC QUALIFICATIONS: MA, PETC
PROFESSIONAL QUALIFICATIONS: FRCO, ARAM
MEMBERSHIPS: ISM, RSM, IAM
HOBBIES AND INTERESTS: Cinema, theatre, food and wine, country walks
EMAIL: Carl.jackson@ccis.org.ok
PERSONAL PROFILE: Carl was senior music teacher at St Paul's Girls School for nine years before becoming director of music of Kingston Grammar School in 1988. He was appointed director of music of the Chapel Royal, Hampton Court Palace in 1996. He is a council member of the Incorporated Society of Musicians.

> ## He was appointed director of music of the Chapel Royal, Hampton Court Palace in 1996
>
> **CARL JACKSON**

MR DAVID JAMES (FOOTBALLER)

Goalkeeper, Aston Villa Football Club, Birmingham

PLACE OF BIRTH: Welwyn Garden, 1.8.70
PROFESSIONAL QUALIFICATIONS: Cap for England, B team, Under 21 and Youth, 212 Appearances for Liverpool
PERSONAL PROFILE: James originally signed as an apprentice for Watford by Graham Taylor after training with Spurs as a schoolboy, David had won 10 England Under-21 caps before his move to Anfield in June 1992. Awarded his first full cap by Glenn Hoddle when he played against Mexico at Wembley. David James will challenge Brad Friedel this season for the number one jersey after seeing his superb run of 212 consecutive appearances (since Bruce Grobbelaar in 1994) ended by the American in February 1998.

MR LENNIE JAMES (ACTOR-WRITER)

c/o ICM, Oxford House, 76 Oxford Street, London, W1V HAX

PLACE OF BIRTH: Nottingham, 11.10.65
MARITAL STATUS: Single
CHILDREN: Three (Romy-Lise, Cezine, Georgia)
COLLEGE: South West London
ACADEMIC QUALIFICATIONS: A-Level Sociology, Government and Politics
PROFESSIONAL QUALIFICATIONS: Diploma In Dramatic Arts
DIRECTORSHIPS: Artistic Direcoriate of the Global Theatre
HONOURS/AWARDS: Persuent Award For Best Supporting Actor 1994
HOBBIES AND INTERESTS: Football, carpentry, playstation, my kids, history
PERSONAL PROFILE: I am the father of three, the partner of one, the son of Phyllis Mary James. I act because I want to, I write because I want to. I believe in God when it suits me and in life always.

REV RENE JARRETT (TEACHER-PRIEST)

Health and Safety Officer, Amherst Primary School, 2 Woburn Mansions, Torrington Place, London, WC1E 7HL

PLACE OF BIRTH: Sierra Leone, 14.7.49
MARITAL STATUS: Married
CHILDREN: Three (Magnus, Oliver, Rene)
COLLEGE: London
ACADEMIC QUALIFICATIONS: B Ed Honours
HONOURS/AWARDS: Pastoral and Teaching Certificates
HOBBIES AND INTERESTS: Reading, writing, swimming, football
PERSONAL PROFILE: I have lived in Camden since 1988. I am attached to St George Parish Church Bloomsbury as an honorary assistant priest. In addition to my current position in school, I am a full-time teacher and a member of the management team and I co-ordinate the affairs of the lower school.

MR LEE JASPER (CHIEF EXECUTIVE)

Director, The 1990 Trust, 90 London Road, London, SE1 6LN

PLACE OF BIRTH: Manchester, 4.11.58
MARITAL STATUS: Married
CHILDREN: Eight (Sarah, Kizzy, Remi, Leah, Kahsha, Jordon, Fabren, Lee)
COLLEGE: Manchester
ACADEMIC QUALIFICATIONS: BA Hons
DIRECTORSHIPS: Jubillee 2000, Discrimination at Law Association, Operation Black Vote
MEMBERSHIPS: Royal Commonwealth Club, Black Jewish Forum
HONOURS/AWARDS: EMMA 1997 Voice, 1997 and 1998 Community Relations
HOBBIES AND INTERESTS: Looking after children, keep fit
EMAIL: jasper@gn.apc.org
PERSONAL PROFILE: Lee Jasper, BA Hons Social Science's. Director The 1990 Trust, a leading policy organisation on issues affecting African, Asian and Caribbean communities living in the UK and Europe. He is currently on the board and is chair of many committees and organisations including the National Black Alliance, National Black Caucus, chair of Operation Black Vote. He is the national secretary of the National Assembly Against Racism. A council member of Charter 88. He has also recently been appointed to the Home Secretary's Race Relations Forum acting as an adviser to government.
NOMINATED BY: Simon Woolley

MR TEE JAYE (Singer, Dancer, Actor)

c/o Paul Spyker Management, 1-2 Henrietta Street, Covent Garden, London, WC2E 8PS

PLACE OF BIRTH: US, 13.11.65
COLLEGE: Graduate Timken Vocational
ACADEMIC QUALIFICATIONS: School Canton Chio
MEMBERSHIPS: Equity Member, AEA of America and British
HONOURS/AWARDS: Dance Magazine Award 1986, Craft of Choreography Conf. NYC
HOBBIES AND INTERESTS: Writing, computers, basketball, drawing, dining out
PERSONAL PROFILE: Professional career began at age 14 years in a production of 'Purlie' by Ossie Davis. Soloist with the 'Canton Ballet' US also with the 'Duluth Ballet of Minnesota'. US leading and featured roles from Broadway to the West End in productions of; 'A Chorus Line'; 'Pippin'; 'Dream Girls'; 'Cats'; 'Song and Dance'; 'The Wiz'; 'Inner City' and 'Five Guys Named Moe'. Plus modelling, commercials, film and TV.

MISS JOCELYN JEE (Actress-Comedian)

In The House Management, PO Box 1253, Ilford, Essex, IG2 6FX

PLACE OF BIRTH: London, 7.5.74
MARITAL STATUS: Single
COLLEGE: Guildhall School of Music and Drama
ACADEMIC QUALIFICATIONS: BA Hons Drama Acting
HONOURS/AWARDS: Comedy Store National Hooch Award Winner 1998
PERSONAL PROFILE: As an actress I have appeared in a number of productions including the feature film 'Baby Mother', 'The Bill' and World Tour Theatre production 'Ticket and Ties' and 'Racing Demons' at the Canada Festival. Current comedy store National New Act of the Year winner the first Black comedian since Lenny Henry to win a National mainstream competitive award.

MS KUNBI JEGEDE (Journalist-Presenter)

News Reporter-Feature Writer, The Voice Group,

PLACE OF BIRTH: London, 17.6.72
MARITAL STATUS: Unmarried
COLLEGE: Trinity College, Cambridge University
ACADEMIC QUALIFICATIONS: 4 A-Levels, English, History, Politics, Sociology, BA Hon, MA Camb. Social and Political Science
PROFESSIONAL QUALIFICATIONS: NVQ Level 2, Information Technology
DIRECTORSHIPS: President/Founder of the Trinity College Writers Circle (1992-94), Founder of the Cambridge Alumnae in the Media Society (1997-to date)
MEMBERSHIPS: At Cambridge active in GEEMA, (Group to Encourage Ethnic Minority) Students and The Black Caucus, National Union of Journalists, Windsor Fellow Graduate, Editorial Committee of CAM (1999)
HONOURS/AWARDS: Writing Competition, Young Haringey to Africa, GLC Summer Arts Festival, National Writing Competition ACER Awards, Cambridge University Writing Awards, Trinity College, Hooper Declaration Prize, President Cambridge Alumnae in the Media. 1999 NUJ winner-2nd prize, Felix Deardem Memorial Prize.
HOBBIES AND INTERESTS: Mentoring, community work, public talks, reading
EMAIL: Kunbi@tesco.net
PERSONAL PROFILE: Writer: New Impact Magazine (1991-1994). 1994 onwards, reporter: BBC World Service and The Daily Telegraph. Editor: The Brief Magazine Reporter: Currently reporter: The Journal Newspaper. Extras, PR: Nubian Jak and Xpress Publishers. TV and presenting: Panellist on BBC programme, 'Reparations to Africa': Panellist on Publishers 4th birthday party.

MARY-THERESA JEROME
(Assistant Priest-Project Manager)

Church of England, 91 Beeches Road, West Bromwich, Birmingham, B70 6HG

PLACE OF BIRTH: Grenada, 23.5.42
MARITAL STATUS: Single
CHILDREN: One (Gail Theresa)
COLLEGE: Queens College
ACADEMIC QUALIFICATIONS: BA Technology
PROFESSIONAL QUALIFICATIONS: State Registered Nurse, State Registered Midwife, Intensive Care of The New Born, Post Registration Psychiatric Nursing, BA Theology
HOBBIES AND INTERESTS: Travel, music, entertaining, spiritual-gospel uplifting
PERSONAL PROFILE: Mary-Theresa came to UK in 1964, qualifications in nursing and midwifery, worked in hospital and community midwifery for several years. Interests in community relations led to work in Lambeth community. Later leading a Black Health Forum in key areas of the country. Her call to the ministry is an ecumenical one steming from a rich RC upbringing to a Methodist lay worker in central London. That led to pioneer the Black Theology course moving on to a BA Degree in Theology at Birmingham University. She is presently assistant priest/project manager St Philips Church, West Bromwich, West Midlands.

REV OSAGUMWENGIE JESUOROBO (Minister)

Pastor-President, God's Time Ministries Ridley Christian Centre, 94 Upton Lane, Forest Gate, London, E7 9LW

PLACE OF BIRTH: Nigeria, 26.1.52
MARITAL STATUS: Married
CHILDREN: Eight (Donovan, Oghosa, Tamara, Jason, Eseosa, Etinosa, Ivie, Orirosa)
COLLEGE: University of Kano, College of Further Education
ACADEMIC QUALIFICATIONS: Certificate in TV Production, Diploma in Technology
PROFESSIONAL QUALIFICATIONS: Certificate in Management, Certificate in International Travel and Services
DIRECTORSHIPS: Pastor / President
MEMBERSHIPS: Evangelical Alliance International Ministerial Council Of Great Britain etc.
HONOURS/AWARDS: TU Cameraman of The Year 1980, Salesman 1994 BCCI, British Chambers of Commerce and Industry 1994
HOBBIES AND INTERESTS: Current affairs, football, human resources
EMAIL: ojesuorobo@Hotmail.com
PERSONAL PROFILE: An honest, hardworking, highly skilled individual with 20 years experience as a professional TV cameraman as well as a wide range of transferable skills obtained in a variety of work situations. A minister of religion with radical faith who is often called to leadership worldwide. Develops and advances human resources.
NOMINATED BY: Sam Jenyo

MR ERROL JOHN (Assistant Director)

Barbados - London East Anglian and South East Region, Bowes Lyan House, St Georges Way, Stevenage, SG1 1XY

PLACE OF BIRTH: St Vincent
MARITAL STATUS: Married
CHILDREN: Two (Emeka, Sukina)
COLLEGE: Stevenage and Middlesex
ACADEMIC QUALIFICATIONS: MA Deviance and Social Policy (MBA Current Herts University)
PROFESSIONAL QUALIFICATIONS: Certificate in Qualified Social Work. Dip Social Sciences
DIRECTORSHIPS: Director of Heights Community Development Agency
MEMBERSHIPS: Director - Jazz Jamaica Ltd
HOBBIES AND INTERESTS: Music, arts politics family, relaxing, entertaining
PERSONAL PROFILE: I have been active in the Black self help movement for over 25 years and founder member of three organisations. Author of two book and several articles (social work/equality). Producer of two plays 'Rainbow Uprising' and 'New Town Boys'. Promoted numerous events and run record labels and manager of artists including Jazz Jamaica and Rico Rodriguez.
NOMINATED BY: Sharon Aitkin

I have been active in the Black self help movement for over 25 years and founder member of three organisations.

ERROL JOHN

MR DANNY JOHN-JULES (Entertainer)

Jonathan Altaras Associates Ltd, 2nd Floor, 13 Shorts Garden, London, WC2H 9AT

PLACE OF BIRTH: London, 16.9.60
MARITAL STATUS: Single
DIRECTORSHIPS: DNA Productions (KMBA) Ltd
MEMBERSHIPS: MU Equity, PRS
HOBBIES AND INTERESTS: Music, theatre, swimming, clubbing
PERSONAL PROFILE: Well what can I say? I just love performing arts and I am fascinated by performers, taking from them what I think I need to progress. Inspired and occasionally put off, I tread onwards in the pursuit of excellence and pray that maybe some other Black kids will take from me too.

DR CHRISTOPHER ADRIAN JOHNSON
(Project Consultant)

Millennium Regeneration Research Institute (MRRI), 69 Oakdale Road, Manor House, London, N4 1NU

PLACE OF BIRTH: Guyana, 22.10.57
MARITAL STATUS: Married
CHILDREN: Three (Angela, Latoya, Mark)
COLLEGE: Cambridge International University of London
ACADEMIC QUALIFICATIONS: MBA (Marketing, PhD in Business Management
PROFESSIONAL QUALIFICATIONS: Industrial Relations, Media Studies, Sociology, PR
DIRECTORSHIPS: I - (MMRI)
MEMBERSHIPS: Cambridge Society Federation of Small Businesses
HONOURS/AWARDS: Nuffield Fellowship, Fellowship of North London Common Purpose, Life long fellowship awarded by the Faculty of Management Science
HOBBIES AND INTERESTS: Cricket, martial arts, research, travel, current affairs
PERSONAL PROFILE: I am journalist, author research and business journalism and with vast experience in economic development and enterprise management. I have developed in recent times a range of strategies and practises for Black business development in the UK. I am still in project management information technology and strategic planning. Recently been awarded a Doctorate in Business Management with Distinction.
NOMINATED BY: Ms Sandra Corbin-Kelly

MR LINTON KWESI JOHNSON
(Poet-Publisher-Record Company)

LKJ Records, PO Box 623, Herne Hill, London, SE24 0LS

PLACE OF BIRTH: Chapelton, 24.8.52
COLLEGE: Goldsmiths University, University of London
ACADEMIC QUALIFICATIONS: Sociology
DIRECTORSHIPS: Founder Member Creation For Liberation
MEMBERSHIPS: Black Panther
HONOURS/AWARDS: Award at the XIII Premo Internazionale Ultimo Novecento for Poetry and Popular Music1990.
PERSONAL PROFILE: In 1977 Linton was awarded a C Day Lewis Fellowship becoming the writer-in-residence for the London Borough of Lambeth for that year. In 1974 Race Today published his first collection of poetry. 1981 LKJ, Johnson's own record label was launched. During the 1980's he became immersed in journalism, working closely with the Brixton-based Race Today collective. From 1985-88 he was a reporter on Channel 4's 'The Bandung File'. In 1998 he released 'More Time'. He is known and revered as the world's first reggae poet. Demand increasing for his voice-overs.
NOMINATED BY: Sharon Aitkin

MR MORGAN JOHNSON (Stunt Arranger-Performer)

British Actors Equity Stunt Register, St Vincents Cottages, Wiltshire Lane, Eastcote, Middlesex, HA5 2CZ

PLACE OF BIRTH: Nottingham, 5.3.58
MARITAL STATUS: Single (Divorced)
CHILDREN: Two (Summer, Stacey)
COLLEGE: Bourneville School of Art
ACADEMIC QUALIFICATIONS: 2 A-Levels, 7 O-Levels
PROFESSIONAL QUALIFICATIONS: Too Numerous To Mention
MEMBERSHIPS: ILAM, IHBC, FHT, NCF
HONOURS/AWARDS: Honorary Citizen of Maryland US, Chief Constables Commedation
HOBBIES AND INTERESTS: Sports, skydiving, music, socialising, keep fit
EMAIL: Mojostunts@AOL
PERSONAL PROFILE: Having served 20 years in the Royal Marine Commandos. Morgan has been a stuntperformer for eight years in such films as: 'Star Wars'; 'Lost In Space', 'Fifth Element' and various TV productions.

MR NEIL ANTHONY JOHNSON (Actor-Singer)

John Markham Associates (Agent),

PLACE OF BIRTH: Gloucester, 25.4.66
MARITAL STATUS: Single
ACADEMIC QUALIFICATIONS: London Studio Centre of Performing Arts
PROFESSIONAL QUALIFICATIONS: Three Year Performance Course, Two Year Vocal Training under the guidance of Tony Pedretti.
MEMBERSHIPS: Full Equity Member
PERSONAL PROFILE: Trained for three years, parts in musical's 'On The Town'; 'Cats'; 'Clockwork Orange'; 'Song and Dance'; 'Soul's In Motion'; 'Fame The Musical'; 'Oklahoma' and 'Chicago'. Television work has included two Royal Variety performances in the honour of the Queen Mother. Neil has taught extensively in the field of jazz dance. He has taught at the West Street Ballet School as well as Sweden and International Dance School, Kent. He has also choreographed works for the Celebration of Dance held in Sardinia.

MISS VERONICA JOHNSON (Parent-Student)

Black Star Housing Association Ltd, 4 Park Avenue, Birmingham, B18 5NE

PLACE OF BIRTH: England, 31.5.62
MARITAL STATUS: Single
CHILDREN: Three (Simone Bowen, Josh Bowen, Nathan Johnson)
COLLEGE: University of Central England
ACADEMIC QUALIFICATIONS: O-Levels, CSE, NVQ Cert HE
MEMBERSHIPS: Board Of Management and Boards Sub Committee
HOBBIES AND INTERESTS: Reading, interested in people
PERSONAL PROFILE: Like most single mothers with three children, I try to balance the social roles that society has bestowed me and balance it with my own education of worth. I am trying to be a female role model for my children. This shows that they can aspire to whatever they need to. I have a stern expression but I am approachable, caring and a good listener. As I am Black Stars' first tenant, being on their Board of Committee and Management was an immense stepping stone for me.

MR WIL JOHNSON (Actor)

PLACE OF BIRTH: London, 18.4.65
HOBBIES AND INTERESTS: Singing, rapping, break-dancing, boxing, jogging, writing
PERSONAL PROFILE: Don Byron in 'Baby Mother' (film); 'Midnight Breaks' (film); TV series 'Cracker' and 'Anna Lee'.
Theatre includes ' A Mad World My Masters' Shakespeare Globe, 'Fuente Ovejuna' at the Royal National Theatre. Co-director in Corazon Productions Ltd film company.

DR CECILY JONES (Lecturer)

Dept. Of Sociology Goldsmiths College, Warmington Tower, Lewisham Way, New Cross, London, SE14 6NW

PLACE OF BIRTH: Barbados, 5/7/60
MARITAL STATUS: Married
CHILDREN: One (Maxine)
COLLEGE: Sussex, Warwick, University of London
ACADEMIC QUALIFICATIONS: BA; (1988) M.A. (1990); PhD (1998), Sociology
HOBBIES AND INTERESTS: Caribbean slavery, history, gender, race
EMAIL: Cecily.forde@virgin.net

'Having served 20 years in the Royal Marine Commandos. Morgan has been a stuntperformer for eight years in such films as: 'Star Wars'; 'Lost In Space', 'Fifth Element' and various TV productions'

MORGAN JOHNSON

MR QUINCY JONES (Artist)

WEA Records, The Warner Buildings, 28 Kensington Church Street, London, W8 4EP

HONOURS/AWARDS: 25 Grammies (second in the all-time list) and Most Nominated Grammy Artist with 77 nominations in total
PERSONAL PROFILE: In a career that has spanned four decades, Quincy has fused pop, soul, hip-hop, jazz, classical, African and Brazilian music and has traversed virtually every medium from records, live performances, movies and television. As a producer of the historic 'We Are The World' and Michael Jackson's solo albums 'Off The Wall', 'Bad' and 'Thriller', Quincy Jones is undoubtedly one of the most successful and respected figures in the entertainment world. Multi-Grammy award winning legend returns with a spectacular double album.

MR VALENTINO JONES (Director-Teacher)

Josina Machel Supplementary School,

PLACE OF BIRTH: Grenada, 17.7.40
MARITAL STATUS: Married
CHILDREN: Two (Radifa, Lumumba)
COLLEGE: Roehampton Institute
ACADEMIC QUALIFICATIONS: Cert. Teacher
PROFESSIONAL QUALIFICATIONS: BA Hons Sociology of Education
DIRECTORSHIPS: Josina Machel Supplementary School
HOBBIES AND INTERESTS: Writing novels, history of Josina School, completing another Caribbean novel
PERSONAL PROFILE: I was born in Grenada. Studied in the UK. Worked as a youth and community worker. Established and member of Black Voluntary Organisation. Also campaigned for race equality, and Black self help organisations. Founded the JMSS School in 1976 which still functions every Saturday. Published a history of the school and a novel based in the Caribbean.
NOMINATED BY: F.Edwards

MS JENNIFER JORDAN (Actor)

14 Eversleigh Road, Battersea, London, SW11 5UZ

PLACE OF BIRTH: England, 10.9.67
MARITAL STATUS: Single
CHILDREN: One (Nyisha)
COLLEGE: Rose-Bruford College
ACADEMIC QUALIFICATIONS: BA Hons 2:1
HOBBIES AND INTERESTS: Writing, directing, music, politics, cooking, travelling
PERSONAL PROFILE: I had to overcome an amazing amount of fears and anxiety in order to achieve my goal in the performing arts. I had to deal with my shyness. Which I was able to do by allowing my determination, focus and creativity to shine.

CLLR BERTHA JOAN JOSEPH (Business Manager)

PLACE OF BIRTH: Dominica, 18.7.55
MARITAL STATUS: Single
CHILDREN: Two (Marcel, Darwin Ramlal)
COLLEGE: College of the Virgin Islands
HONOURS/AWARDS: Hansib Award, Honours US History
PERSONAL PROFILE: Brent councillor since 1986. First African Caribbean mayor for the London Borough of Brent. First female chair of leisure services, first female Black chair of regeneration committee.
NOMINATED BY: Ansel Wong

First African Caribbean mayor for the London Borough of Brent

BERTHA JOAN JOSEPH

MS ELLIN JOYCE JOSEPH (Area Child Protection Officer)

Officer for East Herts, Hertfordshire Local Education Council, 50 Ramsdell, Bedwell, Stevenage, Herts, SS1 1QY

PLACE OF BIRTH: Trindad, 5.4.54
MARITAL STATUS: Divorced
CHILDREN: Five (Michelle, Joe Junior, Nicole, Kyle, Melissa)
COLLEGE: Stevenage College, Warwickshire University CEDC
PROFESSIONAL QUALIFICATIONS: MEd Postgraduate c/e Dip SW, RSA Business/Secretarial Dip.
DIRECTORSHIPS: Magistrate For East Herts Bench (4 Years)
MEMBERSHIPS: Stevenage First Carnival Queen 1982
HOBBIES AND INTERESTS: Music, dancing, community social events
PERSONAL PROFILE: When my parents moved to Stevenage from London in 1968, I remember crying nearly all the way on the journey to Stevenage. The highlight of my life is that as a Black woman and single parent I have been given the opportunities to excel my knowledge and capabilities within Hertfordshire. I have progressed from being a medical secretary to area education child protection officer for east Herts, four years as a magistrate, and in 1997, as a part-time student with Warwickshire University, achieved a postgraduate MEd in Community Education, and over twenty-five years active involvement with Stevenage ethnic minority groups in the community.

MS KAMY JOSEPH (Social Worker-Manager)

(Freelance Trainer), 50 Hillfield Park, Muswell Hill, London, N10 3QS

PLACE OF BIRTH: Brunei, 10.8.49
MARITAL STATUS: Single
COLLEGE: Brunei Teachers College
ACADEMIC QUALIFICATIONS: Teachers: Diploma
PROFESSIONAL QUALIFICATIONS: Social Worker (CQKCCYP)
DIRECTORSHIPS: Own Business -Little Steps Gym
HOBBIES AND INTERESTS: Music, cinema, keeping fit, entertainment
PERSONAL PROFILE: Having worked and trained as a primary schoolteacher, I arrived in England in 1972, worked my way up from a residential social worker to manage residential services in Haringey, Hammersmith and Fulham. First Black woman in Haringey to manage residential services in 1976. I am committed to ensuring equal access for children and families of minority ethnic groups in service provision and delivery.

MR MARC JOSEPH (Footballer)

Cambridge United FC, Abbey Stadium, Newmarket Road, Cambridge, CB5 8LN

PLACE OF BIRTH: Leicester, 10.11.76
PROFESSIONAL QUALIFICATIONS: 87 League Appearances
PERSONAL PROFILE: Marc Joseph was on schoolboy form at Derby County. He came to the Abbey for trials and was accepted for a two year YTS. Marc is quick, cool and comfortable on the ball into the opposition box from the sidelines. Marc was an ever-present this season until he suffered a thigh injury, Marc soon picked up the threads of his excellent partnership with Andy Duncan and he is becoming more composed and a confident player.

MISS MICHELLE JOSEPH (Actress)

Agent Peter Brooks, 19 Denmark Street, London, WC2H 8NA

PLACE OF BIRTH: London, 11.5.70
MARITAL STATUS: Single
COLLEGE: Rose Bruford College
ACADEMIC QUALIFICATIONS: BA Hons 1st Hons Degree, City and Guild in Teaching
PROFESSIONAL QUALIFICATIONS: Seven year experience in TV, radio and theatre
MEMBERSHIPS: Equity
HOBBIES AND INTERESTS: Cinema, theatre, reading
PERSONAL PROFILE: Left drama school with a degree in July 1992. Been working in TV, radio and the theatre professionally since then. Most remembered for 'Della' in 'Eastenders'. I love to sing. I most enjoyed playing Katrina in 'Mother Courage' at The Royal National Theatre (RNT) and Tanya in 'Sounds in Sessions'. by Tyrone Higgins.

MR RICHARD KARLSSON (ACTOR)

Lauderdale House, 11 Gower Street, London, WC1E 2HB

PLACE OF BIRTH: Wales, 20.6.68
MARITAL STATUS: Single
COLLEGE: Webber Douglas Academy
ACADEMIC QUALIFICATIONS: Diploma Professional Acting
EMAIL: Karlsson@lawless.demon.co.uk
PERSONAL PROFILE: Sir Lancelot in 'Merlin' and Pau Puk Keewis in 'Hiawatha' at Royal Lyceum Theatre, Prince of Morocco in 'Merchant of Venice', Ralph in 'Bouncers on the stage':-Dudley Figgis in 'Crisis' (BBC World Service), TV:- 'Cat's Eyes', 'Nigel in Cold Lazarus', Film: 'Two Golden Balls' and 'Going for Broke'.

MS CAROL KENNEDY (TOWN CENTRE MANAGER)

Wood Green Town Centre Management, Unit 91, Shopping City, High Road, Wood Green, London, N22 6YQ

PLACE OF BIRTH: US, 27.11.65
MARITAL STATUS: Separated
COLLEGE: St Petersburg Jnr. College
ACADEMIC QUALIFICATIONS: Diploma Business Studies
PROFESSIONAL QUALIFICATIONS: Qualified Business Advisor, C&G Teaching Qualification
DIRECTORSHIPS: Aim for Business Ltd
MEMBERSHIPS: Association Town Centre Management, North London Chamber of Commerce
HONOURS/AWARDS: Met Police Commander's Commendation
HOBBIES AND INTERESTS: Motorcycling, art, writing, socialising, travel, guitar
PERSONAL PROFILE: As Town Centre Manager, Carol Kennedy has successfully formed a partnership between local business, residents, Haringey Council and the Metropolitan Police to reduce crime drastically and aid in the multi-million pound regeneration project to make Wood Green one of the most up and coming town centres in North London.

MR GLAMMA KID (ARTIST)

WEA Records, The Warner Buildings, 28 Kensington Church Street, London, W8 4EP

HONOURS/AWARDS: MOBO Award for Best Reggae Act 1998
PERSONAL PROFILE: Nineteen year old Glamma Kid is a phenomenon about to go supernova. A native of Hackney, he had already carved a niche as Britain's hottest new reggae star. Over the next few years, he emerged a major talent as the DJ with the Glamma Guard sound system, playing alongside Chris Goldfinger's Asha World Sound System among others. From crafting his own dub plates for the sound system it was a short step to making his own records.

MR DON KINCH (LECTURER-WRITER)

Handsworth College, 28 Grafton Road, Handsworth, Birmingham, B21 9DP

PLACE OF BIRTH: Barbados, 31.10.54
MARITAL STATUS: Married
CHILDREN: Three (Soweto, Oluwaya-Toyin, Mensah)
COLLEGE: University of London
ACADEMIC QUALIFICATIONS: MA Anthropology
PROFESSIONAL QUALIFICATIONS: Teachers Certificate of Education
DIRECTORSHIPS: Harambee, Nu Century Arts
MEMBERSHIPS: NUT; Writers Guild
HONOURS/AWARDS: SOBA Award Theatre
HOBBIES AND INTERESTS: Cricket, tennis, badminton, board-games
EMAIL: donkinch@aol.com
PERSONAL PROFILE: Don Kinch is a seminal figure in the development of Black political theatre in Britain. The Barbados born playwright/lecturer delineates the Black experience in historical terms, and through the forms of music, poetry, and dance. One of his early works, 'Coming up for Air', examined the pathological effect of racism and the crisis of an emergent Black middleclass.
NOMINATED BY: Sharon Aitkin

MISS ROWENA KING (ACTOR)

ICM, International Creative Management,

PLACE OF BIRTH: London, 14.2.69
MARITAL STATUS: Single
COLLEGE: Mountview Theatre School
ACADEMIC QUALIFICATIONS: Three Year Dramatic Diploma

DR AIDA KISANGA (MANAGING DIRECTOR-ARCHITECT)

Managing Director, Builders Resources Ltd, No.17 Kent House, Bourne Road, Bexley, DA5 1LR

PLACE OF BIRTH: Tanzania, 23.3.57
MARITAL STATUS: Married
CHILDREN: Two (Luther, Alexander)
COLLEGE: University of London
ACADEMIC QUALIFICATIONS: PhD, Msc, Dip. (Arch.)
DIRECTORSHIPS: Managing Director, Builders Resources Ltd
MEMBERSHIPS: Management Committee of Barnet Overseas Students Housing Association Ltd
HONOURS/AWARDS: Federation of British University Women, International Development Research Centre, Canada
HOBBIES AND INTERESTS: Travelling
EMAIL: A.Kisanga@btinternet.co
PERSONAL PROFILE: Established and runs a consultancy and procurement company - 'Builders Resources Ltd' with a sister company in Tanzania. Managing editor of 'African Construction Bulletin' a quarterly newsletter on construction news and business opportunities in sub-saharan Africa. Current interests: Working with organisations in East and Southern Africa to develop local capacity of indigenous construction companies.
NOMINATED BY: Mark Anthony Lobban

CARMEN KNIGHT (ACTRESS-DANCER-FITNESS INSTRUCTOR)

c/o Audrey Benjamin Agency, 278A Elgin Avenue, Maida Vale, London, W9 1JR

PLACE OF BIRTH: Bristol, 2.8.64
MARITAL STATUS: Single
CHILDREN: One (Kamau Knight - Delandro)
ACADEMIC QUALIFICATIONS: Basic GCSEs
PROFESSIONAL QUALIFICATIONS: RSA Exercise To Music
MEMBERSHIPS: British Actors Equity, Fitness Professionals
HOBBIES AND INTERESTS: Yoga-meditation, travel, reading, food, films
PERSONAL PROFILE: Trained with Arts Freedom Theatre Bristol, in dance and drama touring England, Germany and Africa. Landed roles in 'One Foot In The Grave' and 'US Girls' for BBC 'Expert Witness' and 'Redhanded' for LWT. Theatre work has taken me all over England and Italy. Film roles include 'Water' and 'Paper Mask'.

MR ARDI KOLAH (PUBLIC RELATIONS-MARKETING)

Director, Maverick (UK) Limited, 32 Kohat Road, London, SW19 8LD

PLACE OF BIRTH: London, 23.10.61
MARITAL STATUS: Single
COLLEGE: Kingston University, Kings College London
ACADEMIC QUALIFICATIONS: BA Hons, LL.M Lond
PROFESSIONAL QUALIFICATIONS: MIPR, MCIM, FRSA, Chartered Marketer
DIRECTORSHIPS: Maverick (UK) Ltd
MEMBERSHIPS: Chartered Institute Marketing Council Member, Institute of Public Relations
HONOURS/AWARDS: CIM/CSSA Marketing Award ABSA Award, Finalist Emma Award, Finalist PR Week Awards
HOBBIES AND INTERESTS: Media, tennis, foreign travel
EMAIL: akolah@amsn.com
PERSONAL PROFILE: Marketing and communication professional. International clients include WHO Cancer Programme. Books include 'Measuring Successful Sponsorship' and 'Maximising the value of sports sponsorship' for the FT. Council member of the Institute of Public Relations, a chartered marketer of the Chartered Institute of Marketing and a Fellow of the Royal Society of Arts.
NOMINATED BY: Tetteh Kofi

AICHA KOSSOKO (Actress)

Method & Madness, Grantham-Hazeldine, 5 Blenheim Street, New Bond Street, London, W1Y 9LB

PLACE OF BIRTH: France, 2.5.67
MARITAL STATUS: Engaged
COLLEGE: Philippe Gauhier School, Jean Darnel School
HOBBIES AND INTERESTS: Reading, sport, walking, music
PERSONAL PROFILE: Currently touring five plays for three years with Mike Alfreds' Method and Madness. Roles include Raeyevskaya in Cherry Orchard. Previous work includes Lucetta in 'The Two Gentlemen of Verona' at the Globe and Octavia (Antony and Cleopatra) and Calphurnia (Julius Caesar) for Vanessa and Corin Redgrave's Moving Theatre in London and US.

MS JOSEPHINE KWHALI (Head of Children's Resources)

London Borough of Greenwich, Social Services Department, Nelson House, 50 Wellington Street, Woolwich, London, SE26 6LY

PLACE OF BIRTH: United Kingdom, 26.2.57
MARITAL STATUS: Partnered
CHILDREN: One (Nadia)
COLLEGE: North London University, Selly Oak Colleges, Brunel University
ACADEMIC QUALIFICATIONS: Master of Philosophy (M.Phil)
PROFESSIONAL QUALIFICATIONS: CQSW, CRCCYP, National Nursery Nursing Board , Master of Philosophy (M.Phil) in Social Work
MEMBERSHIPS: British Association of Social Workers
HOBBIES AND INTERESTS: Travel, reading, political debate, cooking, outdoors, cycling
PERSONAL PROFILE: Learnt at a young age the necessity of strength and struggle in order to achieve and overcome race, class and gender inequalities. Childhood shaped by apartheid struggle, civil rights and lived experience of British racism. Became first Black female manager and first Black holder of M Phil. in Social Work.

MR MICHAEL KYD (Footballer)

Cambridge United FC, , Abbey Stadium, Newmarket Road, Cambridge, CB5 8LN

PLACE OF BIRTH: London, 21.5.77
PROFESSIONAL QUALIFICATIONS: 20 League Goals & 105 League Appearances
PERSONAL PROFILE: Michael Kyd has already completed three seasons as a professional at Cambridge United. He made his league debut as a substitute in August 1994 against Chester City while still a trainee. 1995-96 was an eventful season for the teenager, he scored the first goal of the season. After a bright start to last season, with four goals in the first eight games, Michael signed a new three-year deal.

'Learnt at a young age the necessity of strength and struggle in order to achieve and overcome race, class and gender inequalities. Childhood shaped by apartheid struggle, civil rights and lived experience of British racism. Became first Black female manager and first Black holder of M Phil. in Social Work'

JOSEPHINE KWHALI

Entrants in the Black Who's Who 1999 have been nominated for their achievements and contributions. You can nominate someone who deserves to be in the Black Who's Who 2000, nominate them today.

Entries are free

Send in your nominations, including name, contact address and telephone number to: Books Division, Ethnic Media Group, 148 Cambridge Heath Road, London E1 5QJ

MS YVONNE LAING (Group Advertisement Director)

Sales, Voice Group Limited, Nu Vox House, 370 Coldharbour Lane, London, SW9 8PL

PLACE OF BIRTH: London, 3.11.64
MARITAL STATUS: Single
COLLEGE: Kings College
ACADEMIC QUALIFICATIONS: Health Visiting
PROFESSIONAL QUALIFICATIONS: CAM
MEMBERSHIPS: Institute of Directors
HONOURS/AWARDS: Runner up for Black Business Woman of the Year (1997)
HOBBIES AND INTERESTS: Physical training, vocalist, writing, travel
PERSONAL PROFILE: Dogged determination best describes me. Left midwifery 1985 needed a new challenge. Sold mortgages/pensions for two years for Abbey Life. Group leader at News International working on the Sun and the Times. Voice Publication's from 1992, started as sales executive - managing director in 1995.

MR JUNIOR LANIYAN (Actor-Dancer)

Rossmore Personal Management,

PLACE OF BIRTH: Lewisham, 1.3.82
MARITAL STATUS: Single
HONOURS/AWARDS: Various dance and drama awards while at school
HOBBIES AND INTERESTS: Basketball, skating, ice-skating
PERSONAL PROFILE: I've studied at the Sylvia Young Theatre School, my credits include the solo opening of the William Louthar Memorial at the Cochrane Theatre, touring with the legendary Tobias Tak, the 1990 Brit Awards with Michael Jackson, BBC's 'A Respectable Track' and 'Family Affairs'. I also taught jazz tap at Dance Work, the Sylvia Young Theatre School as well as other professional establishments.

MR DONOVAN K LAWRENCE (Actor-Singer-Designer)

PLACE OF BIRTH: Jamaica, 5.7.68
MARITAL STATUS: Single
COLLEGE: London College of Fashion
ACADEMIC QUALIFICATIONS: ACFI Halute Couture Bespoke Tailoring
MEMBERSHIPS: London Community Gospel Choir
HOBBIES AND INTERESTS: Keeping fit, swimming
PERSONAL PROFILE: I have been privileged to be in a few West End shows ('Mama I Want To Sing', 'Jesus Christ Superstar') I understudied the role of Jesus and Pipin. Also I have sung with quite a number of established singers but am pursuing a recording career with my family band Inesse.

LADY MERANDA M LAWRENCE (Authoress-Writer)

Admin. Receptionist, Age Concern Hackney, Words of Wisdom Publishing, PO Box 6816, Hackney, London, E8 4ST

PLACE OF BIRTH: Jamaica, 22.12.49
MARITAL STATUS: Divorced
CHILDREN: Three (Janet, Pauline, Lee)
COLLEGE: Hackney College
ACADEMIC QUALIFICATIONS: Information Technology Qualification
PROFESSIONAL QUALIFICATIONS: Receptionist/Telephonist, Diploma
DIRECTORSHIPS: Words of Wisdom
MEMBERSHIPS: Hoxton Hall Theatre
HONOURS/AWARDS: Local Community Books Award
HOBBIES AND INTERESTS: Creative writing, poetess, music, storytelling, lyricist
PERSONAL PROFILE: Creative, polite, passionate, honest, outspoken, private, hardworking, thoughtful, intelligent, understanding, giving, communicative, entertaining, love walking, listening to music, debating and discussion. An activist, a very deep thinker. I am a great lover of self-love to help other people in any way I can.

ROYDELLE A J LAWRENCE (Senior Law Lecturer)

Personal Investment Authority, 108 Chandos Avenue, Whetstone, London, N20 9DZ

PLACE OF BIRTH: Cuba, 16.5.21
MARITAL STATUS: Married
COLLEGE: University College London
ACADEMIC QUALIFICATIONS: LLB, LLM
PROFESSIONAL QUALIFICATIONS: Senior Law Lecturer
MEMBERSHIPS: Magistrate Association, MCC Member St Marleybone Rotary Club, West Indies Ex-Service Men and Women's Association
HONOURS/AWARDS: Justice of the Peace
HOBBIES AND INTERESTS: Gardening, sports, TV, music, travel, reading, writer
PERSONAL PROFILE: Jamaican Volunteer Service in RAF, qualified company secretary, graduate University College London, Seconded University Papua New Guinea, Law Professor Cleveland University Ohio US. Founder member Willesden International Association. Also British Caribbean Association, also WI Standing Conference administrator, lecturer, access to law.

MISS DENISE LEARY (Workshop Leader)

Voluntary Group Work Facilitator, Raleigh International Youth Development Programme,

PLACE OF BIRTH: London, 17.5.72
MARITAL STATUS: Single
COLLEGE: University of East London
ACADEMIC QUALIFICATIONS: Dip He Social Sciences Youth and Community
HOBBIES AND INTERESTS: Writing, poetry, drama, theatre, supporting youth organisations
PERSONAL PROFILE: I was brought up in East London of mixed parentage. I have been working to develop young people in the hope of making a positive difference. My background is facilitating youth theatre, theatre in education, young people's social and personal development. This work has extended to environmental, conservation and community charity work in Africa with Raleigh International.

MR SAMUEL RICHARD LEE (Director-Rtd)

Pensioner, Roots of Culture Foundation Registered Charity, 34 Windmill Road, Milton Regis, Sittingbourne, ME10 2NT

PLACE OF BIRTH: West Indies, 16.9.22
MARITAL STATUS: Married
CHILDREN: Six (Cheryl, Sherma, Dianne, Richard, Andrew, Charles)
COLLEGE: Middlesex University
ACADEMIC QUALIFICATIONS: BA Honours Diploma in Social Studies, T.C.
PROFESSIONAL QUALIFICATIONS: Teacher
DIRECTORSHIPS: Roots of Culture Foundation
MEMBERSHIPS: CHC (Medway)
HOBBIES AND INTERESTS: Writing, journalism, reading, philosophy, classics
PERSONAL PROFILE: Studied at Fircroft College, Huddersfield College, Leeds University, Teacher's Certificate, Middlesex University. BA Honours. Director of Roots Charity. Counsellor of Toynbee Hall University Settlement London, E.1. Member of CHC (Medway).
NOMINATED BY: Ansel Wong

MR ADRIAN LESTER (Actor)

Kate Feast Management, 10 Primrose Hill Studios, Fitzroy Road, London, NW1 8TR

PLACE OF BIRTH: Birmingham, 14.8.68
MARITAL STATUS: Married
PROFESSIONAL QUALIFICATIONS: Diploma Hons RADA
MEMBERSHIPS: Equity
HONOURS/AWARDS: Time Out, Olivier
HOBBIES AND INTERESTS: Martial arts, singing, dancing
PERSONAL PROFILE: Extensive theatre work; 'Six Degrees of Separation'; 'As You Like It'; 'Sweeney Todd'; 'Company'. Films Include: Granada's 'Up On The Roof'; Mike Nichol's 'Primary Colors'; Ken Brannagh's 'Loves Labours Lost'; Mary McGuckian's 'Best'; Simon Cellan Jone's 'Storm Damage'.

'Dogged determination best describes me...'

YVONNE LAING

MS LINDA LEWIS (Singer-Songwriter)

Tender Hook Music, Turpin Records, Will Knott & Simon Grace, 76 Brewer Street, London, W1R 3PH

PLACE OF BIRTH: London, 27.9.54
MARITAL STATUS: Single
CHILDREN: One (Jesse)
COLLEGE: St Ursuline's Convent
ACADEMIC QUALIFICATIONS: 3 O-Levels
MEMBERSHIPS: PRS
HONOURS/AWARDS: London Weekend TV Award Best Singer 1995
HOBBIES AND INTERESTS: Movies, reading biogs & self help, astrology, the occult
PERSONAL PROFILE: I believe I have influenced a lot of artists as I was one of the very few Black girl singers/songwriters around when I started in 1970.
NOMINATED BY: Sharon Aitkin

MS THELMA LEWIS (Parish Lay Assistant)

Parish Lay Assistant, St Anselm Roman Catholic Church, 28 Noyna Road, Tooting, London, 7PH

PLACE OF BIRTH: Guyana, 19.3.33
MARITAL STATUS: Single
COLLEGE: Polytechnic North London
ACADEMIC QUALIFICATIONS: Home Economics
PROFESSIONAL QUALIFICATIONS: General Nursing Medical Techn. Public Health
MEMBERSHIPS: Commonwealth Countries League, Royal Commonwealth Society, British Caribbean Association, Guyanese Nurses Association
HONOURS/AWARDS: Who's Who in America Science & English, Who's Who in the World
HOBBIES AND INTERESTS: Reading, dining out, meeting people, sport
PERSONAL PROFILE: Ms Lewis who is involved in a number of charities in the UK which help to improve living conditions in Guyana, has indeed been making sterling contributions to the improvement of life in communities in Guyana and the United Kingdom.

MR NAMASIKU DONALD LIANDU
(Director of Flexible Learning)

University of Abertay Dundee, Kydd Building, Bell Street, Dundee, DD1 1HG

PLACE OF BIRTH: Zambia, 13.4.59
MARITAL STATUS: Married
CHILDREN: Three (Joshua, James, Gabriella)
COLLEGE: Loughborough University
ACADEMIC QUALIFICATIONS: BSc Hons, M Ed
PROFESSIONAL QUALIFICATIONS: Chartered Accountant
MEMBERSHIPS: Institute of Chartered Accountants in England & Wales
HOBBIES AND INTERESTS: Chess, Christian way of life
EMAIL: Aetndltay.ac.uk
PERSONAL PROFILE: Currently, chair of the STUC Blackworkers Committee. A chartered accountant with a BSc. Hons in Computer Studies (Loughborough, 1984) and a Master of Education (Dundee 1998). Currently, director of Flexible Learning, lecturing in accountancy and finance in the Dundee Business School of the University of Abertay, Dundee.

MR ERIC LLOYD LINTON BEM (Engineer)

89 Dulverton Avenue, Chapelfields, Coventry, CV5 8HH

PLACE OF BIRTH: Jamaica, 17.2.28
MARITAL STATUS: Divorced
CHILDREN: Six (Eric, Howard, Michael, David, Madjorie, Yvonne)
MEMBERSHIPS: CWICA, AEUW, CREC
HONOURS/AWARDS: British Empire Medal
HOBBIES AND INTERESTS: Reading, walking, gardening
PERSONAL PROFILE: Chairman of the WICC for 14 years, official member Glen Parva Youth Custody for ten years. Trade Union member for 35 years, member of racial equality council for 20 years, Coventry City councillor.

MRS RUTH LLOYD GARRISON (Advertising Consultant)

Creative Services Consultant, Lloyd Garrison Advertising Consultancy, 46 Lakeside Road, Brook Green, London, W14 0DN

PLACE OF BIRTH: Cheshire, 14.8.64
MARITAL STATUS: Married
ACADEMIC QUALIFICATIONS: 7 O-Levels, 2 A-Levels
DIRECTORSHIPS: Creative Services Director of Wieden & Kennedy
MEMBERSHIPS: Amsterdam working on Accounts such as Nike, Coca-Cola, Microsoft
HOBBIES AND INTERESTS: Alternative health, cooking, socialising
EMAIL: Ruth@Tapestry.co.uk
PERSONAL PROFILE: In seventeen years I have risen through the ranks of the very competitive advertising media world to that of a highly respected business consultant. Although referred in Europe and the US as a skilled professional who empathises with all factors, I have managed to retain my sweet unspoilt nature.

D. GREAT ALEXANDER LOEWENTHAL
(Composer-Producer-Calypsonian)

Lion Valley Records, c/o Kingston Management, Hawks House, School Passage, Kingston-Upon-Thames, KT1 3DU

PLACE OF BIRTH: Trinidad, 14.11.48
MARITAL STATUS: Married
CHILDREN: Two (Carey, Joy)
COLLEGE: Dartington College of Arts
ACADEMIC QUALIFICATIONS: BA Hons Music, PGCE
PROFESSIONAL QUALIFICATIONS: PGCE
MEMBERSHIPS: Musicians Union, BASCA, Equity
HOBBIES AND INTERESTS: Music, cricket, politics, education
EMAIL: gm@psa.org.uk
PERSONAL PROFILE: The UK's foremost calypsonian, famous for treading on the corns of people in power, Alexander runs a community based record label 'Lion Valley Records', which is heading the new British calypso/soca/blues scene, Alexander is a regular contributor on radio and TV.

MR WYLLIE LONGMORE (Actor-Teacher)

Head of Acting, The Arden School of Theatre, 19 Torbay Road, Chorlton-Cum-Hardy, Manchester, M21 8XE

PLACE OF BIRTH: Jamaica, 2.11.40
MARITAL STATUS: Married
CHILDREN: Two (Katharine, Jessica)
COLLEGE: Rose Bruford College
ACADEMIC QUALIFICATIONS: Diploma Rose Bruford College
PROFESSIONAL QUALIFICATIONS: LRAM
DIRECTORSHIPS: Chairman Board Of Directors Contact Theatre
MEMBERSHIPS: British Actors Equity, Arts Council Advisor
HONOURS/AWARDS: Best Actor Manchester Evening News Award 1995
HOBBIES AND INTERESTS: Gardening, yoga
PERSONAL PROFILE: Resident in England since 1961. Worked with youth and community groups and in schools as a teacher of drama, in the major London drama schools a tutor and director, special lecturer in drama at University of Manchester 1977-81. As an actor worked in repertory across the country and at the Royal National Theatre. Head of acting at the Arden School since 1991.

CLLR ALISON LOWE (Housing Manager)

Manager, Leeds City Council, Timble Housing Project, 3rd Floor, Fraternal House, 45 Cheapside, Bradford, BD1 4HP

PLACE OF BIRTH: Leeds, 4.9.64
MARITAL STATUS: Engaged
CHILDREN: Two (Adam, Rosy)
COLLEGE: Leeds University
ACADEMIC QUALIFICATIONS: BA Hons in History, MA in Medieval Studies
DIRECTORSHIPS: HALT - Domestic Violence
MEMBERSHIPS: Various Women's Groups, Labour Party
HOBBIES AND INTERESTS: Keep fit, reading, eating out, cinema
PERSONAL PROFILE: Alison Lowe has been a councillor for ten years and an activist for women's rights for many more. She was also responsible for banning the racist comic Bernard Manning from all Leeds City Council's own venues. Cllr Lowe was featured in an ITV docu soap 'Family Life' which detailed the lives of her family over an eight month period in the run up to the Millennium.

MR VIBERT CLARENCE LUTHERS (Social Worker)

L & B Associates, 25 (A) Wellington Gardens, Charlton, London, SE17 7AD

PLACE OF BIRTH: Guyana, 7.9.32
MARITAL STATUS: Married
CHILDREN: Three (Stephen, Derek, Kenneth)
COLLEGE: West London College of Higher Education, Brunel University
ACADEMIC QUALIFICATIONS: CQSW/Dip Social Work Practise
PROFESSIONAL QUALIFICATIONS: Approved Social Worker, Practise Teacher, Manager of the Mental Health Act 1983, PATH founder (NHS)
DIRECTORSHIPS: Director L&B Assocaites
MEMBERSHIPS: Association of Black Social Workers and Allied Professions, Member of the Labour Party
HOBBIES AND INTERESTS: Current affairs, music, sports
PERSONAL PROFILE: I came to England in 1952. I worked in an electrical factory for 14 years and then worked in the retail trade John Lewis Partners. I also worked for the Met Police and Inner London Magistrates Court in 1973. I was elected a ward councillor for London Borough of Wandsworth as a Labour councillor. I stood down in 1990 (17 years). I was the first Black councillor for Wandsworth council. I got married in 1956 to Doreen who is white English and we are still together.

> She was also responsible for banning the racist comic Bernard Manning from all Leeds City Council's own venues
>
> **ALISON LOWE**

MR REUBEN SIMEON LYNCH
(Toastmaster-Event Consultant)

Chairman of College of Toastmasters, R.L Event Consultant, 12 Perkins Close, Salford Priors, Nr Evesham, WR11 5UZ

PLACE OF BIRTH: Montserrat, 3.3.47
MARITAL STATUS: Married
CHILDREN: Two (Natalie, Marcus)
ACADEMIC QUALIFICATIONS: City & Guilds, Food & Beverage, Work Site Management, Human Kinetics
PROFESSIONAL QUALIFICATIONS: Fellow of the College of Toastmasters
MEMBERSHIPS: Member of Northern Guild of Toastmaster, Chamber of Commerce
HONOURS/AWARDS: Army Appreciation Award, Service To Tourism for LEM/Spad Warwick
HOBBIES AND INTERESTS: Cricket, music, punch making
PERSONAL PROFILE: Was born on the Caribbean island of Montserrat, arriving in England 1963. After leaving school joined British Army serving for twenty-two and half years, the last ten as manager of an officers mess. Since leaving the army worked five years in large Midlands hotel as conference and banqueting manager. Now works as events consultant and Britain's only Black professional toastmaster.

> After leaving school joined British Army serving for twenty-two and half years, the last ten as manager of an officers mess
>
> **REUBEN SIMEON LYNCH**

Entrants in the Black Who's Who 1999 have been nominated for their achievements and contributions. You can nominate someone who deserves to be in the Black Who's Who 2000, nominate them today.

Entries are free

Send in your nominations, including name, contact address and telephone number to:

Books Division, Ethnic Media Group,

148 Cambridge Heath Road, London E1 5QJ

Carribbean Times

Caribbean Times
Incorporating African Times

Friday 5 February 1999 · BRITAIN'S ONLY QUALITY BLACK NEWSPAPER · Issue 920 · 50p

COUNTDOWN TO MISS UNIVERSE

This year's pageant in Trinidad may reach three billion people

Emmaruel Duneeath

AS THE clock ticks louder and louder towards the May 26 Miss Universe 1999 Pageant, national unease heightens about whether Trinidad can deliver, especially in light of the $57 million penalty they may pay if the facilities for the pageant are not ready on time.

But Chairman of the Trinidad and Tobago Pageant Company, Carlos John, believes such unease is unfounded and that the country would neither have to look for monies to pay the penalty, nor face failure in its plans.

He believes that the country will make the event happen and the 12 minutes which Trinidad and Tobago has been allotted to showcase various aspects of the country during the live two-hour Miss Universe show will make the country wish for more than five billion people around the world. While the details of what those 12 minutes will contain have not been

worked out, John expects that it will represent the country's variety and diversity. He outlined the plans and expectations in an interview with Trinidad's Sunday Guardian.

"It was our original intention that the private sector, not Government, would finance the pageant, but this year we have seen it as just a beauty pageant. The strategy has changed to showcase Trinidad and Tobago and highlight its investment potential and to promote the country as a unique tourist destination. The infrastructural cost improvements that we initially conceptualised are now being planned on a larger scale."

"We estimate that the cost to Government will be approximately US$12 to US$13 million. However there will be revenue from sponsorships, sale of local television rights, sale of tickets for the shows and related activities, so that may not be the final cost to the taxpayer. At this time, we anticipate that the net expenditure by Government - the net cost to the taxpayer - will be about US$8 million, or less."

With the show estimated to reach 3 billion people, one thing is certain is that the morning after the pageant, the world will know Trinidad and Tobago exists. "If that is all that is achieved in one quantum leap, it will be worth the time and the effort," John concluded.

Miss Universe 1998, Wendy Fitzwilliam, arrived last Sunday at the Norman Manley International Airport in Jamaica and made a special appearance at the Jamaica Fashion Collections on Tuesday at the French Embassy.

Carlos John: chief organiser

1998 winner, Wendy Fitzwilliam in her role Trinidad hosts this year's contest

NEED A NEW JOB? SEE **Jobs Direct** **ON PAGES 17-26**

COUNTDOWN TO THE MILLENNIUM

MRS EDITH JOAN CHRISTABEL MACAULEY JP
(Legal Administrator)

Communication Workers Union, 150 The Broadway,, Wimbledon, London, SM4 4JR

PLACE OF BIRTH: Sierra Leone, 11.4.49
MARITAL STATUS: Married
CHILDREN: One (Patricia)
COLLEGE: Anglia University
ACADEMIC QUALIFICATIONS: BA Hons
PROFESSIONAL QUALIFICATIONS: BA Hons Business Studies and Marketing
MEMBERSHIPS: Trade Union and Labour Party
HONOURS/AWARDS: Justice of the Peace
HOBBIES AND INTERESTS: Current affairs, politics, football
EMAIL: emacauleyatcwuorg
PERSONAL PROFILE: I am a magistrate at Wimbledon and I enjoy doing this work. I'm also a local councillor in Morden and I assist people of all races: I have been in my employment for 26 years. Lastly I am a Manchester United supporter.

MR CECIL BUNTING MACCORMACK
(Singer-Songwriter)

Bunny Mack, Beemac Productions, 87 James Riley Point, Carpenters Road, Stratford, London, E15 2HZ

PLACE OF BIRTH: Sierra Leone, 3.12.45
MARITAL STATUS: Married
CHILDREN: Three (Cecilia, Tracy, Kevin)
PROFESSIONAL QUALIFICATIONS: Had a hit with 'Let Me Love You' (My Sweetie) Went Gold in 1981
MEMBERSHIPS: Performing Rights Society PAMRA MCPS & and Songwriters Guild (BASCA)
HONOURS/AWARDS: Gold Disc for 'Let Me Love You'. Several other trophies
HOBBIES AND INTERESTS: Driving, dancing, guitar playing, puzzles, quizs
PERSONAL PROFILE: Third son of the late Rev. EG MacCormack and Mrs Hannah MacCormack. Started singing in the choir at Christ Church, Sierra Leone. Started playing the guitar in early 1960s, and joined 'The Echoes' band. Soon after I came to England in 1966 with 'The Sound Casters, and worked all over Europe as lead singer and guitarist. Took up solo recordings in the late 1970s, scored hit in 1980 in UK, toured Africa soon after.

JEROME MACK MBE (Management Consultant)

Managing Director, Equalities Associates Ltd, Centre for Community & Race Relations Training, Laws Hotel, Turvey, MK43 8DB

PLACE OF BIRTH: US, 8.10.44
MARITAL STATUS: Married
CHILDREN: Three (Jerome, Aisha, Charles)
COLLEGE: University of Nebraska
ACADEMIC QUALIFICATIONS: BA Sociology
DIRECTORSHIPS: Equalities Associates Ltd, Board Chamber of Commerce, Beds.
HONOURS/AWARDS: MBE
HOBBIES AND INTERESTS: Reading, travelling
PERSONAL PROFILE: American born, British resident with children of each nationality Jerome established Equalities Associates in 1987, with a view to assisting major organisations and government departments to focus on equality issues. A charismatic, modest and unassuming individual, his name is now known throughout Britain.

MR LOUIS MAHONEY (Actor)

Director-Broadcaster, Elaine Murphy Associates, 310 Aberdeen House, 22-24 Highbury Grove, London, N5 2EA

PLACE OF BIRTH: Gambia, 8.9.38
COLLEGE: King's College Medical School (Left course after 2 and a half years)
ACADEMIC QUALIFICATIONS: Changed to Drama
PROFESSIONAL QUALIFICATIONS: Central School of Speech and Drama (Swiss Cottage)
DIRECTORSHIPS: Artistic Director, Black Theatre Workshop, founder member
MEMBERSHIPS: British Actors Equity Association
HOBBIES AND INTERESTS: Reading, cricket, travel
PERSONAL PROFILE: Chairman Camden Black Artists Group, Equity Afro-Asian Committee 1978-1996, Equity council member 1976-98, vice-president of Equity 1994-96. Active in the Anti-Aparthed Movement campaigned for boycott of British TV programmes sold to apartheid South Africa. Forefront of bringing equal opportunities into the TV and broadcasting industries. Films include: 'Cry Freedom', 'White Mischief', 'Omen III'. TV: 'Faulty Towers', 'Lenny Henry Show', 'Eastenders', 'Harbour Lights'. Theatre: Royal Shakespeare Co., Almeida Theatre, West End.

CLLR YOMI MAMBU (Councillor)

Lead Member on Race, Manchester City Council,

PLACE OF BIRTH: Sierra Leone, 29.4.29
MARITAL STATUS: Divorced
CHILDREN: Five (Victor, Victoria, Valerie, Christopher, Marina)
MEMBERSHIPS: Chair of Bangladeshi Women's Project
HONOURS/AWARDS: Hansib Award 1989
HOBBIES AND INTERESTS: Reading, knitting
PERSONAL PROFILE: Councillor Mambu saw the appointment to Lord Mayor as a challenge and set out to maintain the esteem of the office. She also welcomes it as a chance to meet people throughout Manchester and to get to know them better. 1990-94 Deputy of Equal Opportunities for Manchester City Council, 1994-96 chair of Equal Opportunities for Manchester City Council, governor of Birchfields and St Lukes Schools, member of the Community Health Authority for Central Manchester, 1989-90 first Black mayor, Manchester,1990-91 deputy lord mayor.

MRS CONSTANCE MARK (Medical Secretary Rtd)

PLACE OF BIRTH: Jamaica, 21.12.23
MARITAL STATUS: Married
CHILDREN: Two (Amru Elizabeth, Stanley Roy)
COLLEGE: Cuolmer's High School Jamaica
HONOURS/AWARDS: Assoc. of Jamaicans 1997, Jamaican National 1997
PERSONAL PROFILE: Joined the British Army in 1943, served for ten years. Then joined my husband in 1954, who was playing professional cricket in County Durham. Worked at many leading hospitals, chair of Mary Secole, the Memorial Society Treasurer, Hammersmith and Fulham CRE, Gladioti Families Club.

IMAN ABDUL MASJID (Company President)

Iman Cosmetics, 135 East 55th Street, 5th Floor, New York, 10022

PLACE OF BIRTH: Somalia, 25.7.55
MARITAL STATUS: Married
CHILDREN: One (Zulekha Haywood)
COLLEGE: Nairobi University
HOBBIES AND INTERESTS: Sky diving, scuba - Needle Point
PERSONAL PROFILE: Iman was at the University of Nairobi co-ed working her way towards a degree in political science when Peter Beard (world renowned photographer spotted her) and her career as a supermodel began. After 16 years before the camera lense, Iman pursued a career in Hollywood. She then found her own cosmetic company named Iman and designed exclusively for women with skin of colour. Iman is striving to create an environment where education and communication become the focus.

MR DEAN MONROSE MCCARTHY (Lawyer)

FILEX, Cartwright Cunningham Hasfillgrove & Co. Solicitors, 282/284 Hore Street, Walthamstow, London, E17 QLP

PLACE OF BIRTH: United Kingdom, 6.1.65
MARITAL STATUS: Married
COLLEGE: University of Westminster
ACADEMIC QUALIFICATIONS: O-Level, GCSEs
PROFESSIONAL QUALIFICATIONS: Fellow of Inistitute of Legal Executives, Legal Practise Course Graduate
MEMBERSHIPS: Fellow of the Institute of Legal Executives, Law Society Member
HONOURS/AWARDS: For Best Law Paper on ILEX for year 1990-91
HOBBIES AND INTERESTS: Reading, music, singing
PERSONAL PROFILE: I am conscientious, comprehensive, competent and confident with a willingness to work hard to achieve the best results. In all things I do I put God first. I am actively involved in my local church and I am committed to helping those who need it by giving a helping hand.
NOMINATED BY: Hycinth Rowe

Joined the British Army in 1943, served for ten years

CONTANCE MARK

MISS SHELLY-ANN DESREE MCDERMOTT (STUDENT)

University of Cambridge, 6E Girdlers Road, West Kensington, London, W14 0PU

PLACE OF BIRTH: Jamaica, 21.9.78
MARITAL STATUS: Single
COLLEGE: Cambridge University
ACADEMIC QUALIFICATIONS: 10 GCSEs, inc. 2 A*, 5 Grade A's, 3 B's, A-Levels, 2 A's & 1 B
MEMBERSHIPS: CU Southern African Fund for Education, CU Black & Asian Caucaus, CU Caribbean Society, Link Africa
HONOURS/AWARDS: Outstanding Academic Achievement in the Presence of Prince Phillip
HOBBIES AND INTERESTS: Dance choreography, netball, football
EMAIL: Sadm2@cam.ac.uk

PERSONAL PROFILE: Achieved top five Human Biology A-Level marks in the country. Went up to read archaeology and anthropology at Cambridge University. Awarded first class in preliminary exams; will graduate in the year 2000. Won university prize for an essay on "Race". Working in South Africa with an NGO in summer 1999. Aspires to work with the UN.
NOMINATED BY: Ms Hyacinth A Riley

MISS KATRINA MCDOWELL (SCHOOLGIRL-ACTRESS)

PLACE OF BIRTH: Wycombe, 8.7.88
MARITAL STATUS: Single
MEMBERSHIPS: Jackie Palmer Stage School
HONOURS/AWARDS: Honours in Drama
HOBBIES AND INTERESTS: Rollerblading, reading, art, acting, dancing
PERSONAL PROFILE: A bright enthusiastic girl determined to go to the top, loves acting. She is very confident and very keen and is destined to one day become an actor. Katrina is a fun loving girl and sociable. Awarded and Honour in Drama. Her dream is to become an actor.

BISHOP HAROLD CARL MCFARLANE (MINISTER)

Built on the Rock International Ministeries, 13-19 Herald Street, Bethnal Green, London, E2 6JT

PLACE OF BIRTH: Jamaica, 26.3.39
MARITAL STATUS: Married
CHILDREN: Five (Hugh, Clinton, Angela, Navlehe, Harry)
ACADEMIC QUALIFICATIONS: BD. DD
HONOURS/AWARDS: Many Body-Building Awards
HOBBIES AND INTERESTS: Former body builder

PERSONAL PROFILE: Pasturing for 21 years assistant dean for BTI, for nine-years. Director and founder of BOTRIM Education College. Author of three books. Founder of: Man2Man Woman2Woman Conference of Ministries. Partner with Bilston College AUI for NVQ in the London region.

MR LESPAUL ANTHONY MCKAY (LECTURER)

Topaz Education Consultancy, 103 Stonebridge Road, Tottenham, London, N15 5PB

PLACE OF BIRTH: Jamaica, 23.4.58
MARITAL STATUS: Married
CHILDREN: Two (Janet Ebony, Attallah Y)
COLLEGE: London School of Economics
ACADEMIC QUALIFICATIONS: BSc Hons, Dip. Ap Social Sciences
PROFESSIONAL QUALIFICATIONS: Post Graduate Certificate of Education (PGCE) Soci: Dip Ap.TH

DIRECTORSHIPS: Topaz Education Consultancy
MEMBERSHIPS: London University Alumni Association (IOE), London Diocese Board of Schools, School Home Liaison Project: Afro Caribbean Leadership Council. Afro Caribbean Education Improvement Group: Education Extra Organisation : Caribbean Links Organisation: Researching-Writing Education Articles for Publication: Participating in community seminars arranged by myself or other organisation
PERSONAL PROFILE: My work in the Black community has been focused on raising education aspirations and standards; this includes establishing the organisation Afro Caribbean Education Improvement Group in 1988/89. I have written articles for publication in magazines/media; taken part in seminars I lecture to help raise awareness on issues: I also tutor/teach and mentor students in my programmes, run by Topaz Education Consultancy.

EILEEN MCKEN (TEACHER)

Project Leader, Jennie Lee Professional Centre, Lichfield Road, Wednesfield, Wolverhampton, WV11 3HT

PLACE OF BIRTH: Birmingham, 6.5.56
MARITAL STATUS: Separated
CHILDREN: One (Olukemi)
COLLEGE: West Midlands College of Education
ACADEMIC QUALIFICATIONS: MA in Education
PROFESSIONAL QUALIFICATIONS: Teaching Certificate OFSTED Inspector
DIRECTORSHIPS: The Black Professional Development Forum

MEMBERSHIPS: Race Equality Council, Achievement Network, School governor
HONOURS/AWARDS: Wolverhampton African Caribbean Achievers Award
HOBBIES AND INTERESTS: Reading, gardening, travelling, cultural events, eating out
PERSONAL PROFILE: Teacher for almost 20 years. Have run a supplementary class for children aged 5-15 years for past 15 years at the Afro Caribbean Cultural Centre (Wolverhampton). Established and currently manage an achievement project for African Caribbean youngsters. Invited to meet Prime Minister Tony Blair MP in recognition of contributions to education.
NOMINATED BY: Delva Campbell

MR JOSEPH MCLEAN (MANAGER)

HIV Clinical Nurse Specialist, HIV Service, , Snow Hill Centre, 26A Snow Hill, Wolverhampton, WV4 2AG

PLACE OF BIRTH: Jamaica, 8.12.58
MARITAL STATUS: Married
CHILDREN: Two (Deborah, Nina)
ACADEMIC QUALIFICATIONS: 6 O-Levels, 2 A-Levels
PROFESSIONAL QUALIFICATIONS: Registered Mental Nurse RGN/RN (US)
HOBBIES AND INTERESTS: Jogging, writing, swimming

PERSONAL PROFILE: Joined mother 1966. Trained as psychiatric and general nurse. Took RN exam in US, then got married. Trained as intensive care charge nurse in ITU Wolverhampton. 1991 left NHS to work with homeless men and HIV clients. Now manager of HIV service in Wolverhampton. Give training on HIV to nursing students, colleges and universities.
NOMINATED BY: Hycinth Rowe

MISS SUZANN MCLEAN (ACTRESS)

West Central Management, 4 East Block, Panther House, 38 Mount Pleasant, London, WC1 0AP

PLACE OF BIRTH: London, 12.9.73
MARITAL STATUS: Single
COLLEGE: Italia Conti Academy
ACADEMIC QUALIFICATIONS: 9 GCSEs Grades A & B, Economics A-Level, English A-Level, RE A-Level
PROFESSIONAL QUALIFICATIONS: Lamda Gold Diploma in Acting
MEMBERSHIPS: Equity, Actors Centre

HONOURS/AWARDS: 1990 Young Entertainer
HOBBIES AND INTERESTS: Sports, travel, films, choreography, art
EMAIL: Suzann@zanny.simplyonline.co.uk
PERSONAL PROFILE: As a young performer I have made some excellent achievements in my acting career. My work has been varied as well as challenging and my personal reviews by critics have been superb. I've worked around the UK and abroad and I am happy to be able to put back something in the community by teaching at a children's theatre school.

MRS SYLVIA DOREEN MCLEAN (NURSE-MANAGER)

Anchor Trust, 29 Martin Dene, Bexley Heath, Kent, DA6 8NA

PLACE OF BIRTH: Barbados, 16.9.47
MARITAL STATUS: Married
CHILDREN: Three (Sabrina, Graeme, Jamie)
COLLEGE: East London Certificate in Management
PROFESSIONAL QUALIFICATIONS: RGN, SCM
MEMBERSHIPS: APHA, Barbados High Commission Health & Welfare Group, Headway House-East London, School governor
HOBBIES AND INTERESTS: Helping others.
PERSONAL PROFILE: Full time mother, housewife, with three children. Trained as a nurse and midwife in England. Worked most of my time in the City and Hackney. Lived in Leytonstone for 23 years but recently moved to Bexley Heath, Kent. Still work in London and do all my community work in Hackney and Waltham Forest Still find time for Barbadians in the UK.

MR MAURICE MCLEOD (International Editor)

The Voice Newspaper, 370 Coldharbour Lane, Brixton, London, SW9 8PL

PLACE OF BIRTH: London, 3.7.69
MARITAL STATUS: Single
CHILDREN: One (Jessica)
COLLEGE: Middlesex University, City University
ACADEMIC QUALIFICATIONS: Bsc Hons Psychology
PROFESSIONAL QUALIFICATIONS: Post Graduate Dip. Journalism
MEMBERSHIPS: NUJ
HOBBIES AND INTERESTS: Music, sport, films
EMAIL: maurice.mcleod@hotmail.com
PERSONAL PROFILE: After stints at the Sunday Mirror and Sunday Times Maurice took a staff job at the Voice. He has been political editor, international editor, crime correspondent and letters editor in his time there. He has freelanced for The Express, The Observer, The Times, the Guardian and the Evening Standard and was a finalist in the 1998 Emma Awards (Best Print Journalist).

MRS BERNICE MCNAUGHTON (Counsellor)

Magistrate, Ealing Racial Equality Council, 2 The Green High Street, Ealing, London, W5 5DA

PLACE OF BIRTH: Trinidad, 2.2.31
MARITAL STATUS: Married
CHILDREN: One (Thomas)
COLLEGE: St Joseph's Convent & TVU Trinidad
ACADEMIC QUALIFICATIONS: Senior Cambridge Certificate London
PROFESSIONAL QUALIFICATIONS: Diploma in Counselling
DIRECTORSHIPS: Chair-Ealing Racial Equality Council - Ealing MENCAP
MEMBERSHIPS: Ealing Mediation Service.
TASHA Counselling Service
HONOURS/AWARDS: One - from 'La Petite Musicale' Trinidad
HOBBIES AND INTERESTS: Music, singing, art, antiques, painting, decorating cakes, world affairs
PERSONAL PROFILE: Arrived in London 1961, came from a large family, late parents: Arnold Ward Snr. civil servant JP. Agnes house-wife, community interest. Spent 40 years in voluntary community work in conjunction with full-time employment. Founder: Trinidad Folk Singers, London, Married: Daniel McNaughton, Languages: French, Spanish and French Patois.

REV LEONARD MEADE (Gospel Choir)

London Community Gospel Choir, 9 Greenwood Drive, Highams Park, London, E4 9HL

PLACE OF BIRTH: West Indies, 4.5.51
MARITAL STATUS: Married
CHILDREN: Four (Marlon, Vernetta, Leonn, Stephamie)
HOBBIES AND INTERESTS: Sports & cooking
EMAIL: Greorking@aol.com
PERSONAL PROFILE: Arrived in UK aged nine attended school until 15 years old. Left work and began learning guitar, as a teenager progressed to keyboards, realised a gift in music and began learning voice. Given the responsibility of developing a choir in church, became leader and church m/o. Began gospel band Kainos in the 1970's followed by LCGC in the 1980's.

MR PAUL J MEDFORD (Entertainer)

Actor, Singer, Dancer, c/o Annette Stone Associates, 2nd Floor, 22 Great Marlborough Street, London, W1V 1AF

PLACE OF BIRTH: London
MARITAL STATUS: Single
PROFESSIONAL QUALIFICATIONS: Trained in music, drama and dance at the Barbara Speake Stage School and Italia Conti Academy
DIRECTORSHIPS: Rising Roots Productions
HONOURS/AWARDS: Society of Black Arts Achievements Award
EMAIL: Pjmedford@aol.com
PERSONAL PROFILE: Paul became a professional entertainer at the age of five. Today he continues to sing, dance and act as well as write, direct and produce music, theatre and television. Theatre includes: 'Five Guys Named Moe' for which Paul won a Laurence Olivier Nomination 'Best actor in a Musical'.

MR KOBBY MENSA-KUMA (Chartered Architect)

Director, Kuma Environmental Design Limited, 83 Colliers Water Lane, Thorton Heath, Surrey, CR7 7LF

PLACE OF BIRTH: Ghana, 24.2.49
MARITAL STATUS: Married
COLLEGE: University of Science and Technology in Ghana, Westminster University
ACADEMIC QUALIFICATIONS: BSc Hons Environmental Design & Post Graduate Diploma in Architecture
PROFESSIONAL QUALIFICATIONS: AGIA & RIBA
MEMBERSHIPS: Chair of Society of Black Architects 1996-1998
HOBBIES AND INTERESTS: Voluntary work, travelling, writing, DIY, lawn tennis
EMAIL: Kedesign@aol.com
PERSONAL PROFILE: Kobby Kuma leads a team of four professionals in a newly formed architectural practise. Kuma Environmental Design advocates sensitive design, realistic and practical use of elements in improving the built environment. Kobby was the project architect for the Angel Square development in London.

MS ANGELA MICHAELS (Actress)

Presenter, Rhubarb Personal Management,

PLACE OF BIRTH: Nigeria
MARITAL STATUS: Single
COLLEGE: University of Greenwich
ACADEMIC QUALIFICATIONS: BA Hons Sociology with Psychology
PROFESSIONAL QUALIFICATIONS: Associate of the Imperial Society of Teachers of Dance (ALSTD)
MEMBERSHIPS: Equity
HOBBIES AND INTERESTS: Theatre, opera, travel, writing, eating out
PERSONAL PROFILE: I am committed to the creative arts and also to promoting the use of drama to enable young people to develop their potential. I love meeting people and exchanging ideas and have organised a debating society. Personal and professional development are important but family and friends are invaluable.

MR PATRICK MILLER (Actor)

c/o Jane Lehrer Associates, 100A Chalk Farm Road, London, NW1 8EH

PLACE OF BIRTH: Darlington, 4.10.63
MARITAL STATUS: Partner
CHILDREN: One (Sophie)
COLLEGE: The Bristol Old Vic Theatre School
PROFESSIONAL QUALIFICATIONS: Three Years BOV Theatre School and 13 Years as practising actor
HOBBIES AND INTERESTS: Antiques, home restoration, photography and fine arts, has painted several canvases in spare time
EMAIL: Miller.sheen@virgin.net
PERSONAL PROFILE: After graduating from drama school in 1985 Patrick has worked for the RSC in Stratford and London, the RNT, numerous regional reps including Bristol Old Vic. His last London stage performance was in 'King' . TV credits include 'The Bill', 'Casualty' and 'Prime Suspect 2'. He's currently developing his skills as a writer.

MR NIGEL MOFFATT (Writer-Playwright)

c/o Micheline Steinberg Playwrights, 409 Truimph House, London, W1R 7WF

PLACE OF BIRTH: Jamaica, 22.5.54
MARITAL STATUS: Divorced
CHILDREN: Four (Talita, Nichola, Dee, Sean)
HONOURS/AWARDS: Won The Butler Trust Prison Service Award 1997
HOBBIES AND INTERESTS: Music: playing the blues on my Guild guitar.
EMAIL: Steinplays@aol.com
PERSONAL PROFILE: Nigel began his writing career with poetry and songs. He recorded 'Peace Love And Harmony' with Paul Weller on his Respond record label. He has been writer-in-residence at the National Theatre Studio, and at the Haymarket Theatre where he wrote 'Prime Time'. Nigel is currently writing for BBC radio. He is writer-in-residence at Shrewsbury Prison. He's also literary adviser to West Midlands Arts. Nigel's new play 'Fish Ain't Bitin', was produced by BBC Radio 4.

MS TANYA MOODIE (ACTRESS)

c/o Garricks, 7 Garrick Street, London, WC2E 9AR

PLACE OF BIRTH: Canada, 16.4.72
MARITAL STATUS: Married
CHILDREN: One (Shanti)
COLLEGE: Royal Academy of Dramatic Art
ACADEMIC QUALIFICATIONS: Diploma in Acting
PROFESSIONAL QUALIFICATIONS: Trained at RADA and Graduated in 1993
MEMBERSHIPS: British Actors Equity Association
HOBBIES AND INTERESTS: I am a practising Nichiren Daishonin Buddhist, singing, songwriting, comedy writing
PERSONAL PROFILE: Born in Canada to Jamaican parents, Tanya was one of the youngest students ever to receive a scholarship to attend RADA at the age of 17. Upon graduating in 1993 Tanya has gone on to play leading roles in some of Britain's finest classical theatres for leading directors. Tanya speaks French and Swedish.

MS NICOLE MOORE (WOMEN'S SAFETY DEVELOPMENT OFFICER)

Women's Equality Unit, Nadhari Personal Development Training, 94 Felixstowe, London, N9 0DU

DATE OF BIRTH: 12.10.53
MARITAL STATUS: Single
CHILDREN: One
COLLEGE: University of Westminster, City of London University, Birkbeck College, Middlesex University
ACADEMIC QUALIFICATIONS: Black Women Writers, Motherland to 'Motherland' Black Women's History
PROFESSIONAL QUALIFICATIONS: BA Hons Degree Social Sciences, Business Management Dip., MA Work Based Learning Studies
MEMBERSHIPS: Management Committee Member of Nehanda Black Women's Organisation
HONOURS/AWARDS: Millennium Award for Imagination, Achievement and Commitment to the Community
HOBBIES AND INTERESTS: Creative writing
PERSONAL PROFILE: Nicole was born in London and is mother to a 17-year old son Andrew. Nicole is a woman of African-Caribbean descent with a bi-racial heritage. Nicole has studied Black women's literature and history. This experience has positively contributed towards developing her interest further regarding race, gender and equality issues.

MR ANDREW MORRIS (EMPLOYMENT ADVISER)

New Deal Supervisor, Action for Employment, Civil Rights (UK), 411a Brighton Road, London, SW9 7DG

PLACE OF BIRTH: London, 1.8.76
MARITAL STATUS: Single
COLLEGE: Westminster University
ACADEMIC QUALIFICATIONS: PG Diploma, Community Dev. (Current)
PROFESSIONAL QUALIFICATIONS: Diploma Comp, NVQ Business & Finance, 7 GCSEs
HONOURS/AWARDS: Community Honour 1995, Voice Cert. National and Local Achievement 1998
HOBBIES AND INTERESTS: Youth community development, politics, Black issues
PERSONAL PROFILE: Young, but influential wannabe politico. Advises Jeffrey Archer's team on youth policy in Lambeth. Aged 22, with ambitions for parliament and a keen sense of duty and dedication to Black causes. Solid background in community development and race relations, former right hand to Barrister Rudy Narayan (who sadly passed away in 1998).
NOMINATED BY: Civil Rights UK

TIA MORRIS (SCHOOLGIRL-ACTRESS)

The Jackie Palmer Stage School Agency, 30 Daws Hill Lane, High Wycombe, HP11 1PW

PLACE OF BIRTH: High Wycombe, 26.10.89
PROFESSIONAL QUALIFICATIONS: IDTA Tap Dance Primary Grade
HOBBIES AND INTERESTS: Dancing, singing, swimming, all sports
PERSONAL PROFILE: Tia is ten years old, she enjoys all sports, dancing and singing, Tia and friend dance in talent shows at local youth club. She has passed tap dancing exam hoping to do more exams in tap, ballet and drama.

MR WILLIAM MORRIS (GENERAL SECRETARY)

Transport and General Workers Union, 16 Palace Street, London, SW1E 5JD

PLACE OF BIRTH: Jamaica, 19.10.38
MARITAL STATUS: Widower
CHILDREN: Two (Garry, Clyde)
DIRECTORSHIPS: Hon Executive Bank Of England, Unity Trust Bank
HOBBIES AND INTERESTS: Walking, gardening, jazz music
EMAIL: Billmorris@tgwv.org.uk
PERSONAL PROFILE: General Secretary of the 900,000 - strong T & G. Born in Jamaica, his union career began in the Midlands in the fifties. Full-time official since 1976, culminating in election as GS in 1991. Member TUC General Council, ACAS, New Deal Task Force, Employment Appeals Tribunal and a non-executive director, Bank of England.
NOMINATED BY: Christopher Johnson MBA.

MR MARK MORRISON (ARTIST)

WEA Records, The Warner Buildings, 28 Kensington Church Street, London, W8 4EP

PLACE OF BIRTH: Leicester
HONOURS/AWARDS: Black Music Awards for Best Male Vocalist & Best Single 1996, MOBO Award for Best R'n'B Act 1996
PERSONAL PROFILE: Mark Morrison has established himself firmly at the forefront of a new breed of urban artists creating authentic contemporary British R&B. He reached Number 1 in the UK charts with the single 'Return of the Mack' - which also hit the Number 3 spot in the US. His first single of the year 'Moan 'N' Groan' has continued his chart success with yet another "Top Ten hit - his fifth in a row. Mark has gone on to support RnB giants such as Blackstreet and R Kelly.

PROF DR CHRISTOPHER MULLARD
(COMPANY CHAIRMAN-ACADEMIC)

Focus Consultancy Ltd, Elmsgate House, Steeple Ashton, Nr Trowbridge, Wiltshire, BA14 6HP

PLACE OF BIRTH: Exton, 23.11.44
MARITAL STATUS: Married
CHILDREN: Three (Jay, Jordon, Saul)
COLLEGE: University of Durham
ACADEMIC QUALIFICATIONS: Masters of Arts (MA) Doctor of Philosophy (PhD)
DIRECTORSHIPS: Focus Consultancy Ltd; Focus BV; Zebra; and Osuiosis
MEMBERSHIPS: Royal Commonwealth Society, Royal Horticultural Society, Institute of Directors and National Trust
HOBBIES AND INTERESTS: Art, theatre, gardening, swimming, travelling
PERSONAL PROFILE: Pioneered anti-discrimination laws in the 1960s; developed first UK anti-racist policies in the 1970s; published nine books; including 'Black Britain' (1973) 'Race, Power and Resistance' (1985); held first Royal Chair in Ethnic Studies at the University of Amsterdam; and currently advises clients in UK and abroad in the social management of change.
NOMINATED BY: Dame Jocelyn Barrow

MRS SOPHIA MWANGI (MEDIA RELATIONS CONSULTANT)

Journalist, 85 Daintry Close, Kenton, Harrow, Middlesex, HA3 8PT

PLACE OF BIRTH: London, 22.3.69
MARITAL STATUS: Married
CHILDREN: Two (Muthoni Claire, Adassa Njoki)
COLLEGE: Unversity of Staffordshire
ACADEMIC QUALIFICATIONS: BA Hons International Relations
HOBBIES AND INTERESTS: Reading, films, playing with my children, committed Christian, racial justice, Black history
PERSONAL PROFILE: Have worked as a press officer for the Evangelical Alliance UK and Tear Fund (Relief & Development Agency). First job was in Christian Aid's press office in 1991. Now a freelance journalist and media relations consultant. Also editor of the African and Caribbean Evangelical Alliance.

Aged 22, with ambitions for parliament and a keen sense of duty and dedication to Black causes

ANDREW MORRIS

MR RENVILLE NAYLES (HGV Driving Instructor)

178A Chroument Road, Peckham, London, SE15 4AB

PLACE OF BIRTH: Jamaica, 14.10.55
MARITAL STATUS: Single
CHILDREN: Six (Audrea, Cameka, Nadine, Tia, Aisha, Jonathan)
COLLEGE: Cornwall College
ACADEMIC QUALIFICATIONS: 3 A-Levels English, Maths, Geography
HOBBIES AND INTERESTS: Galaxy Radio presenter, community sports leader
PERSONAL PROFILE: In 1973 I came to England and joined the Army, served for nine years, seven of which were spent with Royal Engineers as a sapper driver. I have since been a driving instructor, HGV driver and a qualified Gym instructor. My main hobby has been working as a radio presenter and DJ, providing a radio station to help unite the community.

MR TREVOR NELSON (Broadcaster-Presenter)

in2music Ltd, 51 Hoxton Square, London, N1 6PB

PLACE OF BIRTH: Hackney, 7.1.64
MARITAL STATUS: Married
CHILDREN: Two (Miles, Mali)
COLLEGE: Kingsway College
ACADEMIC QUALIFICATIONS: 8 GCSESâ
DIRECTORSHIPS: In 2 Music Money Prod
HONOURS/AWARDS: Sony Bronze MOBO Best Radio DJ, Voice Community Award
EMAIL: peelyee@aol.com
PERSONAL PROFILE: Founder member of Kiss FM, he became a shareholder/director and daytime DJ of London's first legal dance station. A leading promoter and club DJ he also was head of Cooltempo Records (EMI) discovering R'n'B Lynden David Hall. Moved to Radio One where he currently hosts two shows, the first national R'n'B chart show and popular Rhythm Nation. Also now hosts two groundbreaking RnB shows, Europe wide on MTV, The Lick Chart & Late Lick.

MR JOSEPH NOBLE (Singer-Actor)

Cast of 'Mamma Mia', 50 Compton Road, Winchmore Hill, London, N21

PLACE OF BIRTH: Birmingham, 14.4.70
MARITAL STATUS: Single
COLLEGE: Middlesex University
ACADEMIC QUALIFICATIONS: BA Hons in Performing Arts
MEMBERSHIPS: Equity, Musicians Union
HOBBIES AND INTERESTS: Songwriter, pianist, new age topics
PERSONAL PROFILE: I have now been professional for nine years, my theatre work has taken me as far as Australia, Germany and throughout the UK. I have appeared in numerous productions in the West End including ' Five Guys Named Moe' and 'Miss Saigon', I continue to push myself forward.

MRS CECILE NOBREGA (Author-Composer)

President, Bronze Woman Foundation, Flat 14, 10 Nealden Street, Stockwell, London, SW9 9QX

PLACE OF BIRTH: Guyana, 1.6.19
MARITAL STATUS: Married
CHILDREN: Three (Keith Anthony, Bruce Malcolm, Eve)
COLLEGE: Hockerill, London University
ACADEMIC QUALIFICATIONS: Teachers Text Book Writer, Art, Music, Poetry
MEMBERSHIPS: International Allliance of Women-Bishops High School Alumni
HONOURS/AWARDS: Music Composition-Classical Songs-Twilight-Poetry
HOBBIES AND INTERESTS: Travel, education of women in arts, heritage, environment
PERSONAL PROFILE: Cecile Nobrega, poet, writer, composer and teacher. Winner of literary and music awards. Author of poem 'Bronze Woman' which has inspired the building of a visual monument to Caribbean and African Women for their community service.

> Author of poem 'Bronze Woman' which has inspired the building of a visual monument to Caribbean and African Women for their community service
>
> **CECILE NOBREGA**

MR TERRY NOEL JP (Steelband Advisor)

Leader BT Melodians, 60 Greenford Gardens, Greenford, Middlesex, UB6 9LZ

PLACE OF BIRTH: Trinidad, 4.2.40
MARITAL STATUS: Married
CHILDREN: Two (Sasha, Jennifer)
COLLEGE: Leicester College of Education
PROFESSIONAL QUALIFICATIONS: Youth and Community Worker
MEMBERSHIPS: Magistrates Association
HONOURS/AWARDS: JP
HOBBIES AND INTERESTS: Steel pans
PERSONAL PROFILE: Mounted police officer, Trinidad 1962-67. Psychiatric nurse Leicester 1967-70. Assistant director youth camp Trinidad 1970-73. Youth and community worker L.B Harrow 1973-65. (JP) Magistrate - Brent Court 1962- present.

MS CELESTE VERONICA NRI OBE (Managing Director)

Age Activity Centre - Wandsworth Black Elderly Project, 966 Garratt Lane, Tooting, London, SW17 0ND

PLACE OF BIRTH: Barbados
MARITAL STATUS: Divorced
CHILDREN: Four (Monique, Mary, Cyril, Debbie)
ACADEMIC QUALIFICATIONS: Cambridge School Certificate
DIRECTORSHIPS: Age Activity Centre CAB Wandsworth
HONOURS/AWARDS: Civil Award from Mayor of Wandsworth, National Council of Barbadian Associations, Barbados Independent Award, OBE
HOBBIES AND INTERESTS: Bridge, scrabble, air, sea travel
PERSONAL PROFILE: Celestri Nri managing director of Age Activity Centre arrived in Britain from Barbados in 1955. Settling in south London, she studied accountancy and later decided to explore Africa. Travelling extensively whilst in West Africa she returned to England during the Biafra war, where she has worked tirelessly towards a better Britain for the Black elderly.
NOMINATED BY: Herbert Yearwood, Barbados HC.

MR TONY IKE NWANJI (Accountant)

Nkosa Associates Ltd, 48 Fiske Court, Lansdowne Road, Tottenham, London, N17 0NA

PLACE OF BIRTH: Nigeria, 21.1.57
MARITAL STATUS: Single
COLLEGE: North London University, Brunel University
ACADEMIC QUALIFICATIONS: BA Hons, MBA, PG Diploma
PROFESSIONAL QUALIFICATIONS: MCIM, MI Mgt., AIMG, FIPFM, FFA, FCEA
DIRECTORSHIPS: Managing Director at Nkosa Associates Ltd
MEMBERSHIPS: Institute of Management & Chartered Institute of Marketing
HONOURS/AWARDS: Chartered Marketer by the Chartered Institute of Marketing
HOBBIES AND INTERESTS: Reading, writing, music, football
EMAIL: Nkosa2@aol.com
PERSONAL PROFILE: I was one of the first group of marketers to be awarded chartered marketer in October 1998 by CIM having worked for five years as a marketing manager. I have also worked for four years as an accountant and now running my own business an accountancy and marketing consultancy. I am currently reading for PhD part-time in financial management.

PRINCE CHINEDU MUNIR NWOKO (Lawyer-Solicitor)

Senior Partner, Ned Nwoko Solicitors, 259 Grays Inn Road, London, WE1X 8QT

PLACE OF BIRTH: Nigeria, 21.12.60
MARITAL STATUS: Married
CHILDREN: Five (Hannah, Omar, Tarik, Jamil, Nassar)
COLLEGE: Keele and KC, University London
ACADEMIC QUALIFICATIONS: BA Hons, LLM
PROFESSIONAL QUALIFICATIONS: Barrister-at- Law, Lincolns Inn Solicitors of Supreme Court England & Wales
DIRECTORSHIPS: LINAS Later (UK) Ltd
MEMBERSHIPS: International Bar Association Law Society, Nigerian Legal Practitioner
HONOURS/AWARDS: Best Solicitor, Best Firm 1993/98
HOBBIES AND INTERESTS: Reading, travelling, politics
PERSONAL PROFILE: Born in Nwoko Royal family in Nigeria, member Vision 2010 in Nigeria, a group put together by the government to chart the country's development into the next century. Represented Nigeria at the International Court of Justice, Hague, and at the UN Geneva. Author of two published books. A writer and social commentator.

Carribbean Times

Caribbean Times

incorporating *African Times*

Friday 8 January 1999   BRITAIN'S ONLY QUALITY BLACK NEWSPAPER   Issue 916   50p

Left: Fidel Castro shows how many decades he has been in charge since the revolution he lead in 1959. Above: Cuban youths enjoy the day's celebrations

CUBANS CELEBRATE CASTRO'S REVOLUTION

It's been 40 years since dictator Batista was overthrown

Emmanuel Dunseath

VETERAN communist leader Fidel Castro — darling of the world's radical left, bogeyman of the capitalist right — last Friday celebrated four stormy and epoch-making decades in power since his 1959 Cuban Revolution.

The one-time fiery, young guerrilla chief, now a greying septuagenarian president, was scheduled to mark the day doing what he has enjoyed most throughout his contentious life: making speeches.

Friday's celebrations of the 40th anniversary of the January 1, 1959, victory centred around a key-note Castro speech in the east of Cuba, where Castro unleashed a two-year guerrilla war against ex-dictator Fulgencio Batista.

Castro, whose oratorical stamina is almost as famous as his trademark beard, was expected to use the speech in Santiago de Cuba — which is officially considered the 'cradle of the revolution' — to underline his political survival despite four decades of US-led opposition and the collapse of his powerful ally, the Soviet Union.

The ruling Communist Party, which Castro heads, has been using this week's anniversary celebrations to pay tribute to the island's official revolutionary heroes, and to urge Cubans to keep faith in their socialist system into the 21st century.

"We are a hope for the peoples, and we represent a fair and viable alternative to solve development problems without exploitation, without neoliberalism and without national catastrophes," said one high-ranking Communist Party official, Esteban Lazo Hernandez, in an interview with state weekly newspaper *Tribuna* published on Thursday.

"For the revolutionaries of the country... to have lived these 40 years is a privilege that many in the world would like to have," added Lazo, first secretary of the Communist Party in Havana province, and member of the central Politburo. "We have faced a variety of difficulties, due to the iron blockade (trade embargo) imposed by Yankee imperialism but we are resisting and we will resist with audacity, intelligence and courage under the sure leadership of Fidel."

Cuba's entirely state-run media was full of such homages, with television playing patriotic music and showing black-and-white footage of Castro's 'barbudos' guerrillas ('the bearded ones') in the last days of the insurgent life war and early days of power.

Since Castro's revolution, he has become one of the world's best-known, longest-serving and most controversial leaders — surviving a 1961 US-backed invasion by Cuban exiles, numerous assassination plots, a 36-year-old US economic embargo, long periods of foreign isolation, the opposition of nine US presidents, and the collapse of crucial aid and trade ties with the Soviet Union.

In the streets of Havana, posters proclaimed "Viva la Revolucion!" ('Long live the Revolution!') next to one of the most famous photo-images of the era — Castro and fellow guerrilla leader Camilo Cienfuegos, both bearded, armed and dressed in the olive-green uniform of the rebel army, riding triumphant into Havana to mass acclaim on January 8, 1959.

Communist Party newspaper *Granma*, the only daily that circulates on the Caribbean

Continued on page 2

COUNTDOWN TO THE MILLENNIUM

MR LEYLAND O'BRIEN (Actor /Student)

Piccadilly Management & City College (Arden Centre), 23 New Mount Street, Manchester, M4 4DE

PLACE OF BIRTH: Manchester, 19.7.82
MARITAL STATUS: Single
COLLEGE: City College (Arden)
ACADEMIC QUALIFICATIONS: School: 7 GCSEs, 3 A's Pass, 1 C Pass
HOBBIES AND INTERESTS: Basketball, kick boxing, actor
PERSONAL PROFILE: At 16 years old focused actor negotiating major film role. At 15 years represented his school (Ducie High, Moss Side) in varied debates including one with Home Secretary Jack Straw. At 14 years competed and won kickboxing competition. At 13 competed in youth basketball league (Runners up). Also performed varied roles TV, radio and theatre.

MR TUNDE ONA OBA (Actor)

PLACE OF BIRTH: Birmingham, 22.2.73
MARITAL STATUS: Married
HOBBIES AND INTERESTS: Reading, writing
PERSONAL PROFILE: From film 'Black On Blue' as Donny Jessup. A retarded murderer to semi-regular in 'Thief Takes All', Danny Lee. Tunde has made his name from playing wild and diverse characters.

MR REX OBANO (Actor)

George Heathcote Management, 58 Northdown Street, London, N1 9BS

PLACE OF BIRTH: London, 28.1.68
MARITAL STATUS: Single
COLLEGE: University of North London
ACADEMIC QUALIFICATIONS: Philosophy (2.1)
MEMBERSHIPS: Equity
HONOURS/AWARDS: 1995 Laurence Olivier Bursary Award
PERSONAL PROFILE: Studied drama at Webber Douglas Academy of Dramatic Art (1993-96) where he was the first Black actor to win the Laurence Olivier Bursary Award (previously won by Micheal Sheen and Ewan McGregor). Member of the Royal Shakespeare Company 'Play for England' and 'Someone's Son'.

MR ANTHONY OFOEGBU (Actor)

The Actors File,

PLACE OF BIRTH: England
MARITAL STATUS: Single
CHILDREN: One (Tigone)
ACADEMIC QUALIFICATIONS: A-Level Art
MEMBERSHIPS: BBC Radio Rep
HOBBIES AND INTERESTS: Try to live well
PERSONAL PROFILE: As a founder member of Four's Company Dance Theatre his work includes 'Vice and Joy' and 'On The Good Foot' at the Theatre Royal Stratford East where he also wrote and performed 'Saxman'. He has been a BBC radio rep member and continues to work with BBC producers. He has also worked with IRDP and LBC Radio.

MR JOHN OGILVIE (Consultant Engineer)

O & O Building Services, Disney Place House, 14 Marshalsea Road, London Bridge, London, SE1 1HL

PLACE OF BIRTH: Jamaica, 26.5.49
MARITAL STATUS: Married
CHILDREN: Four (Ursula, Samantha, Jan, Oliver)
COLLEGE: South Bank University
ACADEMIC QUALIFICATIONS: B.Sc Hons Environmental Engineering
PROFESSIONAL QUALIFICATIONS: Chartered Engineer, European Engineer
DIRECTORSHIPS: Fellow Institute of Mechanical Engineers, Member of Chartered Institute of Building Services
HOBBIES AND INTERESTS: Charities, sports, disabled, community
PERSONAL PROFILE: Born in Clarendon Jamaica immigrated to England with parents in 1960. Studied at Catford Boys, South East London Technical and South Bank University, National College. Youngest project manager at John Laing, Matthew Hall Engineering and Humphries & Glasgow. Designed all building services for projects in UK, US, Canada, Jamaica, Middle and Far East.

MR DELE OGUNTIMOJU (Senior Partner)

Ogun Solicitors, 368 City Road, London, EC1V 2QA

PLACE OF BIRTH: Nigeria, 9.2.62
MARITAL STATUS: Married
CHILDREN: Two (Nike, Demi)
COLLEGE: Polytechnic of North London
ACADEMIC QUALIFICATIONS: LLB, LLM, BL ATII
PROFESSIONAL QUALIFICATIONS: Solicitor and Chartered Taxation Practitioner
DIRECTORSHIPS: Africa Centre North London Mentor Trust
HONOURS/AWARDS: New Business of the Year 1997
HOBBIES AND INTERESTS: Football, boxing, philosophy, debates
EMAIL: Ogun@globalnet.co.uk
PERSONAL PROFILE: When you are playing away (as we in the Black community are) it is unrealistic to expect the home crowd to applaud your efforts, but this should not stop you from playing the game of your life to the very best of your ability.
NOMINATED BY: Dapo Oshiyemi

MS JOYCE OHAJAH (Television Journalist)

Reporter & Presenter, Central TV (Newsroom), Carlton Studios, Lenton Lane, Nottingham, NG7 1DG

PLACE OF BIRTH: London, 24.2.66
MARITAL STATUS: Single
COLLEGE: University of Texas
ACADEMIC QUALIFICATIONS: BA Communications
MEMBERSHIPS: National Union of Journalists
HONOURS/AWARDS: TV News Broadcaster of the Year - (Highly Commended) BT Midlands Press Awards 1998
HOBBIES AND INTERESTS: Travel, badminton, Latin dancing, keyboards
PERSONAL PROFILE: Award-winning producer and presenter recognised in both England and the US. Reporter for ITN and Carlton TV (Central and West Country Television). Hosted TV and radio interview programmes in the US. Born in East London to Nigerian parents. She is the oldest of four children.
NOMINATED BY: Janette Burnette

MR OMAR F OKAI (Artistic Director)

Okai Collier Company, 103 Lexington Building, Bow Qtr, Fairfield Road, London, E3 2UH

PLACE OF BIRTH: London, 8.6.65
MARITAL STATUS: Single
COLLEGE: London Contemporary Dance School
ACADEMIC QUALIFICATIONS: Three Year Certificate In Dance & Arts, City & Guilds-Cuisine, City & Guilds-English
DIRECTORSHIPS: Artistic Director 'Okia Collier Theatre Company'
HOBBIES AND INTERESTS: Fully trained cuisine chef, salsa / lambada enthusiast
PERSONAL PROFILE: Omar is artistic director of the 'Okia' Collier Theatre Company, choreographing and writing the pieces. In addition to other directors posts, he is also an accomplished lead performer. Also international dance tutor and workshop leader. 'Viva O Carnaval'- is about to be staged at the Churchill Theatre Bromley.

FEMI OKE (TV Presenter-Producer)

Weather Presenter LWT, London News Network Television Centre, c/o MPC Entertainment, MPC House, 15-16 Maple Mews, Maida Vale, London, NW6 5UZ

PLACE OF BIRTH: London, 30.6.66
MARITAL STATUS: Married
COLLEGE: Birmingham University
ACADEMIC QUALIFICATIONS: BA Hons Degree English
MEMBERSHIPS: British Academy of Film & Television Arts
HOBBIES AND INTERESTS: Learning languages, going to the cinema, yoga
EMAIL: femoke@hotmail.com
PERSONAL PROFILE: Femi bemused her parents by not taking the typical Nigerian career path into law or medicine. Starting as a schoolgirl reporter for LBC Radio in London, she progressed to reporting and producing for BBC radio, before presenting and producing in television. Television credits include presenting 'Top of The Pops', producing 'The Mag' for Channel 5, and presenting the weather for LWT.

MR UCHENNA O OKEKE (DIPLOMAT)

Acting High Commissioner, Nigeria High Commission,

PLACE OF BIRTH: Anambra State, 4.10.44
MARITAL STATUS: Married
CHILDREN: Four (Lotenna, Ogugua, Dumebi, Chigozie)
COLLEGE: University of Nigeria
ACADEMIC QUALIFICATIONS: BA Hons Journalism
PROFESSIONAL QUALIFICATIONS: French & Italian Courses-Universite Du Benin Lome, Togo
HOBBIES AND INTERESTS: Lawn tennis, music, gardening
PERSONAL PROFILE: Mr Okeke, a Nigerian diplomat, appointed Nigeria's acting High Commissioner to the UK in Nov 1995. Before his current appointment he was the head of consular affairs of the mission in the UK. Mr Okeke's previous diplomatic postings include Rome and New York.

MR INNOCENT OKORO (SENIOR CONSULTANT LIBRARIAN)

Saudi Arabian Oil Company, 217 Winchester Road, Lower Edmonton, London, N9 9ES

PLACE OF BIRTH: Nigeria, 15.12.40
MARITAL STATUS: Married
CHILDREN: Four (Ijeoma .A., Okey A., N. Gozi, P. Okoro)
COLLEGE: Libro Univ. Chioma, C Okoro
ACADEMIC QUALIFICATIONS: Master of Library Studies (MLS) Degree
PROFESSIONAL QUALIFICATIONS: Associateship of The Library Association (ALA)
MEMBERSHIPS: Library Association (ALA) Royal Society, African Caribbean L.A
HONOURS/AWARDS: Library Association Centenary Celebrations Medal
HOBBIES AND INTERESTS: Reading, writing, research on race relations, play chess, hockey, scrabble
PERSONAL PROFILE: I was born in Nigeria, and first came to Britain as a student in December 1964. I became a chartered librarian in August 1967. I have held senior management positions in various libraries in Nigeria, Britain and Saudi Arabia.

MS ROLI MEJEBI OKORODUDU (ACTRESS)

c/o Shane Collins Associates, 39-41 New Oxford Street, London, WC1A 1BH

PLACE OF BIRTH: Surrey
MARITAL STATUS: Married
COLLEGE: UCL The Poor School
ACADEMIC QUALIFICATIONS: Human Sciences BSc Hons, RGN
PROFESSIONAL QUALIFICATIONS: Trained Actress, Trained Nurse
MEMBERSHIPS: Equity
HOBBIES AND INTERESTS: Cat lover, football, film, theatre, vegetarian, cookery, talking
PERSONAL PROFILE: Born Epsom, Surrey and educated Rosebery School, Epsom. Father Rodi Okorodudu, British, born in Nigeria. Mother-Brenda Okorodudu, British born in Morley, Leeds. Brother - Ireto Lori Okorobdudu born in London. An actress living in London with actor husband Graeme Edler. TV, theatre, film credits in drama and comedy.

DR ABDUR-RAHMAN OLAYIWOLA
(LECTURER-RESEARCHER)

Legal Practitioner, Nusra International UK Ltd, PO Box 889, London, SE15 32W

PLACE OF BIRTH: Nigeria, 1.1.55
MARITAL STATUS: Married
CHILDREN: Three (Saidat, Samait, Saeed)
COLLEGE: University of London CLSE
ACADEMIC QUALIFICATIONS: PhD, M.Phil, MSc
PROFESSIONAL QUALIFICATIONS: MCA, PGD, Legal Studies (Hons) Dip/Cert.
DIRECTORSHIPS: Nusra International
MEMBERSHIPS: Law Society Britain, IPSA/RC
HONOURS/AWARDS: First African Muslim councillor to be elected (1994) in Southwark since 1835
HOBBIES AND INTERESTS: Reading, writing, travelling, Arabic language
PERSONAL PROFILE: I was the first African Muslim and first Nigerian to be elected councillor in 1994 to Southwark Council since 1835. I was chair of under 8's committees on education, leisure and social services in Southwark Council 1995-96. I have many scholarly publications by reputable publishers.

CLLR LAZ MADUABUCHI OLEFORO
(ARCHITECT-TOWN PLANNER)

Labour Councillor, London Borough of Hackney, 63 Darville Road, Stoke Newington, London, N16 7PT

PLACE OF BIRTH: Nigeria, 15.1.41
MARITAL STATUS: Married
CHILDREN: Five (Nkechi, Nnamdi, Chima, Nnenna, Udo Ogechi)
COLLEGE: UCL, Westminster. Newcastle-upon-Tyne
ACADEMIC QUALIFICATIONS: BA Hons, Post Graduate. Diploma. UPI, MSc, FRSA
PROFESSIONAL QUALIFICATIONS: Read Architecture and Town Planning
MEMBERSHIPS: FRSA
HONOURS/AWARDS: Special Award by Nigeria Business/Oasis Promotions 1998
HOBBIES AND INTERESTS: Photography, comedy, playwriting
PERSONAL PROFILE: A self-made man. Laz left Nigeria at the age of 25 to work and study architecture and town planning in the UK. He graduated, worked before taking early retirement in 1966. He was first elected in May 1994 as a Labour councillor in East Downward Hackney. He still serves the community as a politician. Currently a senior councillor and the only African councillor in the borough.
NOMINATED BY: Sam Jenyo

MR EKUNDAYO OLOMU (IMPRESSARIO)

CEO, Dayo Olomu Associates, 18 Shirley Road, Stratford, London, E15 4HY

PLACE OF BIRTH: London, 25.6.65
MARITAL STATUS: Married
CHILDREN: Three (Oluwaseyi, Adesewa, Rolake)
COLLEGE: Morris College of Journalism
ACADEMIC QUALIFICATIONS: Diploma in Freelance Journalism
MEMBERSHIPS: National Union of Journalists
HOBBIES AND INTERESTS: Computing, music, reading, meeting people
PERSONAL PROFILE: A music promoter, agent, actor, TV presenter, freelance journalist, writer and trainer. Served as a Black mentor for Soutwark Council between 1997/98. I contribute regularly to Black magazines Focus and Newsmakers where I run a column. I am also at the University of East London in Barking studying computing and business information systems.

REV FEMI OLOWO (MINISTER-PRINCIPAL)

South London Bible College, Skillion Centre, 99-103 Lomond Grove, Chamberwell, London, SE5 7HN

PLACE OF BIRTH: Nigeria, 22.9.61
MARITAL STATUS: Married
CHILDREN: Two (Natasha (10 yrs), Sarah (6yrs))
COLLEGE: University of London, Friends International Christian University, Sheffield University
ACADEMIC QUALIFICATIONS: Bachelors in Theology; MA (Theology) (Candidate)
PROFESSIONAL QUALIFICATIONS: Ordained full-time Minister
DIRECTORSHIPS: South London Bible College, International Churches and Ministers Association
MEMBERSHIPS: Assemblies of God of GB and Ireland Evangelical Alliance; Association of Christian Counsellors
HOBBIES AND INTERESTS: Gospel music, travelling, football, table tennis, photography, guitar playing
PERSONAL PROFILE: Femi Olowo, son of former Nigerian 'Queens Counsel' lawyer and attorney-general, left his University of London law studies to study theology. He is founder and principal of South London Bible College, senior minister of Agape Christian Church, president of International Churches and Ministers Association, author and international travelling preacher.

> I was the first African Muslim and first Nigerian to be elected councillor in 1994 to Southwark Council since 1835.
>
> DR ABDUR-RAHMAN OLAYIWOLA

MR MONSURU ADETUNJI OLUMEGBON
(CHAIRMAN)

Mobak International Promotions, 44 Josephine Avenue, Brixton Hill, London, SW2 2LA

PLACE OF BIRTH: Lagos, 10.6.52
MARITAL STATUS: Married
CHILDREN: Five (Tayo, Lade, Debo, Naomi, Zac)
ACADEMIC QUALIFICATIONS: Post Graduate Diploma in Management Studies
PROFESSIONAL QUALIFICATIONS: Certificate and Diploma in Management (ABE), Associates (ACEA)
DIRECTORSHIPS: Mobak International Promotions WASPAC
MEMBERSHIPS: British Institute of Management, Allied Int. Club
HONOURS/AWARDS: Promoter of the Year 1993, 1995, 1996
HOBBIES AND INTERESTS: Music, football
PERSONAL PROFILE: In Feb 1980, I started working with Nigeria High Commission, London as a local staff. Left in June 1990 to concentrate on my music and arts ambition. I started music and arts promotion in 1985 on a small scale due to my full time job with the embassy.
NOMINATED BY: Sam Jenyo

MS LOLA ONI (NURSE DIRECTOR-LECTURER)

Brent Sickle Cell / Thalassalmia Centre, 122 High Street, Harlesden, London, NW10 4SP

PLACE OF BIRTH: Nigeria
MARITAL STATUS: Single
COLLEGE: South Bank University
ACADEMIC QUALIFICATIONS: BEd Hons
PROFESSIONAL QUALIFICATIONS: Lecturer in Health Visiting & Nursing RGN, RM, Ad.V Cert Counsellors
DIRECTORSHIPS: Brent Sickle, Thal. Centre
MEMBERSHIPS: Chair Sickle, Thalassalmia Association of Counsellors
HOBBIES AND INTERESTS: Sport, reading, writing

EMAIL: Loni@200.co.uk
PERSONAL PROFILE: Ms Oni is actively involved in promoting achievement and support of her Black community. She is currently chair of the Sickle and Thalassalmia Association of Counsellors (STAC) secretary of the Martin Luther King First Twelve. Church worker for the local church. Group leader for the Southwark Diocese Race Relations Annual Youth Conference, plus other community activities. Current chair of Organisation for Sickle Cell Anaemia Research (OSCAR).

MR OLADELE ONIYA (TELEVISION PRODUCER)

Executive Producer Entertainment, Carlton Television, 35-38 Portman Square, London, W1H 0NU

PLACE OF BIRTH: Stoke-on-Trent, 22.10.57
MARITAL STATUS: Married
CHILDREN: One (Omolola)
COLLEGE: Queen's College, Cambridge
ACADEMIC QUALIFICATIONS: MA Hons, Law, MBA in International Business
DIRECTORSHIPS: Citizen Television, Citizen Communications
MEMBERSHIPS: Royal Society

HOBBIES AND INTERESTS: Cooking, ski-ing, antiques
EMAIL: Dele.oniya@carltontv.co.uk

MR JUSTIN ONYEKA MUSIC AND ENTERTAINMENTS EDITOR)

Music & Entertainments Editor, New Nation, 1st Floor, 148 Cambridge Heath Road, London, E1 5QJ

PLACE OF BIRTH: Birmingham, 6.4.66
MARITAL STATUS: Married
CHILDREN: One (Jordan Chibueze)
COLLEGE: University of Westminister
ACADEMIC QUALIFICATIONS: BA Media Studies
HOBBIES AND INTERESTS: Music, entertainments, sport
PERSONAL PROFILE: Justin Onyeka is the music and entertainments editor of New Nation newspaper. He acted as a consultant for the Radio 1 hip-hop documentary 'Fight the Power' and an advisor for the Guinness Book of 'Rap, Dance & Techno'. He has been a music correspondent on Kiss FM's Rap Show and GLR's Upfront programme and in a journalistic career spanning 15 years, Justin has written for numerous publications such as Sunday Times, the Guardian, Blues & Soul, Hip-Hop Connection, Music Week, NME and The Source (in New York).

MISS MARVEL OPARA (WORKSHOP LEADER)

On Site Shiatsu for Co's, Flat 5, 40 Dealtry Road, Putney, London, SW15 6NL

PLACE OF BIRTH: London, 21.4.64
MARITAL STATUS: Miss
CHILDREN: One (Joseph Joyce)
COLLEGE: Kings and Princeton Open University
ACADEMIC QUALIFICATIONS: 3 O-A Levels Started doing degree It's on hold
PROFESSIONAL QUALIFICATIONS: Masters in Reflexology Shiatsu and Actress
DIRECTORSHIPS: Spotlight
MEMBERSHIPS: Equity, Shiatsu Society
HONOURS/AWARDS: Sports Woman Of The Year 1998 For Metro Club
HOBBIES AND INTERESTS: Writing, travelling, craft work, skiing, networking
PERSONAL PROFILE: I'm a woman, a mother and I am a Black VIP, (Visually Impaired). I am an expressive intervisual, with no limitations except for which is imposed on me. There is a time for everything and that is how I live my life.

MR JONATHAN OPPONG-WIAFE (PHOTOGRAPHER)

Spirit Magazine, 2-4 Vestry Street, London, N1 7RE

PLACE OF BIRTH: Britain, 25.9.68
MARITAL STATUS: Single
COLLEGE: Paddington School of Photography
ACADEMIC QUALIFICATIONS: O-Levels, Diploma in Photography
DIRECTORSHIPS: Spirit Magazine
HOBBIES AND INTERESTS: Photography, music, film, martial arts
PERSONAL PROFILE: I studied photography for two years and assisted various photographers for a couple of years after that. I have been working as a photographer in my own remit for ten years and have been fortunate enough to have photography. Many of my heroes are in the jazz world. I am currently photo editor of Spirit Magazine, which is a holistic style magazine.

MR BENSON OSAWE (PRESIDENT NAACS)

National President, National Association of African Caribbean Students, , 50 Winterford Avenue, Ardwick, Manchester, M13 9AF

PLACE OF BIRTH: Nigeria
COLLEGE: Manchester University
MEMBERSHIPS: National Black Students Alliance
HOBBIES AND INTERESTS: Driving, travelling
EMAIL: Benson .Osawe@ stud.man.ac.UK
PERSONAL PROFILE: Current national president/founder National Assoc. of African Caribbean students. Co-founder, National Black Student's Alliance. Current overseas students officer, Manchester University. Strongly involved with the establishment of a Black students officer in the NUS. I have recently sponsored several events on behalf of Black students.
NOMINATED BY: Karen Gabay, Manchester Business School

MS HYACINTH OSBORNE (SOCIAL WORKER)

Gordon House,

PLACE OF BIRTH: Jamaica, 3.2.42
MARITAL STATUS: Divorced
CHILDREN: Three (Denise, Dionne, David)
COLLEGE: University Keele
ACADEMIC QUALIFICATIONS: MA Social Work
PROFESSIONAL QUALIFICATIONS: Social Worker
DIRECTORSHIPS: Oscar B.Ham St Basic
MEMBERSHIPS: Labour Party, Works Employment, Network Europe
HONOURS/AWARDS: Excellence Award Contribution to the Black Community
HOBBIES AND INTERESTS: Theatre, travel, driving
EMAIL: osborneh@globalnet.co.uk
PERSONAL PROFILE: Came to UK 40 years ago, trained as nurse then took degree in social work. First Black officer in charge of home for elders in Birmingham Social Services. Member of various voluntary organisations. Director of Handsworth Employment Scheme 11 YTS. Founder member of Caribbean Women's Association. Jamaica Nationals. Co-ordinator European Contact Group. Women Member Board of Visitors local prison.
NOMINATED BY: Denise James

MR DAPO OSHIYEMI (Managing Director-Publisher)

DBI Communication, Grove House, 82 East Dulwich Grove, London, SE22 8TW

PLACE OF BIRTH: London, 12.9.63
MARITAL STATUS: Single
COLLEGE: University of East London
ACADEMIC QUALIFICATIONS: HNC Business & Finance, Lagos-State Poly: Dip in Agriculture School
PROFESSIONAL QUALIFICATIONS: London Chamber of Commerce & Industry Higher Diploma in Marketing
MEMBERSHIPS: British Institute of Export
HOBBIES AND INTERESTS: Football, lawn tennis, chess
PERSONAL PROFILE: Dapo Oshiyemi set up DBI Communications in 1995 and now the company publishes the influential Africans Around Town magazine, organises the African Awards and Cultural Nites and has just completed its first motion picture, which to date is the biggest independent Black film ever made in the UK. DBI Communications considers itself to be an international organisation already with a subsidiary in Nigeria and one planned for the US.
NOMINATED BY: Sam Jenyo

MR MICHAEL OSHUNGBURE
(Semi Pro Boxer-Clothes Retailer)

Amateur Record, Lion Boxing Gym, 40A Brigstock House, Ilford Road, Brixton, London, SE5 9QF

PLACE OF BIRTH: Leicester, 27.1.74
MARITAL STATUS: Single
ACADEMIC QUALIFICATIONS: 5 GCSE, 1 A-Level City & Guilds, Rec & Leisure Management
HONOURS/AWARDS: 2 Gloden Gloves, 1 Metroplitan Title
HOBBIES AND INTERESTS: Reading, photography, travelling
PERSONAL PROFILE: After being treated unfairly, decided to box in America three and a half years ago. 1996 was New York Golden Gloves finalist. 1998 was Chicago and Springfield, Illinois champion. I'm the third British boxer to win the Golden Gloves title. Also won 1998 New York Metro's title. (I'm the Man), (Amateur Record 31-4)

SIR HERMAN OUSELEY (Chairman CRE)

Commission For Racial Equality, Elliott House, 10-12 Allington Street, London, SW1 5EH

PLACE OF BIRTH: Guyana, 24.3.45
MARITAL STATUS: Married
CHILDREN: Two
COLLEGE: Catford College
PROFESSIONAL QUALIFICATIONS: DMA
DIRECTORSHIPS: Brookknight Security, Kings Health Care Trust
MEMBERSHIPS: IRO, Princes Youth Trust KIO, Preset Trust, Uniting Britain Trust
HONOURS/AWARDS: Flve Hons Degrees
HOBBIES AND INTERESTS: Sport, travelling, cooking
PERSONAL PROFILE: 35 years service in public sector, leading local authority executive, directing the CRE for six years and fronting many charities and voluntary organisations as chairperson or patron. Known as someone with track record of changing organisations, getting results and championing the cause of equality and fair treatment for everyone.

MR OLU OYENIGBA (Manager)

Head of Prospects Association, 28 Magpie Close, Forest Gate, London, E7 9DE

PLACE OF BIRTH: Hackney
MARITAL STATUS: Single
COLLEGE: Hackney College
ACADEMIC QUALIFICATIONS: A-Levels Sociology, History, O-Levels English, Art, History & Numerous CSE Grades
HONOURS/AWARDS: Double Platinum Disc & Gold Disc
HOBBIES AND INTERESTS: Exercise, reading, socialising, cooking, music
PERSONAL PROFILE: Head of Prospects Associations (artist management company). Recipient of Double Platinium Disc and Gold Disc Award (German). Artistes: Shahin Badar featured on the biggest selling album of 1997 and controversial song 'Smack My Bitch Up'. Tania Evans: Entered for Grammy Award nominations (99); Echo Prize; Bravo Award etc. DA-Banned (hip hop group). He is currently working as music columnist co-writer for the Asian newspaper the Weekly East.
NOMINATED BY: Kiran Lyall

35 years service in public sector, leading local authority executive, directing the CRE for six years and fronting many charities and voluntary organisations as chairperson or patron. Known as someone with track record of changing organisations, getting results and championing the cause of equality and fair treatment for everyone.

SIR HERMAN OUSELEY

MS SUSANNE PACKER (ACTRESS-TEACHER)

Teacher, 7 St Georges Square, London, SW1V 2HX

PLACE OF BIRTH: Cardiff, 26.11.62
MARITAL STATUS: Married
COLLEGE: Warwick University and Goldsmiths College
ACADEMIC QUALIFICATIONS: BA, PGCE
PROFESSIONAL QUALIFICATIONS: Qualified Teachers Status
HOBBIES AND INTERESTS: Yoga, reading, travelling
PERSONAL PROFILE: Suzanne qualified with a BA Hons in Theatre and Drama and entered Webber Douglas Academy & Dramatic Art to study acting. Her extensive career spans comedy, West End musicals, theatre, radio and TV. She is probably best known as Josie Johnson, in Channel 4's 'Brookside'. A drama supply teacher when not acting.

CLLR STEPHEN PADMORE (CRO EMPLOYMENT OFFICER)

Greenwich Council for Racial Equality,

PLACE OF BIRTH: Guyana, 24.1.54
CHILDREN: Three (Sabina, Simeon, Tesslyn)
COLLEGE: Brunel and Goldsmiths
PROFESSIONAL QUALIFICATIONS: Politics and Law
DIRECTORSHIPS: Chair of Policies and Equalities Committee (LBL), Deputy Chair of Equalities Panel
MEMBERSHIPS: Association of London Government
PERSONAL PROFILE: Without Black and Asian people, there will be no Britain. I welcome a better Black education community. More black entrepreneurs for tomorrow. Black and Asian young people must be more involved in politics. Only when we are involved in politics in a high profile, will we begin to break down the barriers of racism.

MR CARL PALMER (DIARY EDITOR)

Manchester Evening News, 164 Deansgate, Manchester, M60 2RD

PLACE OF BIRTH: Manchester, 23.3.58
MARITAL STATUS: Married
CHILDREN: Two (Elliott Alexander, Hayden Benjamin)
COLLEGE: Central Lancashire
ACADEMIC QUALIFICATIONS: 7 O-Levels, 3 A-Levels
PROFESSIONAL QUALIFICATIONS: NCTJ Proficiency
MEMBERSHIPS: NUJ
HOBBIES AND INTERESTS: Music, theatre, soccer, poetry, travel, writing
PERSONAL PROFILE: The first Black staff journalist employed in the Manchester Evening News having joined the paper in 1984. Solid news background but now working in features department. I have a great weakness for chocolate, a profound dislike of bad manners and great respect for my elders.
NOMINATED BY: Karen Gabay, Manchester Business School

MR EMMANUEL (KING MASCO) PALMER
(ARTISTE SINGER-BANDLEADER)

Vetma Records & Promotion, 128 Gordon Road, Nunhead, SE15 3RP

PLACE OF BIRTH: Sierra Leone
MARITAL STATUS: Married
CHILDREN: Three (Emma, Evette, Nathan)
ACADEMIC QUALIFICATIONS: HND Business Studies
PROFESSIONAL QUALIFICATIONS: Musician
HONOURS/AWARDS: Musical Awards
HOBBIES AND INTERESTS: Music, football
PERSONAL PROFILE: King Masco an outstanding singer, performer and entertainer in African dance music. He entertains all races and cultures both young and old. Portraying the beauty of Africa with a difference.

PROF GEOFFREY HENRY PALMER (PROFESSOR)

Prof. of Grain Science, Heriot-Watt University Brewing & Distilling Dept., Riccarton, Edinburgh, EH14 4AS

PLACE OF BIRTH: Jamaica, 9.4.40
MARITAL STATUS: Married
CHILDREN: Three (Catherine, Susan, Ralph)
COLLEGE: Heriot Watt University
ACADEMIC QUALIFICATIONS: BSc, PhD, Dsc
PROFESSIONAL QUALIFICATIONS: F Inst. Brew, FRSA
DIRECTORSHIPS: Lothain of Edinburgh Racial Equality Council
MEMBERSHIPS: Inst. of Brewing AM Soc. Brewing Chemists (ASBC)
HONOURS/AWARDS: Master Brewers Assoc. of America, Distinguished Research Award from The ASBC
HOBBIES AND INTERESTS: Reading, charity work, films
EMAIL: G.tt.Palmer@Gw.ac.uk
PERSONAL PROFILE: Emigrated to London 1955. Playing cricket for London School Boys 1955. Junior technician London University 1957-1961. BSc Hons Leicester University, 1964. PhD, Edinburgh University 1967. DSC, Heriot-Watt University 1983. Recognised as world expert on the science and technology of cereal grains. Has worked actively to improve race relations.
NOMINATED BY: CM Brown

MRS JANICE PANTON MBE (MONTSERRAT REPRESENTATIVE)

Information Officer, Montserrat Government UK Office, Lauderdale House, 30B Wimpole Street, London, W1M 7AE

PLACE OF BIRTH: Montserrat, 22.1.48
MARITAL STATUS: Married
CHILDREN: Two (Stuart, Kevin)
COLLEGE: Middlesex
ACADEMIC QUALIFICATIONS: BA Hons Social Policy and Administration
PROFESSIONAL QUALIFICATIONS: Post Graduate Certificate in Research Methods
HONOURS/AWARDS: MBE
HOBBIES AND INTERESTS: Gardening, reading, community work
EMAIL: panton@globalnet.co.uk
PERSONAL PROFILE: Born in Montserrat I have been involved in community work in the UK from 1984 and raised funds for the Montserrat victims of Hurricane Hugo. As a founder member of Mac 89 and it's co-ordinator from 1995-98 assisted Montserrat communities affected by the erupting volcano. Opened Montserrat Government Office UK in 1998.

MICIA PARIS (SINGER SONGWRITER)

Blacklist Entertainments, The Old Church Hall, 67 Studdridge Street, London, SW6 3DT

PLACE OF BIRTH: Islington, 27.4.69
MARITAL STATUS: Single
CHILDREN: One (Monet Alannah)
HOBBIES AND INTERESTS: Reading, drawing, movies, cooking
PERSONAL PROFILE: Started at 17 years old with my first album, which went Platinium and I've just completed my 5th album which is due to come out later this year. I've also done a West End play 'Mumma I Want To Sing'.

MRS YVETTE LORRAINE PARISH (AROMATHERAPIST)

Calmarama Health & Music, 43 Salisbury Road, Heath Park, Romford, RM2 5TP

PLACE OF BIRTH: West Indies, 24.7.53
MARITAL STATUS: Married
CHILDREN: One (Vanessa)
PROFESSIONAL QUALIFICATIONS: Physiology, Anatomy, Reflexology, Aromatheraphy
MEMBERSHIPS: ITPI
HOBBIES AND INTERESTS: Exercise, reading
PERSONAL PROFILE: On-site aromatherapy massage for the business environment, in the City and West End area. Using natural sounds, relaxation and mood music recorded and produced by ourselves. Given our own channel on BWIA Inflight entertainment. Interviewed on Talk Radio appeared in Pride, the Voice, the Gleaner and Voyage magazine.

Recognised as world expert on the science and technology of cereal grains. Has worked actively to improve race relations.

PROF GEOFFREY HENRY PALMER

MR SHAUN PARKES (Actor-Musician)

Lakeside Agency, 21 Poplar Road, Leatherhead, Surrey, CRO 7UD

PLACE OF BIRTH: London, 9.2.73
MARITAL STATUS: Single
COLLEGE: RADA
ACADEMIC QUALIFICATIONS: 4 GCSEs, A-Levels English, Drama
PROFESSIONAL QUALIFICATIONS: Diploma in Acting
HOBBIES AND INTERESTS: Writing, music
PERSONAL PROFILE: I have been acting for about fifteen years, four and half of those years professionally. I have turned to writing music because I find I have more freedom to express myself. My ultimate plan is to be involved with an organisation where Black people can work with each other for each other, not be scared to open up, recognise each others talents positively.

REV MABEL CHRISTOBEL PARRIS (Minister)

Pastor, Bethel United Church of Jesus Christ (Apostolic), 3 Ontario Place, King George Avenue, Leeds, LS7 4LL

PLACE OF BIRTH: Dominican Republic, 29.5.26
MARITAL STATUS: Widow
CHILDREN: Nine (Victor, Reuel, Irma, Amogene, Otis, Arundell, Joyce, Paul, Floyd)
DIRECTORSHIPS: Bethel Day Care Centre, Kenyan Orphan Sponsorship Trust
HONOURS/AWARDS: Community Work
HOBBIES AND INTERESTS: Baking
PERSONAL PROFILE: I came to England 1958 to work in tailoring as a machinist. I was ordained first women minister in our organisation 1982. I am also equal opportunity member of West Yorkshire Caribbean Council of Churches. Member of Technorth Advisory Committee, member of Police Forum. Set up the Kenyan Orphan Sponsorship Trust.

MS YVONNE PASCAL (Actor)

Frewin Associates, 65 Rectory Lane, London, SW17 9PY

PLACE OF BIRTH: Bristol, 15.9.63
MARITAL STATUS: Single
COLLEGE: Welsh College of Music and Drama
ACADEMIC QUALIFICATIONS: Graduate Diploma in Drama
EMAIL: YvonnePasc@aol.com

MRS SHIRLEY DOREEN PATTEN (Travel Clinic Advisor)

British Airways Travel Clinic, 24 Melrose Gardens, Edgware, Middlesex, HA8 5LN

PLACE OF BIRTH: Jamaica, 8.12.48
MARITAL STATUS: Married
CHILDREN: Two (Paul, Donna Marie)
COLLEGE: Westminster University
ACADEMIC QUALIFICATIONS: Certificate in Management, Certificate in Counselling
PROFESSIONAL QUALIFICATIONS: RGN/Obstetrics, PPA
HONOURS/AWARDS: Quality Awards-Reday Service, Quality Awards Equal Opportunity
HOBBIES AND INTERESTS: Reading, theatre, badminton, swimming, dancing, holidays, gardening
PERSONAL PROFILE: Joined parents in 1964 at the age of 14 years, attended a secondary modern school achieved 6 GCEs. Trained and qualified RGN. Married 1969, reared two very talented children. Worked within the community with local borough council with children and families 1971, achieved middle management 1989-1994. Director private nursery 1986-1989. School governor three years.

Marta has financial and IT responsibility for over £700 million expenditure in 6000 projects in 35 structural fund programmes

MARTA R PHILLIPS

MR COLIN ROY PATTERSON (Singer-Actor)

Writer-Dancer, 21 St Marys Road, South Norwood, London, SE25 6UT

PLACE OF BIRTH: London, 26.2.65
MARITAL STATUS: Single
PROFESSIONAL QUALIFICATIONS: Trained Mechanic
DIRECTORSHIPS: Spotlight
MEMBERSHIPS: Equity PRS
HONOURS/AWARDS: LBC Award for Best Song
HOBBIES AND INTERESTS: Music, computers, cars, keeping fit, gymnastics
PERSONAL PROFILE: Born in London, parents from Jamaica, two sisters and three brothers. Originally trained mechanic, took open classes at Pineapple Dance Studios and numerous acting workshops. As a singer/writer, wrote music for Channel 4 Black shows in theatre and appeared in West End in several shows - new project 'Soul Devine' vocal group.

MR DREW JOHN PERIGRINE PATTERSON (Managing Director)

Skin Culture Ltd, Weaver House, 19-21 Chapel Road, West Norwood, London, SE27 6TP

PLACE OF BIRTH: England, 15.9.63
MARITAL STATUS: Single
CHILDREN: Three
COLLEGE: Hull
ACADEMIC QUALIFICATIONS: MBA DMS
DIRECTORSHIPS: Skin Culture
MEMBERSHIPS: Member of the Institute of Management (MIMgt)
HOBBIES AND INTERESTS: Chess, football
PERSONAL PROFILE: I specialise in management consultancy. Worked as a project manager for a local authority. Nominated for business of the year. I have also been interviewed by Skin News which also featured the Minister for Small Firms, Michael Wills.

MR PAUL PEARSON (Managing Director)

Pearson Communications, Southbank House, Black Prince Road, London, SE1 7SJ

PLACE OF BIRTH: Wolverhampton, 21.11.70
MARITAL STATUS: Divorced
COLLEGE: Radbrook College
ACADEMIC QUALIFICATIONS: BTEC in Business & Operational Studies
DIRECTORSHIPS: Pearson Ltd, Alexander Marketing Ltd
MEMBERSHIPS: Prince's Youth Business Trust
HONOURS/AWARDS: Order of Brancoveau, Romania. Order of the Elephant, Swaziland, Star of Bengazi, Libya
HOBBIES AND INTERESTS: Music, swimming
EMAIL: Paul@pearson.pr.com
PERSONAL PROFILE: Coming from a hotel sales and marketing background I have been able to merge these skills with media relations to head a creative and professional team working for the likes of Naomi Campbell, Nelson Mandela's Childrens Fund and Prince's Youth Business Trust.
NOMINATED BY: Sharon Aitkin

MS SONIA M PETERS (Health Visitor)

Wolverhampton Health Care (NHS) Trust, 12 Fairview Crescent, Wednesfield, Wolverhampton, WV11 1BU

PLACE OF BIRTH: Jamaica, 25.4.44
MARITAL STATUS: Divorced
CHILDREN: Three (Micheal, Charmain, Vincent)
COLLEGE: University of Wolverhampton
PROFESSIONAL QUALIFICATIONS: RGN, CMB (Part 1) Cert., RHV, FWT. Cert., Dip. M Prof. Studies (HV)
DIRECTORSHIPS: Wolverhampton Poly Training Limited
MEMBERSHIPS: Board of governors University of Wolverhampton
HONOURS/AWARDS: Wolverhampton African Caribbean Achievers Award (Oct 1998)
HOBBIES AND INTERESTS: Music, reading, dancing, education
PERSONAL PROFILE: I came to England in 1963 appointed a Justice of the Peace in 1977, and to the board of governors of the University of Wolverhampton 1986. Currently secretary of education foundation. A member of Harmony Project and WCCR. A former member chair of WIFA. Vice chair of WCCR. Former secretary of African Caribbean CC and African Caribbean Community Initiative.
NOMINATED BY: Delva Campbell

MR MARTIN RAY PHILBERT (Photographer)

30 Wilbury House, Carleton Road, London, N7 0QT

PLACE OF BIRTH: London, 5.10.69
MARITAL STATUS: Single
COLLEGE: Lancashire University
ACADEMIC QUALIFICATIONS: BTEC National Diploma Photography, Degree in Photography
MEMBERSHIPS: Association of Photographers
HOBBIES AND INTERESTS: Swimming, running
PERSONAL PROFILE: Since graduating from university I have sought to develop my individual style as a people/portrait photographer I have worked for editorial, design and advertising clients in studio and on location. My current and future aim is to establish myself within corporate photography.

MR DARELL PHILIP (Student)

183a Sandringham Road, Hackney, London, E8 2HS

PLACE OF BIRTH: London, 1.8.81
MARITAL STATUS: Single
COLLEGE: Hackney Community College
ACADEMIC QUALIFICATIONS: 5 GCSE's
HONOURS/AWARDS: Daily Mirror Young Sports Writer, Semi-finalist of a BBC Young Journalist Competition
HOBBIES AND INTERESTS: Reading, writing, sport (I am a mad Arsenal Fan)
PERSONAL PROFILE: I feel privileged to have been nominated for a book of this prestige and honour of Black achievers. My ability to write is a gift from God. I feel a sense of pride and satisfaction in people commending my written articles and print journalism is a career I hope to pursue.
NOMINATED BY: Eileen Philip

MISS BARBARA PHILLIPS (Managing Director)

Brownstone Communications Ltd, Suite12, The Lux Building, 2-4 Hoxton Square, London, N1 6NU

PLACE OF BIRTH: London
MARITAL STATUS: Single
COLLEGE: BirkBeck University of London
ACADEMIC QUALIFICATIONS: BA Hons Media Studies and Linguistics
DIRECTORSHIPS: Brownstone Communications, Segueway and The Big Event
HOBBIES AND INTERESTS: Voluntary work, cinema, music, sports
PERSONAL PROFILE: Has spent the last eight years working in the media and set up Brownstone in 1996 to bridge the gap between mainstream organisations and diverse communications. About to study for MA in communications management, is chair of Brent lay visiting panel. Has worked in press, radio and outdoor.

MR DAVE-BENSON PHILLIPS
(Childrens Entertainer & TV Presenter)

Mr Phil Dale, AMG, 11-13 Broad Court, Covent Garden, London, WC2B 5QN

PLACE OF BIRTH: London, 3.2.65
MARITAL STATUS: Single
COLLEGE: English, Art, Sociology, GCSE/Statistics CEE
MEMBERSHIPS: Pre-School Learning Alliance, NSPCC, Makaton Vocabulary Development Project
HOBBIES AND INTERESTS: Motor enthusiast, writing, videos, helping children with special needs, charity work both here, and overseas
EMAIL: ada93@dial,pipex.com
PERSONAL PROFILE: Started career in 1982 presenting shows for children and spent two years performing at the famous Polka Children's Theatre in Wimbledon. His talents soon became noticed, he was asked to appear on LWT's 'Saturday Action'. In 1990 Dave co-presented for 'Children In Need'. Big break 'Playdays' for the BBC. This has led to appearances in 'Nick Jr' for Nickelodeon, 'Cat's Eyes', 'Q & A' and 'Go For It' for BBC, 'Ratkan' and 'Jack In The Box' for Sky and his own successful BBC series 'Get Your Own Back' now in it's ninth year. Dave has also featured in many radio programmes including BBC's popular 'Playtime', '12345' and 'Stories and Rhymes'.

MISS MARTA R PHILLIPS (Chartered Accountant)

Head of Finance EST Unit, European Social Fund Unit, Department For Education & Employment, Caxton House, Tothill Street, London, SW1H 9NA

PLACE OF BIRTH: Guyana, 9.10.52
MARITAL STATUS: Single
COLLEGE: Newscastle-upon-Tyne
ACADEMIC QUALIFICATIONS: BA Hons Economics and Accounting, MSc Computer Science
PROFESSIONAL QUALIFICATIONS: Member of the Institute of Chartered Accountants of Scotland
DIRECTORSHIPS: Servite Houses, Newham Riding School
HOBBIES AND INTERESTS: Horse-riding, reading, gardening, my family
EMAIL: marta.phillips@dfee.gov.uk
PERSONAL PROFILE: Marta has financial and IT responsibility for over £700 million expenditure in 6000 projects in 35 structural fund programmes. She is honorary treasurer for two registered charities - a riding school in East London where she lives and a large housing association.

MR RICHARD PHILLIPS (Engineer-Clubmaker)

Class Clubmaker, Golf Works, 31 Fairfield Road, West Drayton, UB7 8EY

PLACE OF BIRTH: London, 10.3.52
MARITAL STATUS: Married
CHILDREN: Two (Derek, Joseph)
ACADEMIC QUALIFICATIONS: Mechanical Engineer (Hamburg)
PROFESSIONAL QUALIFICATIONS: Specialized in Surbmissible Pumps became Clubmaker eight years ago
DIRECTORSHIPS: Golf Works
MEMBERSHIPS: Farnham Park and Richings Park Golf Club
HONOURS/AWARDS: Clubmaker of the Year 1995 PCF
HOBBIES AND INTERESTS: Music, all kinds of sports especially golf
EMAIL: RichardPhillips1@.vexgin.com
PERSONAL PROFILE: Schooled in Neasden. College in West Africa. University in Hamburg. Specialised in pumps, became clubmaker in 1991 qualified in 1992 as a class A. A clubmaker worked for Callaway and still working for Taywormadi as subcontractor customising clubs.
NOMINATED BY: Mark Anthony Lobban

MR LAURENT PHILLPOTTS
(Lino-type Operator, Graphics Designer, Composer)

Rtd, West Indian Ex-Servicemen's and Women's Association, 20 Windsor Court, Moscow Road, London, W2 4SN

PLACE OF BIRTH: Jamaica, 31.8.23
MARITAL STATUS: Married
CHILDREN: Three (Norma, Tex, Yvonne)
COLLEGE: Kingston Technical College, Notian and District Technology College, Leeds College of Technology
ACADEMIC QUALIFICATIONS: City and Guilds Final
MEMBERSHIPS: W.I Ex-Service's British Caribbean Association, Association of Jamaicans, Mary Seacole Memorial Association, Westminster Carers Forum
HONOURS/AWARDS: Community Awards
HOBBIES AND INTERESTS: Cricket, music, reading, socialities, human welfare
PERSONAL PROFILE: Born in Kingston, Jamaica, attended Mico Practising School and Kingston Technical College. Joined Gleaner Co. apprentice composition, arrived in England in 1944, served in Royal Air Force as a telephone operator, demobbed in 1947. Worked in commerce and newspaper printing in Nottingham left in 1959 for London. Joined Mirror Group Newspapers, published a monthly newspaper "Colonial News" 1956 to 1959.

MISS MARCIA PHINN (Vocal Tutor)

Destiny Vocals, OTR Studios, 143 Mare Street, Hackney, London, E8 3RH

PLACE OF BIRTH: London, 2.3.66
MARITAL STATUS: Single
COLLEGE: London College of Fashion, YTS Diploma (Secretarial)
ACADEMIC QUALIFICATIONS: 4 GCSEs-Maths, English, Social Studies, Child Development
PROFESSIONAL QUALIFICATIONS: BTEC Nat. Business & Finance, BTEC First Business & Finance Business Training Workshop
HOBBIES AND INTERESTS: Dressmaking, designing, hairdressing
PERSONAL PROFILE: Marcia has been singing for eleven years and has sung to audiences of up to three thousand. Marcia is a vocal tutor and has been tutoring since 1996 when she established Destiny Vocals. To date, thirty students have graduated and preparations are being made for the next course.
NOMINATED BY: Anthea Lee

MS SYBIL PHOENIX MBE (MAYORESS)

Marsha Phoenix House, 90/92 Tressillian Road, Brockley, London, SE4 2BA

MARITAL STATUS: Widow
COLLEGE: Fellowship of Goldsmiths
ACADEMIC QUALIFICATIONS: MS
PROFESSIONAL QUALIFICATIONS: MS
DIRECTORSHIPS: Marsha Phoenix House
MEMBERSHIPS: Freeman of Lewisham, Freeman City of London
HOBBIES AND INTERESTS: Helping hands, author
PERSONAL PROFILE: First Black woman living in Britain to receive an MBE. Founder of Marsha Phoenix House. Community leader and racism awareness facilitator.
NOMINATED BY: Pam Donovan, Goldsmiths University

MR JUSTIN PICKETT (ACTOR-MUSICIAN)

PLACE OF BIRTH: Liverpool, 21.6.72
MARITAL STATUS: Single
COLLEGE: Sussex University
ACADEMIC QUALIFICATIONS: BA Hons Degree in American Social Studies
MEMBERSHIPS: Equity
HOBBIES AND INTERESTS: Reading, teaching, sports
PERSONAL PROFILE: A young man, a performer. I am Justin Pickett dedicated to breaking down barriers in the performance industry. Everybody knows me from Desmonds. However, I am determined to display my versatility especially through my music. I have been performing since I was 12 years old and I am still a young man with a bright future, I hope.

YOYO POLLENDINE (ACTRESS-SINGER)

Linkside Agency, 21 Poplar Road, Leatherhead, Surrey, KT22 8SF

COLLEGE: School of Creative Ministries Performing Arts Course
PERSONAL PROFILE: Theatre: 'Dick Whittington' (Ensemble) 'Notting Hill Gate', multi-cultural evening (Singer) Paul Robeson Theatre, Hounslow, Equality Day (Singer) Hounslow Civic Centre. Other experience: Brit Awards (1998) sang with 'All Saints', workshop leader, Seagull Theatre of the Gorge. Special skills: singing; alto (singing teacher Paul Knight); dancing; contemporary dance; ballet; flamenco and good movement.

MR JASON PETER POLLITT (ACTOR-EDUCATIONALIST)

Director, Central Line, 18 Oakland Street, Nottingham, NG7 5JQ

PLACE OF BIRTH: England, 22.2.73
MARITAL STATUS: Single
ACADEMIC QUALIFICATIONS: BA Hons Dramatic Art, Diploma in Theatre Studies
DIRECTORSHIPS: Encompass
MEMBERSHIPS: Equity
PERSONAL PROFILE: Born of Elizabeth Pollitt (Masemola) and John Pollitt. After university began an extensive career in theatre as an actor performing throughout Europe. In the last two years has set up an educational facilitatory role working in the arts with young people especially young men through dance.

MR STEPHEN POPE (PUBLISHER)

The X Press, 6 Hoxton Square, London, N1 6NV

PLACE OF BIRTH: Barbados, 27.11.60
CHILDREN: Two (Sophie, Luke)
COLLEGE: Polytechnic of Central London
ACADEMIC QUALIFICATIONS: BA Hons Media Studies
DIRECTORSHIPS: The X Press, Acreforce Ltd, X Press Entertainment Ltd
HOBBIES AND INTERESTS: Motorcycling, fly fishing, topless darts, big game hunting
EMAIL: Vibes@Xpress.co.uk
PERSONAL PROFILE: Former editor of the Voice newspaper. Co-owner of Europe's largest Black books publisher The X Press. Journalist and friend of royalty. Founder of the Black Disabled Lesbian Motorcycle Action Group. Believes he was a lottery winner in a former life.

MISS VALERIE POTTINGER-NOBLE (HEADTEACHER)

Headteacher, Croydon Education Authority, Tollgate JMI & Nursery School Malling Close, Stockbury Road, Addiscombe, Croydon, CR0 7YD

PLACE OF BIRTH: London, 14.2.56
MARITAL STATUS: Single
CHILDREN: Two (Desmond Kwame Douglas-Noble, Tahira Elizabeth-Mae Douglas-Noble)
COLLEGE: University of London, Goldsmiths College
ACADEMIC QUALIFICATIONS: Bachelor of Education Honours Degree
PROFESSIONAL QUALIFICATIONS: Advanced Diploma in Education, Qualified Teacher
MEMBERSHIPS: National Association of Headteachers
HONOURS/AWARDS: Assoc. Teachers of Dancing Silver Medal for Tap Dancing, Blue Belt:Wushu Kwan, Martial Arts
HOBBIES AND INTERESTS: Dancing, singing, dressmaking, reading
PERSONAL PROFILE: I have been involved in children's education for over 20 years, both in state and community based projects. I am a mother of a 20 year old son and a six year old daughter and very proud grandmother of a baby grandson. My hobbies include dance, reading and dressmaking when I get time.

MR DANIEL POYSER (ACTOR)

JLM Personnal Management, 242 Acton Lane, London, W4 5DL

PLACE OF BIRTH: Sheffield, 3.11.75
MARITAL STATUS: Single
COLLEGE: Manchester
ACADEMIC QUALIFICATIONS: BA Hons Acting Studies
MEMBERSHIPS: Equity
HOBBIES AND INTERESTS: Cinema, weight training
PERSONAL PROFILE: Daniel Poyser studied drama at the Arden School of Theatre. He has made several television appearances including: 'Coronation Street' and 'Band of Gold'. Currently he is in rehearsals for 'Street Story' a thought provoking piece exploring the life and times of Ken Saro-Wina the Nigerian political activist.

MS CORRINA PREECE (ACTRESS)

David Daly Associates, 586a Kings Road, London, SW6 2DX

PLACE OF BIRTH: London, 21.11.74
MARITAL STATUS: Domestic Partnership
CHILDREN: One (Taero Robertson)
COLLEGE: Drama Centre London
ACADEMIC QUALIFICATIONS: GCSE & A-Level
PROFESSIONAL QUALIFICATIONS: Diploma in Dramatic Art. RSA, Exercise to Music
HOBBIES AND INTERESTS: Writing, fitness, child development, interior design
PERSONAL PROFILE: Left drama centre in July 1996 has since worked consistently in film, theatre and television. Took a year out to have son Taero, during pregnancy studied exercise to music at YMCA. Became a qualified instructor at six months pregnant. Also busy writing and creating own projects.

CLLR MICHAEL SINCLAIR PRESCOD (SOCIAL WORKER RTD)

Borough Council of Wellingborough, Council Offices, Swanspool, Wellingborough, NN8 1BP

PLACE OF BIRTH: Barbados, 15.4.38
CHILDREN: Four
COLLEGE: University of Wales
PROFESSIONAL QUALIFICATIONS: Diploma in Social Studies & Bachelor of Arts Degree, Post Graduate Social Studies in Social Work
DIRECTORSHIPS: Neighbourhood Officer, The Afro-Caribbean Association, Vice President Race Equality Council
MEMBERSHIPS: REC, London Group Advisers to the Social Services Inspectorate, Black Social Workers Association
HOBBIES AND INTERESTS: Sports, music, reading good literature, travel, issues relating to community work
PERSONAL PROFILE: During his spell in the army, he served in Malaysia, Hong Kong, Singapore and units in England. Mike arrived in Wellingborough in 1975 as a community development social worker. In 1980 Mike was lead officer for Ethnic Minority Unit. In 1992 he joined Islington Borough Council as principle officer for race equality work in social services. Mike is credited for innovative work in London. Appointed in 1993 as manager for four offices with the rank of assistant director. Mike took early retirement in 1994 and now works as a freelance consultant.

DR WORDSWORTH LAWRENCE VICTOR PRICE
(SENIOR LECTURER IN PHYSICS)

PLACE OF BIRTH: West Indies, 10.8.30
MARITAL STATUS: Married
PROFESSIONAL QUALIFICATIONS: BSc, MSc, PhD, C Phys, M Inst.P, C Eng, MIEE
MEMBERSHIPS: Member of Committee of Wimbledon Bridge Club
HONOURS/AWARDS: Awarded the Trinidad and Tobago High Commission's Scarlet Ibis Award & Gold Medal in 1990 for " Outstanding & Meritorious Service"
HOBBIES AND INTERESTS: Violinist in the Kensington Philharmonic Orchestra, bridge
PERSONAL PROFILE: National winner of the Macallan Trophy at Level 5 1997. In individual events at Bisley, in addition to the St George's Challenge Vase and Gold Cross, I have on occasion won the Sudan and the Faunthorpe, and am probably the only person to have won the University of London Full-bore Rifle Championship on two occasions. In team events I have represented Trinidad and the West Indies and have been on winning teams for the Junior Kolapore, Junior Mackinnon and Nobel Trophy on more than one occasion. I have also in the past represented London in county events. In 1994 captain of London and Middlesex Rifle Team.
NOMINATED BY: Sarah Bunch - The National Rifle Association

MR BOB PURKISS (TRADE UNION OFFICIAL)

National Secretary, Transport & General Workers Union, 16 Palace Street, Victoria, London, SW1E 5JD

PLACE OF BIRTH: Winchester, 11.11.45
MARITAL STATUS: Separated
CHILDREN: Two (Tanya, Melanie)
COLLEGE: P/T Southampton
ACADEMIC QUALIFICATIONS: TV Education Courses
PROFESSIONAL QUALIFICATIONS: A/B Certified
DIRECTORSHIPS: Search High SCAR.
MEMBERSHIPS: TUC, CRE, Searchlight, JCWI , SCG
HONOURS/AWARDS: T/U Awards. National Day in Washington D/C Muslim School
HOBBIES AND INTERESTS: Football Referee, swimming, travelling
EMAIL: BPurkiss@TGWU.Org.uk
PERSONAL PROFILE: Joined merchant navy aged 15. Left the navy and worked for a local ferry company. After various courses at TUC colleges and Southampton University, he joined the Industrial Society as a trade union tutor. 1974, he became the national research officer for the National Workers Union of Jamaica. Back to Britain in 1976, and became the regional research and education officer for the southern region of the TGWU. Appointed to the National Working Party on Race in 1988, he was then co-opted in 1989 on a national basis to establish the union's Race Advisory Committees. In 1990, he was appointed national equalities officer.
NOMINATED BY: T & G

MRS BARBARA VAN PRAAG
(CLASSICAL MUSICIAN - COMPOSER)

14 Rosedene Avenue, London, SW16 2LT

PLACE OF BIRTH: Guyana
MARITAL STATUS: Married
CHILDREN: One (Silra)
COLLEGE: Roehampton University of Surrey
ACADEMIC QUALIFICATIONS: BA Hons, MA Music and Religious Studies
PROFESSIONAL QUALIFICATIONS: Voice Creations (Performing Arts)
HOBBIES AND INTERESTS: Music, religion, all art forms
EMAIL: barpraagbur@easynet.co.uk
PERSONAL PROFILE: Barbara Van Praag has been a primary schoolteacher, a registered nurse, midwife and hospital matron. She studied German Lieder with Madam Ziegler in Minnesota, and opera in Italy under the guidance of Madams Cimmino, Alfani Tellini and Maria Carosio. She sang in concerts and opera in Italy, Spain, US, Caribbean. She has composed two folk operas, two musical suites and several songs and hymns, she founded Voice Creations.

'I have on occasion won the Sudan and the Faunthorpe, and am probably the only person to have won the University of London Full-bore Rifle Championship on two occasions.
In team events I have represented Trinidad and the West Indies'

DR WORDSWORTH LAWRENCE VICTOR PRICE

Barbara Van Praag has been a primary schoolteacher, a registered nurse, midwife and hospital matron. She studied German Lieder with Madam Ziegler in Minnesota, and opera in Italy under the guidance of Madams Cimmino, Alfani Tellini and Maria Carosio. She sang in concerts and opera in Italy, Spain, US, Caribbean. She has composed two folk operas, two musical suites and several songs and hymns, she founded Voice Creations

BARBARA VAN PRAAG

Carribbean Times

COUNTDOWN TO THE MILLENNIUM

MS HEATHER RABBATTS (Chief Executive)

Chief Executive, London Borough of Lambeth, Town Hall, Brixton, London, EC1A 4JA

PLACE OF BIRTH: Kingston, 6.12.55
MARITAL STATUS: Single
CHILDREN: One (Euan)
COLLEGE: London School of Economics
ACADEMIC QUALIFICATIONS: BA Hons, MSc International Relations
PROFESSIONAL QUALIFICATIONS: Barrister-at-Law
DIRECTORSHIPS: British Council, Economic Social Research Council
HOBBIES AND INTERESTS: Music, film, walking, stress reducing shopping
PERSONAL PROFILE: Born in Jamaica, educated England, driven by the idea of making a difference. Worked all my life in the public sector. Believe in family, friends and love to truly have a balanced and whole life.
NOMINATED BY: Sukhvinder K Stubbs

DR RON RAMDIN (Historian-Biographer-Writer)

c/o The British Library, 96 Euston Road, London, NW1 2DB

PLACE OF BIRTH: Trinidad
ACADEMIC QUALIFICATIONS: D. Litt; BSc
PROFESSIONAL QUALIFICATIONS: FRHS
MEMBERSHIPS: Society of Authors; Fellowship of Historical Society; Fellowship of Royal Society of Arts
HONOURS/AWARDS: Trinidad & Tobago High Commission Scarlet Ibis (Gold) Medal; Hansib Award. Doctor of Literature from the University of London 1996
HOBBIES AND INTERESTS: Reading, listening to music
PERSONAL PROFILE: Ron Ramdin is a historian, biographer and novelist who was the first elected secretary of the Whitley Council when the British Library was formed in 1973. He has sat on many London and National committees relating to education and the arts. His books include: 'From Chattel Slave To Wage Earner' (1982); 'The Other Middle Passage' (1995); 'Arising From Bondage'; 'History of the Indo-Caribbean People' (1999). He has given academic papers at universities including the 150th anniversary conference on the arrival of the east Indians in the Caribbean.

MR JIMI RAND (Director-Writer-Producer)

Head Of Simba Centre, 61A Temple Road, Cricklewood, London, NW2 6PN

PLACE OF BIRTH: Barbados, 18.6.47
MARITAL STATUS: Married
COLLEGE: London (Goldsmiths)
ACADEMIC QUALIFICATIONS: BSC Sociology
PROFESSIONAL QUALIFICATIONS: Diploma Performing Arts DMC, CMS, Business & Management Studies
DIRECTORSHIPS: Direct Arts Co. Ltd
MEMBERSHIPS: Equity
HOBBIES AND INTERESTS: Driving, cricket, debates, current affairs
EMAIL: Jimi@DAeP.Demon.co.uk
PERSONAL PROFILE: Actor, stage and film director, playwright, poet, lecturer and producer. Worked extensively both in the UK and the US. Was director and chief executive of YAA Asantewaa Arts Centre until October 1998. Left to take up new post at Simba.

MR NEIL RAYMOND (Careers Officer)

Adviser Outreach, Guildline Careers, 24-32 Carlton Street, Hockley, Nottingham, NG1 1NN

PLACE OF BIRTH: Huddersfield, 16.3.64
MARITAL STATUS: Single
COLLEGE: MSc Race and Education
ACADEMIC QUALIFICATIONS: Degree Public Admin, Degree BA Hons Applied Social Studies
PROFESSIONAL QUALIFICATIONS: Postgraduate Diploma in Careers Guidance
MEMBERSHIPS: Institute of Careers Guidance
HOBBIES AND INTERESTS: International football supporter
EMAIL: neilraymond@guildline.careers.co.uk
PERSONAL PROFILE: I have worked as a careers adviser providing support to Black communities not commonly catered for in terms of providing. Strong Outreach facility for the past 12 years. I have provided a link between corporate, local authority bodies and the community, particularly clients in need who may otherwise never access careers guidance support. I have also produced videos for BBC e.g. 'Fair Guidance which tackles racist issues'.
NOMINATED BY: David Alexander

MR ANTHONY GEORGE REDDIE (Academic Researcher)

Christain Education Development Officer, The Methodist Church, Queens Theological College, Somerset Road, Edgbaston, B15 2QH

PLACE OF BIRTH: Bradford, 10.10.64
MARITAL STATUS: Single
COLLEGE: University of Birmingham
ACADEMIC QUALIFICATIONS: BA Hons Degree in History, Writing up Doctoral Thesis
HONOURS/AWARDS: Awarded an International Fellowship as a Pan-African Christian Educator
HOBBIES AND INTERESTS: Creative writing, drama, reading
EMAIL: Anthonyreddie@compuserve.com
PERSONAL PROFILE: I have been and continue to be engaged in research pertaining to the Christian education of African Caribbean children. This research has been carried out (sponsored by the Methodist Church and others). In order to create a new theory and methodology for an Afrocentric approach to teaching the Christian Faith. Have written and published two books as part of this pioneering, innovative research.
NOMINATED BY: Jill Brown

MISS SHERELLE REECE (Schoolgirl-Dancer)

The Jackie Palmer Agency, 34 Brandon Road, Holmers Farm Way, High Wycombe, HP12 4PS

PLACE OF BIRTH: High Wycombe, 25.7.90
HOBBIES AND INTERESTS: Ballet, tap and jazz dancing, swimming
PERSONAL PROFILE: I am eight years old and attend Jackie Palmer stage school where I do tap, ballet, jazz dancing and drama. I appeared at the Wycombe Swan Theatre in 'The Magical, Musical Mystery Tour'.

MR CARL REID (Actor)

25 Selbourne Close, Reddish, Stockport, SK5 6LJ

DATE OF BIRTH: 10.7.59
MARITAL STATUS: Married
PROFESSIONAL QUALIFICATIONS: Diploma LAMDA
MEMBERSHIPS: British Actors Equity
HONOURS/AWARDS: Gold, Silver & Bronze Medals
HOBBIES AND INTERESTS: Jazz, dance, martial arts, singing, theatre
PERSONAL PROFILE: Highly involved over the years in fundraising for Children In Need, Childline and the Zeebruger Disaster. Always striving as a Black actor to break down stereotypical roles. First leading role working with an inner city production company dealing with real life issues of Black versus white tribulations, sponsored by Camelot and supported by Granada.

MR STEVEN REID (Footballer)

Millwall Football Club, The Den, Zampa Road, London, SE16 3LN

PLACE OF BIRTH: Kingston, 10.3.81
PROFESSIONAL QUALIFICATIONS: 1 League Appearance
PERSONAL PROFILE: England under 16 international striker who made his pro debut at the age of 17, coming on as a substitute in the final game of last season against Bournemouth. One of a significant number of local products who will be looking to force his way into contention at the start of the new campaign.

'Born in Jamaica, educated England, driven by the idea of making a difference. Worked all my life in the public sector'

HEATHER RABBATTS

CLLR MRS BERNICE REIDS (COUNCILLOR)

Manchester City Council, 62 Bowdon Avenue, Fallowfield, Manchester, M14 7HD

PLACE OF BIRTH: Jamaica, 1.11.38
MARITAL STATUS: Married
CHILDREN: Five (Lloyd, Heron, Antony, Janice, Lindel)
ACADEMIC QUALIFICATIONS: O-Level in English & Business Studies, Maths, History, Science
HOBBIES AND INTERESTS: Volunteer, holidays, gardening, reading
PERSONAL PROFILE: I came to England in 1961. Worked for GEC. Switchgear Ltd as secretary for 27 years. I was a volunteer / co-ordinator for Central Manchester Home Start for two years. School governor for St Philip's Primary School for over 12 years. Elected councillor in 1995, re-elected on 6th May 1999. Councillor in council and serve on educational, social services and equal opportunities

MASTER BENJAMIN A H RENNIS (STUDENT-ACTOR)

Boden Agency, 6 Windmill Hill, Enfield, London, EN2 6TZ

PLACE OF BIRTH: London, 2.11.82
COLLEGE: Queen Elizabeth II Boys
HONOURS/AWARDS: Nominated for BBC Bafta Award
HOBBIES AND INTERESTS: Basketball, singing, playing piano, flute, play station.
PERSONAL PROFILE: Eldest son of Pearline and Basil Rennis. Started acting at the age of four. Have enjoyed success in commercials, lead roles in BBC's: 'Think About Science Central' ; 'The Ledge'; ' Childs play'; 'Pirates'. Series and many theatre productions. Will be taking 11 GCSEs in 1999. Wants a career in acting and producing.

CLLR RICHARD REYNOLDS (LEGAL ADVISER)

Councillor, London Borough of Haringey, Richard Reynolds & Associates, International House, 223 Regent Street, London, W1R 8QD

PLACE OF BIRTH: Jamaica, 18.10.54
MARITAL STATUS: Married
CHILDREN: Two (Sabrina, Tanya)
COLLEGE: Middlesex
ACADEMIC QUALIFICATIONS: Cirtus ME Cert.
DIRECTORSHIPS: Richard Reynolds & Associates
MEMBERSHIPS: LGA
HOBBIES AND INTERESTS: Politics, reading, chess, sports, alternative medicine
EMAIL: Reynolds@Inter77.Freeserve.uk
PERSONAL PROFILE: Legal advisor employment law and human resources. Local authority councillor. Local school governor. Vice chair Scrutiny Committee. Chair local area forum with interests in regeneration.

MR DONALD RICHARDS (COMMUNITY ACTIVIST)

Chair SPUG, St Peters Unemployment Group, 31 Allen Road, Whitmore Reans, Wolverhampton, WV6 0AW

PLACE OF BIRTH: Guyana, 28.5.23
MARITAL STATUS: Married
CHILDREN: Three (Donald, Steven, Natalie)
PERSONAL PROFILE: Worked in Guyana as a construction worker, then worked for five years in military police. Came to Britain from Guyana and worked at Goodyears for 25 years, retired 1981. Community activist 1986 to present, St Peters Unemployment Groups and Credit Union Pension's Group.
NOMINATED BY: Delva Campbell

MS JUDY RICHARDS (POLICY DEVELOPMENT OFFICER)

c/o 10 St Georges Mews, Brighton & Hove, BN1 4EU

PLACE OF BIRTH: Chelmsford, 21.5.57
MARITAL STATUS: Single
COLLEGE: University of Liverpool
ACADEMIC QUALIFICATIONS: Diploma in Race & Community Relations (Certificate)
HONOURS/AWARDS: The 1990 Trust, Ujima Pookar Award for Community Development - African & Asian Unity 1994
HOBBIES AND INTERESTS: Music, computers, Black voluntary sector development, people
PERSONAL PROFILE: Has helped develop and support Black community groups, anti-racist networks and other equal opportunities initiatives locally, nationally and internationally . Early 1970's started voluntary work, predominantly with Ugandan Asian refugees. 1988, a founding member of Brighton and Hove Black Women's Group. 1992-1995, Chair NALGO/ Unison National Black Members Committees.
NOMINATED BY: J. Hunte, Brighton & Hove Women's Group

MRS SANDRA RICHARDS (DEVELOPMENT CONSULTANT)

Development Consultant, Reaching Out,

PLACE OF BIRTH: London, 4.8.59
MARITAL STATUS: Married
CHILDREN: Two
MEMBERSHIPS: African Caribbean Community by Birthright
HOBBIES AND INTERESTS: Dancing, singing, travelling
EMAIL: Sandra.richards@easynet.co.uk
PERSONAL PROFILE: Sandra Richards is a development consultant 'Reaching Out' to bring a unifying professionalism to her community work. 'Reaching Out' spearheads 'The Regeneration Village' (African centred people committed to making a difference in the community). A deeply spiritual African woman this Sistah is honoured to have been titled 'Common Unity Mother'.

MISS SHANNEN RICKETTS (SCHOOLGIRL-ACTRESS)

The Jackie Palmer Stage School Agency, 30 Daws Hill Lane, High Wycombe, HP11 1QW

PLACE OF BIRTH: High Wycombe, 31.7.93
HOBBIES AND INTERESTS: Gymnastics, music, tap dancing, ballet
PERSONAL PROFILE: Shannen is a happy and very bright child, she has a lively and outgoing personality. She's confident and mixes well with others. She has a good imagination, Shannen likes dancing, music and dressing up. She also took part in her agency's 'Rhythm of Life' at the Wycombe Swan Theatre (1997) she thoroughly enjoyed this.

MRS ADRIENNE PATRICIA ROBERTS (PROPRIETOR)

Haroldene Residential Home, 75 Harold Road, Leytonstone, London, E11 4QX

PLACE OF BIRTH: Barbados, 26.1.46
MARITAL STATUS: Married
CHILDREN: Three (Theodore, Riccardo, Denise)
ACADEMIC QUALIFICATIONS: TYPR Elementary, Intermediate, Advanced
PROFESSIONAL QUALIFICATIONS: RMN
MEMBERSHIPS: National Care Homes. UK, Barbados Overseas Citizens Association
HOBBIES AND INTERESTS: Travel, reading, music
EMAIL: cprobi@aol.com
PERSONAL PROFILE: Born in Barbados, 1946. Educated at St Boniface/ Alexandra and Community High . London 1962. Married: obtained nursing qualification in 1974 - Ward sister 1979. Management Course 1980 - Opened first residential home for the elderly in 1987 - Second home in 1984-85 - Presently continue to co-own residential homes for the elderly.
NOMINATED BY: B O C A

First person of African ancestry to be appointed Queens Counsel at the English Bar 1988

DR JOHN ANTHONY ROBERTS

First Black sheriff of Notts. First person to hold the office three times:

CLLR ANTHONY ROBINSON

DR JOHN ANTHONY ROBERTS QC (BARRISTER)

Head of Chambers, Chambers of Dr John Anthony Roberts, 45 Thorny Hedge Road, Chiswick, London, W4 5SB

PLACE OF BIRTH: Sierra Leone, 17.5.28
MARITAL STATUS: Married
CHILDREN: One (Ritson John Anthony)
COLLEGE: City University London
ACADEMIC QUALIFICATIONS: Doctor of Civil Law called to Bar (England) & Wales 1969
PROFESSIONAL QUALIFICATIONS: Barrister (Queen's Counsel)
DIRECTORSHIPS: Member of Bar, Sierra Leone, Jamaica, Trinidad & Tobago, Bahamas, St Kitts & Nevis
MEMBERSHIPS: West Indian Ex Servicemen's & Womens Associations, Fellow Chartered Inst. of Arbitrators
HONOURS/AWARDS: Recieved 1st African Achievers Award 1997
HOBBIES AND INTERESTS: Flying, music, choral singing, athletics, playing piano, organ , reading, public speaking, mentoring, helping people, former boxer, sprinter
PERSONAL PROFILE: Brazilian father and Sierra Leone mother (Creole). Royal Air Force 1952-62, UK, Far East, East Pacific, Australia. Assistant recorder, Recorder Crown Court 1983-87. First person of African ancestry to be appointed Queens Counsel at the English Bar 1988. Judge - Supreme Courts of British Virgin Islands and Anquilla 1992-93. Freeman, City of London, Hon. Citizen-Atlanta US. Master of the Bench, Grays Inn, London. Qualified Air Traffic Controller. Qualified pilot. Grassroots Man. Parachutist, Ex RAF boxer and sprinter
NOMINATED BY: Christopher Johnson MBA

MRS NORMA ROBERTS (NURSE-RTD)

89 Sandbroke Road, Stoke Newington, London, N16 0SL

PLACE OF BIRTH: Jamaica, 31.1.43
MARITAL STATUS: Married
CHILDREN: Two (Sheon Andrew, Mark Anthony)
COLLEGE: Princess Mary School
ACADEMIC QUALIFICATIONS: NVQ in Business, Shorthand and Typing
PROFESSIONAL QUALIFICATIONS: Computer Course
MEMBERSHIPS: Ruach Ministries
HONOURS/AWARDS: Feb 1995 Voice Newspaper Community Honors Annual Achievers Award 1993
HOBBIES AND INTERESTS: Writing, reading, travelling, organising
PERSONAL PROFILE: I have written ten plays and two books, one is my life story, one ministry of ushering, released on the market in the first week in December 1998. I am at present working as a voluntary worker for the Ruach Ministry Church in Brixton. I also run a travel agent which I started in June 1998. I am a lay visitor to police stations.
NOMINATED BY: Shean Andrew Roberts

CLLR ANTHONY ROBINSON (COUNCILLOR)

Nottingham City Council, Market Square, Nottingham

PLACE OF BIRTH: Jamaica, 28.1.21
MARITAL STATUS: Married
CHILDREN: Four (Carol, Earl, Eddie, Marcus)
HOBBIES AND INTERESTS: Politics
PERSONAL PROFILE: First Black city councillor. First Black sheriff of Notts. First person to hold the office three times: May 1989-90, May 1993-94, May 1997-98. Co-founder of Afro Caribbean Centre, vice chair CRC, vice chair East Midland Museum. School governor for Eastglade Primary School.
NOMINATED BY: Beryl Robinson

MISS MAE-LOUISE ROBINSON (ACTRESS)

Trilogy Productions, 61 Mill Bridge, Dollis Valley Way, Barnet, EN5 2UG

PLACE OF BIRTH: London, 31.1.71
MARITAL STATUS: Single
COLLEGE: The Urdang Academy of Ballet
ACADEMIC QUALIFICATIONS: 4 O-Levels in English, Biology, Sociology, Dance
PROFESSIONAL QUALIFICATIONS: Diploma in Dance and Theatre Studies
MEMBERSHIPS: Equity, Musicians Union
HOBBIES AND INTERESTS: Ceramics, reading, charity work
PERSONAL PROFILE: I am a young actress and co-founder of Trilogy Productions. My vision for the new Millennium is to see more and more Black artistes writing, producing and creating our own Arena for providing ourselves with the quality of work our European compatriots have so long enjoyed.

VIVIENNE ROCHESTER (ACTOR-TEACHER-DIRECTOR)

Lecturer of Rambert, Freelance Actor, Hilary Gagan Associates, 140a Shaftesbury Avenue, Cambridge Circus, London, WC2H 8HD

PERSONAL PROFILE: Actor, teacher, director, contemporary dancer and choreographer. Creativity is central to my life and work. It inspires me to explore, to communicate with language whether it be verbal physical, emotional, intellectual. The desire to communicate to connect has also led me to study an MA in psychotherapy and counselling in order to improve my work and deepen the connections I make in whatever field.
NOMINATED BY: Sharon Aitkin

MISS LISA ROCK (ACTOR)

PLACE OF BIRTH: England, 8.1.80
MARITAL STATUS: Single
COLLEGE: The Henley College
ACADEMIC QUALIFICATIONS: BTEC National Diploma in Performing Arts
DIRECTORSHIPS: Raksha & Talent Show
HOBBIES AND INTERESTS: Tae Kwondo, street dancing and African dancer
PERSONAL PROFILE: Having decided to take a year out after completing the BTEC National Diploma in Performing Arts at Henley, where I gained three distinctions, eight merits and one pass, I have been performing in the musical 'Godspell': I had to be a diverse character playing different roles trying to separate identities. Godspell is on a tour of England and then Europe. I am currently in the midst of co-hosting a talent show with Richard Blackwood at the Wycombe Swan Theatre.

MISS AMY ROCKSON (ACTRESS)

c/o Vincent Shaw Associates, 20 Jay Mews, South Kensington, London, SW7 2EP

PLACE OF BIRTH: Ghana, 6.8.66
MARITAL STATUS: Single (Engaged)
COLLEGE: Sunderland Polytechnic, Universite De Tours, France
ACADEMIC QUALIFICATIONS: 11 O-Levels, 2 A-Levels, Joint BA Hons in French & English
PROFESSIONAL QUALIFICATIONS: Diploma in Dramatic Art
MEMBERSHIPS: Equity
HOBBIES AND INTERESTS: Cinema, theatre, yoga, computer games, animal welfare
EMAIL: VincentShaw@Clara.net
PERSONAL PROFILE: It hasn't been easy, but I never thought it would be. My mother taught me the value of personal achievement. I watched her battle against illness and misfortune and adopted a belief in perseverance and commitment. Life isn't perfect but I'm working on it and I'm proud of my success.

MR ADRIAN STEWART ROLLINS (CRICKETER)

Opening Batsman, Derbyshire County Cricket Club,

PLACE OF BIRTH: Barking, 8.2.72
MARITAL STATUS: Engaged
CHILDREN: Stepdaughter one (Gemma)
ACADEMIC QUALIFICATIONS: 10 GCSEs, 4 A-Levels
PROFESSIONAL QUALIFICATIONS: Diploma Sports Psychology.
MEMBERSHIPS: Professional Cricketers Association, Derbyshire Representative 1997
HONOURS/AWARDS: Derbyshire Young Player of the Year (1993), Player of the Year (1995) CCPR Community Sports Leaders Award, NCA Coach Award
HOBBIES AND INTERESTS: Music (R 'n' B, ragga, hip hop), basketball (NBA), West Ham United supporter
PERSONAL PROFILE: Grew up in East End in council accommodation with brothers Gary and Robert. Raised by single mother (Marva) who went from machinist to headteacher in primary school. I've played for Derbyshire since 1993 and made my first team debut in June of that year. In first class cricket I have scored over 5000 runs at an average of 35+ with a highest score of 210 versus Hampshire in 1997. In total to date in all cricket I have scored 30 fifties and ten hundreds, two of which have been two hundreds. I expect to play for England.

MS MARVA YVONNE ROLLINS (HEADTEACHER)

Headteacher, Godwin Junior School, 45 First Avenue, Manor Park, London, E12 6AW

PLACE OF BIRTH: Barbados, 14.12.51
MARITAL STATUS: Divorced
CHILDREN: Three (Adrian, Gary, Robert)
COLLEGE: North London
ACADEMIC QUALIFICATIONS: Bachelor of Education Hons
PROFESSIONAL QUALIFICATIONS: MA Education, Certificates in Counselling, Theory & Practise
MEMBERSHIPS: BOCA - ELBWO
HONOURS/AWARDS: Honorary Licentiate College of Preceptors (Teachers)
HOBBIES AND INTERESTS: Reading, personal-professional training, walks
PERSONAL PROFILE: Came to England in 1964. Member of a very supportive family headed by my mother Myrtle Hurst. A mature student who gained headship in eighth year in teaching (1995). Active member in local community for over 20 years. Works with individuals and groups on personal and professional development. Speaker on educational issues.
NOMINATED BY: B O C A

MR RYAN ROMAIN (ACTOR-DIRECTOR)

PLACE OF BIRTH: London, 2.10.70
MARITAL STATUS: Single
COLLEGE: Richmond-upon-Thames
ACADEMIC QUALIFICATIONS: 3 A-Level, 5 O-Levels
PERSONAL PROFILE: As well as being an actor Ryan began directing plays after attending Theatre Royal Stratford East's directors course. He has worked as assistant director for respected directors: Kerry Michael, Richard Wilson and director, designer, Ultz. He has also directed a show for Theatre Royal Stratford East.

MR KEN ROMANO (STUDENT-ACTOR)

143 Thackeray Avenue, London, N17 9DX

PLACE OF BIRTH: London, 8.8.80
MARITAL STATUS: Single
COLLEGE: Trent Park Middlesex University
ACADEMIC QUALIFICATIONS: 9 GCSEs, 3 A-Levels
MEMBERSHIPS: Anna Scher Theatre, Under Agency
HONOURS/AWARDS: Best Actor, Best Play, Festival of Plays, AST, 1996
HOBBIES AND INTERESTS: Reading, swimming, weight training, theatre
EMAIL: jokeluk@aol.com.uk
PERSONAL PROFILE: Since the age of eleven I have been a member of the Anna Scher Theatre and have done various works on TV and radio. Most of all though, is the work I have done in the community. Through the theatre I do many workshops in schools and conferences. These range from AIDS awareness to bullying and depression. As well as this I am experienced in lighting and sound. Peace promotion is our aim at the theatre and I have often stage managed and done lighting and sound for special talks eg. Yolanda King.

MISS CHRYSTAL ROSE (ENTERTAINER)

Businesswoman, 96 George Street, London, W1H 5RH

PLACE OF BIRTH: Lagos, 16.10.62
MARITAL STATUS: Single
CHILDREN: One (Louise Rose)
ACADEMIC QUALIFICATIONS: 6 O-Levels, 2 CSEs, one Diploma
DIRECTORSHIPS: Chrystal's Diamonds, Rose Records UK Ltd
HOBBIES AND INTERESTS: Backgammon, scrabble, netball
EMAIL: Chrystalrose@compuserue.com
PERSONAL PROFILE: Chrystal Rose was not just the first Black person to host a talk show that bore her name in Britain, she was the first woman. She was also the first Black woman to own an evening wear shop in the West End and own her own record label.

MISS MARCIA ROSE (ACTRESS)

PLACE OF BIRTH: London, 8.3.65
MARITAL STATUS: Single
COLLEGE: Rose Bruford College of Speech & Drama
ACADEMIC QUALIFICATIONS: A-Levels, O-Levels
PROFESSIONAL QUALIFICATIONS: BA Hons Degree in Community Theatre Arts
HOBBIES AND INTERESTS: Music all aspects, reading all aspects
PERSONAL PROFILE: Since leaving drama school I have been involved in many theatre productions including Carmen Jones at the Old Vic Theatre, as well as many companies i.e. Black Theatre Co-op and Red Shift. I've worked on films both controversial and rewarding, 'Skin' by Sarah Kane and most recently 'Tube Tale'. I am currently appearing in 'Brothers and Sisters' for the BBC.

MISS CATHERINE ROSS (MANAGEMENT CONSULTANT)

Managing Director, Ross Consultancies, Welland House, Fosdyke, Lincs, PE12 6LH

PLACE OF BIRTH: St Kitts, 25.9.51
MARITAL STATUS: Single, Divorced
CHILDREN: Two (Joanna, Lynda-Louise Burrel)
COLLEGE: Redditch College, Worcestershire
ACADEMIC QUALIFICATIONS: HND Business Studies, Post Graduate Certificate in Law
PROFESSIONAL QUALIFICATIONS: ACCA, City & Guilds Teachers Certificate, NVQ Assessor
MEMBERSHIPS: Employment Services, New Deal Steering Group, Legal Aid Board
HOBBIES AND INTERESTS: Mentoring young Black people, Collector of Black history memorabilia, author of fiction and non fiction, journalist
PERSONAL PROFILE: In business I facilitate corporate development through staff empowerment in the community, I work to ensure Black people, youth and it's older members' repositories of knowledge and experience are recognised and utilised. In the family I enjoy and share the nurturing of an extensive Caribbean heritage, everything else I do benefits from this.

MR CLIVE ROWE (ACTOR)

c/o Peters, Fraser & Dunlop, Chelsea Harbour, Lots Road, London, SW10 0XF

PLACE OF BIRTH: Shaw, 27.3.64
MARITAL STATUS: Single
COLLEGE: Guild Hall School of Drama & Music
HONOURS/AWARDS: Olivier Award Best Supporting Performance 1997
HOBBIES AND INTERESTS: Eating, films, hot summer days
PERSONAL PROFILE: Born Clive Mark Rowe, youngest of seven children raised by mother a woman of great strength and love. Introduced to theatre at age of 14. A hobby that became my passion and profession from Play House to Royal National Theatre; from Sondiem to Shakespeare; from Oldham Chronicle to Who's Who. Thank you

MRS HYACINTH ROWE (HEALTH PROMOTION SPECIALIST)

Health Promotion Service Steps To Health, 3 Coalport Road, East Park, Wolverhapton, WV1 2DE

PLACE OF BIRTH: Jamaica, 20.6.46
MARITAL STATUS: Married
COLLEGE: SR. Dora School of Nursing, University of Wolverhampton
ACADEMIC QUALIFICATIONS: 3 O-Levels, 730 C+G, MSc Health Studies, Current Student
PROFESSIONAL QUALIFICATIONS: Registered Nurse/Midwife
DIRECTORSHIPS: Board Member Deep Co. Ltd. Vice Chair Educare
HONOURS/AWARDS: Health Awards Outstanding Community Service. International Recognition Hypertension in Blacks
HOBBIES AND INTERESTS: Reading, singing, cooking, gardening
PERSONAL PROFILE: I emigrated to England in 1964 to join my parents. Entered nursing in 1966, married, went back to Jamaica, nursed in both rural and urban hospitals. Returned to England in 1980. Converted to RN, midwife. Worked as liaison officer to develop a post natal visiting service, research into health needs of African Caribbean women's health. Founder of Mt Shiloh Health Advisory Centre. Served on CHC and on many community organisations committees.
NOMINATED BY: Andrew Rowe

MR JOHN SALAKO (FOOTBALLER)

Fulham Football Club, Craven Cottage, Stevenage Road, London, SW6 6HH

PLACE OF BIRTH: Nigeria, 11.2.69
PROFESSIONAL QUALIFICATIONS: Caps for England (5)
PERSONAL PROFILE: Winger signed under the Bosman ruling in July from Coventry City to add some much needed width to the Fulham attack. Made his mark under the management of Steve Coppell and provided the ammunition for the Ian Wright and Mark Bright partnership as Crystal Palace were promoted via the play-offs to the old First division.

MR ELIJAH SYLVESTER SALMON (ACTOR-SINGER)

18 Tether Down, Muswell Hill, London, N10 1NB

PLACE OF BIRTH: Warwickshire, 14.10.65
MARITAL STATUS: Single
COLLEGE: Mountview
ACADEMIC QUALIFICATIONS: History, Art, Biology, Design
PROFESSIONAL QUALIFICATIONS: Performing Arts Diploma
MEMBERSHIPS: Equity
HOBBIES AND INTERESTS: Tennis, photography
PERSONAL PROFILE: Trained at Mountview Theatre. Working in film, TV and theatre working with such people as Derek Griffiths, Grace Kennedy, Ruby Turner, Simon Callow, Jude Kelly and Nigel Havers. In 'Paradise Club', 'The Bill' and 'The Heart Surgeon' on TV.. 'The Wicked Old Man', 'Carmen Jones' in Theatre.

MS BRIDGIT AGATHA SAM-BAILEY (EDUCATIONALIST)

Rtd, 41 Blagdon Road, Lewisham, London, SE8 7HH

PLACE OF BIRTH: Guyana, 25.9.36
MARITAL STATUS: Divorced
CHILDREN: One (Jacob O'Brien Yosafa Sam-Larose)
COLLEGE: London
ACADEMIC QUALIFICATIONS: BA Hons Soc of Education, MA Comparative Education
PROFESSIONAL QUALIFICATIONS: Private Secretary's Diploma LCC
MEMBERSHIPS: (Chairman) Guyana Friends Association, Association of Teachers & Lecturers
HOBBIES AND INTERESTS: Singing, travelling, meeting interesting people
EMAIL: BSambailey@aol.com
PERSONAL PROFILE: I have been proactive in equal opportunities issues. I was the first and only Black executive officer of the ATL, and have addressed annual assembly for several years. I am on the governing body of a primary and a secondary school where I am respected . GFA is a fundraising educational charity.

MR ANSLEM SAMUEL (LECTURER FE)

London Borough of Hackney, 28 Cecile Park, London, N8 9AS

PLACE OF BIRTH: Trinidad, 30.11.38
MARITAL STATUS: Single
CHILDREN: Four (Bionda, Nagaat, Zarelle, Monefa)
PROFESSIONAL QUALIFICATIONS: MA Socio Legal Studies
DIRECTORSHIPS: Front Line Housing Advice
HOBBIES AND INTERESTS: Travel, music, local politics, theatre
PERSONAL PROFILE: I have been involved in race relations and community work for over 25 years. Islington CRC, Hackney CRE and Haringey CRE.
NOMINATED BY: Ansel Wong

MR ALEX SANDY-LEE (ADMINISTRATOR)

Charity Commission, PAF Promotions, PO Box 13736, Tottenham, London, N17 9WA

PLACE OF BIRTH: Islington, 6.1.67
MARITAL STATUS: Married
CHILDREN: Two (Jerome, Shanice)
COLLEGE: 6 O-Levels
ACADEMIC QUALIFICATIONS: 1 A-Level
MEMBERSHIPS: Sickle Cell Society
HOBBIES AND INTERESTS: Collecting records (Vinyl Junkie)
EMAIL: a.Lee2@ukonline.co.uk
PERSONAL PROFILE: A civil servant - The Charity Commission since 1990. Educated at Highbury Grove School 1978. City and East London College 1985. Fundraiser for the Sickle Cell Society since 1996. Company PAF Promotions owned with sister Inkla Sandy Lee. Helping to develop artists, promoting fashion and talent shows, exhibitions and media TV programmes.

MISS INKLA SANDY-LEE (PROMOTION MANAGER)

PAF Promotions, PO Box 13736, Tottenham, London, N17 9WA

PLACE OF BIRTH: London, 2.6.69
MARITAL STATUS: Single
COLLEGE: City & Islington/Lambeth
ACADEMIC QUALIFICATIONS: 2 O-Levels, 1 A-Level Diploma (NVQ) 4
PROFESSIONAL QUALIFICATIONS: NVQ 1, 2, 3
DIRECTORSHIPS: None
MEMBERSHIPS: Sickle Cell Society
HOBBIES AND INTERESTS: Photography, reading, socialising
EMAIL: A.LEE2@UKONLINe.Co.uk
PERSONAL PROFILE: Educated at Barnsbury School in Islington I studied creative arts, media and journalism. Reading books by Black authors has inspired me to enjoy writing. I've always believed everyone has the potential to do what they want in life. As one half of PAF Promotions I write scripts for short films and documentaries.

DR MICHAEL SANTIAGO (ASSOCIATE LECTURER)

University of Surrey, 6 Goldsmith Close, Woking, Surrey, GU21 3HF

PLACE OF BIRTH: Trinidad, 25.4.58
MARITAL STATUS: Married
CHILDREN: Three (Richard, Christopher, Olivia)
COLLEGE: Open University of Surrey
ACADEMIC QUALIFICATIONS: BA, MA, PhD
MEMBERSHIPS: International Police Association
HOBBIES AND INTERESTS: Football, table tennis
EMAIL: Micheal.Santiago@net.ntl.com
PERSONAL PROFILE: I migrated to the UK in 1983. I was a police officer with the Surrey constabulary for nine years. I am a committed Christain, I am about to have my first book published on Euro Poll, The European Criminal Intelligence Agency.
NOMINATED BY: Santiago

BALA MOHAMMED SANUSI (MANAGEMENT CONSULTANT)

President, Nigeria National Union, 101 Ansell Road, London, SW17 7LT

PLACE OF BIRTH: Nigeria, 4.5.60
MARITAL STATUS: Married
CHILDREN: Four (Amina, Aisha, Kamal, Azaria)
COLLEGE: South Bank University
ACADEMIC QUALIFICATIONS: Masters in Business Administration
DIRECTORSHIPS: Associate Director BMS Consultancy Ltd
MEMBERSHIPS: MI Mgt (Member Institute of Management)
HOBBIES AND INTERESTS: Tennis, reading, horse-riding
EMAIL: BMSrands@aol.com
PERSONAL PROFILE: President, Nigeria National Union, an umbrella organisation representing over 300,000 Nigerians in the UK, is a man of vision and a quiet achiever. He has been the leader of the union since 1996. Within this period, he had managed to transform the union which was in disarray into a strong and vibrant organisation. He is married to Dr Carcus Douglas-Sanusi, a distinguished management consultant, like himself.

President, Nigeria National Union, an umbrella organisation representing over 300,000 Nigerians in the UK

BALA MOHAMMED SANUSI

MR DANNY KWESI SAPANI (ACTOR)

Marina Martin Associates,
12-13 Poland Street, London, W1V 3DE

PLACE OF BIRTH: London, 15/11/70
MARITAL STATUS: Single
ACADEMIC QUALIFICATIONS: Diploma Drama Arts Degree
MEMBERSHIPS: Equity

MR ADE SAPARA (ACTOR)

Kate Feast Management, 10 Primrose Hill Studios, Fitzroy Road, London, NW1 8TR

PLACE OF BIRTH: Barnet, 28.1.64
MARITAL STATUS: Married
CHILDREN: Three (Indios, Xoa, Shae)
COLLEGE: Central School Speech & Drama
ACADEMIC QUALIFICATIONS: Diploma in Drama
MEMBERSHIPS: Equity
HOBBIES AND INTERESTS: Sport, history
PERSONAL PROFILE: 'Crusoe' co-starring with Aiden Quinn 'The Fatherland' - Riverside, 'Solomon & The Big Cat' Young Vic RSC. 'Riff-Raff' - Ken Loach. 'London's Burning', 'Casualty', 'The Bill' (TV), ESC - Africa Tour. Shared experience. World tour. 'Supply & Demand' - Lynda La Plante (TV). Globe Theatre - Opening seasons Holder Festival, Barbados 'The Tempest'.

MR KWASI SARPONG (PUBLISHIER)

African Pages Ltd, 49 Copeland Road, Wembley, HA0 4YH

PLACE OF BIRTH: Ghana, 14.3.54
MARITAL STATUS: Married
CHILDREN: Three (Nancy, Yaw, Leona)
COLLEGE: Hebrew University of Jerusalem
ACADEMIC QUALIFICATIONS: Diploma; MSc
DIRECTORSHIPS: African Pages Ltd Awbad Settlement; Awbad Publication
MEMBERSHIPS: Directory Publishers Association
HOBBIES AND INTERESTS: Political meetings
EMAIL: Ksarpong@aol.com
PERSONAL PROFILE: Attended Mohnt Mary College (1972); Accra Teacher Training College (1994); University of Ghana (1978) and Hebrew University of Jerusalem (1995). Teacher in Ondo State of Nigeria, have been property sales agent and publisher since 1990.

MR JOSEPH SEALY (BUSINESS PLANNER)

KPMG Transformation Planning, 8 Salisbury Square, London, EC4Y 8BB

PLACE OF BIRTH: London, 27.8.63
MARITAL STATUS: Married
COLLEGE: Leeds
ACADEMIC QUALIFICATIONS: BA Hons, Class 2:1 Master in Business Administration MBA
PROFESSIONAL QUALIFICATIONS: Chartered Institute of Public Finance & Accountancy
HOBBIES AND INTERESTS: Sking, scuba diving, flying, reading, fitness training
EMAIL: Joseph.Sealy@Kang.co.uk
PERSONAL PROFILE: My achievements to date have been built on the foundations of inspiration, family support, education, and good fortune. My passion for life is driven by a belief that 'there are no limits to what people can achieve'. My dream for the Millennium is for the power and value of ethnic diversity to be recognised and treasured throughout all walks of life.
NOMINATED BY: Tetteh Kofi

Senior Tourism Adviser, CBI,1994. Present Secretary, Trade Association Council CBI

DR JUNE-ALISON SEALY JP

DR JUNE-ALISON SEALY JP (ADVISOR TOURISM TRADE CBI)

Advisor Tourism & Trade Association Affairs, Confederation of British Industry (CBI), , Centre Point, 103 New Oxford Street, London, WC1A 1DU

PLACE OF BIRTH: London
MARITAL STATUS: Divorced
COLLEGE: London University
ACADEMIC QUALIFICATIONS: PhD, MMus, B Mus Hons
PROFESSIONAL QUALIFICATIONS: ARCM, LTCL
DIRECTORSHIPS: Springboard UK
MEMBERSHIPS: Fellow Royal Society of Arts (FRSA)
HONOURS/AWARDS: Justice of the Peace, Harrow Care Middlesex. Appt 1995
HOBBIES AND INTERESTS: Music, gardening, swimming
EMAIL: June-Alison.Sealy@CBI.Org.UK
PERSONAL PROFILE: Senior Tourism Adviser, CBI,1994. Present Secretary, Trade Association Council CBI 1999-.Achieved Bachelors, Masters and PhD at Goldsmiths College London University, all through part-time, self-funded study. PhD on Indian, Jewish culture and Biblical Heritage hailed as pioneering work in field. School: Copthall County Girls Grammar, first black pupil, parents from Guyana.
NOMINATED BY: Frances Keenan

MR PHILEMON SEALY JP (CHIEF OFFICER LOCAL GOVT RTD)

JP Lay Magistrate, 5 Lewgars Avenue, Kingsbury, London, NW9 8AR

PLACE OF BIRTH: Barbados, 28.6.34
MARITAL STATUS: Married
CHILDREN: Two (Pamela, Hilda)
COLLEGE: LSE
ACADEMIC QUALIFICATIONS: RGN (SRN) RMN, Dip Soc. Admin
PROFESSIONAL QUALIFICATIONS: SRN, RMN, Dip Soc. Admin
HOBBIES AND INTERESTS: All sports, politics, civic affairs, race relations
PERSONAL PROFILE: Barbadian and Old Combermerian Phil Sealy celebrates 25 years as a Justice of Peace and lay magistrate in London. Phil, the longest serving Black lay-magistrate in Britain came to London in 1956. He joined the Bench at Brent Magistrates' Court in 1973 where he currently serves. First elected as a local Labour Party councillor from 1978 - 86. Phil has been a socialist and political activist. Chairman of the national race relations branch of a leading British trade union. He also served as the first secretary of the UK branch of the Barbados Labour Party.

MR MARK SETCHFIELD (ART DIRECTOR)

Maxim Magazine, Dennis Publishing, 19 Bolsover Street, London, W1P 7HJ

PLACE OF BIRTH: Peterborough, 21.6.70
MARITAL STATUS: Single
COLLEGE: Reading College
ACADEMIC QUALIFICATIONS: HND Graphic Design
HOBBIES AND INTERESTS: Music, film, gym training
EMAIL: Art.Maxim@Dennis.co.uk
PERSONAL PROFILE: I have worked in London in publishing for the last six years, in lifestyle mags. I hope to work abroad and work on new launch ideas.
NOMINATED BY: Jon Daniel

MR JIMMY SHARPE (COMMUNITY SERVICES)

PLACE OF BIRTH: Kingston, 3.3.15
MARITAL STATUS: Married
HOBBIES AND INTERESTS: Sports, cricket enthusiast
PERSONAL PROFILE: Arrived in England 1939, worked as a munition worker, started a tailoring business but due to illness was abandoned. Travelled to Sweden in 1949 and spent a year in Stockholm. On return to London I found work with some of the leading clothing manufacturers. I am an ardent, socialist Anglican, very sociable. Have been involved in all forward movements to intergrate Black people. I am happy to have lived the 'Dream' of Martin Luther King and hope that my good deeds will not be forgotten.

MR BABAFEMI OLATUNDE SHODEKE
(ACCOUNTANT)

Senior Lecturer- Rtd, South East London College, 7 Pasteur Gardens, Edmonton, London, N18 1JN

PLACE OF BIRTH: Nigeria, 24.5.24
MARITAL STATUS: Divorced
COLLEGE: Birmingham London
ACADEMIC QUALIFICATIONS: B.Com (B.Ham); MEd (Multicult) CNAA. Dip. Ed; Cert EDYEE
PROFESSIONAL QUALIFICATIONS: MCIM, MBIM, FFA; ACCS, SAT ACCT.
DIRECTORSHIPS: Adun Society (1985) Trustee; Enfield Race Equality Council
MEMBERSHIPS: OGUN State Union, EGBA United Society; Nigerian Council of Elders
HONOURS/AWARDS: ICOBA UK Merit Award UK
HOBBIES AND INTERESTS: Reading, crosswords, swimming, debates
PERSONAL PROFILE: Community involvement: Co-ordinator and chief executive office of Enfield African Association. Hon treasurer-Enfield Racial Equality Council. Trustee- St Martins La Tour -Housing Association for mentally disturbed persons. 1983-85 Chairman board of trustees- Adun Society (Black Women Dress Design Association). Awards. 1998-Igbobi College Old Boys' Association (ICOBA) UK merit award for services to the association. Lisabi Award for services to EGBAS in the UK and Ireland.

NOMINATED BY: Sam Jenyo

MR CHRISTOPHER SHOKOYA-ELESHIN (CHIEF EXECUTIVE)

Shokoya-Eleshin Group,

PLACE OF BIRTH: Lagos, 24.5.61
MARITAL STATUS: Single
COLLEGE: Ahamodu Bello, Liverpool, Warwick
ACADEMIC QUALIFICATIONS: BENG, MSC Eng.
DIRECTORSHIPS: PYBI S+E Const. Dingle Opps
MEMBERSHIPS: MCC, East India
HOBBIES AND INTERESTS: Cricket, football
PERSONAL PROFILE: Chris is chief executive of one of the few Black construction companies in the UK. He is an authority on urban regeneration and securing socio-economic benefits to targeted communities. He stresses the participation of Black, ethnic minority and disadvantaged groups throughout the construction process. Shokoya-Eleshin Group has championed by example, the concept of utilising local labour within construction works. The company has thus gained National and International recognition for its efforts in building communities.

MISS MELISSA SIMON-SARKODEE (COSTUME DESIGNER)

Artist, 1 Alpha House, Alpha Place, London, NW6 5TE

PLACE OF BIRTH: London, 27.5.77
MARITAL STATUS: Single
COLLEGE: Barnet College / London College of Fashion
ACADEMIC QUALIFICATIONS: BTEC National Diploma In General Art & Design
PROFESSIONAL QUALIFICATIONS: Higher National Diploma In Theatre Studies (Costume Interpretation)
HONOURS/AWARDS: Awards of Distinction For ERTE, Art-Deco Reproduction
HOBBIES AND INTERESTS: Interior design, ceramics, pottery, decorative paint finishes
PERSONAL PROFILE: Theatre studies graduate. Creator of award winning costumes for Notting Hill Carnival. Was nominated for the Alan Young Award for Art Student of the Year. Made garments for the Queen's Golden Wedding Anniversary. Tutored art projects at V & A Museum. Participated in Trinidad & Tobago exhibition held at the Commonwealth Institute.
NOMINATED BY: Ansel Wong

> ## Chris is chief executive of one of the few Black construction companies in the UK
>
> **MR CHRISTOPHER SHOKOYA-ELESHIN**

MR GEORGE SMALLING (LEARNING & DEVELOPMENT SPECIALIST)

Manager, Management Development Centre, Birmingham City Council, Council House Extension, Birmingham, B3 3PL

PLACE OF BIRTH: Wednesbury, 11.8.66
MARITAL STATUS: Single
CHILDREN: One (Jordan)
ACADEMIC QUALIFICATIONS: HNC in Public Administration (1986/87), ONC in Public Administration
PROFESSIONAL QUALIFICATIONS: MA in Human Resource Management (1994/96),TDLB Vocational Assessor Award - D32/D33 (1996), Certificate of Competence in Occupational Testing (1994), Diploma in Training of Competence in Occupational Testing (1994), Diploma In Training Management (1989/90), Institute of Personnel Management (1987/88)
MEMBERSHIPS: MIPD (Member of the Institute of Personnel Development), British Psychological Society
HOBBIES AND INTERESTS: Sports, reading
PERSONAL PROFILE: I am a self-motivated Black man. I have many professional achievements to date. This satisfaction is not gained from the material reward that achievement within formal organisation structures bring but, from the way that I have maintained my integrity and honesty, and grown in individuality and Blackness.
NOMINATED BY: Birmingham City Council

MRS ALMA SMITH (HEALTH PROJECTS MANAGER)

The Independent African & Caribbean Health Research Group, Grove House Family Centre, Bagleys Lane, Fulham, London, SW16 1QB

PLACE OF BIRTH: Aruba, 25.5.48
MARITAL STATUS: Married
CHILDREN: Two (Deborah, Alison)
COLLEGE: South Bank London
ACADEMIC QUALIFICATIONS: MSc in Health Services Management
PROFESSIONAL QUALIFICATIONS: RGN, RM, Dip HSM
DIRECTORSHIPS: Chair - Grenada Health Workers Association (UK), Vice Chair Professional Afro-Asian Women's Association (PAAWA), Health Adviser - Vince Hines Foundation
HOBBIES AND INTERESTS: Singing, travelling, swimming
PERSONAL PROFILE: For the past 25 years I have been actively involved in community work in a voluntary capacity, primarily focusing on the health needs on the Black community. I serve on many committees advising on health issues and managing community health projects. I am a qualified marriage counsellor providing help to families from our community with relationship problems.
NOMINATED BY: Maria Thersa Gerome

MR JASON JUSTIN SMITH (DANCER-DUTY MANAGER)

London School of Contemporary Dance - The Place, Danceworks, 16 Balderton Street, London, W1Y 1TF

PLACE OF BIRTH: London, 27.10.77
MARITAL STATUS: Single
COLLEGE: London School of Contemporary Dance
ACADEMIC QUALIFICATIONS: 9 GCSEs, 3 A-Levels
PROFESSIONAL QUALIFICATIONS: GNVQ Hairdressing
HONOURS/AWARDS: Certificate 1st Level Teaching Volleyball
HOBBIES AND INTERESTS: Disc jockey, fitness, clubing, climbing, Tai-Chi
PERSONAL PROFILE: School - First Black headboy in eight years. College member of student union. First year GNVQ, First in photographic competition. Hairdressing first in Show Case Competition. Currently studying a degree at London Contemporary Dance School. Receiver of William Louther Scholarship.

MR MICHAEL SMITH (ENVIRONMENTAL SERVICES MANAGER)

Evironmental Services Manager, London Borough of Lewisham (Housing), 167 Boleyn Road, Forest Gate, London, E7 9QH

PLACE OF BIRTH: Barbados, 8.6.47
MARITAL STATUS: Married
CHILDREN: Two (Samantha, Susan)
PROFESSIONAL QUALIFICATIONS: Post Grad. Cert. Housing Managament
MEMBERSHIPS: MC.T
HOBBIES AND INTERESTS: Politics

NOMINATED BY: B O C A

COUNT OSSIE OSWALD SMITH (DISC JOCKEY)

Count Ossie, 26 Neale House, Blakenhall Gardens, Wolverhampton, WV2 3HB

PLACE OF BIRTH: Jamaica, 13.1.29
MARITAL STATUS: Single
CHILDREN: Four (Gladson, Presus, Denton, Vernon)
PROFESSIONAL QUALIFICATIONS: Disc Jockey
MEMBERSHIPS: Culture Club
HONOURS/AWARDS: BBC Radio WM & BBC Midlands Today
HOBBIES AND INTERESTS: Music
PERSONAL PROFILE: I arrived in England in 1962 and started to play African Caribbean music in Wolverhampton and I still carry on playing it for the Wolverhampton Culture Club for the entertainment on Fridays and Sundays. I love my music, still after all these years.

MR TSAGAZA HAB SNAPE (SINGER-SONGWRITER)

c/o Connecting Routes, 109 Edison Road, Stafford, ST16 3NH

PLACE OF BIRTH: England, 3.2.61
MARITAL STATUS: Single
HONOURS/AWARDS: Voice Community & Arts Awards, black Music Award
HOBBIES AND INTERESTS: Humanitarian, music, songwriting, God, The Bible

MR BILL SPENCER (ACTOR SINGER)

Music Producer, BMS Recording Studio & Productions, Unit G9 Shakespeare Business Centre, 245A Coldharbour Lane, London, SW9

PLACE OF BIRTH: Jamaica, 4.7.60
MARITAL STATUS: Single
COLLEGE: Morley City Lit.
ACADEMIC QUALIFICATIONS: GCSE 4
PROFESSIONAL QUALIFICATIONS: Equity
DIRECTORSHIPS: Studio Owner
MEMBERSHIPS: Equity/PRS
HOBBIES AND INTERESTS: Football, cricket
PERSONAL PROFILE: Appeared in 'London's Burning', 'Eastenders' and many other programmes and TV commercials. Written and produced several singles to date and own BMS Recording Studio. Bill also gives advice and helps young talent to get a head start in the entertainment industry.

MRS DOROTHY SPRINGER (COMMUNITY WORKER)

Barbados & Friends Association, 16 Beresford Road, Reading, RG30 1DD

PLACE OF BIRTH: Barbados, 5.3.35
MARITAL STATUS: Married
CHILDREN: Four (Sherwyn, O'Neil, Janice, Alison)
HONOURS/AWARDS: Community Award
HOBBIES AND INTERESTS: Reading, cooking, travelling, community work with the elderly, children
PERSONAL PROFILE: A dedicated and committed individual working within the Black community on a voluntary basis for over 30 years. Stalwart member of the Barbados & Friends Association (Reading); trustee of the West Indian Women's Circle: Sunday schoolteacher and group leader providing care and counselling for members who need support.
NOMINATED BY: Patricia Cutting, Barbados & Friends Assoc

He has recently completed a book on African Caribbean elders, entitled 'Cold Arrival, Life In A Second Homeland'

STEVE STEPHENSON MBE

MR MARK SPRINGER (ACTOR-WRITER)

N.T Ensemble Member, Royal National Theatre, 6 Hallam House, Gostling Way, London, SW9 9PX

PLACE OF BIRTH: Reading, 8.5.74
MARITAL STATUS: Single
COLLEGE: Manchester Metro University
ACADEMIC QUALIFICATIONS: BA Hons in Theatre Arts
MEMBERSHIPS: A Member of the First National Theatre Ensemble Company for over ten years
HOBBIES AND INTERESTS: Football, reading
PERSONAL PROFILE: I was born in Reading but have spent most of my life in London. Early career choices included professional football but things didn't work out. However after stumbling across acting in 1990 I eventually enrolled in drama school in 1995, graduating in 1998. My job at the National Theatre is my sixth.

MR ENRICHO ALPHANSO STENNETT (COMMUNITY ACTIVIST RTD)

1 Howard Road, Llandudno, Wales, LL30 1EA
PLACE OF BIRTH: Jamaica, 9.10.26
MARITAL STATUS: Married
CHILDREN: Two (Robert Antony, Paul Raymond)
COLLEGE: Cornwall College
ACADEMIC QUALIFICATIONS: Youth Officer
PROFESSIONAL QUALIFICATIONS: Youth & Community
MEMBERSHIPS: Member Westminster Labour Party & National Union of the Furniture Trade Operators
HOBBIES AND INTERESTS: Ballroom dancing, Latin American dancing, walking.
PERSONAL PROFILE: Spoke in Sabina Park as the voice of young Jamaica at the age of 12. Aged 17 was employed by the Jamaican Nationalist Party, headed by Norman Manley. Came to England 1947, joined Colonial Service, assisting with the settlement of newly arrived West Indians. Between 1950-60, spoke in Hyde Park as the only voice of Black people at the time. Became a demonstration dancer for Mecca Ballroom, appeared in a play 'How Deep Are The Roots'. Founder of Cosmopolitan Social Association, co-founder of the African League, co-founder 'Help' and founded first Black newspaper 'African Voice'.
NOMINATED BY: Mary Stennett

MR STEVE STEPHENSON MBE (MANAGER-SOCIAL WORKER)

Manager, Ashanti Community Support Team, 86 Barkers Lane, Goldington, Bedford, MK41 9SU

PLACE OF BIRTH: Kingston, 10.12.53
MARITAL STATUS: Married
CHILDREN: Two (Andrea, Simone)
COLLEGE: University of Hertfordshire
ACADEMIC QUALIFICATIONS: BA with Commendation
PROFESSIONAL QUALIFICATIONS: CQSW. and Diploma in Management
DIRECTORSHIPS: Patron Cornwall College Old Boy Association
MEMBERSHIPS: Institute of Jamaica
HONOURS/AWARDS: MBE, Hansib Award, Citizen Award, Gleaner Award, Two Voice Awards
HOBBIES AND INTERESTS: Sports, charity work
PERSONAL PROFILE: Steve made a significant contribution to community development and race relations as leader of the Starlight Youth Club in Luton. He has helped to Kick Racism Out Of Football by running a Saturday Club for Black and Asian youth. He has recently completed a book on African Caribbean elders, entitled "Cold Arrival, Life In A Second Homeland". His most recent event was a ground breaking tribute to the Pioneers of Black British Football in 1998. He received six National awards including MBE from the Queen. He is chairman of the Victoria Mutual Cricket Cup.
NOMINATED BY: Mrs M Griffiths

OLIVE STRACHAN (TRAINING CONSULTANT)

Olive Strachan Resources,

PLACE OF BIRTH: Dominica, 30.9.61
MARITAL STATUS: Married
CHILDREN: Two (Rhia, Ricky)
COLLEGE: Salford University
ACADEMIC QUALIFICATIONS: Grad IPD HR Qualifications
PROFESSIONAL QUALIFICATIONS: Diploma in HR Management, Member of Employment Consultants Institute
MEMBERSHIPS: Grad IPD, MECI
HOBBIES AND INTERESTS: Working, dancing, cooking, reading

MS CAROL STRAKER (Dancer-Choreographer)

Artistic Director, Carol Straker Dance Foundation, 136-142a Lower Clapton Road, Hackney, London, E5 0QT

PLACE OF BIRTH: London, 11.6.61
MARITAL STATUS: Married
CHILDREN: One (Jessica)
COLLEGE: Urclang Academy, Legat School of Russian Ballet
ACADEMIC QUALIFICATIONS: O-Level Eng., Art, GCE
DIRECTORSHIPS: Carol Straker Dance Foundation, ICPA, Ground Level Theatre Trust
MEMBERSHIPS: Imperial Society of Teachers of Dancing
HONOURS/AWARDS: Outstanding Contribution to the Performing Arts, Alternative Arts Best Dance Entertainers
HOBBIES AND INTERESTS: Reading, drawing
PERSONAL PROFILE: She has performed as an International artist with Alwin Ailey Dance Theatre, Martha Graham Co. and Michael Clark Co. Her school and dance company are based in Hackney and has over 200 students attending classes and performances. She trained in classical ballet style tap, modern Jazz and drama.
NOMINATED BY: Sharon Aitkin

MR RALPH ADOLPHUS STRAKER JP
(Race Relations Advisor)

Southwark Diocese, 48 Claverley Grove, Finchley, London, N3 2DH

PLACE OF BIRTH: Barbados, 16.3.36
MARITAL STATUS: Married
CHILDREN: Three (Carol, Diana, Jean)
COLLEGE: Barbados Evening Institute
ACADEMIC QUALIFICATIONS: English, Maths Agles Bary Agriculture-Horticulture
PROFESSIONAL QUALIFICATIONS: Diploma in Race Relations
MEMBERSHIPS: Sam Uriah Morris Society
HONOURS/AWARDS: BSM (Barbados Service Medal), Justice Of The Peace
HOBBIES AND INTERESTS: Black history, reading, toastmaster/MC, verger, watching cricket
PERSONAL PROFILE: Known as the Red Master. Worked with London Transport, The Post Office, Hackney CRE. Alexandra Palace as race relations manager. President of Sam Morris Society Black History Museum. Verger at St Paul's Church, Finchley. JP and a board of visitor to Holloway Prison. Twinning Link Person For Friendship (Hackney & Barbados).
NOMINATED BY: Christopher Johnson M.B.A.

MS MARGARET STUBBS (Manager-NHS)

General Manager, Community Health Sheffield, Fulwood Road, Sheffield, S10 1NZ

PLACE OF BIRTH: Jamaica, 14.8.47
MARITAL STATUS: Divorced
CHILDREN: One (Richard)
ACADEMIC QUALIFICATIONS: MBA, BA Hons
PROFESSIONAL QUALIFICATIONS: RN RM HV
MEMBERSHIPS: NIM, 300 Group
HOBBIES AND INTERESTS: Reading, debates, walking
PERSONAL PROFILE: Senior manager with the NHS, worked on issues around women's development and positions within private and public sector organisations and the government and Opportunity 2000. Involved with mentoring as a form of learning tool, development and achieving goals. I enjoy public speaking and being a role model and a mentor.
NOMINATED BY: Sunita Ram

MS SUANDI OBE (Writer-Poet)

Black Arts Alliance, PO Box 88, SDO, Manchester, M20 1BX

DIRECTORSHIPS: Cultural Director - Voluntary of the Black Arts Alliance
MEMBERSHIPS: Board of NWAB, Institute of Directors & British Equity
HONOURS/AWARDS: OBE 1999 New Years Honour's List
PERSONAL PROFILE: SuAndi has been a performance poet since 1985 and in recent years has worked in Live Arts. Her work was recognised with an OBE following her Winston Churchill Fellowship. In 1998 she was sole producer for Manchester Festival, a two day event which included eight performances and an exhibition. 1996-98 she was co-ordinator and editor for There Are No Limitations - a Black disabled initiative. SuAndi is a writer whose words have been described as 'sussed' humorous and to the point. 'I Love The Blackness Of My People' is her fourth collection of work.

MRS CARMELETTA SUBRYAN (Teacher)

Head of French Dept, Rokeby School, Pitchford Street, Stratford, London, E15 4RZ

PLACE OF BIRTH: Guyana, 6.1.56
MARITAL STATUS: Divorced
CHILDREN: Four (Ancel, Selena Monplaisir, Ray, Anthony)
COLLEGE: University of Guyana, UEL
ACADEMIC QUALIFICATIONS: French & English
PROFESSIONAL QUALIFICATIONS: PGCE French
MEMBERSHIPS: Dr. C.C. Nicholson FD / ELBWO / Soc. of Black Lawyers
HOBBIES AND INTERESTS: Community work, athletics, reading
PERSONAL PROFILE: I have taught for 18 years in Guyana, France and England. I am a head of department. I am a school governor, I work with charities, I am mentor and I am a teacher advocate training agency. I also have four children.

MR LANRE ADIO SUNMONU (Marketing Consultant)

Twin-Track Marketing Services (TMS), PO Box 12638, Southwark, London, SE17 22Q

PLACE OF BIRTH: Lagos, 4.5.63
CHILDREN: Two (Rachel, Rebecca)
COLLEGE: Middlesex University
ACADEMIC QUALIFICATIONS: MA in Marketing
PROFESSIONAL QUALIFICATIONS: Chartered Marketer
DIRECTORSHIPS: TMS
MEMBERSHIPS: MCIM-Full Member Chartered Institute.
HONOURS/AWARDS: Special recognition at The 2nd African Business Awards
HOBBIES AND INTERESTS: Sports, reading
PERSONAL PROFILE: I have been in the marketing (business) management as a manager and freelance consultant for seven years. As one of the leading freelance business/marketing consultants, I very much notice the pace of change in the world of business is accelerating. I am undertaking continuous professional development (CPD) to attain my masters degree (MA).
NOMINATED BY: Sam Jenyo

MR DALE SUPERVILLE (Actor)

PLACE OF BIRTH: London, 26.11.68
MARITAL STATUS: Single
COLLEGE: Mountview Theatre School
PROFESSIONAL QUALIFICATIONS: Diploma in Theatre
MEMBERSHIPS: Equity
PERSONAL PROFILE: Before leaving school my teacher suggested that if I wanted to get in to acting, I should wait until I was 22-23, so when I graduated there would be a larger percentage of Black people who had to be in arts. Im so glad he was right.

MS JUNE SUTHERLAND JP (Senior Staff nurse)

Alexandra Hospital, 33 Rockford Close, Oakenshaw South, Rebbitch, B98 7LY

PLACE OF BIRTH: Jamaica, 15.7.46
MARITAL STATUS: Married
CHILDREN: Two (Ginika Okorafor, Jason Okorafor)
COLLEGE: Liverpool Polytechnic
ACADEMIC QUALIFICATIONS: RGN, RCNT
PROFESSIONAL QUALIFICATIONS: Diploma Management
HOBBIES AND INTERESTS: Walking, learning African and Caribbean history
PERSONAL PROFILE: At present I chair the Black History Group which have been in existence for about five years. The current aim is to extend the membership to the wider community of Redditch. I am also a volunteer to the probation service in a advisory capacity on racial matters. Along with caring for two children and doing two jobs, I sit on the local Bench as a Justice of the Peace.
NOMINATED BY: Mrs J M, Chief Probation Officer

Carribbean Times

COUNTDOWN TO THE MILLENNIUM

MR MICHAEL TACHIE - MENSON (CEO)

Taussh, 57 Hampton Road, Forest Gate, London, E7 0PD

PLACE OF BIRTH: London, 8.8.63
MARITAL STATUS: Single
COLLEGE: University of Buckingham, University of New Haven, US
ACADEMIC QUALIFICATIONS: BSc Hons, MBA
HOBBIES AND INTERESTS: Black history, economic development issues, Black music, martial arts, travel
PERSONAL PROFILE: Born in London to Ghanaian parents attended Stratford School. Whilst doing his MBA had an idea for a crease-free way to carry suits. Developed idea into a prototype. Patented the design concept, founded Taussh (designing manufacturing). Developing production in Ghana.

MISS NATALIE TAPPER (ACTRESS-SINGER-SONGWRITER)

Rossmore Personal Management, Rossmore Road, Marylebone, London, NW1 6NJ

PLACE OF BIRTH: London, 18.9.79
MARITAL STATUS: Single
COLLEGE: Sir George Monoux College
ACADEMIC QUALIFICATIONS: A-Levels in Performing Arts & Law
MEMBERSHIPS: Musicians Union
HONOURS/AWARDS: (1997) Hackneys Young Singer of the Year, Award sponsored by the Hackney Gazette
HOBBIES AND INTERESTS: Singing, acting, dancing, going out shopping, partying and keeping fit
PERSONAL PROFILE: Fortunately I am blessed with my talents which I illustrate to achieve success in both drama 'Grange Hill' and also music. I have displayed the ability to not only sing but to write songs. Therefore my destiny is to share my blessing with the world, never losing sight of who I am.

MRS SHIRLEY TATE (SENIOR LECTURER)

Senior Lecturer (Sociology), Leeds Metropolitan University,

PLACE OF BIRTH: Jamaica, 22.3.56
MARITAL STATUS: Married
CHILDREN: Two (Damain, Soraya)
COLLEGE: York University
ACADEMIC QUALIFICATIONS: MA, M Phil.
PROFESSIONAL QUALIFICATIONS: Qualified Teacher, ITD Diploma
DIRECTORSHIPS: Chair West Yorkshire Metropolitan Ambulance Service NHS Trust
HOBBIES AND INTERESTS: Travel, reading, decorating, going to the gym
PERSONAL PROFILE: Born in Jamaica and educated to A-Levels. Voluntary work with Black organisations, arts, HIV and AIDS, youth and community work. 14 years as a sociology lecturer with a special interest in Black studies. Completing a PhD at Lancaster University on Black British identities, six years as a non-executive director on CMH, NHS Trust in Leeds.
NOMINATED BY: Emma Leech

LORD JOHN TAYLOR OF WARWICK
(BARRISTER, COMPANY DIRECTOR)

Member of House of Lords, Unit 3, New House Business Centre, Old Crawley Road, Horsham, RH12 4RU

PLACE OF BIRTH: Birmingham, 21.9.52
MARITAL STATUS: Married
CHILDREN: Three (Laura, Alexandra, Mark)
COLLEGE: University of Keele, University of Warwick
ACADEMIC QUALIFICATIONS: BA Hons Law, Doctor of Laws (LLD)
PROFESSIONAL QUALIFICATIONS: Barrister-at-Law
DIRECTORSHIPS: Director Warwick Consulting International Ltd; Director Warwick Leadership Foundation
MEMBERSHIPS: Committee Member SCAR (Sickle Cell Charity)
HONOURS/AWARDS: Peerage, Freedom of London 1999 (Awarded)
HOBBIES AND INTERESTS: Soccer, cricket, singing, reading
EMAIL: taylorjdb@parliament.uk
PERSONAL PROFILE: Member of House of Lords; Vice president of British Board of Film Classification; Vice president of the Small Business Bureau; Barrister-at-Law; Non-executive director of North West Thames Regional Health Authority; President Ilford Town FC. Patron Kidscape; Patron of Parents for Children.

MR TODD TERRY (DJ)

Smash Press, 99c Talbot Road, London, W11 2AT

PERSONAL PROFILE: Todd Terry, a DJ with a discography most would die for, is about to blow away all of our preconceptions, with an outstanding new single and album to follow. Todd is mainly associated with his house remixes, with tracks like 'Everything But The Girl's', 'Missing' and Grace Jone's 'Slave To The Rhythm', as well as working with the likes of Robert Plant, George Michael, Bjork, David Bowie and Michael Jackson.

GLORIA PATRICIA THEODORE (BUSINESS CONSULTANT)

Standalone, 415 Lincoln Road, Enfield, EN3 4AQ

PLACE OF BIRTH: Trinidad, 10.12.55
MARITAL STATUS: Divorced
CHILDREN: Two (Robert, Mark)
ACADEMIC QUALIFICATIONS: O-Levels, CSE's
PROFESSIONAL QUALIFICATIONS: Balanced Business Leadership
MEMBERSHIPS: ACFF, EFBBWO
HONOURS/AWARDS: Solid Silver Award For Innovation
HOBBIES AND INTERESTS: Writing poetry
PERSONAL PROFILE: My education really started in the school of life in 1971. I worked for NatWest Bank for 24 years achieving junior management at 32, senior management at 35. Due to ill-health (Sarcoidosis). I left the bank in 1997. In June 1998 I formed Standalone Business Consultancy.

EBONY THOMAS (ACTRESS-CHOREOGRAPHER)

10 Tasman Road, London, SW9 9LT

PLACE OF BIRTH: London, 3.2.82
MARITAL STATUS: Single
COLLEGE: Sylvia Young Theatre School
ACADEMIC QUALIFICATIONS: GCSEs
HONOURS/AWARDS: LAMDA Awards (London Academy of Music & Dramatic Arts)
HOBBIES AND INTERESTS: Reading, dancing and socialising, also theatre
PERSONAL PROFILE: Ebony Thomas is known to friends as "Bunny". Actress/dancer. Currently appearing in TV soap 'Family Affairs' Channel 5 character, 'Yasmin McHugh'. Appeared in several television programmes, including 'Grange Hill', 'Sampson Superslug', 'Chalk', 'The Real McCoy' and was a presenter for the BBC series 'Global Gatecrash' filmed in St Vincent. Appeared in Mark Rylance production 'Macbeth' as third witch at Greenwich Theatre. One of Tammy Girl's main campaign models. Founder of the south London dance group Farinhite - which I also teach.

MISS KATRYNA THOMAS-SHELL (ACTRESS)

Rossmore Personal Management, Rossmore Road, Marylebone, London, NW1 6NJ

PLACE OF BIRTH: London, 21.7.79
MARITAL STATUS: Single
COLLEGE: Queen Margaret College
ACADEMIC QUALIFICATIONS: 10 GCSEs (all above C), 2 A-Levels, currently studying for BA Hons Acting
PROFESSIONAL QUALIFICATIONS: Leading Roles in: 'Junk' (1998), 'Stone Cold' (1996) For The BBC, Supporting Roles in 'Grange Hill' (1992-93), 'Eastenders' (1996), 'Bodyguards' (1996) - (except 'Bodyguard' for Carlton), Radio 4: Bullseye Babes. (principal role) and Listen & Write for BBC Schools. Presented Li's For Love - BBC
HOBBIES AND INTERESTS: Acting, singing, dance, reading, cinema, music
EMAIL: Kattythomasshell@hotmail.com
PERSONAL PROFILE: I am currently at drama school studying for a BA as I want to learn all I can about my chosen profession. I feel that I am living proof that it is possible to stay in school and gain excellent qualifications whilst pursuing and succeeding in making your dreams come true.

> ## Todd Terry, a DJ with a discography most would die for
>
> **TODD TERRY**

MS MARSHA THOMASON (ACTRESS)

William Morris Agency, Stratton House, 1 Stratton Street, London, W1X 6HB

PLACE OF BIRTH: Manchester, 19.1.76
MARITAL STATUS: Single
COLLEGE: Manchester Metropolitan
ACADEMIC QUALIFICATIONS: 8 GCSEs, 3 A-Levels, English Lang. A, Media Studies B, Theatre Studies B
MEMBERSHIPS: Equity
HOBBIES AND INTERESTS: Music, playing the guitar, books, fashion, photography
PERSONAL PROFILE: I landed my first job acting in television at the age of 14 and realised I could make a living doing something that I loved. Nine years later I find myself feeling just as passionate about acting, this is just the tip of the iceberg. To infinity and beyond.

MS YVONNE THOMPSON (MANAGING DIRECTOR)

MD, ASAP Communications Ltd,

PLACE OF BIRTH: Guyana
MARITAL STATUS: Single
CHILDREN: One
DIRECTORSHIPS: Choice FM, ACWI, Enterprise Forum
MEMBERSHIPS: IPR, IOD
HONOURS/AWARDS: EFBWBO, Voice Newspaper Business '98, Board Member - Southside Chamber of Commerce
EMAIL: asapcoms@dircon.co.uk
PERSONAL PROFILE: Yvonne Thompson
Credentials:- ASAP Communications; MD, EFBWBO; President, Communications and London Executive Comms; Commission For Racial Equality, Women's Committee; Small Business Bureau, Vice President; Women into Business; Vice Patron; African Caribbean Westminster Initiative - Chair For London, Board of Governors, Catford County Girls School; London First - Skilling London Programme, nominated for the EU and Social Committee

NOMINATED BY: Olivia Aouboshim

MR LEN TRUSTY (ACTOR)

Bruna Zanelli, Mansfield House, 376-378 The Strand, London, WC2R 0LR

PLACE OF BIRTH: London, 16.9.64
MARITAL STATUS: Single
COLLEGE: Rose Bruford
ACADEMIC QUALIFICATIONS: BA Hons in Theatre Arts
PROFESSIONAL QUALIFICATIONS: Trained Actor
MEMBERSHIPS: Equity
HOBBIES AND INTERESTS: Football, boxing, music, reading
PERSONAL PROFILE: Trained at Rose Bruford Drama College and graduated in 1992. Worked extensively in theatre, television and films as an actor, TV credits include: 'Eastenders'; 'Wizzi Wig Manson'; with Ian McShane, 'Rumble', 'Lovejoy', 'The Detectives'. Theatre Credits include: 'Twelfth Night'; Royal National Theatre; 'Romeo & Juliet', 'World Tour'; 'My Children My Africa'; 'Watermill Theatre'.

CLLR AKQIWA CATHERINE TUI-TT (LAWYER)

Councillor-Public Affairs, Town Hall,

PLACE OF BIRTH: Ghana, 16.7.69
MARITAL STATUS: Single
CHILDREN: One
COLLEGE: LSE, University of London
ACADEMIC QUALIFICATIONS: LLB Hons, LLM & MSc
PROFESSIONAL QUALIFICATIONS: BVC
MEMBERSHIPS: Society of Black Lawyers, Inner Temple and Labour Party
HOBBIES AND INTERESTS: Singing, athletics
PERSONAL PROFILE: Young, ambitious and spiritual, committed to community and personal development of the Black man and woman. Enjoys life and a firm belief in self determination. A republican in philosophy.

MISS CHARLENE TURAY (STUDENT-ACTRESS)

PLACE OF BIRTH: Wycombe, 9.1.85
HOBBIES AND INTERESTS: Horse riding, swimming, football
PERSONAL PROFILE: I am very active and quite a sporty person with many hobbies one of which is horse-riding and I have a few horses of my own. My ambition in life is to be a successful singer and maybe a part-time actress like Whitney Houston who is my idol.

MISS RUBY TURNER (SINGER-SONGWRITER-ACTRESS)

Satta Music Company, 8 Bottevill Road, Birmingham, B27 7YU

PLACE OF BIRTH: Jamaica
MARITAL STATUS: Single
COLLEGE: Drama College Bilkem
ACADEMIC QUALIFICATIONS: Acting Public Speaking
PROFESSIONAL QUALIFICATIONS: Drama
PERSONAL PROFILE: Professional singer, eight albums, Gold in New Zealand. Number one R'n'B in the US in 1990. Theatre: 'Carmen' Jones; 'Tame', 'West End.' 'Blue Brothers;' 'Soul Sisters,' Bristol Old Vic.

SISTER MONICA-JOAN TYWANG (REV. SISTER)

Caribbean London Pastoral Assistant,
La Sagesse Convent, 20 Dawson Convent, London, NW2 6UA

PLACE OF BIRTH: Trinidad & Tobago, 18.12.38
ACADEMIC QUALIFICATIONS: Trained Nurse, pastoral worker
PROFESSIONAL QUALIFICATIONS: Mary Secole Memorial Association
DIRECTORSHIPS: Notting Hill Carnival Trust, British Caribbean Association
HOBBIES AND INTERESTS: People, music, arts
PERSONAL PROFILE: In 1977 as member of an international religious congregation - the Daughters of Wisdom - Monica - Joan Tywang was the first woman chaplain of the Caribbean, appointed by Cardinal Basil Hume Arch-diocese of Westminster; following 1976 Notting Hill race riots: from a Christian perspective bringing about creativity and healing. Carnivalist and steelband promoter. Role model for spiritual welfare: historically, and future impact in redressing negative imagery of Caribbean peoples, employment, awareness and caring, her life's work.
NOMINATED BY: Ansel Wong

'Young, ambitious and spiritual, committed to community and personal development of the Black man and woman'

CLLR AKQIWA CATHERINE TUI-TT

MR GUS UHLENBEEK (FOOTBALLER)

Fulham Football Club, Craven Cottage, Stevenage Road, London, SW6 6HH

PERSONAL PROFILE: Dutchman Gus was another summer signing under the Bosman ruling for Kevin Keegan's men. His previous club Ipswich had been keen to hang onto the attacking left wing-back but once again the lure of playing for Keegan proved too much to refuse. The Paramaribo-born player established himself in his home country with his appearances for SV Tops and joined Portman Road outfit in the summer of 1995.

DR N H R UMANA (MANAGEMENT CONSULTANT)

Principal, Robertson International Consulting Limited, 11 Salford Road, Streatham Hill, London, SW2 4BJ

PLACE OF BIRTH: Oron, 16.11.56
MARITAL STATUS: Married
CHILDREN: Three (Eteyen, Emmanuel, Katie)
COLLEGE: South Bank, London College of Advanced Transport Studies, Clayton University, Missori, US
ACADEMIC QUALIFICATIONS: BSc Hons, MSc, PhD
PROFESSIONAL QUALIFICATIONS: MCIT, M Mgt Araes, AIMC (England)
DIRECTORSHIPS: Vice-Chairman, First Line Consulting & Management Services
MEMBERSHIPS: Royal Overseas League, Peoples Club of Nigeria
HONOURS/AWARDS: Listed: 14th Edition, Marquis Who's Who International Professionals in the World
HOBBIES AND INTERESTS: Attending professional seminars, tennis, badminton, Reading - current affairs, classics of western philosophy
PERSONAL PROFILE: Dr Umana is a qualified transport and energy professional working as a management consultant since 1990. He has worked on various projects both in the private and public sector. His research and consulting concerns technical and service management with clients and serves an international market. He is committed to the distillation of best practise from many parallel situations.
NOMINATED BY: E Johnson

Entrants in the Black Who's Who 1999 have been nominated for their achievements and contributions. You can nominate someone who deserves to be in the Black Who's Who 2000, nominate them today.

Entries are free

Send in your nominations, including name, contact address and telephone number to:

Books Division, Ethnic Media Group, 148 Cambridge Heath Road, London E1 5QJ

Carribbean Times

Caribbean Times

Incorporating African Times

Friday 30 October 1998 · BRITAIN'S ONLY QUALITY BLACK NEWSPAPER · Issue 907 · 50p

NEED A NEW JOB? SEE Jobs Direct ON PAGES 18-29

JAMAICA SPARED MITCH'S FURY

Islanders fortunate as 150mph winds skirt coastline

could have been far worse: the side effects of Hurricane Mitch were increased rainfall and rising sea waters, enough to cause flooding in some areas

Emmanuel Dunseath

FIFTY people were being accommodated in a church hall in Spanish Town after being forced to flee their homes because of flood waters triggered by Hurricane Mitch, Jamaica's Office of Disaster Preparedness and Emergency Management (ODPEM) reported.

Jamaicans breathed a sigh of relief as Hurricane Mitch, the most powerful of the season, bypassed the island. The hurricane veered westward from a northward track that would have brought 150 mph winds and probable devastation.

The hurricane skirted Jamaica's south-west coast on the weekend dumping several inches of rain on the island.

A flash flood watch remained in effect over much of the island on Monday afternoon as intermittent showers continued, and the Met office predicted more heavy rain in mid-to-late afternoon.

Residents of low-lying areas in particular were warned to remain on alert to deal with homes to assess damage.

Two families in the Black River area of St. Elizabeth, south-western Jamaica, who fled their homes and took refuge in a designated shelter on Sunday, had since returned to their homes, the ODPEM reported.

Government agencies were moving to clear blocked and partially blocked roads in a number of communities.

Anna Treasure, General Manager of the Metropolitan Parks and Markets (MPM) which cleans streets, gullies and drains in the capital Kingston, called on people to desist from throwing garbage and other debris in drains.

She said the anti-social

coming into The Met Centre said that although Mitch was slowly drifting away north-west of Jamaica, outbands associated with the hurricane would affect the island especially sections of southern and western parishes.

Forced

The ODPEM said food and bedding had been provided for the 50 people from 15 families who were forced to leave their homes in the Nightingale community of St Catherine on Sunday in the face of rising water.

A welfare team from the ODPEM was scheduled to inspect the flooded-out

practice had led to the clogging of some drains resulting in flooding.

Flooding was reported at Marcus Garvey Drive, Lorean Avenue, off Olympic Way, in the Three Miles Area, the Spanish Town Road near Denham Town Police Station, and the entrance to the Kingston Public Hospital (KPH).

Debris

Sections of Windward Road were blocked by debris. The Palisadoes Road was littered with debris thrown on the city by the sea and Harbour View and Windward Road were also blocked with debris.

The police force's Emergency System was activated by Commissioner Francis Forbes in preparation for the effects of the hurricane. The Commissioner also placed the force on full alert.

The National Water Commission (NWC) advised customers to store water for use as it would have had to shut down its pumping facilities during the passage of the hurricane. The NWC also placed its disaster management team on alert, filled storage tanks and assigned personnel to secure the facilities and shut down the inslte gates of surface sources....

INSIDE: Caribbean News · African News · UK News · Letters · Sports

COUNTDOWN TO THE MILLENNIUM

DR CLINTON VALLEY (HEADTEACHER)

The John Loughbrough School, Holcombe Road, London, N17 9AD

PLACE OF BIRTH: Trinidad, 22.12.53
MARITAL STATUS: Married
CHILDREN: Two (Clintelle, Clinson)
COLLEGE: Nottingham University
ACADEMIC QUALIFICATIONS: BA, MA, MSA US Ed.D
DIRECTORSHIPS: Operation Reachback UK
MEMBERSHIPS: Middlesex University for an NAHT
HOBBIES AND INTERESTS: Cricket, football, table tennis
PERSONAL PROFILE: A minister educator of the Seventh Day Adventist Church. Has turned around John Loughborough School and steered it in to GM status. Got 100% increase in GCSE results. School regularly featured in media.

MR NEVEL ANTHONY VASSEL (EDUCATION MANAGER)

Cross Country Manager, Bilston Community College of Further Education, 37 Ennerdale Road, Palmers Cross, Wolverhampton, WV6 9DJ

PLACE OF BIRTH: Wolverhampton, 22.4.57
MARITAL STATUS: Married
CHILDREN: Two (Kay Leigh, Wrayon)
COLLEGE: University of Wolverhampton
ACADEMIC QUALIFICATIONS: MA (Edu. Mgt.) BEd (I.ED), Certificate Educ, Diploma Agric.
PROFESSIONAL QUALIFICATIONS: Diploma in Agriculture
MEMBERSHIPS: Black Professional Development Forum
HOBBIES AND INTERESTS: Music, agriculture, poetry, Black history, travelling
EMAIL: Neville.Nassel@cablenet.co.uk
PERSONAL PROFILE: Nevel is the first Black person to research and grow commercial Sedtch Bonnet pepper in England covered by Channel 4 TV, Radio 5. Co-founder of Jamfolak Performing Company in song, drama, Jamaica style. He is pleasant, easygoing and enjoys discussion on Black issues. He produced his own reggae record, and publication of poetry. Has wide range of skills, works with the unemployed; he plays guitar. Has 18 years experience in education field.
NOMINATED BY: Vilma Okotieboh

MR WINSTON THEODORE VAUGHAN (ENGINEER (BT))

Technical Officer, BT (BTSS) Plc, 81 Newgate Street, London, EC1A 7AJ

PLACE OF BIRTH: Barbados, 8.5.42
MARITAL STATUS: Married
CHILDREN: Three (Shaun, Mark, Samantha)
COLLEGE: City & East London
ACADEMIC QUALIFICATIONS: ONC Telecommunications National Cert. Business & Finance
MEMBERSHIPS: Labour Party Member, Member of the Communications Workers Union
HOBBIES AND INTERESTS: Jazz music, cricket, theatre, travelling
PERSONAL PROFILE: I came to the UK in 1962 and served in the British Army for six years. I am currently employed by BT as a technical officer in a commercial environment. I am an active Labour Party member and chair of West Ham CLP. I am a local councillor in the Borough. Member of the communications workers union equal opportunities committee.

MR JOE VERA (ACTOR)

Magnet Personal Management, Flat C, 10 Noel Road, Edgbaston, Birmingham, B16 GP5

PLACE OF BIRTH: Zimbabwe, 5.7.53
MARITAL STATUS: Single
ACADEMIC QUALIFICATIONS: 4 O-Levels
PROFESSIONAL QUALIFICATIONS: Qualified Operating Department Technician
MEMBERSHIPS: Equity Actors Union
HOBBIES AND INTERESTS: Music, cinema, the arts, TV
PERSONAL PROFILE: Two years nurse training, nine years operating theatre technician, seven years residential social work since 1988. Came into acting and developed musical experience TV and radio work and theatre storyteller. Teach children drama and music, writer of children's stories, guitar, congas, mbira, djembe, percussionist and community drama.

MISS DANIELLE MERISSA VICTORY (SCHOOLGIRL-ACTRESS)

The Jackie Palmer Stage School Agency, 30 Daws Hill Lane, High Wycombe, HP11 1PW

PLACE OF BIRTH: High Wycombe, 28.7.92
HOBBIES AND INTERESTS: Ballet, tap, drama, gymnastics, music, dancing, playing the recorder
PERSONAL PROFILE: Danielle is a very lively, bright, outgoing girl, she loves to dance and sing, she has a very wide imagination and very confident. She has just finished playing one of the children in 'Showboat' at The Prince Edward Theatre, London.

MR DENNIS VICTORY (ACTOR-DANCER)

24 Hunt Road, High Wycombe, HP13 7RE

PLACE OF BIRTH: High Wycombe, 12.12.70
MARITAL STATUS: Single
MEMBERSHIPS: Equity

MISS GRACE FRANCESCA VICTORY (SCHOOLGIRL-ACTRESS)

The Jackie Palmer Stage School Agency, 30 Daws Hill Lane, High Wycombe, HP11 1PW

PLACE OF BIRTH: High Wycombe, 29.8.90
PROFESSIONAL QUALIFICATIONS: Primary Tap IDTA 77% Ballet Primary IDTA 76% Both Commended
HOBBIES AND INTERESTS: Singing, dancing
PERSONAL PROFILE: Grace is a lively child who enjoys all aspects of song, dance and acting. She has done work for C4 TV and has appeared in a Christmas edition of a magazine. She has also done shows for the Stage School. She is friendly and energetic.

MISS LUDMILLA VULI (ACTRESS)

c/o Tim Scott Personal Management, Unit 5, Cloisters Business Centre, 8 Battersea Park Road, London, SW8 4GB

PLACE OF BIRTH: Doncaster, 4.1.69
MARITAL STATUS: Married
COLLEGE: London Studio Centre & The Drama Studio, London
ACADEMIC QUALIFICATIONS: 5 O-Levels
PROFESSIONAL QUALIFICATIONS: Two years Dance Performance Dip. (LSC) one year PG Acting Dip. (DSL)
MEMBERSHIPS: British Equity, International Dance Teachers Association
HONOURS/AWARDS: Carlton Hobbs Radio Competition (1992, Commended)
HOBBIES AND INTERESTS: Handknitting, complementary medicine
PERSONAL PROFILE: Credits Include: Theatre: 'June' in Chicago, English Theatre in Frankfurt 'Helena' in 'A Midsummer Nights Dream' with Northern Broadsides Theatre Company. Television: 'Roz' in 'Watching', Granada TV, 'Eastenders' for BBC TV, Trish in 'Cracker' for Granada TV, Polly in 'Peak Practise' for Carlton TV. Radio: 'Susan' in the 'Hairy Hand of Dartmoor' - BBC Radio 4.

Carribbean Times

Caribbean Times

incorporating African Times

Friday 21 May 1999   BRITAIN'S ONLY QUALITY BLACK NEWSPAPER   Issue 935   50p

James Wolfensohn: The World Bank president has reform plans for Guyana

GUYANA IS POOR ENOUGH FOR AID

The World Bank says penniless nation will get cash for reforms

WASHINGTON - Debt-strapped Guyana on Thursday became only the third country to meet terms for a key international debt relief programme for reformist poor countries, winning immediate financial help from multilateral lenders.

A World Bank spokesman said the Caribbean country had reached the 'completion point' for the Heavily Indebted Poor Countries initiative, which rewards debtor countries that toe the line with Western 'democratic' policies with the money to ease debt relief to enable it to meet on offer.

The bank said Guyana would receive some $256 million of debt relief, at the present value of its $1.09 billion debt. This includes $27 million of World Bank debt relief and $245 million of debt relief from the International Monetary Fund.

'The HIPC debt relief agreed this week will release resources from debt servicing and enable us to increase budgetary allocations toward improving the health, education and living standards of all Guyanese,' Finance Minister Bharrat Jagdeo said in a statement released by the World Bank, without mentioning the added conditions and controls that

Khalil Omunudu

Guyana would now be subject to.

'On behalf of all Guyanese, I would like to thank the international community to have made this possible.'

Eliot

Guyana is the third country to start receiving debt relief under the much-criticised HIPC programme, which was introduced with fanfare in 1996 and 'rewards' countries that follow IMF-sponsored reform programmes generally designed to open economies up to the 'global market' and support governments that uphold the elite status quo.

Aid organisations say the terms are too tough and the money is paid too late, while a report to the boards of the IMF and the World Bank last month admitted the initiative 'in absolute terms may not be

significantly reducing debt service from current levels paid.

The 'international community' is currently looking at ways to reform the HIPC programme, although no final decision is likely before the June summit in Cologne of the Group of Seven industrialised nations — Britain, Canada, France, Germany, Italy, Japan and the United States.

G7 countries have already put forward overlapping, and at times competing, proposals on debt relief and they promise to reach for a deal ahead of the Cologne summit

Bolivia and Uganda are the only other countries which have already started receiving debt relief under the HIPC programme although four other countries — Burkina Faso, Ivory Coast, Mali and Mozambique — could reap the 'benefit' of the programme in the coming months anyway.

Guyana had originally been due to receive the HIPC debt relief in December last year but the payments were delayed after economic reforms stalled slightly.

Bharrat Jagdeo: delighted to be getting money

COUNTDOWN TO THE MILLENNIUM

MR KEITH WAITHE (Composer/ Flautist)

Bandleader, Essequibo Music, 20 Cantley Road, Hanwell, London, W7 2BQ

PLACE OF BIRTH: Guyana, 21.12.49
MARITAL STATUS: Married
CHILDREN: Four (Ashley, Mark, Ayesha, Adam)
COLLEGE: Surrey
ACADEMIC QUALIFICATIONS: LR SM & PGCE (Teaching)
DIRECTORSHIPS: Watermans Arts Centre
MEMBERSHIPS: MPO, MU
HOBBIES AND INTERESTS: Gardening, visiting places of interest
PERSONAL PROFILE: During the past two years, Keith Waithe and the Mascusi Players has been participating in many major festivals and venues in and around the British Isles, ranging from Glastonbury, Bracknell, The TUC's Respect Concert, The Blackie (Liverpool), Croydon Clock Tower, The Purcell Room, South Bank Centre, Birmingham MAC, Ealing Jazz Festival and the Barbican.
NOMINATED BY: Eric Huntley

MR LARRINGTON WALKER (Actor-Writer-Director)

Afrosax,

PLACE OF BIRTH: Kingston, 1.8.46
MARITAL STATUS: Married
CHILDREN: Two (Alando, Larrington Delandro)
MEMBERSHIPS: Equity, Musicians Union, MCPS. BASCA., SBA
HOBBIES AND INTERESTS: Tennis, swimming, keeping fit, theatre, travel
EMAIL: AFROSAX@ Dircon.co.uk
PERSONAL PROFILE: Television: 'Black On Black'; 'Moon Over Soho'; 'You & Me'; 'Playdays'; 'Inspector Morse'; 'Peak Practise'; 'The Bill'; 'Beck'. Theatre: 'The Wizard of OZ'; 'Beggars Opera'; 'Jesus Christ Superstar'; 'Jean'. Film: 'Burning An Illusion'; 'Lamb Yanks'; various shorts. As Director: 'Let There Be Love/Unforgettable'; 'Blood Ties'; 'Busy In The City'; 'Ears Tails & Common Sense', 'Jazz Variations', 'Blues In The Night'. Writer: 'Let There Be Love/Unforgettable'; CH4 'Busy In The City'; 'Ears Tails & Common Sense'.

MR RUDOLPH WALKER (Actor)

c/o Mayer & Eden Ltd, 34 Kingley Court, London, W1R 5LE

PLACE OF BIRTH: Trinidad, 28.9.39
MARITAL STATUS: Married
CHILDREN: Two (Darren, Sheona)
HONOURS/AWARDS: Joint ITV Personality of Year 1972 Time Out Best Actor 1988
HOBBIES AND INTERESTS: Lawn tennis, cricket
PERSONAL PROFILE: Rudolph Walker is one of Britain's most eminent actors. He immigrated to Britain in 1960 and by 1970 gained international recognition with the successful television comedy series 'Love Thy Neighbour', followed with a succession of other major roles and also became a member of 'The Royal Shakespeare Company'. Honoured with many awards and accolades including 'ITV Personality of the Year 1972': Time Out - Best Actor Award 1988: Scarlet IBIS Award 1992 for outstanding service by Trinidad & Tobago: 'The Thin Blue Line' - Best British comedy series award 1996 and deservedly received a 'Lifetime Achievement Award 1996 and deservedly received a 'Lifetime Achievement Award in 1998' for his contribution in film, television, radio, theatre and as a pioneering inspiration to others.

MR SAM WALKER (Director-Museum & Archives)

Black Cultural Archives,

PLACE OF BIRTH: Sierra Leone, 17.4.54
MARITAL STATUS: Married
COLLEGE: Open University, University of North London
ACADEMIC QUALIFICATIONS: BA, PG, Dip
HOBBIES AND INTERESTS: Reading, jogging, cinema
PERSONAL PROFILE: I have been working at Black Cultural Archives for more than 14 years. Written articles on the need for a National Black Cultural Archives and museum and on the history of Black people in Britain. I have served as trustee/director the boards of voluntary organisations.

Received a 'Lifetime Achievement Award in 1998' for his contribution in film, television, radio and theatre

RUDOLPH WALKER

CLLR ROY BLAKE WALTERS JP BEM (Operations Manager Rtd)

Councillor, Non Ex Director, 130 Great Western Street, Manchester, M14 4RA

PLACE OF BIRTH: Jamaica, 6.12.37
MARITAL STATUS: Married
CHILDREN: Four (Gillian, Dahlia, Precelia, Valdimir)
PROFESSIONAL QUALIFICATIONS: Royal Society of Arts in Transport Diploma
HONOURS/AWARDS: Magistrate, British Empire Medal
HOBBIES AND INTERESTS: Cricket, tennis, football, classical, soul music
PERSONAL PROFILE: 1963-1991 Worked on buses, retired as depot operations manager. 1982 to present, secretary and member of management of Moss Care Housing Ltd. 1983- Received BEM for services to transport and community. 1985 - Appointed Justice of the Peace. 1990 - to present, appointed non-executive director for Central Manchester Healthcare Trust. 1998 - Present became a councillor Manchester City Council.

MR TONY WARNER (Footballer)

Goalkeeper, Liverpool Football Club, Anfield Road, Liverpool, L4 0TH

DATE OF BIRTH: 11.5.74
PERSONAL PROFILE: Tony spent 18 months at the club on a non-contract basis (while training as an accountant) before signing full-time at the end of 1993. Originally spotted while playing for the Liverpool FA side, his first ever game at Anfield was for his local football association as they beat Cornwall FA to claim the National Cup. Tony spent a short spell on loan at First Division Swindon Town last season, teaming up with ex-Liverpool player Steve McMahon who was then in charge at the County ground.

MISS MAXINE ELIZABETH WATSON (Senior Producer)

Series Producer Current Affairs, BBC Television, , Room 1173, 201 Wood Lane, White City, London, W12 7TS

PLACE OF BIRTH: Birmingham, 21.6.62
MARITAL STATUS: Married
COLLEGE: Essex University
ACADEMIC QUALIFICATIONS: Comparative English Literature BA Hons
PROFESSIONAL QUALIFICATIONS: CAM Marketing & Media
MEMBERSHIPS: BFI, Women in Film & Television
HONOURS/AWARDS: CRE Media Award 1996/97, Woman in Film Nominee 1998
EMAIL: Maxine.watson@bbc.co.uk
PERSONAL PROFILE: Currently series producer of the BBC's award winning current affairs programme Black Britain. A ten year career in television has lead to over 40 short films for some of the BBCs prime time shows like 'Watchdog' and 'Here and Now' as well as production credits cross television genre's. More recently are documentaries produced for BBC News and Current Affairs, such as 'Scott Sherrin - story of a Black man' (runner up for the Mental Health in Media Award 1997). Executive producer of Blacks Firsts and producer/director of 'Love in Black & White' (BBC Windrush season) nominated for Women in Film and Television Award '98. Producer/director of a timely and well received documentary 'Why Stephen' which preceded publication of the Macpherson report.
NOMINATED BY: Patrick Younge, BBC Television

MRS NESLYN WATSON-DRUEE MBE (Consultancy & Training)

Director, Beacon Organisational DVT & Training Services, 1 Rowlls Road, Kingston-upon-Thames, Surrey, KT1 3ET

PLACE OF BIRTH: Jamaica
MARITAL STATUS: Married
COLLEGE: London University
ACADEMIC QUALIFICATIONS: MSc, BA Hons
PROFESSIONAL QUALIFICATIONS: RGN, RM, RHV, Dip, HEd, MIPD
DIRECTORSHIPS: Lambeth Healthcare Trust London Health Partnership
MEMBERSHIPS: Institute of Directors, Chambers of Commerce
HONOURS/AWARDS: National Training Award British Diversity Gold Standard; Consultancy & Training Business Excellence, BDA Merit Award
EMAIL: bo53@dial,pipex.com
PERSONAL PROFILE: High achieving Jamaican businesswoman. Key achievements include: Development of a leadership and management demonstration programme for the NHS targeted to staff from Black and minority ethnic communities; development of action for opportunity programme for London Enterprise Agency I won five awards during 1986-1988. MBE for nursing leadership.
NOMINATED BY: Sunita

MS CLAUDIA WEBBE (DIRECTOR WREC)

Director, Westminster Race Equality Council, 1st Floor, Piccadilly Mansions, 1-17 Shaftesbury Avenue, London, W1V 7RL

PLACE OF BIRTH: Leicester, 8.3.65
MARITAL STATUS: Single
COLLEGE: Leicester University
ACADEMIC QUALIFICATIONS: BA Hons Social Science Post Graduate Cert Socio - Legal Studies
PROFESSIONAL QUALIFICATIONS: Training & Development, Certificate in Youth & Community Work
DIRECTORSHIPS: Path (West Midlands) Ltd, (Chairperson) Yaa Asantewaa Arts Centre, Mangrove Trust Ltd
MEMBERSHIPS: Associate of the Institute of Personnel & Development
HONOURS/AWARDS: UK Chairperson (1995/'96) of the Council of Europe, European Youth Campaign Against Racism Xenophobia, Anti-Semitism & Intolerance Entitled "All Different / All Eqaul"
HOBBIES AND INTERESTS: Reading, current affairs, mentoring, voluntary, working with young people, community carnivals
EMAIL: Claudia-Webbe@hotmail.com
PERSONAL PROFILE: Claudia provides racial discrimination and racial harassment casework and policy development advice. She is founding member of National Black Caucus and a founding trustee of the 1990 Trust. At 22 she founded the first National conference for young Black people entitled 'The Raw Truth', which attracted in excess of 500. She is also an executive member of the National Assembly Against Racism.
NOMINATED BY: Christopher Johnson MBA

MISS EMMA WEBLEY (SCHOOLGIRL-ACTRESS)

c/o The Jackie Palmer Agency, 30 Daws Hill Lane, High Wycombe, HP11 1PW

PLACE OF BIRTH: Ascot, 19.3.90
MARITAL STATUS: Single
PERSONAL PROFILE: Attends Jackie Palmer Agency for singing, drama, dancing and acrobatic training. Performances: 'Joseph & The Amazing Technicolour Dreamcoat' at Wycombe Swan and Oxford Apollo. Warburtons Bread Commercial and many local performances.

MR PAUL WEEKES (CRICKETER)

County Cricketer, Middlesex County Cricket Club, Lords Cricket Ground, London, NW8 8QN

PLACE OF BIRTH: Hackney, 8.7.69
MARITAL STATUS: Partner
CHILDREN: Two (Cherie, Shyann)
COLLEGE: Hackney College
ACADEMIC QUALIFICATIONS: 3 O-Levels
PROFESSIONAL QUALIFICATIONS: NCA Senior Cricket Coach
HOBBIES AND INTERESTS: Listening to music, gym work, watching boxing
PERSONAL PROFILE: I've been a county cricketer since 1987, for Middlesex, one of the top teams in the country. I have also represented England A and B teams overseas in Australia and Zimbabwe. As a qualified coach I do lots of coaching throughout the inner cities.

MS KAREN MARIE WEIR (SENIOR BROADCAST JOURNALIST)

Active FM Radio, 23A Warwick Road, Earls Court, London, SW5 9UL

PLACE OF BIRTH: Gloucester, 14.8.68
MARITAL STATUS: Single
CHILDREN: One (Boji-Alexandre)
COLLEGE: UNL
ACADEMIC QUALIFICATIONS: First Class BA Hons
HOBBIES AND INTERESTS: Films, TV, music, radio, keeping fit, meditation, reading
PERSONAL PROFILE: She began her media career ten years ago in the marketing and advertising departments (respectfully) at the Voice Communications. She took a short career break to train as a broadcast journalist and currently enjoys freelancing as a broadcast journalist and press and public relations consultant.

MR ROBERT ANTHONY WHEELER (INFORMATION OFFICER)

Cashain David African Caribbean Mental Health Services, Joint Effort Promotion Ltd, 69 Broad Lane, Tottenham, London, N15 4DJ

PLACE OF BIRTH: London, 23.12.62
MARITAL STATUS: Cohabiting
CHILDREN: Four (Naomi, Tahrik, Teheran, Omar-I)
COLLEGE: East London University
ACADEMIC QUALIFICATIONS: BSc Hons in New Technology, Social Policy Research & Information
HOBBIES AND INTERESTS: Computers, reading, sports, looking after the well being of my children, travelling whenever possible
PERSONAL PROFILE: I am an ambitious practical person who will climb to great heights. It's the climb down that's hard for me. I was not well supported throughout my music career. However, myself and a few business partners have set up a music promotion company. To uplift the local talent in our community. I will be working hard with my business partners to achieve the above aims and objectives.
NOMINATED BY: Anthea Lee

DENSIGN WHITE (MORTGAGE CONSULTANT)

c/o Dream World Leisure, 29-30 Queens Street, Wolverhampton

PLACE OF BIRTH: Wolverhampton, 21.12.61
CHILDREN: Two (Adre, Brett)
ACADEMIC QUALIFICATIONS: BA Politics, Psychology
MEMBERSHIPS: Life - British Judo Association
HONOURS/AWARDS: Olympics - 5th Place - 1988, 1984, Commonwealth Games - Gold, 1990, World Championship - Bronze, 1987, European Championship - Bronze 1990, Silver 1988,1987
HOBBIES AND INTERESTS: Reading - novel's, biography's, sport - football, running, swimming, weight training
PERSONAL PROFILE: Started competing at international level at the age of 16. Competed in three Olympic games. After retiring became nightclub owner, while continuing own contracts of teaching judo and self defence. Recently retired as director British Judo Association. Most challenging time in life was supporting family while still competing and studying.

MRS JEAN VETA WHITE (NURSE-RTD)

Leeds City Council, 23 Dorset Road, Hare Hills, Leeds, LS8 3QL

PLACE OF BIRTH: Barbados, 13.7.30
MARITAL STATUS: Married
ACADEMIC QUALIFICATIONS: Diploma in First Line Management at DABTAC
PROFESSIONAL QUALIFICATIONS: SRN, RMN, RGN (M)
DIRECTORSHIPS: Leeds Racial Equality Council, Leeds College of Building, Yorkshire & Humberside Low Pay Unit
MEMBERSHIPS: Unity Housing Association, Association of Local Councillors
HONOURS/AWARDS: BBC Yorkshire Black Achievers Award, National Black Women's Achievement Awards 1994
HOBBIES AND INTERESTS: Singing, writing poetry, reading, drama, youth, community work, sports
PERSONAL PROFILE: Over many years Jean has selflessly given her time for the benefit of the community. Her opposition to disadvantage, inequality and discrimination has lead to her involvement in the community health council, West Yorkshire Low Pay Unit, Unity Housing Association race equality committee and women's committee. In 1994 her work in Leeds was recognised by a local and a national achievement award. Jean has written a book 'When Our Ship Comes In'.

MISS PATSY WHITE (EVENTS ORGANISER)

Executive Officer, RAP Management, 29a Rhodes Place, Oldbrook, Milton Keynes, MK6 2LW

PLACE OF BIRTH: London, 14.7.59
MARITAL STATUS: Single
COLLEGE: Hackney College
PROFESSIONAL QUALIFICATIONS: Business Studies, Radio Presentation
HONOURS/AWARDS: New Ideas Award
HOBBIES AND INTERESTS: Travelling, meeting people
PERSONAL PROFILE: Currently managing male group called Prestige and starring in the annual Miss Elegance & Mr Debangir competitions. Over the coming months I will be opening an exclusive dress hire boutique. I enjoy dancing for fitness.
NOMINATED BY: Anthea Lee

MS LORNA WHYTE (Police Complaints Authority)

Member, Youth Justice Board For England & Wales, Police Complaints Authority (PCA), 10 Great George Street, London, SW1 3AE

PLACE OF BIRTH: London, 29.12.57
MEMBERSHIPS: RSA (Royal Society Arts)
HOBBIES AND INTERESTS: Reading, theatre, fitness
PERSONAL PROFILE: I have worked with young people in trouble for most of my adult life within the disciplines of youth work, play work, youth justice and recently with the Youth Justice Board. I have written articles on 'Race and Criminal Justice' and 'The Needs of Young Women in the Criminal Justice System'. My spare time includes involvement within community based organisations, for example, being a governor at a further education college. My current position as a member of the Police Complaints Authority brings together the principles from earlier posts.
NOMINATED BY: Simone Barnett

MRS ANTHEA WILKINSON (Social Worker-Counsellor)

Manager (Social Education), VOISE - Voluntary Organisations in Social Education, 218 Tulketh Road, Ashton, Preston, PR2 1ES

PLACE OF BIRTH: Lancashire, 3.10.67
MARITAL STATUS: Married
CHILDREN: Two (Bradley Micheal, Ebony Rosemary-J)
COLLEGE: University of Central Lancashire
ACADEMIC QUALIFICATIONS: BA Hons 2:1 Social Worker & Community Studies
PROFESSIONAL QUALIFICATIONS: CQSW. (Social Work); Diploma in Counselling; C+Guilds in Teaching (7307)
MEMBERSHIPS: BAC - British Association of Counsellors (Associate)
HOBBIES AND INTERESTS: Expressive therapy; art work, creativity, spirituality
PERSONAL PROFILE: Self-determination, trust intuition and belief in self, have lead me to discover my confidence, self-esteem, spirituality and individuality. I have succeeded in life without initial formal qualifications. I am a qualified social worker, lecturer, counsellor and manager. I will start my PhD soon. We all can achieve!
NOMINATED BY: Phillip Birch

MR ALEX WILLIAMS (Footballer-Community Officer)

c/o Manchester City FC, Maine Road, Moss Side, Manchester, M14 7WN

PLACE OF BIRTH: Manchester, 13.11.61
MARITAL STATUS: Married
PROFESSIONAL QUALIFICATIONS: D32/D33 City & Guilds Assesor FA Full Badge Holder
HOBBIES AND INTERESTS: All sports
PERSONAL PROFILE: Played for Man. City FC 1981-1985. Port Vale FC 1985-1988. On loan at Queen of South FC 1986. Represented England Youth, England U21 winning European championship medals at both levels.
NOMINATED BY: Gordon Taylor - PFA

MS DENISE WILLIAMS (Voluntary Sector-Manager)

Dash (Drug Advice & Support), Zion Chrc, Royce Road, Hulme, Manchester, M15 5FQ

PLACE OF BIRTH: Manchester, 12.5.65
MARITAL STATUS: Single
CHILDREN: Two (Lee Ivan Junior Proverbs, Wesley Leon Henderson Proverbs)
COLLEGE: Manchester Metropolitan University
ACADEMIC QUALIFICATIONS: Diploma in Community Health CNNA, Youth & Community
DIRECTORSHIPS: Chair, Black Drug Workers Forum (N.W)
MEMBERSHIPS: Black Drug Workers Forum (Hulme & Moss Side)
HONOURS/AWARDS: Moss Side & Hulme, Service to the Community
HOBBIES AND INTERESTS: Interior decorating, community development, issues
EMAIL: DWill25633@aol.com
PERSONAL PROFILE: I am a 34 year old mother of two boys. I was born and raised in Moss Side, Manchester. My professional background is youth and community, health promotion and voluntary sector management.

MS MARCIA WILLIAMS (Author)

The X Press, 6 Hoxton Square, London, N1 6NU

PLACE OF BIRTH: Bromley, 7.2.69
MARITAL STATUS: Single
CHILDREN: Two (Kaisha, Letitia)
COLLEGE: Woolwich College
ACADEMIC QUALIFICATIONS: A-Level Sociology
PROFESSIONAL QUALIFICATIONS: Adminstration Supervisory Management (NEBSM)
HONOURS/AWARDS: Nomination Black Women Of The Year, Greenwich
HOBBIES AND INTERESTS: Keep fit, writing, poetry, photography
EMAIL: Mwilliams@greenwich.opu.uk.
PERSONAL PROFILE: I wanted to be a published author since age fifteen. My ambition became fruitful when I entered the Xpress Yourself competition in 1995 with my first novel, 'Flex, Babymother' written (1996), then 'Waiting For Mr Wright' (1998). I give talks to inspire aspiring authors and young people to what they can achieve with dedication.
NOMINATED BY: Ms L Simpson

MISS NADIA WILLIAMS (Actress-Children's TV Presenter)

University Student, Rossmore Personal Management, Rossmore Road, Marylebone, London, NW1 6NJ

PLACE OF BIRTH: London, 15.7.80
MARITAL STATUS: Single
COLLEGE: Reading University
ACADEMIC QUALIFICATIONS: 10 GCSEs (A-C), 3 A-Levels (A-B)
PROFESSIONAL QUALIFICATIONS: Lamda Grade 1, To Gold
HOBBIES AND INTERESTS: Dance music, singing, going to live gigs, reading, writing
PERSONAL PROFILE: I've been involved in media from the age of six. I've done television work (mainly children's programmes for the BBC/ITV) radio plays, theatre, and most recently, film. I'm now doing a degree in English and sociology, and hope to establish a career as a presenter or journalist.

SABRA WILLIAMS (Actress)

c/o Emptage Hallet, 24 Poland Street, London, W1V 3DD

PLACE OF BIRTH: London
MARITAL STATUS: Married
COLLEGE: Arts Educational School & Rambert Academy
ACADEMIC QUALIFICATIONS: 2 A-Levels
MEMBERSHIPS: Equity
HONOURS/AWARDS: IVCA Best Presenter Award
HOBBIES AND INTERESTS: Buddhism, films
EMAIL: Sabrawilliams@hotmail.com
PERSONAL PROFILE: Sabra Williams has achieved professional excellence in the worlds of dance, TV presenting and acting. Primarily known as an actor, she has appeared extensively in film, television and theatre in UK and internationally. Her passion is film and includes, 'Thin Ice' and 'Elephant Juice'. Sabra is a partner in presenter-led productions and is a practising Buddhist.

MR GARY WILMOT (Actor)

Dee O'Reilly Management Ltd, 112 Gunnersbury Avenue, Ealing, London, W5 4HB

PLACE OF BIRTH: London, 8.5.54
MARITAL STATUS: Married
CHILDREN: Two (Katie, Georgia)
MEMBERSHIPS: Equity / PRS / MCPS / Pamra
HOBBIES AND INTERESTS: Football, DIY
PERSONAL PROFILE: Achieved fame with innumerable TV appearances, including several own series. 1989 left television to concentrate on theatre. Lead appearances include: 'Me & My Girl' (West End & Tour), 'Carmen Jones' (West End), 'Copacabana' (Tour & West End), 'The Goodbye Girl' (West End & Tour), plus major concert tours.

I am a 34 year old mother of two boys. I was born and raised in Moss Side, Manchester. My professional background is youth and community...'

DENISE WILLIAMS

MISS CARMEN WILSON (Actress)

PLACE OF BIRTH: Germany
MARITAL STATUS: Single
COLLEGE: Guildford Tech
ACADEMIC QUALIFICATIONS: HND Business & Finance Studies As - German
HOBBIES AND INTERESTS: Music, travelling, yoga, walking, gardening
PERSONAL PROFILE: I have worked extensively across the country and in Europe; performing in schools and theatres. Providing a vital part of education in sexual health, medical science and language. Travelling is a passion of mine and six months across Africa is the most thrilling and rewarding expedition to date.

MS EILEEN WILSON (Principal-Director)

Learning Tree Montessori Nursery School, 309 Preston Road, Harrow, HA3 0QQ

PLACE OF BIRTH: Jamaica
MARITAL STATUS: Single
CHILDREN: One (Micheal Carvin)
COLLEGE: State University New York
ACADEMIC QUALIFICATIONS: BA Psychology 6 CSEs Montessori Graduate, Diploma, Food Hygiene
DIRECTORSHIPS: Above Company
MEMBERSHIPS: NW Chamber of Commerce
HONOURS/AWARDS: EFBWBO Business Owner 1998
HOBBIES AND INTERESTS: Travelling, golf, ski-ing, reading, arts, writing
PERSONAL PROFILE: Left home at 16. Signed by Sarah Cape Modelling Agency. Appeared in films and TV i.e. 'Bond', 'Star Wars', entered or placed in many competitions. Joined Playboy Club as croupier. By 21, made enough money to buy a flat, had a child, moved to New York. Attended State University of NY, BA Psychology. 1987 back to England, Montessori College. Gained graduate Dip. private tutor. 1995, set up own Montessori Nursery School. 1998 won EFBWO award.

MR GRANVILLE A WILSON (Senior Citizen-Ex-RAF)

PLACE OF BIRTH: Jamaica, 17.4.27
MARITAL STATUS: Widower
CHILDREN: Two (Sharon, Vanessa)
COLLEGE: Elementary School
ACADEMIC QUALIFICATIONS: Was Engineering Hearing Worker
HONOURS/AWARDS: I received The Caribbean Achievers Award
HOBBIES AND INTERESTS: Listen to jazz & dance jazz, betting on horses
PERSONAL PROFILE: After serving in the RAF from 1944 to 1947. I went back to Jamaica to demob, then I was amongst the first to return to England on the S S Windrush. I have lived and worked in an around Wolverhampton ever since.
NOMINATED BY: Delva Campbell

MS PRECIOUS WILSON (Recording Artiste)

Businesswoman, Rise Enterprises Ltd, PO Box 17129, London, SW12 9WJ

PLACE OF BIRTH: Jamaica, 18.10.57
MARITAL STATUS: Single
CHILDREN: One
COLLEGE: Goldsmith College
ACADEMIC QUALIFICATIONS: Open University
PROFESSIONAL QUALIFICATIONS: International Recordings and Stage Work
DIRECTORSHIPS: Rise Enterprises Ltd
MEMBERSHIPS: MU, PRS, MCPS, Equity
HONOURS/AWARDS: Gold & Silver Awards for Outstanding Record Sales
HOBBIES AND INTERESTS: Reading, writing, singing, painting, smelling roses
PERSONAL PROFILE: Precious Wilson recording artiste/composer for over 20 years. International hits include 'I Can't Stand The Rain', 'One Way Ticket', 'I'll Be Your Friend' and the title track from the movie 'The Jewel of The Nile'. She heads her own company and is principal of a childrens theatre arts school.

MISS LORRAINE WOODLEY (Student-Actor)

The Jackie Palmer Agency,

PLACE OF BIRTH: Buckinghamshire, 2.2.78
MARITAL STATUS: Single
COLLEGE: Amersham & Wycombe College
ACADEMIC QUALIFICATIONS: A-Level English & Theatre Studies, A/s Level Dance & Psychology-Currently Studying
PROFESSIONAL QUALIFICATIONS: Musical Theatre HND
HOBBIES AND INTERESTS: Mixing vinyls on turntables, reading, singing, swimming
PERSONAL PROFILE: I have worked professionally in television and theatre from the age of six. I have taken several dance exams in ballet, tap and gymnastics. In my final year of A-Levels I got a part in 'Grange Hill' which marked my destiny for a career in acting.

MISS STEPHANIE WOODLEY (Schoolgirl-Actress)

Jackie Palmer Agency,

PLACE OF BIRTH: Buckinghamshire, 9.8.84
COLLEGE: School Lord Williams's
ACADEMIC QUALIFICATIONS: Studying For GCSEs
HOBBIES AND INTERESTS: Dancing, singing
PERSONAL PROFILE: I am currently at school studying for my GCSEs. I have real love for music and I have taken several exams successfully. My goal so far in life is to learn many styles of dance and enjoy it.

MISS CHARLOTTE WOOLFORD (Actress)

PLACE OF BIRTH: England, 2.8.72
MARITAL STATUS: Single
COLLEGE: Theatre Studies 'A' Level
ACADEMIC QUALIFICATIONS: GCSE Maths, English Lit., Drama
PROFESSIONAL QUALIFICATIONS: Acting Diploma (Drama Centre)
HOBBIES AND INTERESTS: Roller blading, ballet
PERSONAL PROFILE: I trained at drama centre and have not stopped acting since. I also joined a theatre company called The Riggs O'Hara Theatre Company and have done several Black plays, that have been written by Courtia Newland.

MR JOHNNY WORTHY (Actor-Director)

Dancer-Singer, Flat G, 30 Brunswick Square, Hove, BN31 1EO

PLACE OF BIRTH: Bristol, 19.6.44
MARITAL STATUS: Single
DIRECTORSHIPS: Rising Roots Productions
MEMBERSHIPS: British Actors Equity
PERSONAL PROFILE: Fourth generation to make the theatre a career. Been an actor for forty years. British Actors Equity Council eight years. Founder Equity Afro Asian Committee-member accreditation board of British Drama schools - Save London Theatre's-Director Equity Trust Fund, founder/director Actors Centre - Appointed observer 'Dancers Trust'.

MR NEAL WRIGHT (Actor)

Paul Telfords Management, 23 Noel Street, London, W1V 3RD

PLACE OF BIRTH: Gloustershire
MARITAL STATUS: Single
COLLEGE: Arts Educational
PROFESSIONAL QUALIFICATIONS: Diploma
MEMBERSHIPS: Equity
HOBBIES AND INTERESTS: Music, dancing, eating out
PERSONAL PROFILE: Did a National tour of 'Joseph and Amazing Techni coloured Dream coat', then worked on 'Smokey Joe's Cafe' at the Prince of Wales Theatre, London. Now currently working in the new musical 'Mamma Mia!' with the songs from ABBA playing the part of 'Pepper'.

MR SALIM-GEDDES YATES (Arts Coordinator-Bandleader)

Freelance Consultant, Tropical Heatwave Music & Arts Development, 25 Dodson Street, Bermondsey, London, SE7 7QL

PLACE OF BIRTH: Trinidad, 22.3.45
MARITAL STATUS: Married
CHILDREN: Five (Rebecca, Deanna, Ashley, Christopher, Jamilah)
COLLEGE: Manchester Polytechnic, Fatima College (TNT)
ACADEMIC QUALIFICATIONS: 4 GCSE, Community Arts Diploma Certificate
MEMBERSHIPS: Society of Caribbean Arts CAMMA Arts
HONOURS/AWARDS: Medal (European Carnival Cities Committee) for services to carnival, A.C.G.B -Bursary
HOBBIES AND INTERESTS: Keep fit, crosswords, reading, pan-tuning, writing poetry, politics, current affairs
PERSONAL PROFILE: Cultural & Community Arts (Non European) Office; Development: education, drama, literature, music, fine art, youth arts, elderly arts project, prison at risk youth arts work, carnival arts projects. Music - bandleader 'Tropical Heatwave' workshops, demonstrations, discussions, percussion. Folk poet, calypso lyricist, singer and steelpannist.

MS AFUA YEBOAH (Director)

ASC Recruitment, Suite 243, The Linen Hall, 162-168 Regent St, London, SW2 1PU

PLACE OF BIRTH: London, 28.2.69
MARITAL STATUS: Married
CHILDREN: Two (Afi, Kojo)
COLLEGE: Southbank University
ACADEMIC QUALIFICATIONS: Bsc Product Management
PROFESSIONAL QUALIFICATIONS: BPS Level A & B
MEMBERSHIPS: Recruitment Society BBC Advisory Council

EMAIL: justasck@hotmail.com
PERSONAL PROFILE: Much of my working career has been spent committed to the personal development and progression of Black and Asian people. In my increasing concern and desire to empower my community I recently launched a recruitment consultancy removing barriers for those wanting to find employment in IT.

MR BABATUNDE YINUSA (Director Financial Services)

Director, Beautex Ltd, 53 Riverdale Centre, Lewisham Shopping Complex, London, SE13

PLACE OF BIRTH: Ososa, 10.11.55
MARITAL STATUS: Married
CHILDREN: Four (Lola, Segun, Muyiwa, Tobi)
COLLEGE: City & Guildhall University
ACADEMIC QUALIFICATIONS: Certificate in Banking
PROFESSIONAL QUALIFICATIONS: Associate Chartered Institute of Bankers England & Wales (ACIB)
MEMBERSHIPS: Institute of Administrative Accountants, Association of Banking Teachers
HOBBIES AND INTERESTS: Travelling, driving, music
PERSONAL PROFILE: Started banking career in 1976 with National Bank of Nigeria, overseas branch. Later joined Manufacturers Hanover Trust at Stratford in Documentary Credits Department. Worked for various banks in the City until he joined in ING Bank in 1988, where he worked as a documentation officer until he resigned in 1994. He is now self employed as director of Beautex Ltd and agent of Money Gram (international money transfers). He is scheduled to go fully into financial services and bureau de change. He is also actively involved in the entertainment industry.
NOMINATED BY: Sam Jenyo

MR JASON YOUNG (Student-Theology)

President, Kings College London, University of London Athletics Club, 86 Park View Road, Tottenham, London, N17 9DP

PLACE OF BIRTH: Clapton, 17.10.72
MARITAL STATUS: Single
COLLEGE: Kings College London
ACADEMIC QUALIFICATIONS: BA Theology
PROFESSIONAL QUALIFICATIONS: Diploma in Theology, Food Hygiene Certificate
DIRECTORSHIPS: Captain UL Athletics Club, President KCL Theology Society
MEMBERSHIPS: Publications Officer, University of London Union Sports Executive
HONOURS/AWARDS: Offered a place at Wycliff Hall Oxford University Nov 1995
HOBBIES AND INTERESTS: Listening to music, going cinema, photography
EMAIL: Jason.young@kcl.ac.uk
PERSONAL PROFILE: Jason Young is the prototype of the 21st Century Black Englishman. He has a dynamic personality and enjoys working in a team. He plans to produce films about London in order to create a history and an identity for Black English people in the 21st Century.
NOMINATED BY: London Athletic Club

CLLR VINCE YOUNG (Councillor)

Manchester City Council, Town Hall, Lloyd Street, Manchester, M60 2LA

PLACE OF BIRTH: Jamaica, 16.4.26
MARITAL STATUS: Married
CHILDREN: Four (Karl, Kurt, Suzanne, Katarina)
COLLEGE: Wolverhampton
DIRECTORSHIPS: Five
MEMBERSHIPS: Trade Union
HOBBIES AND INTERESTS: Reading, football, cricket
PERSONAL PROFILE: Trade union since 1948. Manchester councillor for 12 years elected to Moss Ward in 1988, was also a Labour candidate for Levenshulme ward. School governor of infant and junior schools. Chair and deputy of equal opportunities. Deputy chair personnel committee. Deputy chair education. Serves on personnel, social services education and finance.

> Manchester councillor for 12 years elected to Moss Ward in 1988, was also a Labour candidate for Levenshulme ward
>
> **CLLR VINCE YOUNG**

DR BENJAMIN ZEPHANIAH (Playwright-Poet)

1 Kingsway House, Albion Road, London, N16 0TA

PLACE OF BIRTH: Birmingham
MARITAL STATUS: Married
ACADEMIC QUALIFICATIONS: Honorary Doctorate, University of North London
DIRECTORSHIPS: Vegan Society, Penrose HA, Blackliners (AIDs Helpline)
MEMBERSHIPS: Equity, Performing Rights Society, Musicians Union
HOBBIES AND INTERESTS: Kung-Fu, numismatics, classic car restoration
PERSONAL PROFILE: Author of nine books of poetry, one book of prose and one teenage novel. Writer and performer of eight musical recordings and eight plays. But he is most renowned for his live poetry performances and for popularising poetry in Britain. His performances are very energetic and highly political.
NOMINATED BY: Sharon Aitkin

Abbey	Nathaniel	105	Eboda	Michael	111	Martin	George	117
Abou	Samassi	105	Ebohon	Christinia	111	Massive	Mikey	117
Adams	John	105	Emmanuel	Heather	111	Mastin	Jay	117
Adebola	Bamberdele	105	Emmanus	Brenda	111	Maynard	Michael	117
Aden	Mohamoud	105	Eshun	Ekow	111	Mcalmont	Anthony	117
Adeniran	Abi	105	Euba	Tunde	111	Mcdonald	Trevor	118
Alexander	Dounne	105	Evaristo	Bernardine	111	Mcpherson-Sulaiman	Stephanie	118
Allison	Wayne	105	Eversley	Owen	111	Mills	Gloria	118
Andrew	Rene	105	Fairclough	Foston	111	Monu	Nicholas	118
Andrews	Fitzroy	105	Femi-Ola	John	112	Murray	Errol	118
Anthony	Kirk	105	Fisher	Annette	112	Murray	Valerie	118
Antoine	Roselle	106	Fleming	Curtis	112	Myers	Andy	118
Appio	Isabel	106	France	Thomas Arthur	112	Nasah	Chris	118
Augustin	Simon	106	Francis	Jenny	112	Newton	Edward	119
Babayaro	Celestine	106	Frater	Nelda	112	Nisbett	Stephen	119
Bain	Allister	106	Gayle	Mike	112	Omar	Rageh	119
Baxter	Nicholas	106	George	Kadija	112	Opeyokun	Victor	119
Bell-Gam	Hope	106	Gichigi	John	112	Osei-Bonsu	Maame	119
Bent	Colin	106	Gordon	Dean	113	Palmer	Donna	119
Beresford	Randolph	107	Graham	Aubyn	113	Parke	Elaine	119
Beswick	Lincoln	107	Grant	Bernie	113	Patterson	Clive	119
Blair	Veronica	107	Gray	Andy	113	Pedro	Rotimi	119
Blango	Michael Joe	107	Griffiths	Jaye	113	Phillips	Trevor	119
Boateng	Kwasi	107	Griffiths	Mathew	113	Powell	Wilton	120
Boateng	Ozwald	107	Griffiths-Brown	Colin	113	Ramroop	Madan	120
Boateng	Paul	107	Grosset	Simeon	113	Raphael	Nick	120
Bonsu	Henry	107	Gulam	William	113	Ricard	Hamilton	120
Boulaye	Patti	107	Hall	Stuart	114	Richardson	Pikay	120
Boyce	Lewis	108	Hamilton	Lewis	114	Robinson	June	120
Boye-Anawomah	Micheal	108	Hanley	Ellery	114	Robinson	Lionel	120
Brennan	Fernie	108	Harrison	Audley	114	Robinson	Trevor	120
Brown	Miquel	108	Hayfron-Benjamin	John	114	Rollins	Elizabeth	121
Brown	Pamela	108	Henriques	Julian	114	Ross	Matthew	121
Brown	Selwyn	108	Hinds	David	114	Sampsons	Alfred	121
Campbell	Sandra	108	Howe	Darcus	114	Sealy	Clinton	121
Campbell	Vince	108	Hughes	Ella	114	Schloss	Donald	121
Cannonville	Dean	108	Ipaye-Sowunmi	Yemi	115	Shillingford	Ron	121
Charlery	Kenneth	109	Isfort	Jane	115	Simms	Sheryl	121
Charles	Faustin	109	Jennings	Brenda	115	St. Hill	Dionne	121
Clarke	Pamela	109	Johnson	Gerald	115	St. John	Joan	121
Chinegwundoh	Francis	109	Jones	Jennifer	115	Thompson	Geoffrey	122
Coker	Alexander	109	Jordan	Diane	115	Weir	Mark	122
Crooks	Joy	109	King	Adebayo	115	Williams	Nicola	122
De Banya	Simon	109	King	Oona	115	Williams	Roy	122
D'Souza	Neil	109	King	Samuel	116	Wilson	Paul	122
Da Cocodia	Louise	109	Knight	Beverley	116	Wood	Wilfred	122
Datson	Fidelix	110	Kumi	Yvonne	116	Wright	Ian	122
Davis	Karle	110	Lawrence	Doreen	116	Wright	Ola	122
Day	Berril	110	Lawrence	Neville	116	Younge	Patrick	123
Deane	Brian	110	La Mothe	Anthony	116	Zack-Williams	Alfred	123
Desailly	Marcel	110	Lambourd	Bernard	116	Zack-Williams	Dorothy	123
Dixon-Fyle	Dora	110	Lamont	Matt	116			
Duberry	Michael	110	Laurence	Daoud	116			
Duncan	Lyndon	110	Laurent	Burt	116			
Dunseath	Emmanuel	110	Le Roc	Kele	117			
Dunson	Gregory	110	Lee	Anthea	117			

MR NATHANIEL ABBEY (Footballer)

Goalkeeper, Luton,

PLACE OF BIRTH: Islington, 11.7.78
PERSONAL PROFILE: Made his debut for Luton in the Coca Cola Cup against Colchester as an 18-year old. Later he enjoyed an impressive spell on loan at Woking.

MR SAMASSI ABOU (Footballer)

West Ham United,

PLACE OF BIRTH: Ivory Coast, 4.8.73
PROFESSIONAL QUALIFICATIONS: Caps for Ivory Coast
PERSONAL PROFILE: Following a series of unconvincing performances as substitute, Abou settled in and began silencing his critics. Abou broke his duck with his first goal for the Hammers during the fourth round of the Coca Cola Cup in 1997, Abou's dynamic display gave the fans a taste of things to come.

MR JOHN ADAMS

PERSONAL PROFILE: John Adams is an information and communications technology specialist. He has worked on numerous IT projects including the development of a multimedia video server for Reuters International, setting up mission critical systems for Blue Chip companies in the City and other communications training projects. He has set up and runs the Black Information Link web site. His graphics and web designing skills are self taught and applied to the site.

MR BAMBERDELE (DELE) ADEBOLA
(Footballer)

Birmingham City,

PLACE OF BIRTH: Nigeria, 23.6.75
PERSONAL PROFILE: Having made great strides over the past couple of years, and becoming Crewe's leading scorer in 1996-97, despite several clubs expressing an interest in him during the 1997 close season he remained at Gresty Road.

MR MOHAMOUD ADEN (Project Officer)

Somali Youth Project, Priory Community Centre, Acton Lane, London, W3 8NY

PLACE OF BIRTH: Somalia, 10.10.61
MARITAL STATUS: Married
CHILDREN: Three (Amal, Muna, Ahmed)
COLLEGE: Somali National University
ACADEMIC QUALIFICATIONS: MSc, Bsc, Water Engineering and Civil Engineering
PROFESSIONAL QUALIFICATIONS: MSc, Bsc, BBTS-Youth & Community
HONOURS/AWARDS: Lara Dec 1996
HOBBIES AND INTERESTS: Football, reading
PERSONAL PROFILE: I used to be assistant lecturer at Somali National University and civil engineer as well as contractor in the construction industry in Somalia. I did my BSc in Somalia and MSc in the Netherlands as a Fellowship. I started community work in 1992 and got full-time employment in 1995 in the Somali Youth Project.

NOMINATED BY: Joseph Anastacio

MR ABI ADENIRAN (Research Consultant)

Hot House Market Research Ltd, 24 Highbury Grove, London, N5 2EA

PLACE OF BIRTH: Lagos, 28.12.69
COLLEGE: LSE
ACADEMIC QUALIFICATIONS: BA Hons
PROFESSIONAL QUALIFICATIONS: MCIM, MRs
DIRECTORSHIPS: Hot House Market Research Ltd; Titan Oil & Gas Ltd
MEMBERSHIPS: ARRP, MRS, IOD, Member of RFO Advisory Committee
HONOURS/AWARDS: RIMA
HOBBIES AND INTERESTS: Sports, Chair of St John's Youth Project
EMAIL: abi@hothouse.ndirect.co.uk
PERSONAL PROFILE: Educated at Kent College Canterbury and studied marketing at the London School of Economics. New employment with NOP as a research assistant and promoted to projects controller within four years. Then joined Voice Group Ltd as marketing manager, left to establish Hot House Market Research which pioneers ethnic minority social, economic and consumer research projects for both the private and public sector.
NOMINATED BY: Nicola Loftus, Whittman Hart (UK) Ltd

MS DOUNNE ALEXANDER (Herbal Food Manufacturer)

Managing Director, Gramma's UK, PO Box 218, East Ham, London, E6 4BG

PLACE OF BIRTH: Trinidad, 28.1.49
MARITAL STATUS: Married
CHILDREN: Two
COLLEGE: Rush Green Tec
ACADEMIC QUALIFICATIONS: 4 O-Levels, Laboratory Technician
DIRECTORSHIPS: Own business
MEMBERSHIPS: Food from Britain, Tastes of Anglia, Small Business Federation, Women Mean Business
HONOURS/AWARDS: Women of Achievement, Most Outstanding Black Business Woman
HOBBIES AND INTERESTS: Travel, food, exercise
PERSONAL PROFILE: Dounne started her unique manufacturing business GRAMMA's in 1987 - immediately stocking her Herbal Pepper Sauces in Britain's most prestigious stores, Harrods and Fortnum & Mason, capturing extensive national media coverage, thus raising the profile, quality, standards and presentation of Black foods. Winner of several national awards, gained recognition as a British speciality food producer and recorded in the American Chile Institute's Hall-of-Fame to become an inspiration to other budding Black entrepreneurs.
NOMINATED BY: Christopher Johnson MBA

MR WAYNE ALLISON (Footballer)

Huddersfield Town,

PLACE OF BIRTH: Huddersfield, 16.10.63
PERSONAL PROFILE: A typically big, strong figure who holds the ball up well and creates the space and chances for others, Wayne was quickly dubbed the battering ram of the front line.

MR RENE ANDREW (Graphic Designer- Illustrator)

Production Editor, New Nation, 1st Floor, 148 Cambridge Heath Road, London, E1 5QJ

PLACE OF BIRTH: London, 28.12.67
MARITAL STATUS: Single
COLLEGE: Newham College
ACADEMIC QUALIFICATIONS: HND in Graphic Design
HOBBIES AND INTERESTS: Sports, TV trivia
PERSONAL PROFILE: Designer and illustrator with over ten years experience. Major clients include New Nation, Ms London, Nicklelodeon UK. Currently embarking on a TV career.

FITZROY ANDREWS (Chief Executive)

The Windsor Fellowship,

PERSONAL PROFILE: Scheme where first year degree students of African-Caribbean and Asian origin are linked up with companies for work placements and skills workshops.
NOMINATED BY: Sunita Ram

MR KIRK ANTHONY

PERSONAL PROFILE: Kirk Anthony's Chinese-Jamaican parentage coupled with years of living in Toronto has enabled him to blend an accent that has been called "smooth and unique". His radio career started in 1977 and over the years he moved from pirate radio to nightclubs. His big break came in 1989 when he approached Choice with a demo cassette. The rest is history!

> Dounne started her unique manufacturing business GRAMMA's in 1987 - immediately stocking her Herbal Pepper Sauces in Britain's most prestigious stores, Harrods and Fortnum & Mason
>
> **DOUNNE ALEXANDER**

ROSELLE ANTOINE (Director)

TCS Educational Trust Limited, 21 Broadwalk, Pinner Road, North Harrow, HA2 6ED

PLACE OF BIRTH: Grenada, 12.3.58
MARITAL STATUS: Single
CHILDREN: One (Cyrus)
COLLEGE: University of North London
ACADEMIC QUALIFICATIONS: BA Hons, MA (Part 1), PhD in progress
PROFESSIONAL QUALIFICATIONS: Lecturer, advisor, remedial specialist
DIRECTORSHIPS: TCS Educational Trust
MEMBERSHIPS: Board member of National Record of Achievement, member Harrow Area Board
HONOURS/AWARDS: Winner Young Black Writer 1981, Award for Outstanding Contribution to Multiculturalism and Education
HOBBIES AND INTERESTS: Writing childrens literature, music, theatre, oral cultures
PERSONAL PROFILE: An educator with tenacious will and steely determination, Roselle ensures the younger generations are given every opportunity to succeed. A children's writer, with several publications, local board member positions in the community, she's been teaching for over 15 years - all levels to post graduate. Roselle's involvement in the local and international community helps her to continue in the tradition of our ancestral pioneers.

MS ISABEL APPIO (Director)

Publisher, Soho Publishing,

PLACE OF BIRTH: London, 30.6.63
COLLEGE: Central College
ACADEMIC QUALIFICATIONS: BA Communications
PERSONAL PROFILE: Isabel Appio has worked as a journalist, editor and publisher in both the mainstream and ethnic press. Formerly editorial director of the Voice group she now runs her own publishing company

MR SIMON AUGUSTIN (Managing Director)

Carib Globe Real Estate Consultant, Stanmore House, 35 Stanmore Road, Tottenham, London, N15 3PR

PLACE OF BIRTH: St Lucia, 18.7.49
MARITAL STATUS: Single
COLLEGE: East Ham Tech
ACADEMIC QUALIFICATIONS: Eletcronic Business Studies - Hendon Tech
PROFESSIONAL QUALIFICATIONS: Business Studies - Hendon Tech
HONOURS/AWARDS: Sam Tec Dance 1998
HOBBIES AND INTERESTS: Theatre, sports, debates
PERSONAL PROFILE: Set up company in 1993, after leaving BT in 1992, as PR for dealing systems throughout BT network. Have been promoting St Lucia and other Caribbean islands real estate, also encouraging ex patriots to purchase land on their respective islands.
NOMINATED BY: Christopher Johnson MBA

MR CELESTINE BABAYARO (Footballer)

Chelsea Football Club, Stamford Bridge, Fulham Road, London, SW6 1HS

PLACE OF BIRTH: Nigeria, 29.8.78
PROFESSIONAL QUALIFICATIONS: 10 Nigerian Caps, 18 Nigerian U21 and Olympic Caps
HONOURS/AWARDS: Belgian Young Player of the Year 1995 and 1996, Best African in Belgium 1996, Olympic Gold Medalist 1996
PERSONAL PROFILE: Signed to Chelsea Footbll Club. Two stress fractures in the foot after a groin muscle tear is not the best way to start life at a new club when you've joined for its teenage transfer record of £2.25m aged 18. But that was Baba's lot last season. He showed himself be more at home at left-back than in midfield, but can play either and is very strong, good in the air, and excellent both defensively and in keeping possession. His last appearance, at Tottenham on December 6, was followed by Chelsea's slump in form. He got himself fit enough to play in the World Cup.

> 'Having only played rugby since I was 19 I believe I have achieved a great deal in 1997/98 season. I was named player of the season and broke the national try scoring record for trys in a season (29) and tries in a game (6)'
>
> **NICHOLAS ANTHONY BAXTER**

MR ALLISTER BAIN (Actor)

Britt Management,

PERSONAL PROFILE: TV credits include: 'Fords on water'; 'Vanity Fair'; 'US Girls'; 'South of the border and black silk'. Stage: 'The Cherry Orchard'; 'Midsummer Nights Dream'; 'Sweet Talk'; 'Two Can Play'; 'Remembrance' and 'The Pied Piper' at the National Theatre. One man pieces: Ova-Ya; La La and Dear Mister Shakespeare.
NOMINATED BY: Malet MSe

MR NICHOLAS ANTHONY BAXTER (Pro Rugby Player)

Worcester Rugby Club, Sixways, Pershore Lane, Hindlip, Worcester, WR1 1RB

PLACE OF BIRTH: Edgbaston, 13.4.73
MARITAL STATUS: Single
COLLEGE: University of Derby
ACADEMIC QUALIFICATIONS: HND Business & Finance BA Hons (2i) Business Administration & Marketing
PROFESSIONAL QUALIFICATIONS: Chartered Institute of Marketing Diploma
MEMBERSHIPS: CIM
HONOURS/AWARDS: Jawson Player of the Season 1997/98
HOBBIES AND INTERESTS: Golf, tennis, DIY
PERSONAL PROFILE: Having only played rugby since I was 19 I believe I have achieved a great deal in 1997/98 season. I was named player of the season and broke the national try scoring record for trys in a season (29) and tries in a game (6). I am inspired as a role model for Black children who would like to play a game which is principally dominated by players from a privileged background.
NOMINATED BY: Mr Cusroth, Worcester Rugby Club

DR HOPE BELL-GAM (Doctor GP)

PLACE OF BIRTH: Nigeria, 29.4.54
MARITAL STATUS: Married
CHILDREN: Three (Winston, Margaret, Karl)
COLLEGE: Ahmuda Bellouniv, Nigeria
ACADEMIC QUALIFICATIONS: MB BS, MRCP, DGM, MRCGP, FWACP, DNH, DGM
PROFESSIONAL QUALIFICATIONS: MB BS, MRCP, DGM, MRCGP, FWACP, DNH, DGM
MEMBERSHIPS: BMA, British Geriatrics Society, RCPGP, NMA, RCPI
HOBBIES AND INTERESTS: Counselling, speeches, cooking, film and video
PERSONAL PROFILE: I am a physician with a special interest in hypertension and neurology. I am also a geriatrician. I am currently practising as a freelance GP.

FLYING OFFICER COLIN BENT (H M Forces)

Engineering Officer, Royal Air Forces, RAF Air Squadron, Royal Military College of Science, Shrivenham, Wiltshire, Swindon, SN6 8LS

PLACE OF BIRTH: Huddersfield, 12.4.70
MARITAL STATUS: Single
COLLEGE: RMCS Shrivenham University
ACADEMIC QUALIFICATIONS: HNC Electronics, OWD Avionics. Currently reading for a Degree
MEMBERSHIPS: Institute of Electrical Engineers (IEE) and Incorporated Engineers (AMIIE)
HONOURS/AWARDS: BTEC Student of the Year 1993 (Gold), Sasson Flying Award 1994
HOBBIES AND INTERESTS: Great Britain and England athlete (Athletics high jump)
EMAIL: BENT.C.G@Rmcs.CRANFIELD.ac.UK
PERSONAL PROFILE: Electrical apprentice of the Year 1986-87 and 1987-89. Territorial Army Best Recruit 1988. BTEC Student of the Year 1993, Gold Medalist. Philip Sasson Flying Award 1994. Great Britain & England Athlete since 1995 (High Jump). Became an RAF Officer in April 1998. Currently at university studying electrical engineering.
NOMINATED BY: Sir Richard Johns, Ministry of Defence

MR RANDOLPH BERESFORD MBE/BEM

London Borough of Hammersmith and Fulham,

PLACE OF BIRTH: Guyana, 20.3.14
CHILDREN: Seven (Vanrick, Ulric, Esther, Ethel, Elaine, Elezabeth, Gregery)
COLLEGE: Ruskin College
ACADEMIC QUALIFICATIONS: Branch Official Correspondence Course, Industrial Relations in the Workplace with the TUC and a Course in English Local Government
PROFESSIONAL QUALIFICATIONS: Trade Union, Political Studies
MEMBERSHIPS: Member of Lions International, Chairman of the London Borough of Hammersmith Black Senior Citizens Group
HONOURS/AWARDS: Awared the BEM 1979, Caribbean Times Award 1986, Awarded MBE January 1987
HOBBIES AND INTERESTS: Writing
PERSONAL PROFILE: Awarded the BEM June 1979. Chairman of the London Borough of Hammersmith Black Senior Citizens Group. Awarded Member of the British Empire (MBE) January 1987. My biography 'A Journey Through Life from Guyana to Ghana' compiled with the assistance of Dr Christopher A Johnson, MBA was published in 1995.
NOMINATED BY: Christopher Johnson MBA

MR LINCOLN BESWICK (TELECOM TECHNICIAN)

Councillor, London Borough Brent, Town Hall, Forty Lane, Wembley, HA9 9HD

PLACE OF BIRTH: Jamaica, 8.5.47
MARITAL STATUS: Single
CHILDREN: One (Kenrick Jason Martin)
COLLEGE: City of Guilds London Institute
ACADEMIC QUALIFICATIONS: Part 1,2 & 3. (CGLI)
PROFESSIONAL QUALIFICATIONS: Telecommunication Technician
HONOURS/AWARDS: Award of Investors in People (IIP), Medal Awarded Local Business Partnership, Long Service & Good Conduct (LSGC), Health & Safety Certificate for Contribution to Company Staff
HOBBIES AND INTERESTS: Politics, current affairs, travelling, cultural pursuits including art, antiques, walking
PERSONAL PROFILE: Astute politician, long distinguished public service, high achiever, totally into servicing and empowering the community in order to achieve greater democracy, believe in equity and is practically involved in promoting greater democracy and economic and social justice for all. He is one of the longest serving persons in the public services from the Black community.
NOMINATED BY: Chris Mullard

MRS VERONICA EVADINE BLAIR
(NON EXECUTIVE DIRECTOR DUDLEY NHS)

PLACE OF BIRTH: Jamaica, 22.10.37
MARITAL STATUS: Widow
CHILDREN: Four (Wilton, Joy, Velda, Venetia)
COLLEGE: Dudley Technical College
ACADEMIC QUALIFICATIONS: 6 O-Levels at Grade C, above, GNVQ Level 5
PROFESSIONAL QUALIFICATIONS: State Enrolled Nurse, State Certified Midwife
DIRECTORSHIPS: Non Exeutive Director Dudley Group NHS Trust
HOBBIES AND INTERESTS: Water colour painting, crocheting

PERSONAL PROFILE: I am a magistrate on the Dudley Bench. I have been a local councillor for the past four years and the chair of social services for the last twelve months. (I have just lost my seat). I am an executive member of a minority ethnic group called the Dudley Caribbean and Friends Association.

COLUMBA MICHEAL JOE BLANGO (SPORTS TEACHER)

59 Elgar Street, Rotherhithe, London, SE16 1QR

PLACE OF BIRTH: Sierra Leone, 23.4.56
MARITAL STATUS: Married
CHILDREN: Three (Christian, Columba, Yaenie Martha)
COLLEGE: Kiev State Institute of Sports
ACADEMIC QUALIFICATIONS: MSc, PhD, Certificate in Education (PGCE)
PROFESSIONAL QUALIFICATIONS: Athletics Coach in Multi Events (Decathlon)
DIRECTORSHIPS: British Amateur Athletics Board (BAAB)
HONOURS/AWARDS: Assistant club coach
HOBBIES AND INTERESTS: Sports, reading, politics, computers
EMAIL: C65641@aol.com
PERSONAL PROFILE: 1977 - 1st West African Games - Lagos Nigeria. 1980 - Moscow Olympic Games (Decathlon). 1981 - Kiev State Institute of Sports. 1982-89 - High profile competitions. 1986 - MSc in Sports. 1991 - PhD Theory & Methods of Sports. 1992 - Executive member (Sierra Leone) People's Party UK & Ireland Branch. 1996 - Vice chair Sierra Leone People's Party, UK & Ireland Branch. 1998 - Southwark Liberal Democrat councillor for Dockyard Ward.

MR KWASI AMPONSAH BOATENG (CHARTERED ARCHITECT)

Director, Knak Design Architects & Development Consultants, Laser House, 132-140 Goswell Road, London, EC1V 7DY

PLACE OF BIRTH: Ghana, 24.12.61
MARITAL STATUS: Married
CHILDREN: Two (Akua Amponsa, Kwaku Gyimah)
COLLEGE: South Bank University, University College London
ACADEMIC QUALIFICATIONS: BA Hons Architecture 2.1, Dip Arch with Commendation, MSc. (Econs)
PROFESSIONAL QUALIFICATIONS: Urban Development Planner (Development Economics), RIBA
DIRECTORSHIPS: Society of Black Architects, Black International Construction Organisation
HONOURS/AWARDS: UK Black Link Business of the Year 1999-2000, RIBA Award Ideal Rooms
HOBBIES AND INTERESTS: Collect hats, play tennis, basket ball and oware
PERSONAL PROFILE: Practise in architecture and the wider built environment. Chair of the Society of Blacks Partners, KNAK Design, Architects and Development Consultancy. Visiting Fellow in Urban Development at South Bank University, with a focus on 'Good Governance' in the construction industry. Alumnus of the United Nation Leadership Academy, Amman Jordon.

MR OZWALD BOATENG (FASHION DESIGNER)

PERSONAL PROFILE: Ozwald Boateng is regarded as a radical modernist in the closed world of bespoke tailoring. Ozwald's work reflects his Anglo Ghanaian heritage. His clients include lawyers, politicians and artists. He recently launched the UK's first Couture House in Wimpole Street, London, W1.

MR PAUL BOATENG MP (BARRISTER-AT-LAW)

Minister of State, House of Commons,

HONOURS/AWARDS: EMMA Award for 'Politician For The Year', Martin Luther King Memorial Prize
PERSONAL PROFILE: Paul Boateng was appointed Minister of State for Home Affairs in 1998. Previously, he was Under Secretary of State at the Department of Health. He joined Parliament as Member for Brent South in 1987. In 1988, he received the Martin Luther King Memorial Prize for his contribution to the field of social, economic and racial justice at home and abroad. He also won an EMMA Award last year for 'Politician For The Year'.

MR HENRY BONSU

HONOURS/AWARDS: EMMA Award for Best Audio Journalist.
PERSONAL PROFILE: Henry Bonsu is the winner of the 1998 EMMA award for Best Audio Journalist. Henry became a freelance writer and broadcaster after a six year stint with the BBC. Currently, he presents 'Upfront Word Up!' on Radio 5 Live and 'Talking Africa' on Spectrum Radio.

PATTI BOULAYE (ENTERTAINER)

Boulaye Entertainment Ltd,

PLACE OF BIRTH: Nigeria
MARITAL STATUS: Married
CHILDREN: Two (Emma, Sebastian)
COLLEGE: Lagos
DIRECTORSHIPS: Five
HONOURS/AWARDS: Numerous show business awards including Female Vocalist of the Year
PERSONAL PROFILE: Patti Boulaye has been writing a musical dance show 'Patti Boulaye's Sun Dance' for which she has written the music, script and designed the costumes. The show is planned for production in 1999. Patti is now established as a successful jewellery designer and has a regular programme on QVC. She will be introducing her new 'Paradise' Autumn range on QVC. She will stand as candidate for the greater London assembly.

MR LEWIS BOYCE (PROJECT MANAGER)

Project Manager, 261 B Sheringham Avenue, Manor Park, London, E12 6HJ

PLACE OF BIRTH: Barbados, 9.11.44
HOBBIES AND INTERESTS: Walking, reading, music
PERSONAL PROFILE: Born in Barbados in 1944. Resident in UK, since 1964. Employed at London Underground 1964 to 1995. Currently a project manager in the voluntary sector. Gained NEBSM certificate and diploma in supervision and management in 1991 and 1994. Local councillor, Newham, 1982 to 1994. Chair Newham African Caribbean Alliance 1990-1996, Barbados Overseas Citizens Association 1988-1989; Monega primary school governor 1990 to present.
NOMINATED BY: B O C A

CLLR MICHAEL BOYE-ANAWOMAH JP
(ACADEMIC ADMINISTRATOR RTD)

Councillor, London Borough of Islington, 5-7 Marlborough Road, London, N19 4NA

PLACE OF BIRTH: Ghana, 4.2.35
MARITAL STATUS: Married
CHILDREN: Three (Margo, John Philip, Samuel)
COLLEGE: Oriel Oxford University
ACADEMIC QUALIFICATIONS: MA (Oxon), Dip. Pol. Econ. Social Studies
PROFESSIONAL QUALIFICATIONS: Teachers Certificate B (Ghana)
DIRECTORSHIPS: North Islington Law Centre, Peter Bedford Housing Assocaition
MEMBERSHIPS: Justice of the Peace
HOBBIES AND INTERESTS: Music, voluntary work, local politics
PERSONAL PROFILE: Mayor of Islington 1994-95. Justice of the Peace, Harrow since 1979. Member, Home Secretary's race relations forum. Chair, environment, leisure and transport committee, Islington. Member, London Fire and Civil Defence Authority. Former faculty administrator, polytechnic, now University of North London. Former secretary to the Prime Minister of Ghana.

MS FERNNE BRENNAN (LECTURER IN LAW)

Department of Law, University of Essex, Wivenhoe Park, Colchester, CO4 3SQ

PLACE OF BIRTH: London, 31.7.56
MARITAL STATUS: Married
CHILDREN: Two (Ashley, Jonathan)
COLLEGE: King's College, Greenwich University
ACADEMIC QUALIFICATIONS: Sociology BA Hons, Law LLB & LLM
PROFESSIONAL QUALIFICATIONS: Solicitor PGDL
MEMBERSHIPS: SPTL, EALDHR, UK/ELU Monitoring Centre
HOBBIES AND INTERESTS: Reading, music, travel, theatre, horror movies, good food
EMAIL: joash@essexac.UK
PERSONAL PROFILE: Academic lawyer. Graduate of King's College and Greenwich University. Trained at the College of Law as a solicitor before appointment to the University of Essex Department of Law. Specialist in criminal justice, European community law and medical law. Published in European law and criminal justice. Inspiration mother, Mr Chaterjee and God.
NOMINATED BY: Elle Sarply

MS MIQUEL BROWN (ACTRESS-SINGER)

LWA, 18 Elliot Square, London, NW3 3SU

PLACE OF BIRTH: US, 8.2.49
MARITAL STATUS: Married
CHILDREN: Two (Sinitta Renet, Gail Rhyette)
COLLEGE: University Washington Seattle/Wayne, Detroit
ACADEMIC QUALIFICATIONS: Attended American College in London & Classes at Royal Academy DA
PROFESSIONAL QUALIFICATIONS: 28 Years on stage
HONOURS/AWARDS: Gold Records from around the world
HOBBIES AND INTERESTS: Golf, chess, tennis, ski-ing, painting
PERSONAL PROFILE: Miquel was the first Black female to play the traditionally white role of Sheila in the musical 'Hair' on the London West End stage. Miquel and her daughter Sinatta were the first mother and daughter to be in the charts (music) at the same time. Miquel was voted the sixth top female vocalist in the world by Bill Board magazine in 1984.

> ## Qualified mechanical engineer, who was awarded special commendation by the Queen in 1979
>
> **VINCE CAMPBELL**

MS PAMELA BROWN (MANAGEMENT CONSULTANT)

Director, Pamela Brown Associates, 4 Foxhill Gardens, Upper Norwood, London, SE19 2XB

PLACE OF BIRTH: Kenya, 8.11.55
MARITAL STATUS: Divorced
CHILDREN: One (Nathan Amir Daniel)
COLLEGE: Hull
ACADEMIC QUALIFICATIONS: BA Hons American Studies, MA Criminology
DIRECTORSHIPS: Chair of Housing Association Ombudsman service
HOBBIES AND INTERESTS: Race relations, travel, history, politics
PERSONAL PROFILE: Pam Brown has worked on race strategies in Britain and Bermuda. Her work in Bermuda has been continued by the government and several major businesses who employed her to develop codes of practise and business strategies. She continues to work all over the country and abroad on equality issues.
NOMINATED BY: Chris Mullard

MR SELWYN BROWN (MUSICIAN)

Keyboards-Vocals, Steel Pulse/Pulse Music Ltd, 42 Upper Dean Street, Digbeth, Birmingham, B5 4SG

PLACE OF BIRTH: London, 4.6.56
MARITAL STATUS: Divorced/co-habitee
CHILDREN: Four (Derrick, Joshua, Naomi, Aliyah)
COLLEGE: Tamworth College
ACADEMIC QUALIFICATIONS: 5 O-Levels
DIRECTORSHIPS: Pulse Music Ltd
MEMBERSHIPS: PUSH
HONOURS/AWARDS: Naras-Grammy
HOBBIES AND INTERESTS: Football, computers, word games
EMAIL: steelpulse2000@hotmail.com
PERSONAL PROFILE: Attended Handsworth Wood Boys School then Tamworth College. As a child introduced to music by his parents who encouraged Selwyn to take piano lessons. After leaving school formed Steel Pulse along with David Hinds, Alphonso Martin, Michael Riley, Basil Gabbidon, Colin Gabbidon and Ronnie McQueen.

MS SANDRA CAMPBELL

PERSONAL PROFILE: Sandra Campbell is a freelance graphic designer who has been credited for her work on behalf of recruitment consultants CCG (Corporate Consultancy Group). She designed the company logo and brochure. Sandra took two C's and interlocked them to convey the idea of linking people and business.

MR VINCE CAMPBELL
(MECHANICAL ENGINEER)

Chair, Black Business Association Waltham Forest Ltd, 5 Black Horse Lane, Walthamstow, London, E17 6DS

PLACE OF BIRTH: Jamaica, 28.9.28
MARITAL STATUS: Married
CHILDREN: Six
DIRECTORSHIPS: Black Business Association, Charterhouse Merchant Bank
MEMBERSHIPS: Institute of Management
HONOURS/AWARDS: Awards for Industry
PERSONAL PROFILE: Qualified mechanical engineer, who was awarded special commendation by the Queen in 1979 for pioneering work in product design and development. Active community worker who represented Black people on a number of organisations including CRE. Now actively developing partnerships to promote economic development within the black communities of Waltham Forest and Enfield.
NOMINATED BY: Christopher Johnson MBA

MR DEAN CANONVILLE (FOOTBALLER)

Millwall Football Club, The Den, Zampa Road, London, SE16 3LN

PLACE OF BIRTH: Perivale, 30.11.78
PROFESSIONAL QUALIFICATIONS: 2 League Appearances
PERSONAL PROFILE: Dean suffered a heartbreaking season in 1997/98. Having just broken through to the first team squad the previous year he was sidelined for the entire campaign through injuries to his back and shin. A pacy, skilful player, he will be hoping to pick up where he left off and force his way into the first team once more.

MR KENNETH CHARLERY (Footballer)

PLACE OF BIRTH: London, 28.11.64
PROFESSIONAL QUALIFICATIONS: Over 400 appearances and over 200 goals
PERSONAL PROFILE: At the age of 24 Ken started his professional football career with Maidstone FC. At the age of 34 Ken fulfilled his dream when he played for his home country St Lucia. Barnet FC is his present club and Ken intends to continue his footballing career for at least another three or four years as well as coaching at a professional level.

MR FAUSTIN CHARLES (Writer-Storyteller-Dramatist)

Community Literacy Officer, Enfield Borough Library Services, 10 Kemplay Road, Hampstead, London, NW3 1SY

PLACE OF BIRTH: Trinidad, 15.9.44
COLLEGE: Kent University, Canterbury
ACADEMIC QUALIFICATIONS: BA Hons
PROFESSIONAL QUALIFICATIONS: None
DIRECTORSHIPS: None
MEMBERSHIPS: Society Of Authors
HONOURS/AWARDS: None
HOBBIES AND INTERESTS: Music, art, ballet plays, operetta, reviews and children's books. I have performed poetry and stories all over Europe.
NOMINATED BY: Christopher Johnson MBA

MS PAMELA CLARKE (Child Care Assistant)

London Borough Of Brent,

PLACE OF BIRTH: Birmingham, 17.6.61
MARITAL STATUS: Divorced
CHILDREN: Two (Darrell, Dominique)
MEMBERSHIPS: Brent South Black Parents Association
HOBBIES AND INTERESTS: Interior decorating, keeping fit, dance
PERSONAL PROFILE: I am a divorced mother of two boys Darrell and Dominique. I enjoy keep fit, dance and have worked in the medical field for over fourteen years.

DR FRANCIS CHINEGWUNDOH (Surgeon-Urology)

Consultant, St Bartholomew's Hospital, 144 Harley Street, London, W1N 1AH

PLACE OF BIRTH: London, 11.3.61
MARITAL STATUS: Married
CHILDREN: One
COLLEGE: St George's Medical School, London
ACADEMIC QUALIFICATIONS: MBBS MS
PROFESSIONAL QUALIFICATIONS: FRCS (Urol) FRCSEd, FEBU
DIRECTORSHIPS: Chairman Cancer Black Care
MEMBERSHIPS: BMA, Royal Society of Medicine, African Caribbean Medical Society
HOBBIES AND INTERESTS: Sports, chess
PERSONAL PROFILE: I was appointed as a consultant urologist in 1996 to two trusts in east London. Duties involve outpatient clinics, operating, teaching, research and lecturing. I have an interest in prostrate cancer and ethnicity. Voluntary work is for the charity Cancer Black Care

REV DR ALEXANDER BRYAN COKER
(Anglican Priest-Uni. Lecturer)

Director, Community Mission Chaplaincy (Ecumenical/Greater London), The Mission House, 149 Henley Avenue, North Cheam, SM3 9SD

PLACE OF BIRTH: Sierra Leone, 12.10.48
MARITAL STATUS: Married (Separated)
CHILDREN: Two (Adopted) (Wilhelmina Coker, Emmanuel Coker)
COLLEGE: King's College London
ACADEMIC QUALIFICATIONS: BD Hons, PhD, MA, MTH, MED
PROFESSIONAL QUALIFICATIONS: L Div (Licentiate In Divinity) 73, PGCE (77)
DIRECTORSHIPS: Thames Educational Institute, Mabwin Supplementary School, College of Preceptors (MPhils.), Associate of King's College 1976, Fellow Thames Educ. Inst. 1990
HOBBIES AND INTERESTS: A variety of music (piano), table tennis, Black organisations support
EMAIL: CMC@AnnRhodes.businesscentre.co.UK
PERSONAL PROFILE: Community chaplain to CACFO 1998. Croydon African Caribbean Organisation, Anglican Ministry 1970-the present. Ordained priest at St Paul's Cathedral 1987. Taught RE in Brent (MOD) 1979-85. Academic dean: Overstone Theological College, Northampton 1982-87. Visiting lecturer, Uni. St John's College with Cranmer Hall, Uni. of Durham 1983-88. Guest lecturer, Uni. London Inst. of Educ. 1984-85. Consultant, England Board of Social Responsibilities. Associate Professor Greenwich Uni., Sch of Theology 1987 to present.

MISS JOY CROOKS (Registered General Nurse)

Sickle Cell Counsellor, Sickle Cell Haematology Department, Sickle Cell & Thalassaemia Support Project, Haematology Dept, New Cross Hospital, Wolverhampton, WV10 0QP

PLACE OF BIRTH: Jamaica, 27.10.58
MARITAL STATUS: Single
CHILDREN: One (Latisha Shanice Reid)
COLLEGE: Wolverhampton University
ACADEMIC QUALIFICATIONS: 4 O-Levels, 2 A-Levels
PROFESSIONAL QUALIFICATIONS: State Enrolled Nurse, Ophthalmic Proficiency Certificate, State Registered Nurse
MEMBERSHIPS: Sickle Cell & Thalassaemia Association of Counsellors
HONOURS/AWARDS: African Caribbean Achievers Award, Windrush (BBC Nov 1998)
HOBBIES AND INTERESTS: Gardening, photography, art
PERSONAL PROFILE: Came to Britain age nine. Worked as nurse 1978-1990. Post of sickle cell and thalassaemia counsellor Sept 1990. Was full time until 1996 - now works part-time for Sickle Cell Project and part-time as disabilities counsellor for Wolverhampton Health Care Trust. Caring, confident, bright personality, encourages young people to do their best.
NOMINATED BY: Delva Campbell

MR SIMON DE BANYA

PERSONAL PROFILE: Simon De Banya is a freelance media consultant working on press and PR for a range of social policy campaigns, mainly within the Black community. Simon has highlighted the plight of murdered teenage Stephen Lawrence and his family to a worldwide audience, precipitating a change in British law and changing the way the judiciary perceives racist crimes in this country.

MR NEIL D'SOUZA (Actor)

c/o Waring & McKenna, Lauderdale House, 11 Gower Street, London, WC1E 2HB

PLACE OF BIRTH: Teddington, 4.5.70
MARITAL STATUS: Single
COLLEGE: University of Ulster
ACADEMIC QUALIFICATIONS: BA Hons Theatre Studies and Philosophy
PROFESSIONAL QUALIFICATIONS: RADA Dip. From The Royal Academy of Dramatic Art
HONOURS/AWARDS: Morphy Richards Award for Philosophy University of Ulster
HOBBIES AND INTERESTS: Piano, reading, cinema, keeping fit
PERSONAL PROFILE: Born Teddington, educated locally gained BA Theatre Studies/Philosophy from Ulster University. Spent one and half years living and working in Milan on returning to England won a place at RADA, graduated 1996. Work as an actor since includes 1998 Globe Season , Richard III (Leicester) and The Red Slender (Radio 3).

MRS LOUISE A DA-COCODIA JP BEM
(Project Development Consultant)

9 Arliss Avenue, Levenshulme, Manchester, M19 2PD

PLACE OF BIRTH: Jamaica, 9.11.34
MARITAL STATUS: Widow
CHILDREN: Two (Richard, Sarah)
COLLEGE: Bolton Technical College
PROFESSIONAL QUALIFICATIONS: RGN, SCM, QN, NDN, H/V Certs
DIRECTORSHIPS: Cariocca Enterprises PA.CT, Arawak Walton Housing, Womens' Action Forum, General Synod CE Rep.
MEMBERSHIPS: M.M University, University of Manchester Crown Court, Advisory Committee Manchester
HONOURS/AWARDS: BEM, Hon MA, National Anti-Racist Award (1995), JP
HOBBIES AND INTERESTS: Reading, dancing, community activities, travel
PERSONAL PROFILE: Succeeded in nursing career, nurse assistant, director area nursing officer, sat on the Hywtner tribunal; consultant-advisor government MS&H, Task Force 1991-95. Non executive director M/C Health Commission. Assessor M/C County Court. M/C city magistrate. Deputy chair voluntary action initiated enterprise workspace, housing association. Positive Action Training Ethnic Minorities, Womens Action Forum. Agency for Economic Development. Care Group for Elderly. Education review group majoring in public relations role.
NOMINATED BY: Karen Gabay, Manchester Business School

CAPTAIN FIDELIX DATSON MBE (Army Officer)

British Army,

PLACE OF BIRTH: Ghana, 26.2.72
MARITAL STATUS: Single
COLLEGE: Barnet FE College
ACADEMIC QUALIFICATIONS: A-Level, Sports Studies, English
HONOURS/AWARDS: MBE
HOBBIES AND INTERESTS: All sports, reading
PERSONAL PROFILE: From September 1997 to October 1998 was officer commanding the Army's Ethnic Minorities Recruiting Team. Born in Accra - Ghana, moved to England aged three. Lived in North London until joining the Army in October 1991. Attended Sandhurst from May 1992 to April 1993. Promoted to captain in September 1997. Awarded an MBE in the 1998/99 New Year's Honour's List.
NOMINATED BY: W R Harber Lieutenant Colonel, ARMY

MRS KARLE DAVIS (General Secretary)

The Royal College Of Midwives, 15 Mansfield Street, London, W1M 0BE

PLACE OF BIRTH: Jamaica, 10.10.46
MARITAL STATUS: Married
CHILDREN: One (Andre)
ACADEMIC QUALIFICATIONS: BEd Hons, MA
DIRECTORSHIPS: RN, RM, MTD
HOBBIES AND INTERESTS: Cooking, reading, theatre
PERSONAL PROFILE: Trained as midwife at Carshalton having undertaken nurse training at Nottingham. Became midwifery teacher and then director of midwifery education at Guy's St Thomas and Lewisham. Midwifery adviser to SE Thames Regional Health Authority, the deputy general secretary at RCM until 1996. Wife to Victor and mother to Andre.
NOMINATED BY: Malcolm MacMillan RCM

MRS BERRIL FRANCES DAY (Art Director, Afrikart)

c/o Lloyds, TSB, 79 Brompton Road, London, SW3 1DD

PLACE OF BIRTH: London, 21.1.38
MARITAL STATUS: Married
COLLEGE: Rose Bruford College of Speech and Drama
ACADEMIC QUALIFICATIONS: Acting Diploma, Teaching Diploma
MEMBERSHIPS: Equity, Friend of various art galleries and museums
EMAIL: afrikart@bitnternet.com
PERSONAL PROFILE: Entered Rose Bruford College aged 16 and was first Black female student. Acting debut at Royal Court Theatre, 1958. Theatre, film, TV roles followed. Praised by Kenneth Tynan for performance in 'Mr Johnson', Lyric, Hammersmith. Directed by Robert Helpman, Tony Richardson and Tony Garnett. Currently promoting Yoruba wood carvers through Afrikart. The mission of Afrikart is to encourage and promote the wood carvers and their carvings and create a commercial outlet for their sculptures.

MR BRIAN CHRISTOPHER DEANE (Footballer)

Middlesbrough Football Club, Cellnet River Side Stadium, Middlesbrough, TS3 6RS

PLACE OF BIRTH: Leeds, 7.2.68
MARITAL STATUS: Single
ACADEMIC QUALIFICATIONS: 4 O-Levels
PROFESSIONAL QUALIFICATIONS: 3 England Caps (full international level)
PERSONAL PROFILE: Experienced frontman who returned to England after a spell in Portugal with Benfica - joined Boro for £3 Million in October 1997, capped 3 times for England. Previous clubs Doncaster Rovers, Sheffield United and Leeds United.

MR MARCEL DESAILLY (Footballer)

Chelsea Football Club, Stamford Bridge, Fulham Road, London, SW6 1HS

MARITAL STATUS: 7.9.68
CHILDREN: Ghana
PROFESSIONAL QUALIFICATIONS: 49 Caps for France. World Cup Winner, 5 U21 Caps
PERSONAL PROFILE: The World Cup winner. Big, athletic, a whippet of a tackler, a measured passer, a leader. A defender before that with Marseille. "With Chelsea you can see that they win the Cup Winners' Cup and they are growing, and I'm happy to be at the beginning of the growing, and I hope that in a few years we win the Champions' League. For me this is the ambition."

CLLR DORA DIXON-FYLE (Former FE Lecturer)

Local Government Officer,

PLACE OF BIRTH: Sierra Leone, 14.12.59
MARITAL STATUS: Single
COLLEGE: South Bank Polytechnic
MEMBERSHIPS: Elected member of Southwark Council 1998, Vice chair Social Services 1999
HOBBIES AND INTERESTS: Reading, tennis, talking, watching TV soaps
PERSONAL PROFILE: First African born woman member of Southwark Council.

MR MICHAEL DUBERRY (Footballer)

Chelsea Football Club, Stamford Bridge, Fulham Road, London, SW6 1HS

PLACE OF BIRTH: Enfield, 14.10.75
PROFESSIONAL QUALIFICATIONS: 3 England U21 Caps, England U21 Caps 1996/7
HONOURS/AWARDS: Coca-Cola Winners Medal and European Cup Winners Cup Winners Medal 1998
PERSONAL PROFILE: Still only 23, here is a career full of potential which suddenly needs working on. He finished last season with Bell's-palsy, a difficult affliction, half his face frozen stopping him from speaking or smiling . It certainly didn't stop him from celebrating two winners' medals in the year, however, following missing out on the FA Cup win because of the original injury.

MR LYNDON DUNCAN (Footballer)

England Under 16's, Queens Park Rangers FC, Football Association, South Africa Road, Shepherds Bush, London, W1R 7HH

PLACE OF BIRTH: London, 12.1.83
COLLEGE: Hammersmith, West London
ACADEMIC QUALIFICATIONS: GCSE
PERSONAL PROFILE: Born of Rudy and Eouia Duncan, have a sister called Emma. Started playing football at the age of eight, was scouted by QPR at 12. I was one of 16 young footballers selected and given a scholarship by the Football Association. I spent two years at the School of Excellence in Lilleshall.

MR EMMANUEL DUNSEATH (Sub Editor)

New Nation, 1st Floor, 148 Cambridge Heath Road, London, E1 5QJ

PLACE OF BIRTH: Rwanda, 4.5.72
MARITAL STATUS: Married
CHILDREN: One (Malik)
COLLEGE: Goldsmith College
ACADEMIC QUALIFICATIONS: BSc Psychology
HOBBIES AND INTERESTS: Travel, Islam, Pan-Africanism, reading
EMAIL: emg@eeye.demon.co.uk
PERSONAL PROFILE: Having been born and raised in Africa, I have a keen interest in news on the continent and in the long term development of the individual nations and people. I believe we in the diaspora have a key role to play in making the Pan-African ideology a reality, to bring real liberation to all Black people.

SERGEANT GREGORY DUNSON (Aircraft Technician, RAF)

Management Instructor, Royal Air force, 63 Derwent Drive, Priorslee, Shropshire, Telford, TF2 9QR

PLACE OF BIRTH: London, 2.12.63
MARITAL STATUS: Married
ACADEMIC QUALIFICATIONS: 6 O-Levels, 2 CSE at Grade 1
PROFESSIONAL QUALIFICATIONS: C&G Aeronautical Engineering, NVQ 3 Engineering Maintenance
HOBBIES AND INTERESTS: Athletics
PERSONAL PROFILE: Joined RAF in 1981. Selected for RAF athletics team 1982. Have been RAF 400m Hurdling champion since 1983, became an international athlete for GB in 1992 competing against Kenya . Have since represented England up until 1998 and been a military international champion since 1985. At present hold both 110m Hurdling and 400m Hurdling records in RAF.
NOMINATED BY: Sir Richard Johns

MR MICHAEL EBODA (EDITOR)

New Nation, Ethnic Media Group,

PLACE OF BIRTH: London, 18.10.63
MARITAL STATUS: Single
COLLEGE: City of London
ACADEMIC QUALIFICATIONS: MA (Business Law)
PROFESSIONAL QUALIFICATIONS: Post Grad Journalism
HONOURS/AWARDS: EMMA Journalist of the Year Award 1999
HOBBIES AND INTERESTS: Sport, travel
PERSONAL PROFILE: Michael has worked for the Guardian, the Sunday Times, The Observer, Total Sport and Boxing News. He took over editorship of the New Nation in 1997 and two years later has more than doubled it's circulation.

MISS CHRISTIANA EBOHON (FILM-TV DIRECTOR)

London Management Ltd, 2-4 Noel Street, London, W1V 3RB

PLACE OF BIRTH: England, 21.12.66
MARITAL STATUS: Single
COLLEGE: Bournemouth
ACADEMIC QUALIFICATIONS: BA Hons Communication Media Production 2:1
PROFESSIONAL QUALIFICATIONS: Diploma, National Film and TV School (Fiction Director)
MEMBERSHIPS: BECTU
HONOURS/AWARDS: Kodak Award Emerging Filmmaker 1999, The Short List, US 1998, Lloyd's Bank Channel 4 Film Challenge
PERSONAL PROFILE: Once I decided that I wanted to be a director, that was it. Since then, it has been about hard work and determination. I have come further than I dared to hope, but there is still a long way to go until I have achieved my dreams.
NOMINATED BY: Ron Shillingford

MISS HEATHER EMMANUEL (ACTRESS-RIDING INSTRUCTOR)

Examiner & Judge,

PLACE OF BIRTH: Sri Lanka
MARITAL STATUS: Married
CHILDREN: Two (Christopher, Sarah)
COLLEGE: RADA
ACADEMIC QUALIFICATIONS: Fellow Trinity College London (Speech & Drama), GCSE Japanese
PROFESSIONAL QUALIFICATIONS: BHS A1, Examiner & Judge, Judo 1st Dan
HONOURS/AWARDS: Free Training At RADA
HOBBIES AND INTERESTS: Horse-riding, pottery, woodwork, upholstery, cookery, guitar, judo, signing for the deaf

MR BRENDA EMMANUS (TV RADIO PRESENTER)

Showplay Television,

PLACE OF BIRTH: London, 7.6.63
MARITAL STATUS: Single
COLLEGE: University of Westminster
ACADEMIC QUALIFICATIONS: BA Hon Media Studies
DIRECTORSHIPS: Showplay Television
MEMBERSHIPS: Patron: Body and Soul. Member City and Islington Mentor Scheme, 'Innovative Black Women' Arts Group, Centrepoint.
HONOURS/AWARDS: Nominations: Woman of the Year, 1997 and Cosmopolitan magazine's Woman of Achievement Award, Also media awards from the Voice and Candace.
HOBBIES AND INTERESTS: Travel, creative writing, the arts, sport
PERSONAL PROFILE: One of the most versatile faces on British television. Brenda is also an accomplished print journalist who has contributed celebrity profiles as well as travel and fashion features to national newspapers such as The Observer, New Nation and The Voice. TV shows include ' The Clothing Show', 'Holiday', the Channel Four Daily and Black Britain. She is involved in a number of charities and media projects

MR EKOW ESHUN (EDITOR)

COLLEGE: London School of Economics
PERSONAL PROFILE: Previously, he was the assistant editor of The Face. He was appointed editor of Arena magazine at the age of 28, the youngest editor of a men's magazine. Ekow is now a regular on BBC TV 2's Late Review.

MR TUNDE EUBA (ACTOR)

117 Lockwood House, Kennington Park Estate, Kennington, Oval, London, SE11 5TD

PLACE OF BIRTH: Nigeria, 8.7.62
MARITAL STATUS: Married
CHILDREN: Two (Segun, Sayo)
COLLEGE: University of Badan, Nigeria
ACADEMIC QUALIFICATIONS: BA Hons Theatre Arts
MEMBERSHIPS: Nigerian Association of Theatre Arts Practitioner, Equity
HONOURS/AWARDS: HOFA - Hubert Ogunde Foundation Award
HOBBIES AND INTERESTS: Music, books, swimming
PERSONAL PROFILE: Tunde has lived half his life in England where he was raised and half in Nigeria, where he trained. In 1992 he won 'Best Actor Award' for his role in 'Checkmate' a Nigerian soap which also ran on IDTV for two seasons.

BERNARDINE EVARISTO

MEMBERSHIPS: Poetry Society's Poet in Residence
PERSONAL PROFILE: Has emerged as one of Britain's most original and exciting new writers. Her verse novel 'Lara' was selected as a Book of the Year by The Daily Telegraph and New Statesman. She tours worldwide giving readings of her work.

MR OWEN OSWALD EVERSLEY OBE (DIPLOMAT RTD)

PLACE OF BIRTH: Barbados, 29.8.33
MARITAL STATUS: Married
CHILDREN: Four (Owen Jr, Jennifer, Caroline, Ricardo)
COLLEGE: South East London Technical College, Goldsmith College, Economics and British Constitution
PROFESSIONAL QUALIFICATIONS: Qualified Osteopath, Physiotherapist and Chiropodist
HONOURS/AWARDS: OBE in HM New Years Honours List 1990, The Prestigious 'Hansib Communities Award' 1990, Awarded an Honorary Fellowship of the College of Preceptors 1989
HOBBIES AND INTERESTS: Reading, most sports, debates, voluntary work, loves cooking
PERSONAL PROFILE: Served in the Barbados Youth Movement and rose to the rank of Drum Major: Served in Her Majesty's Royal Corps of Signals at Catterick and Colchester. Played in the Barbados Cricket League for Victoria C.C. and Belfield C.C. Also played semi professional cricket in the United Kingdom and club cricket for Catford Wanderers CC. A founder member of the Barbados Overseas Community and Friends Association which was formed in 1966. Served as vice president, acting president and then president for fifteen years before resigning in 1986 due to my appointment as Deputy High Commissioner.

CLLR FOSTON MALACHI FAIRCLOUGH
(ELECTRICAL ENGINEER)

Supervisor,

PLACE OF BIRTH: Jamaica, 14.5.44
MARITAL STATUS: Married
CHILDREN: Three
COLLEGE: Southgate Tec, Tottenham, Willesden
ACADEMIC QUALIFICATIONS: City & Guilds Licentiateship Electrical & Refrigeration
DIRECTORSHIPS: Midfield Theatre
MEMBERSHIPS: Enfield North Labour Party, London Northwest Tribunal
HOBBIES AND INTERESTS: Reading, gardening, music, community involvement
PERSONAL PROFILE: I spent six years as a lay visitor in community activity, an appointment made by the Home Secretary. I have also been made chairman of the lay visitors panel and representative of Enfield on the National Association. I am a school governor, vice chair of Enfield North CLP, and a member of London Northwest Tribunal and a local councillor for Enfield.

> 'Once I decided that I wanted to be a director, that was it. Since then, it has been about hard work and determination'
>
> **CHRISTIANA EBOHON**

MR JOHN FEMI-OLA (BARRISTER-AT-LAW)

Chambers of Desmond Da Silva QC, 2 Paper Buildings, Temple, London, EC4

DATE OF BIRTH: 25.12.58
MARITAL STATUS: Married
CHILDREN: Two (Benedict, Tobias)
COLLEGE: Inn of Courts School of Law
ACADEMIC QUALIFICATIONS: BA Hons Diploma in Law
PROFESSIONAL QUALIFICATIONS: Barrister-at-Law
HOBBIES AND INTERESTS: Music of Fela Kuti, African literature, football
PERSONAL PROFILE: Considered one of the leading junior criminal defence barristers in the country. Appeared over the last fourteen years in major cases touching and concerning human rights in all aspects of common law.

MISS ANNETTE FISHER (ARCHITECT)

Managing Director, Fisher Associates Ltd, Studio 3, 92 Lots Road, Chelsea, London, SW10 0QD

PLACE OF BIRTH: Glasgow
MARITAL STATUS: Divorced
CHILDREN: One (Francetta)
COLLEGE: Strathclyde
ACADEMIC QUALIFICATIONS: BSc B.Arch
PROFESSIONAL QUALIFICATIONS: RIBA MNIA
DIRECTORSHIPS: One
MEMBERSHIPS: City Property Association, Women's Pioneer Housing
HONOURS/AWARDS: 1997 Natwest Award for African Professional of the Year
HOBBIES AND INTERESTS: Music, dance, reading, theatre
PERSONAL PROFILE: An architect in practise for over 17 years, my greatest achievement to date is being elected to the RIBA Council as a national councillor, I am honoured to be the first Black women ever. This recognition is a strong indication that RIBA is ready for change and diversity within its membership.

MR CURTIS FLEMING (FOOTBALLER)

Middlesbrough Football Club, Cellnet Riverside Stadium, Middlesbrough, TS3 6RS

PLACE OF BIRTH: Manchester, 8.10.68
PROFESSIONAL QUALIFICATIONS: Caps for Ireland & 200 League Appearances
PERSONAL PROFILE: Tough-tackling Republic of Ireland full-back who has been capped ten times for his country having previously represented Eire at under 21 and 'B' levels. Fleming made his name with top Irish side St Patrick's, where he played in Europe. The fans' favourite came close to joining Swindon and Oldham but eventually signed for Boro. He has become a regular and recently topped 200 league appearances for Boro.

MR THOMAS ARTHUR BENJAMIN FRANCE MBE (EMPLOYMENT ACCESS WORKER)

Employment Officer, Tech. North Learning Centre, 39 Lovell Park Hill, Leeds, L7 1DF

PLACE OF BIRTH: West Indies, 16.9.35
MARITAL STATUS: Married
CHILDREN: Three (Mahalia Hema, Karuna Devi, Vinod Ebenezer)
COLLEGE: Leeds Polytechnic University
HONOURS/AWARDS: Ambassador for Community. Fellowship for Yorkshire Black Achievers
HOBBIES AND INTERESTS: Arts, making carnival costumes, politics, cricket
PERSONAL PROFILE: I am a very strong, passionate and committed person to my family and also genuinely believe in welfare and progress of the Black race and am fully committed to education, arts, sports, cricket, politics and seeing the welfare of the Black community in Leeds in progress.
NOMINATED BY: Mrs Geraldine Connor

MS JENNY FRANCIS

PERSONAL PROFILE: Jenny Francis' favourite slogan "sit on it and let it move ya" is now familiar to listeners of her R&B programme on Choice 96.9FM. Jenny started her career via pirate radio and joined Choice FM in 1990. In 1991, she was voted Female Radio Presenter of the Year by Black Celebrities Award and in 1998 was nominated for the Best Radio Presenter at the MOBO Awards.

DR NELDA FRATER (PRIVATE GENERAL PRACTITIONER)

121 Harley Street, London, W1N 1DH

PLACE OF BIRTH: Jamaica
MARITAL STATUS: Married
CHILDREN: One
COLLEGE: University of Cambridge, University of Oxford
ACADEMIC QUALIFICATIONS: BA, MA, PhD, BSc, MBBS
MEMBERSHIPS: Fellow of the Royal Society of Medicine, ACMS
HOBBIES AND INTERESTS: Music, art, collecting antiques, travel, decorating, gardening
EMAIL: neldafrater@hotmail.com
PERSONAL PROFILE: After an early career in biochemistry research, I trained as a doctor at Oxford and Cambridge universities. Worked in hospitals and NHS general practice in London 1990-1997. Set up private general practice in 1997. Committee member of the Afro-Caribbean Medical Society.

MR MIKE GAYLE

PERSONAL PROFILE: Previously an Agony Uncle, Mike Gayle is a freelance journalist who has contributed to a variety of magazines including FHM, Sunday Times Style and Cosmopolitan. He is the author of the best selling novel 'My Legendary Girlfriend'.

MS KADIJA GEORGE (WRITER-EDITOR)

Journalist, SAKS Media, 42 Chatsworth Road, Hackney, London, E5 0LI

PLACE OF BIRTH: Single
MARITAL STATUS: London
COLLEGE: Birmingham University
ACADEMIC QUALIFICATIONS: BA General Honours (major-West African studies)
MEMBERSHIPS: George Bell Fellow, The Ananse Society, Womens Writers Network
HONOURS/AWARDS: Candace Woman of the Achievement 1996, Cosmopolitan Woman of Achievement 1994
HOBBIES AND INTERESTS: My lifestyle is my hobby
PERSONAL PROFILE: Writes as Kadija Sesay on literature and women's issues. Editor, co-editor of three anthologies. Burning Words, Flaming Images, six plays by Black and Asian women writers, IC3. Established SAKS publications, publishing anthologies by writers of African descent and SABLE, a literacy journal. Operates the Writers' Hotspot holidays for writers.
NOMINATED BY: Ron Shillingford

MR JOHN GICHIGI (PHOTOGRAPHER)

Allsport (UK) Ltd, Greenlea Park, Prince Georges Road, London, SW19 2JD

PLACE OF BIRTH: Kenya, 24.12.54
MARITAL STATUS: Married
CHILDREN: Three (Philip, Andrew, Chris)
COLLEGE: University of Westminister
ACADEMIC QUALIFICATIONS: 8 O-Levels, 2 A-Levels
PROFESSIONAL QUALIFICATIONS: Photography Diploma
MEMBERSHIPS: Professional Sports Photographers Association
HONOURS/AWARDS: Winner -Sports Council Award 1986, Runner Up European Sports Picture Award and Highly Commended Nikon Award
HOBBIES AND INTERESTS: Photography, judo, music
EMAIL: jgichigi@allsport.co.uk
PERSONAL PROFILE: Born in Kenya moved to England for A-Level's and university, initially followed architecture before qualifying in photography. Joined Allsport in 1979, has covered five Olympics and worked for all major sports names and newspapers. Currently specialises in studio, sports and sponsor photography using all formats. Has won various awards.
NOMINATED BY: Allports

Considered one of the leading junior criminal defence barristers in the country

JOHN FEMI-OLA

MR DEAN GORDON (FOOTBALLER-DEFENDER)

Middlesborough Football Club, Cellnet Riverside Stadium, Middlesbrough, TS3 6RS

PLACE OF BIRTH: Croydon, 10.2.73
PROFESSIONAL QUALIFICATIONS: England Under 21 & 200 Appearances
PERSONAL PROFILE: One of the most exciting and consistent wing-backs around, Gordon played every single league game for Boro during the 1998-99 Premier League campaign. He was a bargain buy in the summer of 1998, costing just £900,000 from Crystal Palace where he had come through the youth ranks and made over 200 appearances. Quick and athletic, he is capable of delivering quality crosses and scoring spectacular goals and is widely tipped to be England international in the near future.

CLLR AUBYN GRAHAM JP
(COMMUNITY DEVELOPMENT WORKER)

Voluntary Action Westminster, "Kismet", The Gardens, East Dulwich, London, SE22 9QQ

PLACE OF BIRTH: Jamaica
MARITAL STATUS: Divorced
CHILDREN: Two (David, Gui)
COLLEGE: Institute of Education
ACADEMIC QUALIFICATIONS: Adult & Continuing Education MA
PROFESSIONAL QUALIFICATIONS: Youth & Community Worker, Further Education Teachers
DIRECTORSHIPS: London Youth Games
MEMBERSHIPS: Caribbean Youth & Community Association, Southwark Black Elderly Group
HONOURS/AWARDS: Certificate of British Human Society
HOBBIES AND INTERESTS: Sports all, arts, going to the theatre
PERSONAL PROFILE: In my profession I have been very successful in the voluntary sector working as youth and community worker in Lewisham, Southwark and Ealing, active in sports such as football and netball. Long standing councillor elected to the London Borough of Southwark in Lynd Hurst Ward 1982-98. Lane Ward 1998-present. Chair of race and equalities committee, chair of grant committee.

DR BERNIE GRANT MP (MEMBER OF PARLIAMENT)

House of Commons,

PLACE OF BIRTH: Georgetown, 17.2.44
MARITAL STATUS: Married
CHILDREN: Three
DIRECTORSHIPS: Race Equality in Europe Trust, International Centre for Performing Arts, Global Trade Centre
MEMBERSHIPS: Commonwealth Club
HOBBIES AND INTERESTS: Cricket
PERSONAL PROFILE: Bernie Grant MP is the member of parliament for Tottenham, London. Elected to parliament in 1987, he is the senior of the first ever Black MP's elected to the British parliament in that year. He represents the Labour Party, and was re-elected for a third term in May 1997 with a hugely increased majority. He has taken a leading role in making contacts with Black politicians throughout the world.

MR ANDY GRAY (FOOTBALLER)

Millwall Football Club, The Den, Zampa Road, London, SE16 3LN

PLACE OF BIRTH: Lambeth, 22.2.64
PROFESSIONAL QUALIFICATIONS: 12 League Appearances & 1 Cap for England
PERSONAL PROFILE: Andy Gray made an immediate impact in January '98 by adding steel and experience to the midfield. He inspired a dramatic victory at York on his debut, and scored a magnificent winner in another fine display at Fulham. A full England international, Gray won his cap against Poland whilst with his first league club, Crystal Palace whom he also played in an FA Cup Final. Subsequently played at the top level with Spurs and Villa before having spells in Spain and Scotland.

> Simeon Grossett, Mr Network has possibly the widest network of ethnic minority business in the UK. He set up the first National Black Business Awards in 1989 at the Bank of England. Held the largest network event in the UK for over 1000 people

JAYE GRIFFITHS (ACTRESS)

Susan Angel Associates,

PERSONAL PROFILE: 'Love in Black and White' is a powerful documentary produced and directed by Maxine Watson and presented by Jaye Griffiths. The fifty minute documentary looks at the story of an inter-racial love marriage as seen through the eyes of the women who have crossed the racial divide. 'Love in Black and White' explores how these intensely private choices become public talking points and how mixed relationships have changed the cultural and racial identity of modern Britain.

MR MATHEW GRIFFITHS

PERSONAL PROFILE: Mathew Griffiths is the News Editor at The Voice newspaper. He has combined his journalism career as a professional rugby player and last year represented England at the Commonwealth Games in Kuala Lumpur in the first ever sevens tournament at the games.

MR COLIN GRIFFITHS-BROWN (ACTOR)

PLACE OF BIRTH: Croydon, 17.8.64
MARITAL STATUS: Married
CHILDREN: One (Thomas)
MEMBERSHIPS: Equity, PRS
HOBBIES AND INTERESTS: Singing, reading, tennis, football, cricket
PERSONAL PROFILE: Colin has spent the last six years working as an actor. Recent productions include 'Smokey Joe's Cafe', 'Carmen Jones' and 'Les Enfant Du Paradis' (RSC). TV credits include 'The Knock' and 'Raw Soup'. He is currently pursuing a recording contract with his cappella band 'The Magnets'. He is also doing an acting degree at Rose Bruford College.

MR SIMEON AUGUSTUS GROSSETT
(DIRECTOR OF DEVELOPMENT)

Britains Ethnic Minority Business Federation,

PLACE OF BIRTH: Jamaica, 7.7.55
MARITAL STATUS: Married
CHILDREN: Four (Daniel, Patrick, Amanda, Rebecca)
COLLEGE: Brunel University
ACADEMIC QUALIFICATIONS: BSc CQSW
PROFESSIONAL QUALIFICATIONS: Diploma Psychotheraphy
DIRECTORSHIPS: IOD EHB
PERSONAL PROFILE: Simeon Grossett, Mr Network has possibly the widest network of ethnic minority business in the UK. He set up the first National Black Business Awards in 1989 at the Bank of England. Held the largest network event in the UK for over 1000 people.

MR WILLIAM A GULAM (TEACHER-LECTURER)

Salford University, Statham Building, Frederick Road Campus, Salford, M6 6PU

MARITAL STATUS: Married
CHILDREN: Two
COLLEGE: Leicester, Manchester Met, Salford
ACADEMIC QUALIFICATIONS: BA, MA, MSc
PROFESSIONAL QUALIFICATIONS: PGCE
DIRECTORSHIPS: PACT
MEMBERSHIPS: Gov. Body; Mauldeth School; Pendleton College
HOBBIES AND INTERESTS: Jazz, cinema, squash
PERSONAL PROFILE: Has spent his working life as an educator and inspector of education. His support for 'Access', founding of the pioneering Black qualified teachers courses. Initiation of a mentoring programme for Black undergraduates have impacted on Black educational opportunities. He has published on education and was a regular Caribbean/Asian educational writer.
NOMINATED BY: Chris Mullard

PROFESSOR STUART HALL

Open University & Goldsmith College, BBC O U Television Centre, Faculty of Social Sciences, Walton Hall, Milton Keynes, MK7

PLACE OF BIRTH: Jamaica, 3.2.32
MARITAL STATUS: Married
CHILDREN: Two (Rebbecca, Jesse)
COLLEGE: Merton College, Oxford
ACADEMIC QUALIFICATIONS: MA D Phil
HONOURS/AWARDS: Hon D Litt
PERSONAL PROFILE: Rhodes and Jamaican Scholarships to Merton College Oxford. Born Kingston, Jamaica. Rhodes and Jamaica Scholarships to Merton College, Oxford. Editor, New Left Review. Research Fellow, then director of the Centre for Cultural Studies, University of Birmingham. Prof of Sociology, The Open University (rtd 1997). Currently Visiting Prof, Open University and Goldsmiths College. Chair Directors of Autograph. 15 Hons - DLitt. Member of the Commission for Multi Ethnic Britain.
NOMINATED BY: Sharon Aitkin

MR LEWIS HAMILTON (British Junior Kart champion)

Lewis Hamilton Motorsport, 4 Woodfield Road, Stevenage, SG1 4BP

PLACE OF BIRTH: Stevenage, 7.1.85
ACADEMIC QUALIFICATIONS: Still at school
HONOURS/AWARDS: British Junior Kart Championship, Northern Ireland Championship, McLaren Mercedes Champions of the future
PERSONAL PROFILE: Started karting at eight, at the age of ten Lewis was the youngest driver ever to win a British Junior Kart Championship. He is the only driver to have held the British Junior Kart Championship, the McLaren Mercedes Champions of the future, The Sky TV Kart Masters and the UK Five Nations, Northern Ireland Championship at the time. Recognised by McLaren and receives their support and sponsorship, hopefully through to Formula 1.
NOMINATED BY: Ron Shillingford

MR ELLERY HANLEY MBE (Head Coach)

The Rugby Football League, Palm Villa, Grove Lane, Headingley, Leeds, LS6 2AP

PLACE OF BIRTH: Leeds, 27.3.61
MARITAL STATUS: Partner
CHILDREN: Two (Amida, Dyma)
ACADEMIC QUALIFICATIONS: Honorable Fellowship from Preston and Leeds University
PROFESSIONAL QUALIFICATIONS: All Coaching Badges Grade 1
HONOURS/AWARDS: Man of Steel Award, Lance Todd Award
HOBBIES AND INTERESTS: Squash, chess, rollerblading, wildlife programmes, computers, tennis, reading
PERSONAL PROFILE: Height 5ft 11' Weight 13 st 12lbs. I trust everybody once - like honesty in people, good manners are paramount as they are free. Education is very important, good health is important too, not to take anything for granted in life and respect everyone, even the ones less fortunate than yourself. Give your very best in all you do.
NOMINATED BY: Neil Tunnicliffe

MR AUDLEY HARRISON (Commonwealth Games Champion)

Advantage International, Glen House, Stag Place, London, SW1E 5AG

PLACE OF BIRTH: London, 26.10.71
MARITAL STATUS: Single
COLLEGE: Brunel University
ACADEMIC QUALIFICATIONS: BSc Hons Sports Studies and Leisure Management
HOBBIES AND INTERESTS: Reading, music, socialising, eating out, networking and helping people understand themselves
EMAIL: in98ahh@hotmail.com
PERSONAL PROFILE: For those who have not seen me perform in the ring will not know that I will become the next thing in heavyweight boxing after I've won the Olympic World Championship. To be successful in your chosen career requires dedication, commitment, risk taking, plenty of confidence. I have been blessed with them all.
NOMINATED BY: Ron Shillingford

> ## 'I opted out of the course to pursue a music career…The rest is history'
>
> **DAVID HINDS**

DR JOHN MENSAH SARBAH HAYFRON-BENJAMIN

PLACE OF BIRTH: Ghana, 12.1.36
MARITAL STATUS: Married
CHILDREN: Two (Terence Robert Mark, John Mensah Sarbar)
COLLEGE: Guys Hospital London University
ACADEMIC QUALIFICATIONS: LRCP, MRCS, MB BS,(Lon), DCH (Eng)
PROFESSIONAL QUALIFICATIONS: LRCP, MRCS, MB BS (Lon), DCH (Eng)
MEMBERSHIPS: Hunterian Society . Founder Member African Caribbean Medical Society. Medical Defence Union.
HONOURS/AWARDS: Confined Scholar Guy's Hospital, London 1957 Commonwealth CSAAP Scholar 1968
HOBBIES AND INTERESTS: Reading, walking, rugby football, athletics
PERSONAL PROFILE: GP, South London 1971-1998, Educated in Ghana. Medical Registrar, University of Ibadan, Nigeria 1965-1967. Medical Registrar Medical School Ghana 1967.

JULIAN HENRIQUES (Writer-Director)

Formation Films, PO Box 3635, London, NW10 5BW

MARITAL STATUS: Married
CHILDREN: Two (Anan, Mala)
HONOURS/AWARDS: Best Documentary at Mondial Film Festival, Best Asian Documentary at Tokyo Film Festival
PERSONAL PROFILE: Feature film as writer/director, 1994-98 'Babymother', Channel Four. Documentaries as producer/director 1993 'Derek Walcott: The Poet of the Island', 1990 'The Green Man' and 1989 'States Of Exile' and 'Dictating Terms'.

MR DAVID HINDS (Musician)

Lead Vocals - Guitar, Steel Pulse, 42 Upper Dean Street, Digbeth, Birmingham, B5 4SG

PLACE OF BIRTH: Birmingham, 15.6.56
MARITAL STATUS: Single/co-habitee
CHILDREN: Four (Jamilah, Baruch, Shakeel, Wsene)
COLLEGE: Bournville School of Arts
ACADEMIC QUALIFICATIONS: 7 CSE's, 5 O-Levels
DIRECTORSHIPS: Pulse Music Ltd
MEMBERSHIPS: PUSH
HONOURS/AWARDS: Naras - Grammy
HOBBIES AND INTERESTS: Word games, films, do-it-yourself, mind games, black history - world history
EMAIL: steelpulse2000@hotmail.com
PERSONAL PROFILE: Attended Handsworth Boys School, went on to Bournville Art College where I completed two years of a BA in Fine Art. I opted out of the course to pursue a music career…The rest is history.

MR DARCUS HOWE

PERSONAL PROFILE: Trinidadian born Darcus Howe has been active in Black politics since the late 1960's. He writes a column for the New Statesman and has also written for The Sunday Times, The Observer and the Evening Standard. He is best known for presenting 'The Devil's Advocate', the Channel 4 programme. Darcus' most recent television appearance was in the programme 'England My England', which he co-produced.

ELLA HUGHES (Development Officer)

African Caribbean Children's Ed Participation Trust, 35 Luxembourg Close, Luton, LU3 3TD

PLACE OF BIRTH: West Indies, 28.5.60
CHILDREN: Four (Meshach, Liana, Julien, Derrique)
COLLEGE: University of Luton
ACADEMIC QUALIFICATIONS: BA Hons
HOBBIES AND INTERESTS: Photography, expanding my mind
PERSONAL PROFILE: I strongly believe in encouraging and motivating individuals to make the most of the talent they were given, talents are not necessarily physical, the mind is our greatest machine for self-development.
NOMINATED BY: Anthea Lee - New Nation

YEMI IPAYE-SOWUNMI (LECTURE IN LAW)

Presenter, Aiye Productions,

PLACE OF BIRTH: London, 22.3.67
MARITAL STATUS: Married
COLLEGE: Reading University, The College of Law, London School of Economics
ACADEMIC QUALIFICATIONS: LL B Hons, Admitted to Law Society as solicitor, LL M (Masters in law)
MEMBERSHIPS: The Law Society
HOBBIES AND INTERESTS: The arts, photography, debates, human rights, travelling, meeting people, jazz, acting, dance
PERSONAL PROFILE: Qualified as a lawyer, Yemi's interests in the media enabled her to gain experience in producing and presenting legal programmes. She recently set up Aiye Productions as an avenue to focus on a wide range of arts/debate projects. She is presently pursuing her TV presenting career, whilst lecturing in law.

MRS JANE ISFORT (RETAILER OF ORGANIC PRODUCTS)

Shop Owner, Aroma Organics Herbs & Spices, 9 Leigham Court Road, Streatham Hill, London, SW16 2ND

PLACE OF BIRTH: London, 12.10.56
MARITAL STATUS: Married
ACADEMIC QUALIFICATIONS: 4 A-Levels, 3 O-Levels, Diploma in Art
PROFESSIONAL QUALIFICATIONS: Fluent in Spanish and German
DIRECTORSHIPS: Anycompany 'Aroma Organic'
MEMBERSHIPS: London Ladies Club, Arts Club,
HOBBIES AND INTERESTS: Art, music, dancing, swimming, reading, antiques
PERSONAL PROFILE: I have always had an interest in organic foods. More people are interested now in what they eat actually. I try to provide a service to the public that encompasses a reactive way of eating and therefore a healthier lifestyle.
NOMINATED BY: Sharon Aitkin

MISS BRENDA JENNINGS (NURSERY-MANAGER)

African Caribbean Day Nursery,

PLACE OF BIRTH: England, 10.7.66
MARITAL STATUS: Single
COLLEGE: Trinidad, Westminster University
ACADEMIC QUALIFICATIONS: Childcare Qualifications. BA Business Studies currently
HOBBIES AND INTERESTS: Travelling, reading, Church and community work
EMAIL: bpjoi@yahoo.com
PERSONAL PROFILE: Brenda has been manager of the African Caribbean Day Nursery for the past six years. She has been involved in promoting early years education for children between six months and three years, primarily for the Black community. She has successfully built up community links and has made an impact in both her work and local Church. She sees herself as a positive role model.

CLLR GERALD JOHNSON

Borough Councillor, Hammersmith and Fulham Council, Hammersmith Town Hall, King Street, London, 9JU

PLACE OF BIRTH: London, 27.7.47
MARITAL STATUS: Single
COLLEGE: Imperial College
ACADEMIC QUALIFICATIONS: Zoology Degree
MEMBERSHIPS: Old Labour Party, Vice chair London Ecology Committee
HOBBIES AND INTERESTS: Theatre, opera, ballet, real ale, books
PERSONAL PROFILE: I still live in the house where I was born, from my living room window I can see the church where my grandparents were married in 1918. My grandfather was a Black African, my grandmother a white English woman. I have been a political and community activist since my student days.

MS JENNIFER JONES

PERSONAL PROFILE: Jennifer Jones is the publisher of Who What When (WWW) Magazine which she started in 1998. Jennifer felt that unsigned Black talent needed to receive more support and promotion in order to achieve their goals of landing a recording/publishing or even a management deal. The magazine also aims to recognise the work of Black music executives and companies within the industry.

DIANE LOUISE JORDAN

Backbone Productions,

PLACE OF BIRTH: London, 27.2.60
MARITAL STATUS: Single
CHILDREN: One
COLLEGE: Rose Bruford College of Speech and Drama
ACADEMIC QUALIFICATIONS: O and A-Levels, BA Hon Theatre Arts
DIRECTORSHIPS: Property and Production Companies
MEMBERSHIPS: The Diana, Princess of Wales, Memorial Committee, BBC's Children in Need, a vice-president NCH Action for Children, a Patron: Oasis Trust; Great Osmond Street Hospital Jeans for Genes Appeal; Anne Frank Trust and Brambles Bereavement Trust.
PERSONAL PROFILE: In 1989 Diane became the first Black presenter of Blue Peter. In 1997 Chancellor Gordon Brown invited Diane to sit on The Diane, Princess of Wales, Memorial Committee. Known for her humanity and integrity, Diane has been described as a 'presenter across boundaries'. She is at her strongest when addressing and interacting with people.

MR ADEBAYO KING (MARKETING-PR CONSULTANT)

Publisher, Newsmakers Publications Ltd, 7 Serbert Road, Forest Gate, London, E7 0NG

PLACE OF BIRTH: Nigeria, 17.7.56
MARITAL STATUS: Married
CHILDREN: Five (Adeolu, Adedapo, Aderopo, Adejumoke, Adenike)
COLLEGE: University of Strathclyde, South Bank University
ACADEMIC QUALIFICATIONS: MBA, P/Dip. (BITS), Diploma in Marketing
PROFESSIONAL QUALIFICATIONS: Diploma, Chartered Inistitute of Marketing
DIRECTORSHIPS: Newsmakers Publication Ltd, Obatala Arts
MEMBERSHIPS: Member Chartered Institute of Marketing
HOBBIES AND INTERESTS: Travelling, reading, football
EMAIL: newsmakers@btinternet.com
PERSONAL PROFILE: I am an honest, hardworking person who believes strongly in Black total liberation and complete independence from all oppression and dominance. I have always pursued this just cause and will continue to do so. I am quite intelligent and versatile. I am an extrovert, into promotions, entertainment and now publications. The sky is the limit.

OONA KING MP (MEMBER OF PARLIAMENT)

House of Commons, Westminster, London, SW1

MARITAL STATUS: Married
COLLEGE: York University
ACADEMIC QUALIFICATIONS: First Class Degree in Politics
MEMBERSHIPS: House of Commons Select Committee on International Development, Founding Chair of the All Party Group on Rwanda & the Prevention of Genocide
HOBBIES AND INTERESTS: Promotion of human rights, and the elimination of poverty, both in Britain and internationally
PERSONAL PROFILE: Oona King was born in 1967 and elected to the British Parliament when she was 29. She is the second Black woman elected to Parliament in Britain, and the only young Black person (under 30 at the election) elected to Parliament in Europe. She worked at the European Parliament in Brussels for five years as a researcher and political assistant before returning to Britain to become a trade union officer representing low-paid manual workers.

She is the second Black woman elected to Parliament in Britain, and the only young Black person (under 30 at the election) elected to Parliament in Europe

OONA KING

MR SAMUEL KING MBE

Chairman, Windrush Foundation,

PLACE OF BIRTH: Jamaica, 20.2.99
MARITAL STATUS: Married
CHILDREN: Three (Daslin, Michael and Althea)
COLLEGE: Goldsmiths, London University
ACADEMIC QUALIFICATIONS: Certificate in Theology
HONOURS/AWARDS: MBE
HOBBIES AND INTERESTS: Cricket, gardening
PERSONAL PROFILE: Active service in RAF Second World War. 22.6.48 arrived on the Windrush. August 1958. I and Claudia Jones with twelve others set up the first Westindian carnival. 1983 The only minority mayor in the UK (Southwark). Chairperson: Windrush Foundation; Equiano Society. Author: 'Climbing up the rough side of the mountain'.

MS BEVERLEY KNIGHT (VOCALIST-SONGWRITER)

HONOURS/AWARDS: 1998 MOBO Awards for Best R&B Act
PERSONAL PROFILE: Beverley Knight has been dubbed 'the Queen of UK R&B' by Blues and Soul magazine.. Beverley won Best R&B Act at the 1998 MOBO Awards. On her new album 'Prodigal Sista' (Parlophone Records), Beverley takes credit for all lyrics, melodies and vocal arrangement and she regards this effort as "the coming of age" of herself as an artist.

MISS YVONNE KUMI (ADVERTISING EXECUTIVE)

Deputy Manager, Ethnic Media Group, 1st Floor, 148 Cambridge Heath Road, London, E1 5QJ

PLACE OF BIRTH: Forest Gate, 11.2.73
MARITAL STATUS: Single
COLLEGE: Greenwich University
ACADEMIC QUALIFICATIONS: BA Hons Business Administration
HOBBIES AND INTERESTS: Socialing, reading, keep fit
PERSONAL PROFILE: I was promoted from marketing to deputy advertising manager over a two year period. Advertising has many pressures, though I enjoy its challenges as I strive to maintain targets and lead a team. I am someone who is friendly, dependable and dedicated, just your regular media babe. The future is never set in stone. All I can do is plan to always be in a position of strength, resilience and inspiration.

MRS DOREEN LAWRENCE

COLLEGE: University of East Anglia, University of London
ACADEMIC QUALIFICATIONS: Fellowship from Goldsmiths College
PROFESSIONAL QUALIFICATIONS: Hon Degree, Currently studying for an MSc in Therapeutic Counselling
HONOURS/AWARDS: 'Woman of the Year' in 1998
PERSONAL PROFILE: Doreen Lawrence was named 'Woman of the Year' in 1998 and she has also received an honorary degree from the University of East Anglia and a Fellowship from Goldsmith's College, University of London. Currently studying for an MSc. in Therapeutic Counselling.

MR NEVILLE LAWRENCE

COLLEGE: The University of East Anglia and University of London
ACADEMIC QUALIFICATIONS: Fellowship from Goldsmith's College
HONOURS/AWARDS: RADAR, Person For The Year
PERSONAL PROFILE: Neville Lawrence has been honoured many times for his campaigns on behalf of his son; being named a RADAR Person For The Year; receiving a honorary degree from The University of East Anglia and a Fellowship from Goldsmith's College, University of London. Neville and David Lawrence have also set up The Stephen Lawrence Trust that offers support to minority students for studies in architecture.

MR ANTHONY JOHN LA MOTHE (HEADTEACHER)

London Borough of Lambeth Stockwell Park School, Clapham Road, London, SW9 0AL

PLACE OF BIRTH: West Indies, 6.5.42
MARITAL STATUS: Married
CHILDREN: Two (Micheal, Richard)
COLLEGE: East Anglia, Sussex
ACADEMIC QUALIFICATIONS: BA European Studies 2:1
PROFESSIONAL QUALIFICATIONS: PGCE MA, Education
HOBBIES AND INTERESTS: Creative writing
PERSONAL PROFILE: Worked in industry, rising to the position of section manager. As a mature student, went to university. Taught for 22 years, the last eight years as a headteacher. Retired early because of ill health. Currently exploring a new career in writing novels, plays, poetry, children's stories and educational essays.

MR BERNARD LAMBOURDE (FOOTBALLER)

Chelsea Football Club, , Stamford Bridge, Fulham Road, London, SW6 1HS

PLACE OF BIRTH: Guadeloupe, 11.5.71
PERSONAL PROFILE: A difficult first season for Bernard started with an injury which ruined pre-season, and saw him establish himself more as a midfielder, rather than a defender, the position for which he was bought. Mobile and fast, now he has had a year of English leagues' pace to learn from. In his last year in France, Bordeaux came fourth and qualified for the UEFA cup.

MATT 'JAM' LAMONT (DJ-PRODUCER)

Tuff Jam, Fifty First Recordings, Alaska Building, 61 Grange Road, London, SE1 3BA

MEMBERSHIPS: Musicians Institute
HONOURS/AWARDS: BPI. Silver discs for Rosie Gaines and Tina Moore to recognise sales of 100,000
PERSONAL PROFILE: Karl Brown part of duo 'Tuff Jam'. A DJ, production duo who have hit the Top 20 with their remixes of Rosie Gaines 'Closer Than Close' and Tina Moore's 'Never Gonna Let You Go'. Travel the world DJing and they own a recording studio.

MR DAOUD ALFAH LAURENCE (COMMUNITY ACTIVIST)

Black Business Association, 5 Blackhorse Lane, Walthamstow, London, E17 6DS

PLACE OF BIRTH: Dominica, 7.5.39
MARITAL STATUS: Married
CHILDREN: Two (Soliman, Muna)
COLLEGE: Liverpool University
ACADEMIC QUALIFICATIONS: Dip RCR
PROFESSIONAL QUALIFICATIONS: Dip BS
DIRECTORSHIPS: BBA
MEMBERSHIPS: BBA, ACC
HONOURS/AWARDS: WF Civic award
HOBBIES AND INTERESTS: Reading, walking
PERSONAL PROFILE: Dedicated activist in the promotion of community race relations. Former lay visitor and race and community relations officer. Founder, Waltham Forest Homeless Youth Hostels; founder, Black Peoples Mental Health Association; founder, African Caribbean Centre; co-founder, Federation of Black Housing Organisations. Currently active in developing partnerships in area of inner city regeneration to promote economic development within the black communities in Waltham Forest and Enfield.

MR BURT LAURENT (PRODUCER)

Artiste Representation, In The House Production Limited, PO Box 1253, Ilford, 1G2 6FX

PLACE OF BIRTH: London, 28.7.67
MARITAL STATUS: Single
CHILDREN: Two (Jarryde, Joshua)
COLLEGE: Westminster University
ACADEMIC QUALIFICATIONS: BA Television, Film Production
PROFESSIONAL QUALIFICATIONS: Institute of Personnel Management
DIRECTORSHIPS: In The House Production Ltd, Black International Comedy Awards Ltd
HOBBIES AND INTERESTS: Comedy, theatre
PERSONAL PROFILE: Promoting and producing stand-up comedy shows since 1989 both mainstream and Black comedy circuit. Productions include first tour of a major US comedian, in John Witherspoon UK tour. Also represented several comedians, the main producer behind the UK wide growth of the Black comedy circuit. Presenting the Black International Comedy Awards at the London Palladium in November 1999.

KELE LE ROC

PERSONAL PROFILE: Kele Le Roc's debut album, 'Everybody's Somebody', was produced by Wild Card, the soul offshoot of Polydor. At 21, Kele travelled to California eager to appreciate developments in music production techniques but also determined that her music would keep its unique British flavour. She has written and recorded songs alongside some of the biggest names in R&B production. Meanwhile, star guests such as Coolio have dropped by to contribute on an album that fulfils a lifelong ambition.

MS ANTHEA AGATHA LEE (JOURNALIST-RADIO REPORTER)

Deputy Entertainments Editor, Ethnic Media Group, 1st Floor, 148 Cambridge Heath Road, London, E1 5QJ

PLACE OF BIRTH: England, 21.7.75
MARITAL STATUS: Single
COLLEGE: Greenwich
ACADEMIC QUALIFICATIONS: BA 2:1 Media and Communication Studies
HOBBIES AND INTERESTS: Photography, cinema, theatre
PERSONAL PROFILE: I currently write for Britain's number one black newspaper in the entertainment section entitled The Pulse. However my creative skills range from picture researching as well as devising feature photographic shoots. I have a monthly radio slot on BBC Radio Leeds called Phenomenon. The show is about the best news, views and reviews on the Black entertainment scene.

MR GEORGE MARTIN (SOFT FURNISHING)

Wilmart Interiors,

PLACE OF BIRTH: Jamaica, 19.12.37
MARITAL STATUS: Married
CHILDREN: Two (William, Winston (Dr))
PROFESSIONAL QUALIFICATIONS: Motor Engineer
HOBBIES AND INTERESTS: Voluntary work in the community
PERSONAL PROFILE: Came to Britain in 1960. Involved WISC, assistant Jamaican REC, HC Education Committee. Invited to Buckingham Palace garden party 1987. Mayor Award 1994. HBC Award 1997. Chair Haringey Education Mediation Forum.

MR MIKEY MASSIVE (JOURNALIST)

Company Director,

PLACE OF BIRTH: London, 29.7.60
MARITAL STATUS: Divorced-Engaged
CHILDREN: Four (Sasha Adassa, Matthew Makonnen, Lanthe-Sade, Arinaat)
COLLEGE: Southbank Polytechnic
ACADEMIC QUALIFICATIONS: Business Studies BA Hons 8 SCE O-Levels, 4 SCE A-Levels
PROFESSIONAL QUALIFICATIONS: NLTJ Certificate in Journalism
DIRECTORSHIPS: Bright Soul Production, Aclalia Promotions
MEMBERSHIPS: National Union of Journalists
HOBBIES AND INTERESTS: Developing a vibrant independent black entertainment infrastructure maintaining a sixpack into my 50's, eating
EMAIL: mardy@BTinternet.com
PERSONAL PROFILE: Massive combines vocations for writing in the fields of social affairs journalism with ongoing chronicles and commentary on the development of Black Britain's generic culture; Massive has contributed to a vast array of periodicals and electronic media projects in Britain, the US and the Caribbean.

'I have a monthly radio slot on BBC Radio Leeds called Phenomenon. The show is about the best news, views and reviews on the Black entertainment scene'

ANTHEA AGATHA LEE

MR JAY MASTIN (COMPUTER ANALYST)

CEO, Hardware Trade & Technology Ltd, Trade House, Unit 11, I.B. Centre, Southway, Wembley, HA9 0HB

PLACE OF BIRTH: London, 12.7.63
MARITAL STATUS: Married
CHILDREN: One (Olivia)
COLLEGE: Willesden Technical
ACADEMIC QUALIFICATIONS: OND, A-Level
PROFESSIONAL QUALIFICATIONS: MCSE, Internet
DIRECTORSHIPS: Hardware Trade Tech Ltd
MEMBERSHIPS: IEEE, FSB, Tech (CEI)
HOBBIES AND INTERESTS: Golf, badminton, squash, computers, travelling
PERSONAL PROFILE: Entrepreneur and community man. Set up computer maintenance company in 1985 selling and support early networks and systems to banks and health authorities. Today, the company remains a small focused PC consultancy providing services to Buckingham Palace, BBC and Houses of Parliament.

MR MICHAEL CHRISTOPHER MAYNARD (WRITER-AUTHOR)

Television Producer,

PLACE OF BIRTH: Birmingham, 12.7.64
MARITAL STATUS: Single
COLLEGE: University of Wolverhampton
PROFESSIONAL QUALIFICATIONS: BA Hons Politics and Economics
DIRECTORSHIPS: X-Press Entertainment Ltd
MEMBERSHIPS: Writers Guild of Great Britain
HOBBIES AND INTERESTS: Travelling, cricket, weight-training
PERSONAL PROFILE: Michael has directed 'African Portraits', a 30 minute documentary in Zimbabwe for the BBC. He travels the world covering sport. As a producer on Channel 4's Transworld sport. His debut novel 'Games men play' was published by the X-Press in 1996 and his first radio drama 'Shades of Black' was broadcast by Radio 4 in 1998. Michael is currently working on a series of film and television drama scripts.
NOMINATED BY: Ron Shillingford

CLLR ANTHONY MCALMONT (CHARTERED ENGINEER)

Borough Councillor, London Borough of Newham, Newham Town Hall, London, E6

PLACE OF BIRTH: Guyana, 4.12.61
MARITAL STATUS: Single
CHILDREN: Two (Kojo, Marcus)
COLLEGE: South Bank University
ACADEMIC QUALIFICATIONS: B/Eng Hons, Final Year of MSc
PROFESSIONAL QUALIFICATIONS: MI Mec HE, MIRTE, MIMI, Certificate Education
HOBBIES AND INTERESTS: Travelling, cooking, theatre
PERSONAL PROFILE: Anthony, is a self assured local councillor and chartered mechanical engineer who came from Guyana 16 years ago. He believes in equality of opportunity and the empowerment of individuals, families and communities. He takes a keen interest in education.

Entrepreneur and community man. Set up computer maintenance company in 1985 selling and support early networks and systems to banks and health authorities.Today, the company remains a small focused PC consultancy providing services to Buckingham Palace, BBC and Houses of Parliament

JAY MASTIN

SIR TREVOR MCDONALD OBE (Presenter)

Anchor, The Evening News, ITN, 200 Grays Inn Road, London, WC1X 8XZ

PLACE OF BIRTH: Trinidad, 16.8.39
MARITAL STATUS: Married
CHILDREN: Three
ACADEMIC QUALIFICATIONS: 1994 Honorary Degree Doctor of Letters from Southbank University, 1995 from Plymouth University, 1996 Honorary Degree of Doctor of Laws from University of the West Indies
PROFESSIONAL QUALIFICATIONS: 1997 Honorary Degree of Doctor of Letters from Southampton Institute, Autumn 1999 will be appointed Chancellor of Southbank University
MEMBERSHIPS: 1995, 1997 Chairman of a steering group set up to encourage the use of better English in schools
HONOURS/AWARDS: OBE, 1999 received the Richard Dimbleby Award for Outstanding Contribution to Television, Named Newscaster of the Year for the third time by the prestigious TRIC. Royal Television Society, Gold Medal 1998
HOBBIES AND INTERESTS: Cricket, tennis, rugby, football, golf
PERSONAL PROFILE: Sir Trevor McDonald OBE began his television career in 1962 in his native Trinidad. He joined ITN as a reporter in 1973. In 1978 he became sports correspondent, reporting on the Soccer World Cup of that year in Argentina. His next role was ITN diplomatic correspondent in 1980. He took the title diplomatic correspondent to Channel 4 News in 1982 becoming diplomatic editor of the programme in 1987. Over the years he has interviewed people such as Saddam Hussain, President Clinton, General Collin Powell, Nelson Mandela and Chief Buthelezi. Sir Trevor has written biographies of Westindian players Viv Richards and Clive Lloyd, as well as his own autobiography 'Fortunate Circumstances'.

MS STEPHANIE MCPHERSON-SULAIMAN (Counsellor)

Genetic Counsellor, Sickle & Thalassaemia Association of Counsellors (STAC), Wandsworth Community Health NHT, Balham Health Centre, 120 Bedford Hill, Balham, London, SW12 9HP

PLACE OF BIRTH: London, 27.10.50
MARITAL STATUS: Married
CHILDREN: One (Ibrahim)
COLLEGE: South Bank University
ACADEMIC QUALIFICATIONS: MSc Health Studies
PROFESSIONAL QUALIFICATIONS: RN, RM, Dip HED, Dip Couns (London), Cert Management
DIRECTORSHIPS: Market 2000
MEMBERSHIPS: RCN, RCM Unison
HOBBIES AND INTERESTS: Theatre, dancing, gardening, reading
PERSONAL PROFILE: I am a wife, a mother and an advocacy worker. I worked for many years in the NHS. I negotiated and was instrumental on setting up the Sickle Cell Anaemia Counselling Information Service in Wandsworth. I am a active member of the REC. Vice-chair for JHLO and a governor for the local primary school.

MISS GLORIA MILLS (Trade Union Officer)

Director of Equal Opportunities, Unison, 20 Grand Depot Road, London, SE18 6SF

PLACE OF BIRTH: Trinidad, 31.1.58
MARITAL STATUS: Single
MEMBERSHIPS: Fellow Royal Society of Arts; TUC General Council; Department of Employment and Education Race Education and Employment Forum
HOBBIES AND INTERESTS: Photography, music, sports, politics
EMAIL: g.mills@unison.co.uk
PERSONAL PROFILE: Gloria Mills created history in 1994 as the first Black woman elected to the British TUC Ruling General Council in it's 130 years history. A formidable campaigner for equality and against racism her pioneering work has changed the agendas, structure and culture of the British trade union movement. She is the only senior Black woman officer in Unison, the largest British Union. She is the only Black woman in the TUC.
NOMINATED BY: Kerrianne Mills

> She is the only senior Black woman officer in Unison, the largest British Union. She is the only Black woman in the TUC

GLORIA MILLS

MR NICHOLAS MONU (Actor)

RSC Lead, Royal Shakespeare Co., 51b Saltown Road, Brixton, London, SW2 1EW

PLACE OF BIRTH: Nigeria, 25.3.65
MARITAL STATUS: Single
CHILDREN: One (Malik)
COLLEGE: American University Washington D.C, Webber Douglas Academy of Dramatic Art
PROFESSIONAL QUALIFICATIONS: BA Dip. Acting
HONOURS/AWARDS: Nominated for Manchester News Awards
HOBBIES AND INTERESTS: Reading, dance, Japanese martial arts
EMAIL: Nick@ogimonu.demon.co.uk
PERSONAL PROFILE: Arrived in England in early 1970's, schooled at Millfield in Somerset. Then university in America. On return to the UK entered Webber Douglas School and trained to be a professional actor. Career stretches over five countries, top theatres in England, Russia, Germany, America and Nigeria and presently playing at the RSC.

MR ERROL MURRAY (Journalist)

Producer, BBC GLR 94.9, 35c Marylebone High Street, London, W1A 4LG

PLACE OF BIRTH: West Bromwich, 23.10.63
MARITAL STATUS: Single
COLLEGE: University of Westminster
ACADEMIC QUALIFICATIONS: Certificate in Radio Journalism
PROFESSIONAL QUALIFICATIONS: BTEC Telecommunications
PERSONAL PROFILE: Radio reporter and producer of BBC GLR 94.9's Black news programme, upfront, broadcast every week night. Former news editor at Choice 96.9 FM and reporter at Capital FM. Has written for the Independent and The Observer and taught media law.
NOMINATED BY: Sharon Aitkin

VALERIE MURRAY (Actress-Writer)

FT Student Law-History, c/o Essanay, 2 Conduit Street, London, W1R 9TG

PLACE OF BIRTH: Jamaica, 5.8.43
MARITAL STATUS: Widow
COLLEGE: University North London
ACADEMIC QUALIFICATIONS: Under Graduate
HOBBIES AND INTERESTS: People, theatre, visual arts
EMAIL: Valvmceyahoo.com
PERSONAL PROFILE: Still on the road travelling, it is the journey, not the arrival that matters.

MR ANDY MYERS (Footballer)

Chelsea Football Club, Stamford Bridge, Fulham Road, London, SW6 1HS

PLACE OF BIRTH: Isleworth, 3.11.73
PROFESSIONAL QUALIFICATIONS: 4 England U21 Caps
HONOURS/AWARDS: Young player of the Year 1991, FA Cup Winner Medalist, European Cup Winners Medalist
PERSONAL PROFILE: A very accomplished Chelsea player, who can either play as wing back or left side of central defence. Chalked up his 100th game for the Blues at the age of 24 last season, his latest position seems to be central defence where his strength, pace and jumping ability have brought out natural defensive qualities despite his lack of height. His appearances coincide with a remarkable number of clean sheets.

MR CHRIS TAYOU LIFANGI NASAH (Chartered Architect)

Director, Knak Design Architects & Development Consultants, Laser House, 132-140 Goswell Road, London, EC1V 7DY

PLACE OF BIRTH: Nigeria, 22.4.64
MARITAL STATUS: Married
CHILDREN: Two
COLLEGE: South Bank University, University College London, Bartlett School of Architecture and Planning, London
ACADEMIC QUALIFICATIONS: BA Hons Arch. 2.1, MSc Arch (Building Design for Developing Countries), Dip Arch
PROFESSIONAL QUALIFICATIONS: RIBA
MEMBERSHIPS: Royal Institute of British Architects Society of Black Architects
HONOURS/AWARDS: Business of the Year 1999-2000
HOBBIES AND INTERESTS: Keeping design diary, music, life
EMAIL: knaknasah@hotmail.com
PERSONAL PROFILE: Chartered architect and educator. Experience working in Europe and Africa. Ground breaking curriculum development work in architectural education at the University of East London. Building links with African schools of architecture and the United Kingdom through jointly delivered programmes. Partner at Knak Design, winner of the first UK Black Links Business of the Year Award.

MR EDWARD (EDDIE) NEWTON (FOOTBALLER)

Chelsea Football Club, Stamford Bridge, Fulham Road, London, SW6 1HS

PLACE OF BIRTH: London, 13.12.71
PROFESSIONAL QUALIFICATIONS: 2 England U21 Caps
HONOURS/AWARDS: European Cup Winners Cup Winners Medal, FA Cup Winners Medal 1997, Coca-Cola Cup Winners Medal
PERSONAL PROFILE: Two-and-a-half years of never being fully fit took its toll on Eddie towards the end of the last campaign. In the end the mobility, pace and sharpness were something he couldn't maintain, and he had to make do with a substitutes bench place in the European Cup Winners' Cup final. But when he came on with ten minutes to go to help shore up midfield, Stuttgart never got a look in.

MR STEPHEN NISBETT (MUSICIAN)

Drummer, Steel Pulse / Pulse Music Ltd, 42 Upper Dean Street, Digbeth, Birmingham, B5 4SG

PLACE OF BIRTH: West Indies, 15.3.48
MARITAL STATUS: Divorced
CHILDREN: Five (Steve Jnr, Claire, Andrew, Lucas, Jamilah)
DIRECTORSHIPS: Pulse Music Ltd
MEMBERSHIPS: PUSH
HONOURS/AWARDS: National Academy of Recording Arts & Science - Grammy
HOBBIES AND INTERESTS: Electronics, films, sports
EMAIL: steelpulse2000@hotmail.com
PERSONAL PROFILE: Schools: St Saviours, Nevis and Birmingham. Slade Road Secondary Boys, Birmingham. Employed at GBC as floor and production manager. Began music career at 19 years of age playing with various funk bands, Benny Black, jazz, reggae with Candy and Bunny McKenzie and Force 8. Next step Steel Pulse, ever since.

MR RAGEH OMAR

PLACE OF BIRTH: Somalia
PERSONAL PROFILE: Rageh Omar was born in Somalia. He joined the BBC in 1992. In 1997 he was appointed correspondent in Amman and was the driving force in reopening the BBC's access to Iraq. Since 1998, Rageh has been the Developing World Correspondent. Currently, he is part of the team covering the Balkan crisis.

MR VICTOR OPEYOKUN (FREELANCE ANIMATOR)

COLLEGE: Humberside University
ACADEMIC QUALIFICATIONS: BA Degree
PERSONAL PROFILE: Victor ia a freelance animator who began making films whilst studying for a BA (Hons) degree at Humberside University in Hull. In 1998, Victor's animated film 'Rooted' was accepted by the British Film Institute (BFI) which distributes films on an international level. 'Rooted' has been shown at various European Animation festivals and is still shown at London venues.

MAAME OSORIWAA OSEI-BONSU (MANAGEMENT CONSULTANT)

PLACE OF BIRTH: Ghana, 19.9.99
MARITAL STATUS: Single
CHILDREN: One
ACADEMIC QUALIFICATIONS: MBA
PROFESSIONAL QUALIFICATIONS: MBA
HONOURS/AWARDS: The Voice Community Awards 1995 (Nominated 1997)
HOBBIES AND INTERESTS: Reading, cooking, arts, theatre, aerobics, charity events
PERSONAL PROFILE: I am a carer for people with HIV/AIDS and cancer. I like helping others whenever possible. I am also a carer for the disabled. I help the homeless and those in need.
NOMINATED BY: Barbara Thompson

MS DONNA PALMER (ACTRESS)

June Epstein Associates, 62 Compayne Gardens, London, E3 3AE

DATE OF BIRTH: 12.8.69
COLLEGE: Middlesex University
ACADEMIC QUALIFICATIONS: BA Hons Performing Arts and Drama
MEMBERSHIPS: Former Member Lilian Baylis Youth Dance Co and Young Writers and Producers Co - The Cockpit
PERSONAL PROFILE: Donna Palmer's theatre performances include; 'King Lear'; 'The Soul Nation'; 'The Hairpiece'; 'What The Butler Saw'. Her skills include devising performance poetry scripts and devising and performing stand-up comedy.

MS ELAINE PARKE

PERSONAL PROFILE: In 1997, Elaine Parke became the first woman to head the news department at Choice FM Radio. Since taking the helm, she has been at the cutting edge of breaking news including coverage of the Stephen Lawrence inquiry and the Brixton bomb blast. She has interviewed, amongst others, Maya Angelou, Rev. Jesse Jackson, director Spike Lee and actor Samuel L Jackson.

MR CLIVE 'JIGS' PATTERSON

PERSONAL PROFILE: Clive 'Jigs' Patterson has been a DJ since the age of 16. At Choice FM he presents the popular weekday lunchtime show. Jigs is also joint head of music at the station. Nominated for the MOBO Awards in 1996 and 1998, Jigs is also the organiser of the Choice FM's Rapalogy, a teen talent competition -his brainchild-that attracted an audience of 2000. .

ROTIMI PEDRO (BARRISTER-COMPANY DIRECTOR)

Managing Director, Optima Sports Management International UK Ltd, 26 King Edwards Road, Hackney, London, E5 7SF

PLACE OF BIRTH: London, 27.4.66
MARITAL STATUS: Single
ACADEMIC QUALIFICATIONS: LLB, BL, MSc
PROFESSIONAL QUALIFICATIONS: Barrister
DIRECTORSHIPS: Optima Sports Ltd, Optima Securities Ltd, Officetron Co. Ltd
MEMBERSHIPS: Chairman, Nigerian Football Supporters Club (UK), Securities Institute of England & Wales
EMAIL: naijaball@aol.com
PERSONAL PROFILE: Hardworking Nigerian lawyer, businessman responsible for taking Nigerians living in the UK to the last World Cup to support the Nigeria's Super Eagles. Positive outlook of life for this rising but certainly high achiever.
NOMINATED BY: Ron Shillingford

MR TREVOR PHILLIPS (BROADCASTER-JOURNALIST)

MD Pepper Productions, 1 Albion Court, Albion Place, London, W6 0QT

PLACE OF BIRTH: London, 31.12.53
MARITAL STATUS: Married
CHILDREN: Two (Sushila, Holly)
COLLEGE: Imperial College London
ACADEMIC QUALIFICATIONS: BSc
PROFESSIONAL QUALIFICATIONS: ARCS
DIRECTORSHIPS: Pepper Productions
MEMBERSHIPS: Groucho Club, RSA
HONOURS/AWARDS: Royal Television Society OBE. Hon MA
HOBBIES AND INTERESTS: Music, reading
NOMINATED BY: The Runnymede Trust

BISHOP WILTON POWELL OBE (Chartered Engineer)

Chairman - Bishop, Nehemiah Housing Association Ltd,

ACADEMIC QUALIFICATIONS: Chartered Engineer
DIRECTORSHIPS: Chairman, Nehemiah Housing and Black Star Housing Associations.
PERSONAL PROFILE: Bishop Wilton Powell, who is chairman of two Birmingham based Black housing associations, Nehemiah and Black Star. was awarded the OBE (1999) for his extensive work with both associations. Fifty year old Bishop Powell has been active in the social housing movement for the past 13 years and he serves as Bishop for The Church of God of Prophecy.

MR MADAN ANDREW EDWARD RAMROOP (Tailor)

Managing Director, Maurice Sedwell, 19 Saville Row, London, W1X 1AE

PLACE OF BIRTH: Trinidad, 10.11.52
MARITAL STATUS: Married
CHILDREN: Two (David, Marsha)
COLLEGE: London College of Fashion
PROFESSIONAL QUALIFICATIONS: First Class Diploma in Clothing Design, Tailoring
DIRECTORSHIPS: Maurice Sedwell Ltd
HOBBIES AND INTERESTS: Cricket, badminton
EMAIL: maurice_sedwell_19savillerow@compuserve.com
PERSONAL PROFILE: First Black tailor on Saville Row. Chairman of Master Craftsman's Association and Retail Export Group. Teacher at London College of Fashion 1976-1988. Owner: Maurice Sedwell Ltd.
NOMINATED BY: Christopher Johnson MBA

MR NICK RAPHAEL (Artist)

Smash Press, 99c Talbot Road, London, W11 2AT

PERSONAL PROFILE: August 1985 the Manasseh Sound System is unveiled, over the next year its founder members Nick Raphael, Billy T and Eddie Maiden play at many of London's burgeoning warehouse parties of the time linking with the to-be-famous Good Times Sound System (Norman Jay) and Femi Williams (Young Disciples).

MR HAMILTON RICARD (Footballer)

Middlesbrough Football Club, Cellnet Riverside Stadium, Middlesbrough, TS3 6RS

PLACE OF BIRTH: Colombia, 12.1.74
PROFESSIONAL QUALIFICATIONS: Caps for Colombia (18), 18 League & Cup Goals
HONOURS/AWARDS: Cellnet Player of the Year & Supporters' Club Player of the Year Award
PERSONAL PROFILE: The big Colombian international has just enjoyed a brilliant season for Boro and bagged 18 League and Cup goals. His performances earned him not only the prestigious Cellnet Player of the Year Award but also a share of the Middlesbrough Official Supporters' Club Player of the Year Award. Ricard was selected for his country's 1998 World Cup squad and has more than 20 International caps. He signed for £2 million from Deportivo Cali in 1998.

> Trevor shot to fame in the advertising world when he and his partner spearheaded the Tango campaign in 1991, while at Howell Henry Chaldecott Lury (HHCL). Trevor set up his own company, Quiet Storm, which was commissioned by HHCL to create the latest Apple Tango Campaign. He is the recipient of more than 40 awards for advertising

TREVOR ROBINSON

DR PIKAY RICHARDSON (Lecturer)

Director, India Unit, Manchester Business School, Booth Street West, Manchester, M15 6PB

PLACE OF BIRTH: Foso
MARITAL STATUS: Married
CHILDREN: Four (Ebo, Akua, Kofi, Kwesi)
COLLEGE: University of Manchester
ACADEMIC QUALIFICATIONS: BSc (Engineering), MSc, PhD (Economics)
PROFESSIONAL QUALIFICATIONS: MIEEE
DIRECTORSHIPS: (Non-Exec) NCHA
MEMBERSHIPS: AUT
HOBBIES AND INTERESTS: Travel, music
PERSONAL PROFILE: Dr Richardson graduated in engineering in 1977 and worked for three years as a broadcast engineer, before taking up a five year contract appointment in Nigeria. In 1985 he joined the University of Manchest where he studied to his PhD in 1988. Since then, he has been a lecturer and director of the India Research Unit of the Manchester Business School.
NOMINATED BY: Karen Gabay, Manchester Business School

MRS JUNE M ROBINSON (Teacher-Painter)

Head of Lower School Eng, The St Thoma The Apostle College, Hollydale Road, Nunhead, London, SE15 2EB

PLACE OF BIRTH: London, 13.8.58
MARITAL STATUS: Married
CHILDREN: Five (Jason, Robert-Andrew, Stephen-Nicholas, Shana, Crystal)
COLLEGE: Greenwich University, The Jamaica School of Art, Knox College
PROFESSIONAL QUALIFICATIONS: Cert. Ed Dip Fine Art
MEMBERSHIPS: Jamaican Alumni Association UK
HOBBIES AND INTERESTS: Reading, travelling, painting, community work, fundraising for Jamaican organisation
PERSONAL PROFILE: Mrs Robinson is a founding member of JAA UK, Knox Past Students Association (Europe), a partner in Skully's Jamaican Foods, and h paintings are included in the collections of the Jamaican High Commissions in London, Belgium and Jamaica. She exhibits every year in the Telegraph Hill Op Studios. She has been a teacher for nearly twenty years.
NOMINATED BY: Edward Flood

MR LIONEL ALEXANDRA ROY ROBINSON (Caterer)

Owner, Skully's Jamaican Foods, 21 Troutbeck Road, New Cross Gate, London, SE 5PN

PLACE OF BIRTH: Kent, 26.1.49
MARITAL STATUS: Married
CHILDREN: Five (Jason, Robert, Shana, Stephen, Crystal)
MEMBERSHIPS: JAA UK, JCOBA UK
HOBBIES AND INTERESTS: Reading, cooking travelling, school governor, fundraising
PERSONAL PROFILE: Born in England and grew up in Jamaica from age one. Educated Jamaica College in Kingston. Has worked in hospitality industry since 1970's including Air Jamaica, Adventure Inn Hotel, Shakeys Pizza Parlours. Partner in Skully's Restaurant. Owner of Natures Bounty Ja. Returned to UK 1990. Curre business Skully's Jamaican Foods - speciality catering company.
NOMINATED BY: Mark Anthony Lobban

MR TREVOR ROBINSON

PERSONAL PROFILE: Trevor shot to fame in t advertising world when he and his partner spearheaded the Tango campaign in 1991, wh at Howell Henry Chaldecott Lury (HHCL). Trevo set up his own company, Quiet Storm, which was commissioned by HHCL to create the late Apple Tango Campaign. He is the recipient of more than 40 awards for advertising from vari ous UK and European bodies.

> During his spell in the army, he served i Malaysia, Hong Kong, Singapore and units in England

MICHAEL SINCLAIR PRESCOD

MRS ELIZABETH ROLLINS (Artist-Sculptor)

Artist in Residence, Newman House, Grey Court School, Ham Street, Richmond, Surrey, TW10 7HN

PLACE OF BIRTH: England, 17.11.62
MARITAL STATUS: Married
COLLEGE: Middlesex University
ACADEMIC QUALIFICATIONS: BA Hons Constructed Textiles, Fine Arts 'Distinction'
HONOURS/AWARDS: Artist in Residence Grey Court School Ham - Artist in Residence Redless Stables Isleworth 1995-98
HOBBIES AND INTERESTS: Latin music, opera, renaisssance art, the occult
PERSONAL PROFILE: I am inspired by myth, magic and legend in my work, and through it, I look to challenge societies perceptions of stereotypes. My work is currently exploring the subject of angels and devils and the relationship to history, spirituality and ancestry.
NOMINATED BY: Ron Shillingford

MR MATTHEW ROSS (Artist Relations Executive)

Sony Music Entertainment,

PERSONAL PROFILE: Started his career at Sony Music as artist relations executive in 1991 and became head of Black music at Columbia Records in 1996. In his present capacity, Matthew proactively implements an ethnic minority internship programme with a view to providing opportunities and support to young members of the community.

MR ALFRED GYASIES SAMPSONS (Architect)

A G Sampson, 9 Evelyn Court, Stourcliffe Street, London, W1H 5AS

PLACE OF BIRTH: Ghana, 25.4.32
MARITAL STATUS: Divorced
CHILDREN: Five
COLLEGE: A A School of Architecture
PROFESSIONAL QUALIFICATIONS: Dip. Arch (Hons), RIBA
MEMBERSHIPS: Royal Institute of British Architects, Architects Registration Board
HOBBIES AND INTERESTS: Photography
EMAIL: agsampson@USA.net
PERSONAL PROFILE: An architect of several years of international experience in architecture and town planning in UK, Denmark, Ghana and Saudi Arabia on large projects in the public sector. Principal of A G Sampson & Partners with offices in London, UK and Accra, Ghana.

BISHOP CLINTON SEALY (Minister)

Trinity Free Church, Askew Road Church, Shepherds Bush, London, W12

PLACE OF BIRTH: Barbados
MARITAL STATUS: Widower
CHILDREN: Six (Melnese, Shirley, Marlene, Barbara, Clinton Junior, Chester)
ACADEMIC QUALIFICATIONS: Teachers Diploma
PROFESSIONAL QUALIFICATIONS: Certificate Theology, Diploma Theology
MEMBERSHIPS: Variety of Voluntary Organisations
HONOURS/AWARDS: Barbados High Commission Independence Award 1996, Voice Community Award 1996
HOBBIES AND INTERESTS: Community development
PERSONAL PROFILE: I am basically a person who practices my Christianity by serving human kind in a variety of ways. My aim has always been to help people to help themselves. My greatest achievement is in the field of education.
NOMINATED BY: Herbert Yearwood, Barbados H C.

> **'I chose general practice as my career after qualifying in medicine, because I am interested in people'**
>
> **JOAN ST JOHN**

MR DONALD SCHLOSS (Chief Executive)

Adult Dyslexic Organisation,

PLACE OF BIRTH: London, 24.5.59
MARITAL STATUS: Single
DIRECTORSHIPS: Trustee eight charities
HONOURS/AWARDS: Lambeth Civic Award for work in the community
EMAIL: dyslexia.hq@dial.pipex.com
PERSONAL PROFILE: Donald is severely dyslexic and he left school with no formal qualifications. He has an affinity with his local community, hence the number of charities of which he is on the board. He is a member of various government committees. His crowning achievement was to start a local charity for adult dyslexics which has grown to national status.

MR RON SHILLINGFORD (Sports Editor)

Journalist, New Nation, 1st Floor, 148 Cambridge Heath Road, London, E1 5QJ

PLACE OF BIRTH: London, 14.2.58
MARITAL STATUS: Married
CHILDREN: One
COLLEGE: Westminster University
ACADEMIC QUALIFICATIONS: Civil Engineering Communications
HOBBIES AND INTERESTS: Boxing, scrabble, comedy
EMAIL: ron@eeye.demon.co.uk
PERSONAL PROFILE: Experienced print and broadcast journalist who has interviewed many of the top sports people of the past two decades, including Muhammed Ali, Sugar Ray Leonard, Frank Bruno, Linford Christie and John Fashanu. Ron's first book 'No Glove No Love' will be published late 1999 - a promising Blockbuster.

MS SHERYL DAWN SIMMS (Broadcaster)

Freelance Journalist,

PLACE OF BIRTH: London
MARITAL STATUS: Single
CHILDREN: One (Bertie Simms Beisiegel)
COLLEGE: University of Essex
ACADEMIC QUALIFICATIONS: Philosophy BA Hons
PROFESSIONAL QUALIFICATIONS: Various BBC Radio Courses
HOBBIES AND INTERESTS: Writing poetry, walking, running, reading, having fun with my partner
PERSONAL PROFILE: As a broadcaster, journalist I have worked for all the terrestrial TV channels as well as for print (Evening Standard, women's and style magazines) and Radio's 1,2 and 3, GLR and BBC World Service. I have presented on the 'BBC Holiday', 'Clothes Show' and 'Rough Guide to Careers' and also worked as a reporter, director and producer.

MS DIONNE ST. HILL

PERSONAL PROFILE: Managing Editor of Pride - the magazine for people of colour. She joined Pride after four years at the Voice Newspaper, as arts and entertainment editor. Best known for her column Dionne's Diary, she now writes regularly for the New Nation and is working on several broadcasting and book projects.

DR JOAN ST JOHN (Doctor)

General Practitioner,

PLACE OF BIRTH: Manchester, 27.11.58
MARITAL STATUS: Married
CHILDREN: Two
COLLEGE: Birmingham University Medical School
ACADEMIC QUALIFICATIONS: 9 O-Level, 3 A-Levels
PROFESSIONAL QUALIFICATIONS: MBChB, DRCOG, MRCGP, DCH
MEMBERSHIPS: BMA, Chair - ACMS (African Caribbean Medical Society)
HOBBIES AND INTERESTS: Music, sport, theatre, cinema, alternative therapies
PERSONAL PROFILE: I chose general practice as my career after qualifying in medicine, because I am interested in people. I have a busy general practice in Harrow. I have two children and I'm married. I am interested in complementary therapies as well as duopathic medicine. It is my professional aim to facilitate people to have good health.

MR GEOFFREY THOMPSON MBE (Social Entrepeneur)

Executive Chair, Youth Charter for Sport Culture & The Arts, Anchorage 2, Anchorage Quays, Salford Quays, Manchester, M5 2YW

PLACE OF BIRTH: Wolverhampton, 3.2.58
MARITAL STATUS: Married
CHILDREN: Three (Jordon, Luke, Francesca)
COLLEGE: University of Life
ACADEMIC QUALIFICATIONS: School of Hard Knocks, Degree in Common Sense
DIRECTORSHIPS: Sports Council Trust Company
MEMBERSHIPS: Sport England
HONOURS/AWARDS: MBE
HOBBIES AND INTERESTS: Sport, reading, music, travel, philosophy, spirituality, practical Christianity
PERSONAL PROFILE: A former five times World Karate Champion, Geoff Thompson's credentials in sport have made him one of the UK's most respected sporting ambassadors. A member of the English Sports Council and part of Manchester's Olympic and Commonwealth Games bid teams, his contribution to sport was recognised by the award of an MBE in 1996.
NOMINATED BY: Wavery Lloyd

MARK WEIR (Martial Arts Trainer-World Champion)

PERSONAL PROFILE: Set up his own martial arts training centre known as The Mark Weir Fighting Range, based in Gloucester. Mark has also created his own unique training programme. Having gained world championship status, he has become a great role model for young people, particularly in his area. One of the few British-Black martial arts champions.
NOMINATED BY: Sunita Ram

MS NICOLA WILLIAMS

PERSONAL PROFILE: Nicola Williams is of Guyanese descent. An experienced criminal law barrister, she has successfully acted in a variety of serious trials before all levels of the judiciary, including Commonwealth death penalty appeals before the Law Lords in The Privy Council. She is a member of Mensa and other community organisations. 'Without Prejudice' is her first novel.

ROY WILLIAMS

COLLEGE: Rose Bruford College
ACADEMIC QUALIFICATIONS: 1st Class BA Hons, Degree in Writing
PERSONAL PROFILE: Worked as an actor before turning to full time writing in 1990. Starstruck is a comedy drama set in 1960's Jamaica. The play has already won the 31st John Whiting Award and the Alfred Fagan Award in 1997.

INSPECTOR PAUL WILSON (Black Police Association)

Chairman, Black Police Association, New Scotland Yard, Broadway, London, SW1P 0BG

PLACE OF BIRTH: Lincolnshire, 25.12.58
MARITAL STATUS: Single
CHILDREN: Two (Shani, Lewis)
HOBBIES AND INTERESTS: A regular columnist for International Police Review magazine, providing analysis and comment on various internet websities
PERSONAL PROFILE: Inspector Paul Wilson of the Metropolitan Police, is chair of the Black Police Association (BPA) an organisation he helped establish in March 1993. Inspector Wilson has gained wide recognition as a commentator on police and Black community issues. His evidence to the Stephen Lawrence inquiry is formally acknowledged within the published report. He designs and maintains the BPA website at http:/www.bpa.cc

THE RT REVD DR WILFRED DENNISTON WOOD (Bishop of Croydon)

in the Diocese of Southwark,

PLACE OF BIRTH: Barbados, 15.6.36
MARITAL STATUS: Married
CHILDREN: Five
COLLEGE: Combermere School, Codrington College
ACADEMIC QUALIFICATIONS: Ordained deacon, St Michael's Cathedral, Barbados 1961. Ordained priest St Pauls Cathedral, London 1962.
PROFESSIONAL QUALIFICATIONS: Curate: S Stephen with St Thomas, Shepherds Bush,196 66. Hon Curate 1966-74, Bishop of London's office in Race Relations 1966-74
DIRECTORSHIPS: Chairman, Institute of Race Relations 1971-74.
MEMBERSHIPS: Founder-member of Shepherds Bush Social and Welfare Association; Shepherds Bush Credit Union; Islington Harambee; Berbice Housin Association Coop; Carib Housing Association; Martin Luther King Memorial Trust; Non-executive Director of Mayday University Hospital Healthcare NHS Trust.
PERSONAL PROFILE: Vicar of St Laurence, Catford 1974-82; Hon Canon, Southwark Cathedral 1977-85; Rural Dean of East Lewisham 1977-85; Archdeacon and Borough Dean of Southwark 1982-85; Consecrated Suffraga Bishop of Croydon in St Pauls Cathedral 1985; Area Bishop of Croydon 1991; Inner London, 1971-85. Member: Royal Commission on Criminal Procedure, 1978-81; World Council of Churches to Combat Racism, 1975-80 (Moderator 1977-80); Archbishop of Canterbury's Commission on Urban Priority Areas, 1983-85; Doctor of Divinity (Hon) General Theological Seminary 1986; Board c Housing Corporation, 1986-95. He is responsible for 102 parishes in the boroughs of Croydon, Bromley, Sutton, Banstead/Reigate and the districts of Tandridge and the Mole valley.

MR IAN WRIGHT (Footballer-TV Host)

TV Chat Show, Jerome Anderson Management Ltd, , 248 Station Road, Edgware, Middlesex, HA8 7AU

PLACE OF BIRTH: London, 3.11.63
MARITAL STATUS: Married
CHILDREN: Five
HONOURS/AWARDS: League Cup 1993 with Arsenal, FA Cup, 1993 & 1998 with Arsenal, Premiership 1998 with Arsenal 27 Caps For Englan Golden Boot 1992, Premiership & FA Cup Winners 1997-98
PERSONAL PROFILE: Former plasterer Ian Wright was destined to wear the red and white of Arsenal. The club purchased Wright, the biggest bullet of all from Crystal Palace for £2.5m in 1991. Since then h has become record goal-scorer. On the 13 September 1997 when Arsenal bea Bolton Wanderers 4-1, Wright scored a hat-trick and claimed the 50 year reco once held by Cliff Basten of 178 league goals. When it comes to goal-scoring he is up there with the very best of them. Wright made a surprising transfer to West Ham in July 1998. Now TV host and presenter extraordinaire.

NOMINATED BY: Gordon Taylor - PFA

MS OLA WRIGHT

PERSONAL PROFILE: A freelance PR consultant, Ola Wright was responsible for the event management at the launch of Bluewater, Europe's largest and most innovative retail and leisure destination. Based in Kent, Bluewater, with over 320 stores in three malls, will offer a variety of shopping and dining that will be un valled outside Central London.

> He is responsible for 102 parishes in the boroughs of Croydon, Bromley, Sutton, Banstead/Reigate and the districts of Tandridge and the Mole valley

THE RT REVD DR WILFRED DENNISTON WOOD

MR PATRICK YOUNGE (EXECUTIVE PRODUCER BBC)

PERSONAL PROFILE: Patrick was recently appointed Deputy Commissioning Editor for Multicultural programmes at Channel 4 from BBC, where he was series producer of the BBC 1 prime time current affairs programme, 'Here and Now'. His most recent credits include Charles Wheeler's special report 'Why Stephen'.
NOMINATED BY: Maxine Watson

DR ALFRED ZACK-WILLIAMS (UNIVERSITY LECTURER)

Reader in Sociology, University of Central Lancashire, 27 Greenhill Road, Mossley Hill, Liverpool, L18 6JJ

PLACE OF BIRTH: Sierra Leone, 5.9.45
MARITAL STATUS: Married
CHILDREN: Two (Semra, Shomari)
COLLEGE: Liverpool University, Salford University, Sheffield University
ACADEMIC QUALIFICATIONS: BA Hons, MSc, PhD
DIRECTORSHIPS: ROAPE Publications
MEMBERSHIPS: Council of African Studies Association of UK
HOBBIES AND INTERESTS: Reading, thinking Africa, gardening
EMAIL: abzw@cableinet.co.uk
PERSONAL PROFILE: Teaches and has conducted research on the political economy of underdevelopment in Africa and the African Diaspora. He is the author of books and scores of articles on these themes. He has researched and taught in Salford University, Sheffield University, Baycro University of JOS. He is an active volunteer in the Black community in Liverpool.

MRS DOROTHY ZACK-WILLIAMS (HEALTH VISITOR)

Specialist Health Visitor, Centre for Inherited Blood Disorders, , Abercromby Health Centre, Grove Street, Liverpool, L18 7HG

PLACE OF BIRTH: New York, 21.9.49
MARITAL STATUS: Married
CHILDREN: Two (Semra, Shomari)
COLLEGE: University of Lancaster
ACADEMIC QUALIFICATIONS: BSc Hon Psychology
PROFESSIONAL QUALIFICATIONS: Registered Nurse, Midwife, Health Visitor, Community Practice Teacher
DIRECTORSHIPS: Director of Toxteth Community Health Forum
MEMBERSHIPS: Mary Seacole House, Multi-cultural Womens Group Black Health Network
HOBBIES AND INTERESTS: Networking with other agencies, keep fit, cycling
PERSONAL PROFILE: I have always been interested in supporting and promoting leadership in progress and personal developments in the areas of ethnic related health issues. Networking and dialogue have given me the opportunity to apply and further develop my skills to individuals on a programmable and non-programmable manner. A new database has now been devised to assist me with my on going research on inherited blood disorders.

> I have always been interested in supporting and promoting leadership in progress and personal developments in the areas of ethnic related health issues
>
> **DOROTHY ZACK-WILLIAMS**

Entrants in the Black Who's Who 1999 have been nominated for their achievements and contributions. You can nominate someone who deserves to be in the Black Who's Who 2000, nominate them today.

Entries are free

Send in your nominations, including name, contact address and telephone number to:

Books Division, Ethnic Media Group, 148 Cambridge Heath Road, London E1 5QJ

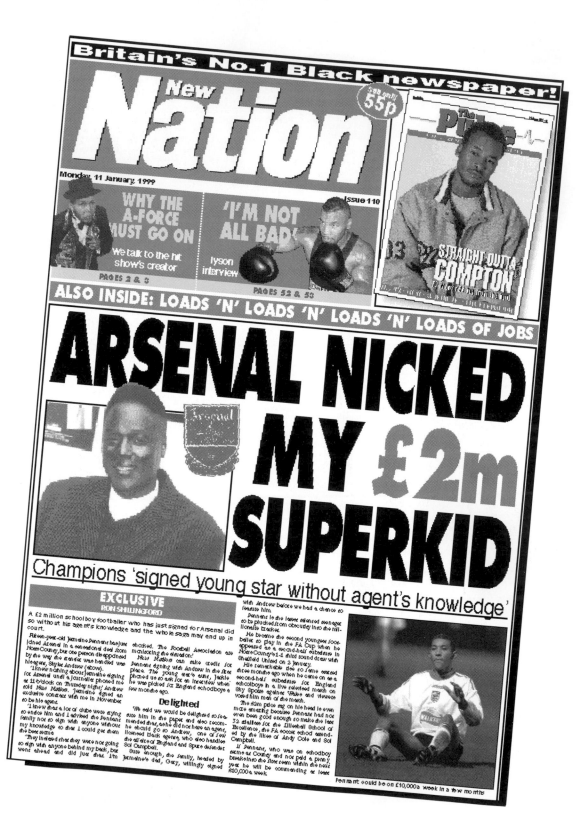

11 January 1999

18 January 1999

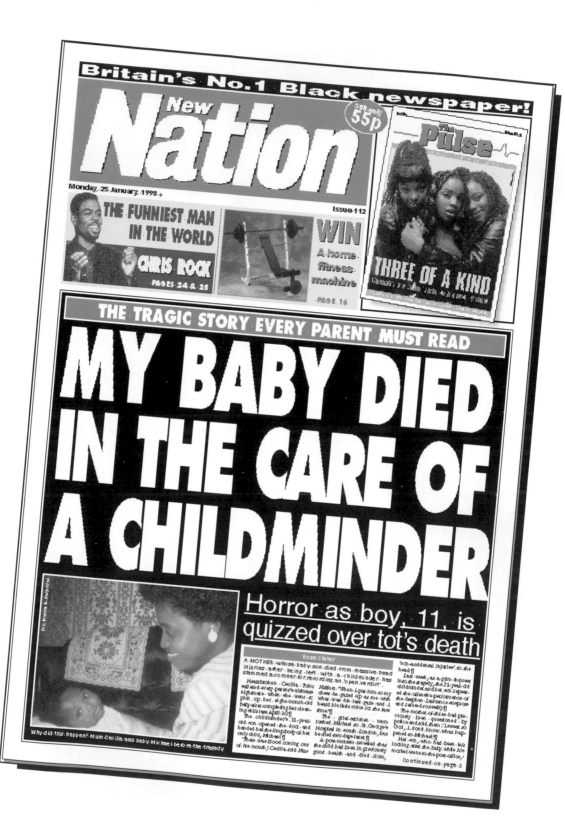

Britain's No.1 Black newspaper!

New Nation

Monday, 25 January 1998

Issue 112

55p

THE FUNNIEST MAN IN THE WORLD CHRIS ROCK — PAGES 24 & 25

WIN A home fitness machine — PAGE 16

The Pulse — **THREE OF A KIND**

THE TRAGIC STORY EVERY PARENT MUST READ

MY BABY DIED IN THE CARE OF A CHILDMINDER

Horror as boy, 11, is quizzed over tot's death

By Ross Slater

A MOTHER whose baby son died from massive head injuries after being left with a childminder has slammed a coroner for recording an 'open verdict'.

Heartbroken Cecilia Toku suffered every parent's ultimate nightmare when she went to pick up her eight-month-old baby after completing her cleaning shift last April.

Her childminder's 11-year-old son opened the door and handed her the limp body of her only child, Michael.

"There was blood coming out of his mouth," Cecilia said. Miss Nation. "When I put him on my chest he gazed up at me with what was his last gaze and I heard his little voice for the last time."

The grief-stricken mum rushed Michael to St George's Hospital in south London, but he died two days later.

A post-mortem revealed that the child had been in previously good health and died from 'non-accidental injuries' to the head.

Last week, at a grim inquest into the tragedy, the 31-year-old childminder and her son repeated the offensive performance of the Stephen Lawrence suspects and refused to testify.

The mother-of-three had previously been questioned by police and told them: "I swear to God, I don't know what happened to Michael."

Her son, who had been left looking after the baby while his mother went to the post office, Continued on page 2

Why did this happen? Mum Cecilia and baby Michael before the tragedy

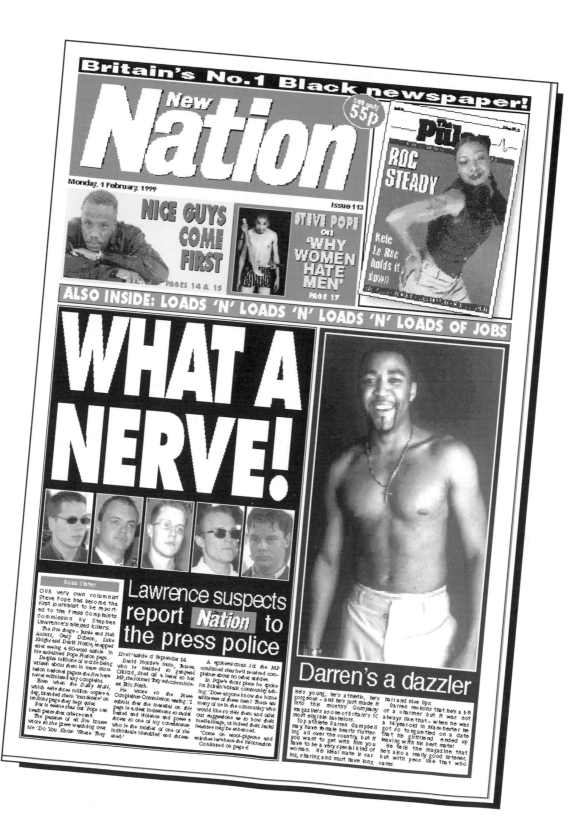

Britain's No.1 Black newspaper!

New Nation

55p

Monday, 1 February, 1999

Issue 113

NICE GUYS COME FIRST
PAGES 14 & 15

STEVE POPE on 'WHY WOMEN HATE MEN'
PAGE 17

ROC STEADY
Kele Le Roc holds it down

ALSO INSIDE: LOADS 'N' LOADS 'N' LOADS 'N' LOADS OF JOBS

WHAT A NERVE!

Ross Slater

OUR very own columnist Steve Pope has become the first journalist to be reported to the Press Complaints Commission by Stephen Lawrence's alleged killers.

The five thugs – Jamie and Neil Acourt, Gary Dobson, Luke Knight and David Norris, snapped after seeing a 60-word article in his acclaimed Pope Nation page.

Despite millions of words being written about them in mass circulation national papers the five have never submitted any complaint.

Even when the Daily Mail, which sells three million copies a day, branded them 'murderers' on its front page they kept quiet.

But it seems that our Pope can reach parts that others can't.

The parents of all five thugs wrote to the press watchdog over his 'Do You Know Where They

lived' article of September 14.

David Norris's mum, Theresa, who is married to gangster Clifford, fired off a letter to her MP, the former Tory schoolteacher Eric Forth.

He wrote to the Press Complaints Commission saying: 'I submit that the material on this page is a clear incitement to racial hatred and violence and poses a threat to one of my constituents who is the mother of one of the individuals identified and threat-

ened.'

A spokeswoman for the MP confirmed that he'd received complaints about no other matter.

In Pope's short piece he spoke for Britain's black community asking: 'Does anyone know the home addresses of these men? There are many of us in the community who would like to visit them and offer our suggestions as to how their medal tinge, or indeed their social functions may be enhanced.

'Come on social-pigeons and enriches let's have the information
Continued on page 6

Lawrence suspects report Nation to the press police

Darren's a dazzler

He's young, he's athletic, he's gorgeous – and he's just made it into this month's Company magazine's as one of Britain's 50 most eligible bachelors.

Top athlete Darren Campbell may have female hearts fluttering all over the country but if you want to get with him you have to be a very special kind of woman. His ideal mate is caring, sharing and must have long

hair and nice lips.

Darren reckons that he's a bit of a charmer but it was not always like that. when he was a 14-year-old in Manchester he got so tongue-tied on a date that his girlfriend ended up leaving with his best mate!

He tells the magazine that he's also a really good listener, but with pecs like that who cares.

Continued on page 6

1 February 1999

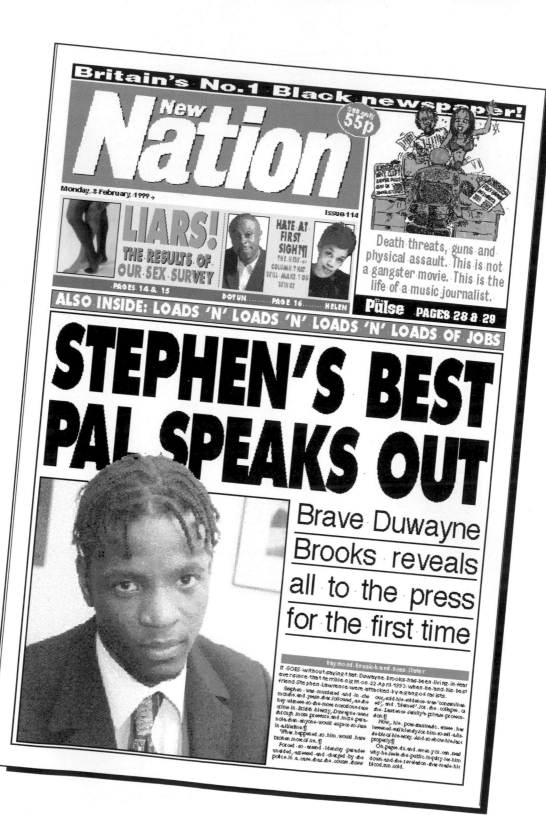

8 February 1999

Britain's No.1 Black newspaper!

New Nation

Monday, 15 February, 1999

Issue 115

Do celebs make good chat show hosts?

PAGES 14 & 15

TYSON: Chump or champ? We decide

PAGES 52 & 53

Sale only 55p

3-PAGE SPECIAL FEATURE

An A to Z of Black comedy in Hollywood in Pulse p.28-36

ALSO INSIDE: LOADS 'N' LOADS 'N' LOADS 'N' LOADS OF JOBS

Trevor P: Back me for Mayor

TV FAVOURITE Trevor Phillips has let it slip that he's serious about being the first-ever Mayor of London.

After months of speculation, the 41-year-old presenter was recently confronted by a supporter who told him he wanted to place a £1,000 bet on him becoming the capital's top politician.

He replied: 'My advice would be to put on £500 because the bet I may need isn't my campaign fund!'

In recent weeks Phillips has held 'sounding out' meetings with leading black figures such as Sir Herman Ouseley of the Commission for Racial Equality and Lee Jasper of Operation Black Vote.

He told them there was impressive for at least half-a-dozen credible black candidates to stand in the Greater London Assembly election, scheduled for May 2000.

Phillips also hopes to secure support from the black churches and trade unionism.

But sceptics fear that he does not have a big enough base of support among traditional Labour Party activists, who oppose him sending his children to private school. An apparent revelation came to light when he came under fire last week when left-wing MP Ken Livingstone went public with his campaign to stop the Labour leadership stopping him from standing.

'COCONUT' JIBES MADE ME SO SAD!

EXCLUSIVE
Delia Dolor

TALK show queen Trisha Goddard has revealed her sadness at never dating a black man.

The successful mixed-race star has criss-crossed the globe as an airline hostess, a journalist and presenter but says that because she has never dated a black man, black people have labelled her a 'coconut'.

Speaking exclusively to New Nation about her sector comment, Trisha, 40, explained: 'I never met any black guys as a girl. The only black guy that I could have dated, fancied etc... was on a holiday and even then, and I'm being honest, there was a bit of to and fro-ed. It's only have in life I've thought, "why didn't I date any black guys?"'

The reverse lies in her formative years with her Dominican mother and English father, who were both psychiatric nurses.

They moved frequently after Trisha's birth in Hackney, near London and apart from living in Tanzania between the ages of five and

Continued on Page 5

---

15 February 1999

22 February 1999

Britain's No.1 Black newspaper!

New Nation

55p

Monday, 1 March, 1999

Issue 117

Lawrence from a black perspective

PAGES 1,2,3,4,5,6&7

The Pulse

BACK TO BASICS

STEPHEN LAWRENCE SPECIAL ••• STEPHEN LAWRENCE SPECIAL ••• STEPHEN LAWRENCE SPECIAL

THE ULTIMATE INSULT

Racist hooligans, blundering cops, and a lame Inquiry Report

1 March 1999

New Nation — BRITAIN'S BEST BLACK NEWSPAPER

Britain's No.1 Black newspaper!

New Nation

Just only 55p

Monday, 8 March, 1999

Issue 118

TREVOR MAC DONALD Writes about his new challenge
PAGES 14 & 15

LENNOX: 'My dream woman'
PAGES 52 & 53

STILL A BACHELOR? Ginuwine reveals what's so different

NEED A FRESH START? JOBS DIRECT, PAGES 37-48

Pulse FREE INSIDE

£1,000 for best West Indian chef in Britain

WINNING FORMULA

Nigerian pays £77m for motor racing team

Ross Slater

AS THE Grand Prix season roared off last weekend, there was a new face strolling around the pit lanes — Malik Ado Ibrahim's.

The Nigerian businessman recently became the majority shareholder of the Arrows team after a £77 million buy out.

And now he is working to do a Tiger Woods and open doors for other black people in a previously white-dominated sport.

He said: "I dont want to paint myself into a corner over the colour issue but I can't deny that being black and being here is going to break the mould.

"I hope my role will act as a stepping stone for other minorities. They don't have to be a team owner or driver, because they could even be a mechanic."

But there are many lapse to go before Prince Ibrahim's dream becomes a reality.

All aspects of motor sport from the Go-Karting circuits to the Formula One track are bereft of black talent and that

Continued on page 2

8 March 1999

COUNTDOWN TO THE MILLENNIUM

Britain's No.1 Black newspaper!

New **Nation**

Just only 55p

Monday, 29 March, 1999

ISSUE 121

SOUL II SOUL Special

10 YEARS ON - WHY CARON WHEELER DOESN'T WANT TO WORK WITH JAZZIE B AGAIN

Pulse

WHO MADE EUBANK WEAR A DRESS?

Find out Pages 14-15

NEED A FRESH START? JOBS DIRECT, PAGES 37-48

Straw's plan for Lawrence Report

JACK STRAW pledged last week that all 70 recommendations done from the Lawrence Inquiry Report would be acted on... but some more quickly than others.

The Home Secretary, who is known to be unhappy with a handful of the proposals in Sir William Macpherson's controversial report, announced that he would chair a steering group to oversee implementation.

It will include representatives from the Commission for Racial Equality and the Black Police Association.

The Government's Action Plan unveiled last week pledged:

★ The police would be covered by freedom of information legislation, but investigation details and the use of informers would be exempt.

★ Documents will be disclosed to victims' representatives before inquests but legal aid will only be available in exceptional cases.

★ All police officers will be trained in race awareness and cultural diversity.

★ To undertake a feasibility study into whether an independent police complaints system can be afforded.

★ To consider giving a written reason to all those stopped and searched.

★ Tough new disciplinary measures to remove racist cops and a review of whether they should be liable for discipline up to five years after leaving the service.

The controversial proposal to allow a suspect to be tried twice for the same offence will be considered by the Law Commission and the Government said it had, 'serious reservations' about making racist language in private a criminal offence.

On education, the Plan promises to record all racist incidents in school under the new definition but says anti-racist education will be covered by new classes in citizenship.

You thought the first one was bad... now New Nation presents:

PATTI: THE SEQUEL

Tory candidate makes amazing new claims

Ross Slater and Janise Elie

POTTY Patti Boulaye relaunched her political career last week with even more crazy claims that are sure to enrage black people.

The showbiz star aimed social comments at the record straight after making one of the most extravagant of political debuts earlier this month.

But, amazingly, as an Invesdan-only meeting of key members of the black group, she managed to trump all that had gone before with a claim that Margaret Thatcher, one of the staunchest allies of South Africa's apartheid regime, had freed Nelson Mandela and brought down the racist system.

The unbelievable outburst comes after her first interview two weeks ago when she announced her candidature as a Conservative for the forthcoming Greater London Assembly elections and stunned the political world by claiming that '90 per cent of Labour people have been prejudiced' as opposed to 20 per cent of Conservatives' adding her assurance that the killers of Stephen Lawrence were, 'either Radical Front or Labour voters.

Full story page 5

29 March 1999

5 April 1999

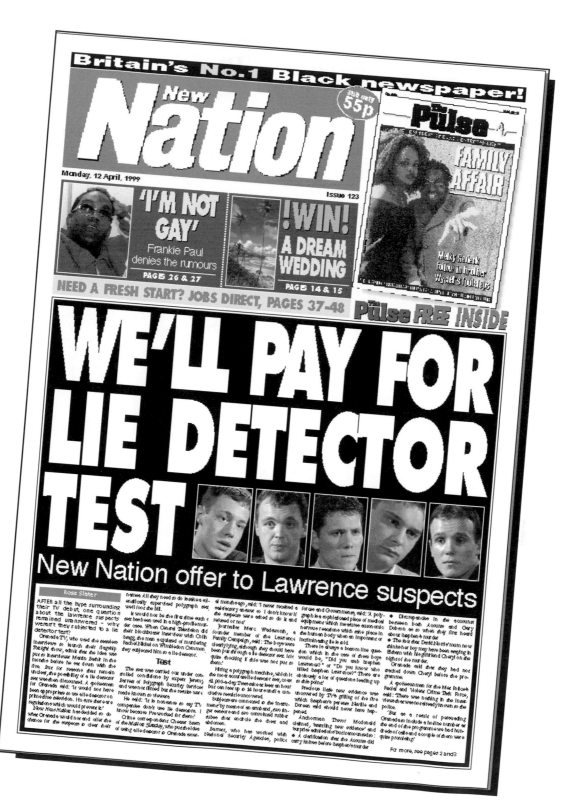

12 April 1999

New Nation
BRITAIN'S BEST BLACK NEWSPAPER

19 April 1999

COUNTDOWN TO THE MILLENNIUM

3 May 1999

Britain's No.1 Black newspaper!

New Nation

Still only **55p**

Monday, 17 May 1999

Issue 128

INSIDE:
BRITAIN'S TOP COLUMNISTS

"Parents must whip their kids mercilessly if they want them to behave properly"

"My opposition to beating children stems from horror stories of evil left unchecked"

HE SAY, SHE SAY PAGE 17

CALLING THE SHOTS

The Pulse FREE INSIDE

FOX OFF!
Black-led hunt faces racial abuse probe

A MIXED RACE worker's valiant efforts to curb fox-hunting cruelty were thwarted when a member of the blood-thirsty New Forest Foxhounds Hunt punched him in the face and called him 'a black bastard'.

Emile French, a 30-year-old Rozhune monitor from Hampshire, was peacefully observing the actions of the Hunt members as they commanded their horses to tear apart a certified fox, when Keith Colbert, a white member of the pack, attacked him.

'I was certified,' said French, who regularly reports on his findings to the Rozvery Commission that governs the pleasuresque forest.

'I feared for my life when he came at me. He kept yelling over and over again, "go back to your own country you black bastard".

'Colbert was literally snatching at me and repeatedly asking me what right I thought I had to be anywhere

Precious Williams

near his hunt. Before I had a chance to move away from him he had lashed out at me.

'It makes me feel even more let down that Derek Laud, a black man, is now the Master of that hunt. It's kind of ironic isn't it.'

Hunted

Now the hunter has become the hunted – as New Forest police confirmed an Colbert about his racist assault on French in November last year. They confirmed to New Nation that charges have been brought against him, and that the case has been brought to the attention of the CPS but Colbert had disappeared.

'He's gone to ground,' said a police spokesperson, without a hint of irony in his voice.

When Laud, the first black man ever to lead a hunt, was made Master of the New Forest Foxhounds earlier this month, he enthused: 'It

French: assault claim

is the most important job that I shall ever do in my life. I am, as master of foxhounds, somebody to whom others will look to for leadership and support.'

Members of the New Forest Foxhounds are eager to promote themselves as non-racists and boasted to New Nation that they are 'oblivious' to Laud's skin colour. But then, if Laud's track record is anything to go by, so is he.

● Laud and Master, see pages 6 & 7

Laud and Master: the controversial Derek Laud is now the leader of the New Forest Foxhounds Hunt

Pic Trevor Mandel

NEED A FRESH START? JOBS DIRECT, PAGES 37-48

17 May 1999

New Nation BRITAIN'S BEST BLACK NEWSPAPER

24 May 1999

COUNTDOWN TO THE MILLENNIUM

7 June 1999

Britain's No.1 Black newspaper!

New Nation

Monday, 14 June, 1999   ISSUE 132

Sell only 55p

WIN!
Two Rolexes still up for grabs
Page 8

WAYNE'S WORLD
FIRST SOLO INTERVIEW: PAGES 28 to 30

Windies Test star 'shot a policeman'

Chanderpaul had gunlicence

BABY-FACED batsman Shivnarine Chanderpaul has been arrested after shooting a cop in Guyana.

The Test star was canoodling with his 16-year-old girlfriend at the Georgetown sea-front just before the incident last Tuesday night.

It is believed that Chanderpaul, 20, thought he was being watched by thieves when the policeman shone a torch in his direction.

Local sea-front is the islands as well as a favourite haunt for young lovers.

Police Commissioner Laurie Lewis confirmed that the young West Indies favourite had been arrested after firing at one of his officers, but was released on police bail after questioning.

He said: 'The officer concerned was not seriously hurt - just minor injuries to his wrist. It seems that he was scared by the officer and believed he was being watched.'

He confirmed that Chanderpaul was a licensed firearm-holder. The scandal is just the latest disaster for West Indies cricket. Indeed, had the side not been eliminated at the group stage of the World Cup, Chanderpaul would have been batting in England rather than cuddling up in Georgetown.

MIRACLE!
Girl, 11, lives after she is shot at point blank range, but parents are killed in bed next to her

Ross Slater

BRAVE little Laura Fisne should be dead. The pretty 11-year-old was sleeping between her mum and dad when a maniac gunman burst into the bedroom and let fire with a high-powered shotgun.

Tragically, both her mum Joy and dad Robert were killed but miraculously Laura cheated death by burying herself in the duvet.

The bullet intended to end her life went through her now coming out the other side.

Last week the plucky youngster came out of hospital, where she had been given plastic surgery, to lead mourners at her mum's funeral in Manchester.

Her gran, Ludie Bogle, who was so upset to attend her own daughter's funeral, said: 'I have never seen any child in all my life so strong as she. She was my strength that day.

'She cried her eyes out at the funeral then came home and gave me a big hug.'

The awful slaughter took place in the German town of Dillingen where Manchester-born Joy, 41, lived with her French husband Robert, 37, and Laura.

Fire

Crazed Gunar Hermann Buene recently released from a rape sentence in prison, began his murder spree by gunning down more than 20 people in the local disco - swodled.

He then broke into the Fisne's flat where he opened fire on Joy, Robert and little Laura as they slept.

From there, Buene shot dead another man who refused to give him his car before fleeing across the border into France then Luxembourg where he ended his own life with a bullet to the head.

Rumours abound that Buene became obsessed with former model Joy after meeting her in a club where she worked as a waitress.

He also bore a grudge against Robert who gave evidence against him in a court case.

Joy's mum, Ludie, said: 'To be killed on the street is one thing but to do it in your own home, in your own bed is something else.

'My daughter was a brilliant girl. Everyone loved her for her sense of humour and caring nature.'

Ludie and husband Clifford first heard about the murders when they were watching the TV news but were

Continued on page 5

HEED A FRESH START? JOBS DIRECT, PAGES 37-48

14 June 1999

21 June 1999

New Nation

BRITAIN'S BEST BLACK NEWSPAPER

Britain's No.1 Black newspaper!

New Nation

Monday 28 June 1999 ISSUE 134

SELL ONLY 55p

IS STAR WARS RACIST?
Pages 26 & 27

K-CI & JOJO
Have they left Jodeci?
Pages 28 & 29

Phillips to pay bail for M25 'killer'

Phillips on the case

SPOULDBB London Mayor Trevor Phillips has agreed to pay part of the bail for a man wrongly convicted of murder.

'SHE DRIVES ME CRAZY!'

Joel stops his bus to propose to his sweetheart

Tessa Joseph

BESOTTED bus driver Joel Burke stunned his passengers when he suddenly did an emergency stop and popped the question to his girlfriend.

True romance: Joel Burke will soon marry Walker down the aisle

NEED A FRESH START? JOBS DIRECT, PAGES 37-48

Special

Continued on page 7

---

28 June 1999

COUNTDOWN TO THE MILLENNIUM

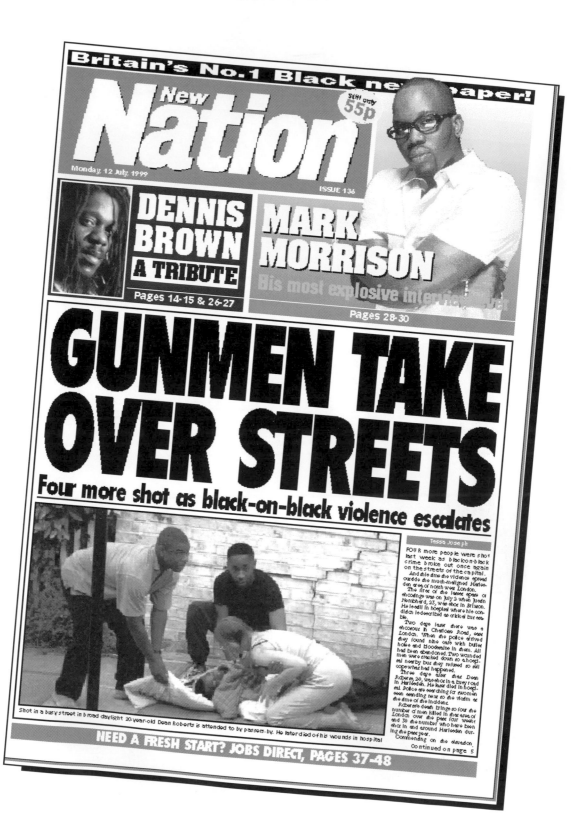

Britain's No.1 Black newspaper!

New Nation

55p

Monday, 12 July, 1999

ISSUE 136

DENNIS BROWN A TRIBUTE
Pages 14-15 & 26-27

MARK MORRISON
His most explosive interview ever
Pages 28-30

GUNMEN TAKE OVER STREETS
Four more shot as black-on-black violence escalates

Shot in a busy street in broad daylight 20-year-old Dean Roberts is attended to by passers-by. He later died of his wounds in hospital

Tessa Joseph

FOUR more people were shot last week as black-on-black crime broke out once again on the streets of the capital.

And this time the violence spread outside the much-maligned Harlesden area of north west London.

The first of the latest spate of shootings was on July 2 when Justin Nembhard, 23, was shot in Brixton. He is still in hospital where his condition is described as critical but stable.

Two days later there was a shootout in Charlotte Road, east London. When the police arrived they found nine cars with bullet holes and bloodstains in them. All had been abandoned. Two wounded men were tracked down to a hospital nearby but they refused to tell police what had happened.

Three days after that Dean Roberts, 20, was shot in a busy road in Harlesden. He later died in hospital. Police are searching for a woman seen standing next to the victim at the time of the incident.

Roberts's death brings to four the number of men killed in this area of London over the past four weeks and 30 the number who have been shot in and around Harlesden during the past year.

Commenting on the situation

Continued on page 5

NEED A FRESH START? JOBS DIRECT, PAGES 37-48

12 July 1999

COUNTDOWN TO THE MILLENNIUM

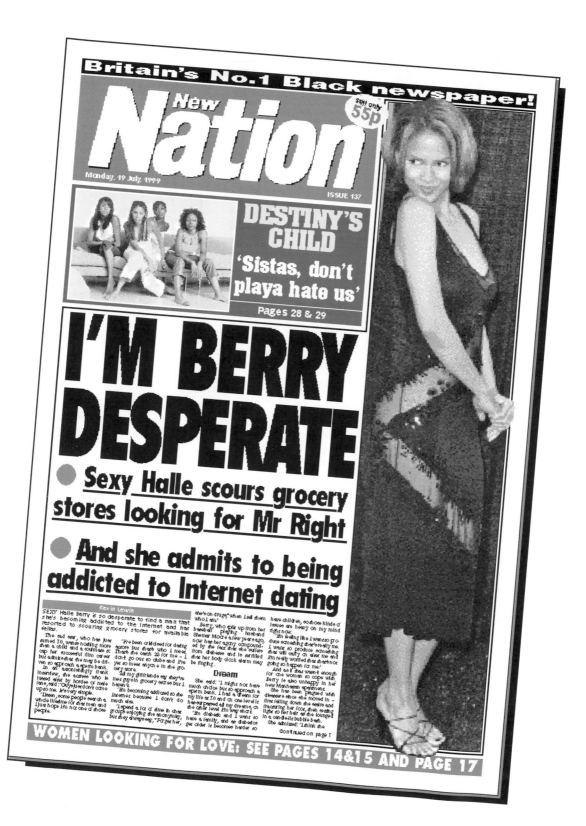

19 July 1999

Britain's No.1 Black newspaper!

New Nation

Monday, 9 August, 1999

ISSUE 140

Self only 55p

600 FREE TICKETS TO SEE EDDIE & MARTIN'S NEW MOVIE

EXCLUSIVE MEGA GIVEAWAY! P. 22

ARCHER: 'BLACK WOMEN WERE TOO FAT'

They couldn't dress well either, says peer

Ross Slater

TORY peer Lord Archer has caused outrage by saying that black women used to be fat and badly dressed.

His amazing remark was made during an interview for The Kwik E programme on Spectrum Radio in which he was explaining why he should be the director Mayor of London.

Asked about institutional racism in the police force, he began by saying that he hoped and believed race relations were improving from generation to generation.

Then he added: "When I was a child to see a black man and a white woman, or a white man and a black woman together is actually something you looked at. Now, let every other person and think, God, isn't it wonderful. That's the way we should be going.

He added: "If you look at African-Caribbeans 30 years ago they had the worse jobs and you know, your head did

not turn in the road if a black woman passed you because they were badly dressed, they were probably over weight and they probably had a lousy job.

"But if you walk down London streets now there are the more exaggeratingly beautiful girls of every nationality. That is part of getting rid of prejudice and making things equal.

His rival for the Mayor job, Trevor Phillips, said: "He is entirely just asking my breath away. It is a quite unbelievable remark."

Continued on page 7

NEED A FRESH START? JOBS DIRECT, PAGES 37-48

9 August 1999

COUNTDOWN TO THE MILLENNIUM

Britain's No.1 Black newspaper!

New Nation

Still only **55p**

Monday, 30 August, 1999

ISSUE 143

Vote for sexiest celebs

HOT BLACK 100

Pages 14 - 15

TEVIN CAMPBELL 'wanted oral sex with a man'!

Pages 28 – 30

$777 TRILLION SLAVE TRADE COURT CASE

Britain to face massive compensation lawsuit

'I don't want your money' – Duwayne's message to Condon

Page 9

Ross Slater

WESTERN countries who took part in the slave trade can look forward to receiving the biggest compensation demand of all time – a whopping $777 trillion.

Modern-day leaders of countries like Britain, America and Spain will be called before the International Court of Justice in the Hague to answer for the crimes of their forbears.

The decision to issue a compensation writ was taken by the African 'World Reparations and Repatriation Truth Commission' at a meeting in Accra, Ghana last week.

Their Chair Debra Kato told New Nation:

'Slavery was the greatest crime against humanity and the African continent and African people in the diaspora are still feeling the effects today.'

'Other groups like the Jews have been compensated for what they went through. How let our sum.'

The Commission have set 2004 as a deadline for having the case heard.

The Pan-Africanists are not the only ones who are using the millennium to bring some colonial childrens home to roost. Mau Mau veterans in Kenya are also planning a law suit as well as Trinidad families who claim Britain dispossessed them to help fight the Second World War.

Full story on pages 6 & 7

NEED A FRESH START? JOBS DIRECT, PAGES 37-48

30 August 1999

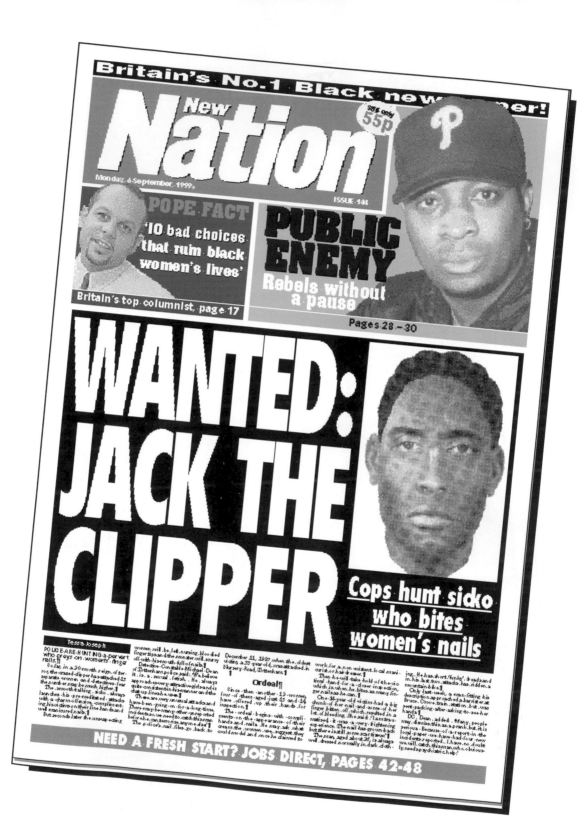

6 September 1999

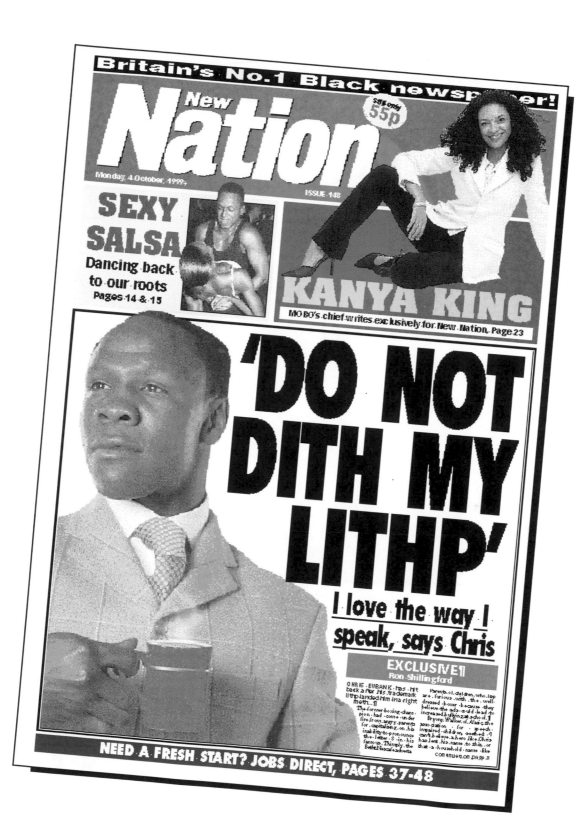

Britain's No.1 Black newspaper!

New Nation

Monday, 4 October, 1999

Still only **55p**

ISSUE 148

SEXY SALSA
Dancing back to our roots
Pages 14 & 15

KANYA KING
MOBO's chief writes exclusively for New Nation, Page 23

'DO NOT DITH MY LITHP'

I love the way I speak, says Chris

EXCLUSIVE!!
Ron Shillingford

CHRIS EUBANK has hit back after his trademark lithp landed him in a right moth...

The former boxing champion had come under fire from angry parents for capitalising on his inability to pronounce the letter S in his famous Thimply the Betht! adverts.

Parents of children who are furious with the well-dressed boxer because they believe the ads could lead to increased bullying at school.

Bryony Walker of Maidstone Asso-ciation for speech-impaired children, seethed: "I can't believe a hero like Chris has lent his name to this, or that a household name like

continued on page 5

NEED A FRESH START? JOBS DIRECT, PAGES 37-48

4 October 1999

digiscan

HIGH END REPRO FACILITY

Unit 2, Bayford Industrial Centre, Bayford Street, London E8 3SE

Dainippon Screen imagesetter
Hercules imagesetter
Hewlett Packard designjet
Dainippon Screen drum scanner

B1 film output

posters
magazines
banner advertising
point of sale
worldwide campaigns

A0 posters

tel 0181 985 9988
tel 0181 986 6072
fax 0181 986 3167
isdn0181 985 7045

email: graphic@digiscan.demon.co.uk

Graphic
Digiscan
Limited

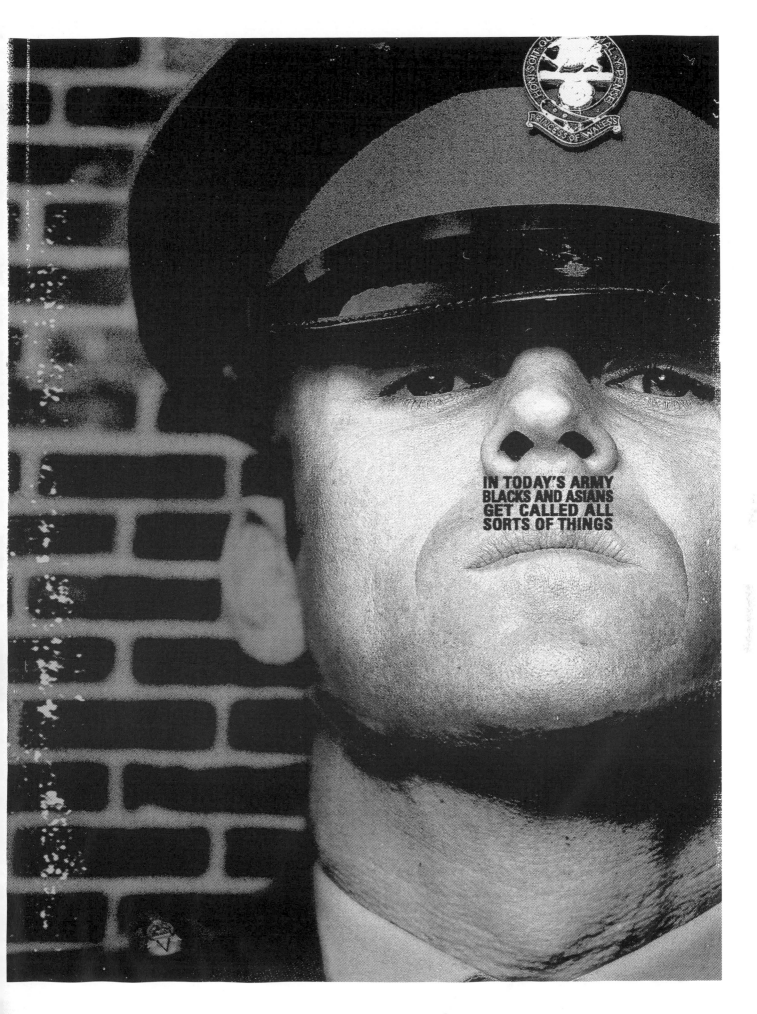

IN TODAY'S ARMY
BLACKS AND ASIANS
GET CALLED ALL
SORTS OF THINGS

**LIEUTENANT
CAPTAIN
MAJOR
COLONEL**

We now have more ethnic minorities in positions of real power than ever before.
So nowadays, there's only one group of people being held back. Racists.
If you think you could be an Officer in today's Army call 0345 3000 111
quoting ref WW001 or write to the Army, Freepost, CV37 9BR.

ARMY
BE THE BEST

http://www.army.mod.uk The Army is committed to Equal Opportunities.

NatWest

has the experience and

understands

how to help African-Caribbeans make their

businesses

a success.

Talk to one of our small business advisers
about how we can help.

PublicSector

An exciting new weekly supplement dedicated to Black and Asian public sector professionals nationwide.

PublicSector Issue 13

PublicSector Issue 8

PublicSector Issue 14

• Are you keen to keep abreast of current issues in the public sector?

• Looking for a new job that matches your professional skills and qualifications?

If the answer is yes, then look no further than Public Sector.

Every week we will bring you topical news and opinions from across the public sector from nursing to teaching, from social work to fire-fighting.

To secure your copy every week, just fill in the form below.

Please send your completed order form to: Public Sector Subscriptions, Ethnic Media Group, 1st Floor, 148 Cambridge Heath Road, London E1 5QJ

Public Sector Subscription Order Form

Name: _____

Job Title: _____

Organisation Name: _____

Delivery Address: _____

Postcode: _____

Telephone: _____ Fax: _____

I would like to order a one-year subscription ☐ £25.00 inc p&p.

I would like to enquire about a bulk subscription ☐ Send no money now

Payment Method

Cash/PO ☐   ☐ Cheque   ☐ Credit Card

Card Name: _____

Card Address: _____

Card No. ☐☐☐☐☐☐☐☐☐☐☐☐☐☐☐☐   ☐☐ ☐☐ Exp

Internal use only: Received _____ Start _____

BUILDING BRIDGES

At the Ethnic Media Group (EMG) we publish Britain's leading ethnically targeted newspapers. With Eastern Eye and Asian Times for the Asian Community and New Nation and Caribbean Times for the Afro-Caribbean communities we reach over 475,000 readers every week.

What's more, those readers are qualified, motivated and socially active - just the sort of employees most organisations need to ensure their workforce reflects the modern market-place.

So we build bridges. Bridges between minority ethnic and Corporate Britain. Call us today and find out how we can help you.

FOR FURTHER INFORMATION PLEASE CALL
0171-702 8012

ASIANS IN THE MILLENNIUM

An extraordinary Who's Who of Asian Achievers in Britain

ASIANS IN THE MILLENNIUM is a Who's Who of Asian Achievers, many of whom are making immense contributions to the wealth and development of Britain. This directory lists over 1,000 profiles and introduces a diverse representation of achievers and positive role models. Also included is a section dedicated to Britain's Richest 200 Asians - a unique insight into the enterprise skills of Asian businesses in Britain.

ASIANS IN THE MILLENNIUM is an essential reference resource for everyone who needs to network and exchange information with Britain's top Asian achievers. It will be useful to media, marketing and PR companies, and will prove ideal for recruitment consultants and organisations seeking members, patrons, specialists and business connections. Students will find an enormous treasure trove of information and inspiration, while the general reader will discover many different dimensions to the Asian community.

The rich and famous, the movers and shakers as well as many lesser known achievers are all included in this unrivalled who's who. ASIANS IN THE MILLENNIUM reveals the tremendous extent of Asian involvement in the life of Britain today.

All entries in Who's Who were nominated by **Eastern Eye** and **Asian Times** readers. Entries include achievers in all fields and professions, those who have received local or national awards and those who work on behalf of the community - the unsung heroes. One thousand stories emerged...

WHO'S WHO OF ASIAN ACHIEVERS

First Edition

Asians in the Millennium

Published by

EASTERN Eye
FOR THE ASIAN PERSPECTIVE

&

ASIAN TIMES

NOTES